JIM PLIM
AMBASSADOR EXTRAORDINARY

JIM PLIM
AMBASSADOR EXTRAORDINARY
A Biography of Sir James Plimsoll

Jeremy Hearder

Connor Court Publishing
Ballarat

Connor Court Publishing Pty Ltd

Copyright © Jeremy Hearder 2015

ALL RIGHTS RESERVED. This book contains material protected under International and Federal Copyright Laws and Treaties. Any unauthorised reprint or use of this material is prohibited. No part of this book may be reproduced or transmitted in any form or by any means, electronic or mechanical, including photocopying, recording, or by any information storage and retrieval system without express written permission from the publisher.

PO Box 224W
Ballarat VIC 3350
sales@connorcourt.com
www.connorcourt.com

ISBN: 9781925138498 (pbk.)

Cover design by Maria Giordano and photo by DFAT

Printed in Australia

CONTENTS

Illustrations	vi
Foreword: Alexander Downer AC	viii
Jim Plimsoll and Australian Diplomacy, 1945-82	x
1. Bondi, Banks and the University Union, 1917-42	1
2. Alf's Army, 1942-47	25
3. The United Nations and Korea, 1948-52	54
4. "A Tiger for Work": Canberra, 1953-59	86
5. The Highlight of His Career: the United Nations, 1959-63	123
6. Indian Indulgence, 1963-65	156
7. The Dutiful Secretary: Canberra, 1965-70	181
8. "A Precious Vase": Washington, 1970-74	227
9. Moscow, 1974-77	263
10. Brussels, London, Tokyo, 1977-82	294
11. "A Great Tasmanian", 1982-87	329
12. Epilogue: Ambassador Extraordinary	362
Acknowledgements	363
Select Bibliography	367
Index	375

Illustrations

1. Plimsoll senior returning from the beach with his sons Jim and John (Plimsoll family) (p. 3)

2. Plimsoll, young bank economist, with his parents and brother John (Plimsoll family) (p. 9)

3. Major Plimsoll's ID card for Australian Joint Staff Mission, Washington DC, June 1945 (Plimsoll family) (p. 38)

4. UNCURK meeting in Pusan, c 1951. Plimsoll is at lower right (Lady Currie) (p. 62)

5. R.G. Casey, on his visit to Korea in 1951, with President Syngman Rhee, Plimsoll and Prime Minister Chang Myun to his right, and with Pote Sarasin (Thailand Representative on UNCURK) and Alan Watt to his left (Australian War Memorial) (p. 69)

6. With UN Secretary General, Dag Hammarskjold, after presenting credentials, June 1959 (UN photo) (p. 122)

7. Visit of Australian Prime Minister, Robert Menzies, to the UN in October 1960. With Frederick H. Boland (Ireland), President of the UN General Assembly, and Plimsoll (UN photo) (p. 129)

8. Plimsoll with UN Secretary General U Thant, Australian Foreign Minister Sir Garfield Barwick, and US Permanent Representative Adlai Stevenson, September 1962 (UN photo) (p. 141)

9. Official portrait as Secretary (DFAT) (p. 180)

10. With Paul Hasluck, Australian Minister for External Affairs, at talks in Tel Aviv in 1966 with Abba Eban (far right), Foreign Minister of Israel. To Plimsoll's right are Bill Landale, Ambassador to Israel, and Geoff Bentley, Acting P/A to Hasluck (Israel Foreign Ministry) (p. 183)

11. Plimsoll and Hasluck with Australia's Heads of Mission in South East Asia, Manila 1968. From left to right: Plimsoll, Allan Eastman (Kuala Lumpur), John Ryan (Vientiane), Max Loveday (Jakarta), Lewis Border (Saigon), David McNicol (Bangkok), Alfred Parsons (Singapore), Hasluck, Francis Stuart (Manila), and Noel Deschamps (Phnom Penh) (DFAT) (p. 187)

12. With President Nixon at the White House after presenting credentials, June 1970 (Richard Nixon Library and Museum)* (p. 226)

13. With Prime Minister Gough Whitlam at Moscow airport (Russian Foreign Ministry)* (p. 268)

14. Being introduced to Soviet leader Leonid Brezhnev (Russian Foreign Ministry)* (p. 278)

15. Call by Australian Parliamentary Delegation in Brussels, 1979, on Roy Jenkins, President of the European Commission. Left to right: Jenkins, Gordon Scholes, Stephen Lusher, Alexander Downer (Third Secretary, Brussels), Jim Short, Sir Billy Snedden, Senator Reg Withers, Ken Fry, Senator Don Grimes and Plimsoll (European Union)* (p. 307)

16. The Governor with Premier Robin Gray and Tasmanian Government Ministers, March 1986. Back row left to right: Peter Hodgman, Julian Green (Secretary, Premier's Department), John Bennett, John Beswick, Roger Groom, Nick Evers, Ray Groom. Front row left to right: Ian Braid, Gray, Plimsoll, Geoff Pearsall, Peter Rae (Newspix)* (p. 334)

* Copy of photo 12 was supplied by the Plimsoll family. Copies of photos 13-15 were supplied by the National Library of Australia, and of photo 16 by Sally Evers.

Foreword

Alexander Downer AC
Minister for Foreign Affairs, 1996-2007

There never was a greater Australian diplomat than Sir James Plimsoll. A shy man in many ways, Plimsoll was not only highly educated but was a true intellectual. Like all intellectuals, he loved to read. His knowledge of English literature was prodigious. But *en poste* he would also master the literature of his host country. When I worked for Sir James in Brussels as his Third Secretary, he developed a greater mastery of Belgian literature than almost any Belgian.

Plimsoll's intellectual interests extended to music and art. Travelling with him was always a delight. The car would stop in small towns so he could explore the local art gallery. Visits to European capitals were timed to coincide with the opera. There was never a significant opera which Sir James did not know.

All this was highly relevant to Sir James's work as an ambassador. In the relatively educated and intellectual world of diplomacy, the unmarried Australian ambassador was able to engage with his interlocutors in ways few could match. In Brussels he built a unique relationship with the president of the European Commission, Roy Jenkins, not by banging on about Australia's sheep meat quota or family ties but through their shared passion for literature. Having built a close friendship based on shared interests, then Plimsoll could bang on about sheep meat quotas so much more effectively than the average diplomat.

Like all good diplomats, Plimsoll was an inveterate networker. After holding most of Australia's most senior diplomatic posts over a period of nearly half a century, he collected a list of contacts and friends which would make the most avaricious name dropper drool. But Plimsoll was, for a man of his distinction, a relatively modest man who did not give his contacts a sense he wanted to use them. They would all have understood that for all the professional benefits he could get from his extensive teledex, Sir James above all liked people for their ideas and conversation.

Professionally, Plimsoll had two other strengths. The first was his extraordinary capacity to describe complex issues in simple, clear language. His despatches often read as simplistic. That was a reflection of the clear, concise way in which he wrote. And his second and more important asset was his wisdom. With a wealth of experience to draw on, Sir James invariably made sensitive and accurate political judgments. He was also a clever tactician, understanding instinctively how other governments would react to Australia's pleadings and representations.

There were times when Plimsoll would judge the instructions coming from Canberra as so futile he would not carry them out. This did not mean he would ignore the government's policy objectives. It did mean, though, that if he thought the government's tactics to achieve its goals were foolish, he would gently bury them.

Finally, Plimsoll was a wonderful mentor to young people. He enjoyed the company of the young and relished giving them advice. In my case, he was one of two people who I could genuinely say was not only a mentor but something of a hero. The other was my father. When I heard on the radio while driving one evening from Adelaide to the Barossa Valley that Plimsoll had died from a heart attack, I stopped the car so I could quietly weep.

I am delighted Jeremy Hearder, with whom I worked in Brussels in the late 1970s, has written this book. It's high time the story of the great Plimsoll is told to all Australians.

Adelaide, February 2013

Jim Plimsoll and Australian Diplomacy, 1945-82

This book is set in an important period of Australia's history: its emergence as a nation internationally giving voice to independent views based on its own interests, and playing an active role in its own right as a member of the international community.

Symbolic of this process was the visit to Asia by John Latham, Minister for External Affairs in the Lyons UAP Government in 1934. In the late 1930s, with the increasing preoccupation of the UK about the "gathering storm" in Europe, Australia was increasingly concerned about the situation in Asia, and was drawn into big events.

Robert Menzies, Prime Minister from 1939 to 1941, pointedly told the nation that what was, to Britain, the "far east", was, to Australia, the "near north". During the anxious first two years of the Second World War, the Australian Government expended much effort in ensuring that preoccupation with Europe was not at the expense of security in the Pacific. Following the Japanese attack on Pearl Harbour in December 1941 and the surrender of Singapore early in 1942, Australia was in direct line of attack. Not only dependent on outside aid for its defence, Australia also looked to having its own voice heard in the post-war settlement of the Asian region.

The Department of External Affairs was established in Canberra as a separate agency in 1935. The first intake of graduate trainees began work in 1936. Australia's first diplomatic missions in the Asia-Pacific were established in Washington, Ottawa and Tokyo in 1940, in Chungking in 1941, and in Wellington and New Delhi in 1944.

The Department, with a slender staff, was the principal organisation for carrying out the new foreign policy. The post-war years were a period of "sudden and dramatic growth." Between mid-1946 and mid-1949 the

Department's total staff more than trebled; between mid-1945 and mid-1949 the number of posts abroad grew from nine to 26.[1]

Even so, External Affairs was still very small and inexperienced, struggling to deal with the responsibilities placed upon it. These continued to grow, reflecting post-war international developments in which Australia became involved or had a close interest. Australia was prominent in establishment of the United Nations (UN) in 1945 and in its subsequent operation. It was one of the first temporary members of the Security Council. In 1948 Dr Evatt, the Minister for External Affairs, became the third President of the General Assembly. Posts established in Europe reflected the need for independent relations with important countries there, as well as a high rate of immigration to Australia from Europe, and the onset of the Cold War.

But Asia was increasingly a major focus, with the peace treaty and subsequent development of a new relationship with Japan, and with other, newly independent, Asian states, notably Indonesia. With the unfolding of the Cold War, concerns about the Communist threat in the region, notably in China, Korea, and Vietnam, demanded increasing attention.

The next 30 years were a defining period in evolution of Australia's engagement with the wider world, and in formulating its foreign policy. It was a period in which successive Australian governments facing this new situation, particularly foreign ministers and prime ministers, grappled with issues as they arose, and tried to develop Australia's relations with the Asia-Pacific region, especially development cooperation, with the USA and with Europe, with an increasing number of multilateral organisations, especially the UN and the Commonwealth, and with the wider world of Africa, the Middle East, and Latin America. Another matter of growing significance was international scientific cooperation in the Antarctic. Governments sought to explain policy to the wider world, and to the Australian people at home. In all these endeavours they received much advice from the Department of External Affairs – Foreign Affairs from 1970.

Among graduate entrants to the department after the war were many who were newly demobilised from the services. Jim Plimsoll was one of these. This book is about Plimsoll's career of 35 years. He held eight important ambassadorial appointments. For five years he was Secretary of the Department under three ministers. After retirement from the diplomatic service he was Governor of Tasmania for more than four years.

His diplomatic career began when, late in 1945, as Major Plimsoll of the Australian Military Mission in Washington, he was unexpectedly recruited to assist in preparations for the inaugural meeting of the Far Eastern Commission (FEC) that was to coordinate Allied policy towards the defeated Japan. Australia was represented by Dr H.V. Evatt, Minister for External Affairs in the Chifley Labor Government. Thrown in at the deep end, Plimsoll nevertheless impressed Evatt who appointed him as Australia's representative to the FEC. Two years later Plimsoll joined the Department of External Affairs in Canberra.

He rose rapidly. Within three years, and aged only 33, he was appointed to his first ambassadorial post. It was as Australian representative on the United Nations Commission for the Unification and Rehabilitation of Korea(UNCURK). During 1950-53 Korea was a war zone, but Plimsoll ensured that this UN civilian presence played a significant role maintaining communications with the Korean Government, especially its despotic head, President Syngman Rhee, with whom he developed a relationship of some influence.

Upon returning to Canberra, Plimsoll found himself, at a very senior level in the department, overseeing development of Australia's relations with Asia, as well as periodically acting as head of the department. From 1959 until 1963 he was Permanent Representative at the UN in New York. Among the matters in which he played a role was persuading the UK not to grant independence to a minority government in Southern

Rhodesia. As High Commissioner to India (1963-65) he made a special contribution fostering a better government-to-government relationship with that major country.

Following his relatively short time in India, Plimsoll was Secretary of the department for five years. He then became Ambassador in Washington (1970-74). Already well known there, he maintained Australia's important relationship with the US during a difficult period, marked by tensions arising from the advent of the Whitlam Government, conclusion of the Vietnam war, crises that erupted in the Middle East and the Indian sub-continent, and Watergate. From Washington, he went to Moscow (1974-77). In addition to the usual diplomatic endeavours in a Communist state he had to deal with the question of the Baltic states. He also lectured at Moscow State University on literature. His later postings were to Brussels, London – the first career officer to be High Commissioner – and Tokyo.

The high regard in which he was held led Sir Paul Hasluck, a minister whom Plimsoll served as department head, to write:

> Over the years, in a succession of diplomatic appointments to the great capitals of the world he was the personification of Australia, spoke for Australia and acted in the name of Australia and always did so worthily. I like to think that, because they knew Plimsoll, there are quite a number of highly placed foreigners who think of Australians as persons of intelligence, understanding, courtesy, consideration and a good intention.[2]

This reflected Plimsoll's exceptional talent, ultra-dedication to the job, including his capacity to remain on top of all current issues and his ability to communicate about them clearly and concisely, frankly yet sensitively. He ghost-wrote two books for ministers he served, Evatt and Casey respectively, in each case while continuing to perform his normal work. Private and upright, he made many friends by his quiet, courteous and accessible manner, yet it was not easy to get to know him well. Two ministers with whom he worked closely for long periods, R.G. Casey for more than six years and Hasluck for four, each felt he did not understand him.[3] In many ways he was by no means the typical diplomat: hardly gregarious, did not play golf or any other sport, and he was often ill at ease with small talk or in conversation with women, especially those he did not know.

Management was not his forte. He worked well with staff at posts but, as department head, the major managerial responsibility of running the department and the posts abroad exposed an area in which he knew he had shortcomings – indeed, it was part of the reason that he was reluctant to become Secretary. His term in the post was by no means the highlight of his career.

Having reached the top of his profession at an early age, both as department head, then Ambassador in Washington, he might have moved to fresh pastures. But he wanted to continue being an Australian diplomat because of his belief in the importance of the work. The last five years of his career, in which he had three postings, were unhappy ones. He was twice required to make way, indirectly while Ambassador in Washington, and later, more directly, as High Commissioner in London, in order to facilitate non-career appointments.

The Cold War provided the background and context of Plimsoll's diplomatic career. But he looked beyond this. He actively sought better relations with India, then a leading non-aligned country, and later with the USSR. And his career is of wider, enduring significance because of his remarkable display of the classical talents of a diplomat, talents which are important regardless of time or circumstances.

Endnotes

1 P.G. Edwards, "The origins and growth of professional diplomacy in Australia." *Australian Foreign Affairs Review,* vol 56, 1985, 1069-76.
2 Hasluck to Crocker 2/6/1987. Courtesy of Nicholas and Sally Hasluck.
3 Casey once wrote to Plimsoll: "Heaven knows, you may be a dyed in the wool dangerous radical, under the guise of a moral, balanced and intelligent individual. I don't think you are – but who really knows?" Hasluck wrote: "One of the most puzzling men whom I have met and I really don't know whether I understood him. Yet we always worked well together." Casey to Plimsoll, 5/6/72. Plimsoll papers, National Library of Australia, 8048/1/38. Hasluck to Sir Walter Crocker, 2/6/1987. Hasluck private papers, courtesy of Nicholas and Sally Hasluck.

1
Bondi, Banks and the University Union, 1917-42

Inclined to be somewhat inhibited by overconscientiousness, but he should be quite well suited for any form of work involving frequent contact with others.[1]

An upright, straightforward and well-behaved young man . . . a youth to be trusted.[2]

Jim Plimsoll's first 25 years were crucial in establishment of his identity and formation of his character and outlook. He was born in 1917, at a time when Australia had been engaged in the Great War for nearly three years. Australia was mainly fighting as part of the British force, on land or at sea, and it did not as yet have settled autonomy in international affairs. But, as Billy Hughes's performance at the Paris Peace Conference of 1919 showed, that time was not far off.

Plimsoll's start was auspicious. He was born on 25 April, Anzac Day, in Sydney, Australia's oldest and best known city. The first Anzac Day commemoration had been held one year before.[3] For his first 25 years he lived in Bondi, Sydney's famous beach-side suburb. His schooling was at institutions which were among Australia's oldest and most venerable – Sydney Boys High School and the University of Sydney.

Family background

His parents had arrived in Australia only three years previously. Plimsoll's great-grandfather, Thomas, was a cousin of Sir Samuel Plimsoll, remembered chiefly for the Plimsoll Line in shipping. His father, James Ernest Plimsoll, was born in 1881, one of the nine children of James

Plimsoll, a butcher of Aylesbeare in Devonshire.[4] When he was three James Ernest and two brothers, Dick and George, went to New Zealand with their father. In 1901 James Ernest moved to Fiji, to work as an accountant.[5] It was said that "Mr Plimsoll takes an active interest in all classes of outdoor sport, particularly cricket,"[6] which proved to be an enduring family tradition.

In Fiji James Ernest met Jessie Arthur, a Scottish bookkeeper in Ba, a town not far from Lautoka, where he was based. Hailing from the family farm near Colliston, a fishing town in Aberdeenshire, Jessie was born in 1877, the seventh child of eight, into a family of modest means. In 1908 she joined a brother who was working in Ba. Her mother had been in domestic service before marrying, while her father, at first a farm servant, had become a tenant farmer by 1891.[7] The accountant and the bookkeeper were married in Lautoka on 2 August 1913.[8]

After a year the couple moved to Sydney where, in 1914, James Ernest became the accountant for the retail store David Jones, rising to become Company Secretary by 1927, a job he retained through the Depression. He became something of an institution at DJs until retirement in 1956 aged 75. His flourishing signature was a work of art which "took five minutes to complete".[9]

In some ways Plimsoll's father was the antithesis of his son. Father was short and stocky, whereas Jim became tall and thin. He went to work smartly dressed in a three-piece suit; he looked every inch the Company Secretary of David Jones.[10] Jim by contrast was less sartorial. His father enjoyed a yarn with a friend over a whisky and a cigar,[11] and was a Mason.[12] The son never smoked, drank sparingly, and did not become a Mason.

Yet there were many similarities. James senior was conscientious, quiet, not outgoing but easy to get on with, and quite unflappable.[13] He was never heard to swear and would not borrow money for anything. He believed that homes were to live in rather than to own, so his family lived in various rented houses in Bondi until 1952 when, at age 71, he bought his first house. He did not own or drive a car, preferring public transport and taxis.¹⁴ His son Jim was influenced by all these idiosyncratic behaviours, as was John, his younger brother.

Jim's childhood was a normal, happy one, in a close and loving family. A love of reading was fostered and one of his earliest memories was of his father reading *Snugglepot and Cuddlepie* to him.¹⁵ At the time of Jim's birth his father was 36 and his mother 39. The relatively older age of his parents to their sons¹⁶ meant parental discipline was not as strict as "the standards of those days". Another factor was that John had a series of illnesses when young, on two occasions life-threatening. Plimsoll thought

Plimsoll senior returning from the beach with his sons, Jim and John (Plimsoll family)

that concern about John led to his own upbringing being anything but spoilt: "If anything I was treated more severely" than was John.[17] When he was about five, John broke his arm. Part of his rehabilitation was that every day he had to fill a bucket of sand at the beach and carry it home. Jim accompanied him on these expeditions to look after him – which included helping him carry the bucket up the street to home, letting John carry it the last stretch.[18]

James Ernest and his sons watched Sheffield Shield and Test matches at the Sydney Cricket Ground, where they all became members. There were family holidays each year at Katoomba in the Blue Mountains, about two hours away in the train, where they stayed at the Balmoral Guest House. The mountain tracks, some of them long and steep, became very familiar to the boys, who would go off together for long walks. There was Sunday School at St Matthew's Church, Bondi, where Margaret Whitlam remembered being in the same class as Jim, but he made no special impression.[19]

Jim Plimsoll was close to both his parents, especially his father. After Jim left home, he and his father exchanged letters at least fortnightly. Having Jim's power-of-attorney while he was abroad, James Ernest looked after his son's financial interests including a share portfolio. Whenever he was home, Jim joined his father in early morning swims in the surf and an afternoon walk.

Plimsoll's mother was described by Lionel Kentwell, his closest school friend, as "lovely, soft, always pleasant, friendly, never cross, a lady". When Kentwell saw Plimsoll after he had been knighted in 1962, Plimsoll had said, with unusual emotion and candour, that he wished that his mother had still been around (she died in 1957).[20]

School

Jim went to primary school at Bondi Commercial in Wellington Street (now known as Bondi Public). Like church and beach, the school was within easy walking distance from home. His last school report, in

December 1928 at age 11, described him as "excellent" in English, History and Geometry, and in overall conduct. The headmaster summed him up as "a quiet, earnest, consistent worker. Displays more than usual ability. Diligent and painstaking."[21]

Jim proceeded to Sydney Boys High, while John later went to Sydney Grammar. From that time their interests and careers took different paths. They saw little of each other for years at a time, both during the War and subsequently, but remained close. After their parents died, John and his wife Patricia and their three daughters, Kathleen, Susie and Jane, were Plimsoll's only close family. John took over looking after Jim's investments.

Sydney Boys High, situated just to the south-east of the city in Moore Park, was about 45 minutes by tram from Bondi. The school today still enjoys a certain feeling of space, thanks to its location in the green belt of Moore Park. The school moved to its present site in 1928. Arriving at the school a year later, Plimsoll and his classmates had the advantage of starting at a venerable old school but at a new site with new buildings and amenities.

The area had previously been known as Billy-Goat Swamps. The previous occupant had been the Sydney Zoological Gardens, which had moved to its present site in Taronga Park. In the school grounds the former zoo bearpit was the sole relic of the earlier animal kingdom and, in Plimsoll's time, boys sometimes fell into it. As if the dangers of the bearpit were not enough, immediately to the south of the school lay forbidden territory, Sydney Girls High. No communication between pupils of the two establishments was allowed during school hours.

Plimsoll's time at the school coincided with the Bodyline Test cricket series of 1932-33. Sir Roden Cutler, a school contemporary of Plimsoll, used to wag school and duck across the road to the SCG when the English team played. This affected Cutler's exam results, and he had to repeat the year.[22] Plimsoll would have followed the matches keenly, but was too conscientious to allow them to interrupt his schooling.

As a selective high school with admission by competitive examination, much of the school's spirit and quality derived from the calibre of students as well as that of the teaching staff.[23] Plimsoll's years at the school, from 1929 to 1933, coincided with the worst years of the Depression, but many of his contemporaries achieved distinction in various walks of life. John Cornforth, Dux of the school, was awarded the Nobel Prize for Chemistry in 1975. The school supplied a number of Australian diplomats, including no fewer than four heads of the department: Sir Alan Watt (1950-54), Alan Renouf (1974-77), Peter Wilenski (1992-93) and Plimsoll himself – more than any other school. A son of the then Country Party leader, Dr (later Sir) Earle Page, was in Plimsoll's classes, and gave him "quite a lot of insights into politics".[24] In sport there were Olympians Mervyn Wood, gold medallist in rowing (also later a NSW Police Commissioner), Alan Metcalf and Basil Dickinson in athletics, and Viv McGrath, the Davis Cup tennis player.

The headmaster, George Saxby, was a firm but fair disciplinarian. Any boys found to have misbehaved on public transport would be named in school assembly on Monday mornings, and given a clear but not savage dressing-down in front of the whole school.[25] Anyone late for assembly would have to go to the gym for six of the best.[26]

Plimsoll was inconspicuous; he made no special impression.[27] A number of his contemporaries who were aware of his achievements in later life could not even recall his being at school with them. In the school records Plimsoll's name does not appear as holding any position of leadership, or for any prominence in sport. Sydney High may have been "a superb school academically", but boys still mainly made their name in sport,[28] at which Plimsoll, although interested and knowledgeable, did not shine.

The only notable mention of Plimsoll in the school records was for "The Portent," a short story, two pages long, in the school magazine for December 1932. For its time, the story must have been somewhat unusual for its sympathetic approach towards the feelings of indigenous people when confronted by the arrival of the first Europeans. It was judged, along with two other entries, as "excellent", the next best to the winning entry for the headmaster's prize for the best short story.[29]

Plimsoll was actively involved in debating and demonstrated an "earnest, logical mind" and knowledge of detail, but without injecting any "drama".[30] Sir John Cornforth recalled a class debate on "Whether the League of Nations was a Good Thing". Plimsoll "made a much better job of rubbishing the League than I did of praising it".[31]

Roden Cutler recalled Plimsoll as "a methodical student with a prodigious memory, serious, gentle and caring with his school fellows, with no interest in taking part in sport and no interest in girls".[32] Even so, Plimsoll liked to talk. He and Lloyd Kentwell talked as they walked in the Bondi neighbourhood where both lived, or walking across Moore Park between school and tram at Victoria Barracks. Subjects included religion – neither was agnostic, but the Anglican Plimsoll and the Methodist Kentwell were questioning the faiths in which each had been brought up;[33] and also world affairs – on the tram from Bondi with his father, Plimsoll was given the first two news pages of the *Sydney Morning Herald*, including the editorial page, to read and hand back before alighting,[34] a procedure that continued during his university years.

Plimsoll was in the top stream for most subjects and his marks were usually above class average. Conscientious, "far above average in the desire to learn", he was a bookworm and at break times he used to walk around the playground studying a textbook.[35] His English and Latin teachers consistently praised his work. He was in the top class in English and learned by heart a lot of poetry which he could still recite in later life.[36] But he did not win any academic prizes, in contrast to school contemporaries John Quinn, Alan Loomes and Alan Renouf, all later diplomat colleagues, and all high achievers scholastically.

He was one of only three in his year to study Greek. In the 1933 Leaving Certificate exams, he managed a pass in Greek, contrary to the headmaster's prediction.[37] Plimsoll was comfortably admitted to university with A's in Latin, Maths I and II and with B's in English, French, Greek and Chemistry. Cornforth recalled that Plimsoll "always seemed to me one of the brighter boys in the class", and was surprised he did not achieve honours. He wondered whether Plimsoll might have been passing through "some illness or crisis at the time of the examination"[38] but there is no evidence of this.

The headmaster's character reference for Plimsoll stated: "This lad has an excellent record for work and conduct. Teachers speak very highly of his character, and conscientiousness. Reliable and painstaking in all he does."[39]

Bank and university

In February 1934, Plimsoll declined an offer from the NSW Education Department of a place at the Teachers College with its financially tempting scholarship.[40] Some inclination towards teaching would have been offset by doubts about or distaste for controlling classes, which he knew, even at Sydney High, could be unruly.[41]

His father probably could have afforded to support Jim at the University of Sydney full-time. Perhaps the Depression led him to advise Jim to take a job. It was decided that he would seek full-time work and study part-time at university. With an accountant father and a bookkeeper mother, parental encouragement was a likely factor in his decision to study economics.

Early in May 1934, his father arranged for him to be tested by the Australian Institute of Industrial Psychology in Sydney, to identify what sort of work might suit him best. The report proved prophetic. Plimsoll received the highest mark, "very superior", in two areas, general intelligence and space relationships – aptitude in reading and interpreting plans and designs. He was "high average" for clerical aptitude, that is, capacity for application and attention to work, both in business and study. For mechanical ingenuity he was judged only "average". His outlook on life was "perfectly normal and healthy". He was "inclined to be somewhat inhibited by overconscientiousness, [but] he should be quite well suited for any form of work involving frequent contact with others". The report said he was "easily of university honours standard" although "approximately a year younger than the average undergraduate".⁴²

Plimsoll, young bank economist, with his parents and brother John (Plimsoll family)

It was difficult to find a job in the wake of the Depression. Plimsoll's father marshalled some strong referees. One, Mr (later Sir) Charles Lloyd Jones, Chairman of the Board of DJ's and Chairman of the ABC, was a leading citizen of Sydney. Another was Mr D. Bradford, a Director of DJ's, who wrote of "the excellent home training" which Plimsoll had received.[43] The other referees were his former headmaster, and the Rev. Pollock of St Matthew's, Bondi. The psychological report was also used.

Plimsoll applied to the Bank of Australasia.[44] He had a medical examination to ensure his fitness for work, in theory anywhere that the Bank had branches "from the tropics to the colder districts of New Zealand". He had an interview, from which the comment was: "Tall, slim, somewhat sallow, earnest rather than bright. Passed his Leaving. However says he plays cricket and tennis. Quite suitable." Finally, on 14 June 1934, six months after leaving school, he was taken on as a supernumerary, effectively an apprentice. For three years a supernumerary was paid no salary but, depending upon good conduct and efficiency, could receive a gratuity at the discretion of the bank.

Supernumeraries "had to have been well brought up, be of good character", while their families had to be "of undoubted respectability and social position". They had to be "presentable" and at least 5 feet 6 inches, or likely to attain that height, and have handwriting that was "properly formed".[45]

For two years Plimsoll worked at the NSW head office branch of the bank on the corner of Martin Place and George Street, starting with some menial daily tasks such as putting out the front doormat.[46] In 1936 he moved to the branch at Marrickville, a suburb to the southwest of the city, involving more travelling time.

After three years, promotion to permanent staff at the bank was normally automatic, but not for Plimsoll. The routine medical examination in June 1937 showed that in the three years since joining the bank, his weight had fallen from 11 stone 4 lbs to 10 stone 5 lbs (68 kilos). In three years he had lost nearly a stone (or six kilos) in weight. In addition his chest measurements had decreased slightly. The doctor commented that he could not find any medical explanation. Plimsoll's branch manager at Marrickville was quick to offer one. Noting that Plimsoll would be sitting his final university exams in Economics at the end of the year, the manager described Plimsoll's daily routine: "Five nights in the week he leaves this office at from 5 to 5.30, thence direct to the university, where he has his dinner, and afterwards attends lectures and studies. It is generally midnight before he arrives home." The loss of weight was thus explained as due to "this stress of study and consequent late hours". He predicted that Plimsoll would pass the exams, and would then relax and "regain any physical setback he may have suffered temporarily".

The bank inspector, who received the bank manager's letter, told the doctor about Plimsoll's part-time studies and that he was "giving up practically the whole of his time outside the office to studying". The doctor's assessment was "lack of exercise and outdoor recreation". He prescribed a course of "physical culture", commenting that, had Plimsoll been an applicant for life assurance, he would have been deferred for 12 months. Ironically, only a few months before, Colonial Mutual had issued Plimsoll with a life assurance policy.[47]

The bank's headquarters in Melbourne, while praising Plimsoll's "zeal and enthusiasm" for achieving an Economics degree, decided to follow the medical advice and defer his permanency for a year.[48]

After such interest in the pressures on Plimsoll, the bank made life even more difficult for him. For the last four months before his final exams, he had to work at the branch at Kogarah, south-west of Kingsford Smith Airport. This was further away from the university and home, causing even longer daily travel. Plimsoll later wondered how he found the time to study, "because in those days it was a 42 hour week and sometimes one had to work overtime".[49]

Plimsoll's problem was partly self-inflicted owing to his increasingly active involvement in student affairs. In his final year of Economics he was President of the Evening Students' Association for Men, Secretary/

Treasurer of the Economics Society, and an active participant in debates at the weekly Union Nights. This was hardly conducive to finding extra time for study, let alone to relax and exercise. He passed his final year's Economics, remarkably without losing more weight. Another medical examination in June 1938 showed he had gained five pounds in weight and that his chest measurements were improved. The doctor pronounced him "fit" and he was finally made permanent.[50]

Economist at the Wales

A month later Plimsoll resigned from the Bank of Australasia and, in October, at the age of 21, he started at the Economics Department of the Bank of New South Wales at a salary of £250.[51] The Wales had long been an institution in Australia. The first bank in Australia, established in 1817, it was then the only wholly Australian-owned bank. The Economics Department, the first research unit of any bank in Australia, proved a stimulating experience, offering a new economics graduate unusually interesting work and colleagues, and some high level attention and encouragement.[52]

The Economics Department had been set up in 1931 by Sir Alfred Davidson, chief general manager. Sometimes referred to as Davidson's kindergarten, the department was just outside his office door, and worked directly to him, although it had wider tasks as well. It was a primitive form of a brains trust, fleshing out ideas rather than creating them. Davidson wanted it to be a vehicle to promote collective thinking about Australia as a whole.[53]

Davidson was full of ideas and had some influence. A few years before, he had played a part in the decision to move the Australian Pound away from parity with Sterling. Later he had taken a prominent role before the Royal Commission into Banking in 1936, drawing on material prepared for him by the Economics Department. Davidson set great store by his department. He hired a succession of economics professors from Australian universities, both to head the department and to advise him more generally. During Plimsoll's tenure Professor Torleiv Hytten from the University of Tasmania occupied the post, also bringing international experience to the task.[54]

Plimsoll had responsibility for a variety of matters. These included analysing political conditions in Australia, North and South America, population and migration, transport and defence, secondary industry and New Zealand, and producing the bank's monthly summary.[55] Research provided experience in interviewing people outside the office. Often bank customers, they were usually helpful. It was "very stimulating" to be independent investigators. Although capable guidance was available, reports (usually two pages maximum) went direct to Davidson.[56] This was invaluable experience for a future diplomat. Plimsoll got to know Dr H.C. Coombs, who was then an economist at the nearby Commonwealth Bank.[57]

For the Economics Department Davidson recruited graduates in economics and related disciplines from Australian and British universities. Arthur Tange, from the University of Western Australia, became one of Australia's most distinguished post-war public servants, and a close colleague and friend of Plimsoll's. Leslie Bury, a federal minister in the 1960s, was recruited from the UK. Unusually for the period, the department included women: Vesta Davies from Sydney University, and Betty Burke, an Australian from Cambridge University. In its heyday the department had nearly 20 graduates. "It was a radical move for a bank in any country of the world outside of Europe to gather such a staff of academics interested mainly in looking at the economy as a whole rather than in counting the bank's funds."[58]

The Economics Department was housed in a newly refurbished part of the bank in George Street, opposite Martin Place. No expense, including imported Italian tiling, had been spared to create a magnificent building. A well-stocked library included many leading newspapers and periodicals from around the world. Every morning members of the department would take turns to go through the newspapers with

Davidson personally, a frightening prospect the first time.[59] Davidson is, however, remembered for the kindly way that he treated them. The Davidsons, who had no children, would invite staff to their home in Leura in the Blue Mountains at weekends.

Davidson encouraged an interest in national and international affairs through participation in various groups and societies which the bank supported. The Economics Society of Australia and New Zealand was one of these. While at the bank, Plimsoll wrote at least one article for its journal, the *Economic Record*, about an aspect of the economic thinking of colonial Governor Gipps of NSW, in which Plimsoll argued that Gipps showed himself as an early proponent of an aspect of Keynesian theory.[60]

Davidson gathered the department together about every two months for a general exchange of views, encouraging spirited discussion. Once, in about 1938, on return from a visit to Britain, he informed assembled members of the department and senior members of the bank that he had been told by Admiral Sir Dudley Pound that another world war was inevitable. Sir Alfred invited discussion of how to ensure that Australia was adequately prepared for war.[61] Tange later co-authored a book which appeared in 1941, *Australia Foots the Bill: War Finance 1939-41*, with R.B. McMillen, S.J. Butlin, and T.K. Critchley of the Rural Bank, later a distinguished diplomat.[62]

Plimsoll was remembered favourably, even affectionately, as a colleague. Betty Burke recalled him as "a tall rather plain young man with a quiet, gentle nature – we called him 'Jimmy the Plim.' He was liked by us all and his opinions respected. We would all have missed something if we had not known him."[63] Vesta Davies recalled that, as fellow cat lovers, they had something in common. (The Plimsoll family cat, called Commo, was named after the first Commonwealth Loan – a subsequent family cat was called Drip, after the Dividend Reinvestment Plan).[64] Arthur Tange found him "always dutiful, unfrivolous, but not a dull man, someone who found humour in lots of situations, yet unworldly and a loner". Tange did not see Plimsoll outside the office. Although not gregarious Plimsoll made friends "because people liked him, but to no great depth".[65]

Tange thought Plimsoll did not make any special contribution in the work of the Economics Department.⁶⁶ Another colleague considered he had no great grasp of economic principles.⁶⁷ Experience there was nevertheless invaluable. It enhanced Plimsoll's research and analytical capability, and broadened his horizons in matters beyond economics. It sharpened his interpreting of current political developments: "He could read a politician's mind."⁶⁸ It widened his circle of friends, staying in touch with many when he moved on.

The perpetual student

Plimsoll spent eight years at university. Having attained a pass degree in Economics, after another three years he graduated in Arts, majoring in History and English, which reinforced a lifelong love of English literature. Apart from intellectual development, the university period was important in other ways. Plimsoll became prominent in debating and student affairs, which enhanced his self-confidence. All this left little time for the usual pursuits of young men, who would have found it hard to contemplate life without socialising at a pub or at parties, or without time to play sport regularly. Plimsoll did not see life without these things as a great sacrifice. Socially, he was shy, he did not dance, and he did not drink. Although tolerant of others, such activities were not for him. The relationships and friendships he formed with men and women were based on mutual respect rather than any degree of closeness. Plimsoll's later work habits and approach to life, that is, almost total absorption in the job at hand, doubtless followed from the disciplined and monastic regime that he adopted during this period.

From the outset he participated actively in weekly Union Night debates, and quickly made a reputation for himself. Speaking as long ago as 1875 about the idea of Union Night debates, Professor Charles Badham had addressed the value of the experience of being able to speak off the cuff:

> To call up the right word from the depths of your consciousness, or indeed to have any internal consciousness at all, while you are standing up to be looked at by an innumerable throng of faces, is a power which scarcely comes by nature, even to those whom nature intends to be public speakers.[69]

Plimsoll learned to speak confidently, with scarcely a note even on complex matters. A prodigious memory enabled him to have considerable detail at his command. He also prepared carefully for set speeches.[70] Owen Davis, later a fellow diplomat, and who first met him at these debates, recalled that Plimsoll was "a well-informed, serious debater, who had a contribution to make".[71] Hugh Robson, later a NSW judge, remembered Plimsoll as very quiet, precise in his comments, "economical with words, but with a feeling for their value. At the same time there was wit and charm".[72]

Plimsoll's acknowledgement of intellectual ability, whether male or female, involved him in decisions that led to the first annual debates between male and female students; in 1940 to the selection of the first woman on the Sydney Inter-Varsity Debating team; and in 1941 to the participation of women students in Union Night.[73] He became a selector of the Inter-Varsity Debating team, although never actually in it, probably due to difficulties in getting leave from the bank. He also became a leader of debates, or an adjudicator or chairman at Union Night and at inter-faculty and inter-collegiate debates. His "genial and forbearing control of the follies" of Union Night were long remembered.[74]

Plimsoll's other involvements on campus gradually increased in extent and responsibility. He became a vice-president of the Students' Representative Council (SRC), and a member of the Inter-Faculty Sports Committee. In SRC meetings, Plimsoll was quiet, brief, and to the point. Never aggressive, more often than not reducing by "negative criticism" the more outlandish or bizarre suggestions of other councillors. He was "already a man of caution and prudence, and considerable intellectual perception".[75] Mainly a Union man, Plimsoll tended to regard the SRC as rather frivolous. He probably had the SRC in mind when he later recalled "how little discussion or division actually occurs in student societies on real fundamentals of social and cultural importance".⁷⁶

The Union became his main focus. He served as honorary treasurer and, at the end of 1940, was elected president, a considerable feat for an evening student. People respected Plimsoll's work on detail, and his sober analysis. He was by no means charismatic, nor was he someone who actively sought publicity or votes. The help of those who nominated him and knew his ability was crucial in mustering support for his election.⁷⁷ He won by two votes.

To Gordon Jockel, later a fellow diplomat, Plimsoll was "a godlike, more senior figure hovering around". Like others he noted Plimsoll had the same facial appearance as he would have for the next 40 years, "a graven quality, which was a striking aspect of his personality".⁷⁸

Plimsoll, then, was "gawky, untidy, anything but elegant". There were soup stains on his waistcoat, and his table manners were poor. Yet he had a "curious capacity for making valuable friends, getting close to older people of influence".⁷⁹ The union president worked with a management committee comprising professors and others to oversee the operations of the union. At the annual general meeting of the union late in 1941, Plimsoll was described by the honorary secretary, Dr A.H. McDonald, as "one of the great Presidents of the Union". P.J. Kenny, a former president and later a prominent Sydney barrister, said it had been a particularly busy year, with the completion and furnishing of building extensions, and new projects such as music recitals. Plimsoll had engendered "a spirit of cooperation amongst the union board" which had despatched its business "with less time and greater efficiency" than he had seen before. Plimsoll was reelected unopposed.⁸⁰

Donald Horne recalled the widely favourable impact made by the changes to the Men's Union, instituted by Plimsoll, bringing in music, art and better food.⁸¹ Plimsoll was serious, but not aloof, friendly in his own way and quietly helpful to anyone around him.⁸² Horne, then a sometimes controversial writer for Sydney University's student newspaper, *Honi Soit*, was surprised and pleased that Plimsoll took some personal interest in him: "His air of thoughtful interest in my future breaks through my pride, and I listen to his advice."[83]

Plimsoll showed courage by strongly criticising the Senate, the university's supreme governing body, for cancelling appointments of two new professors to the law faculty for what he thought to have been dubious reasons, and that the Jewish background of one, Julius Stone, may have been a factor.[84] The appointments finally went ahead a few days later.

Plimsoll thrived at Sydney University, for which he retained a special affection and a strong belief in the virtues of higher education "both as an indicator of intelligence and of discipline and application".[85] He developed a lifelong interest in universities, wherever he was, and was well informed about them.[86]

War

During 1939, out of a sense of duty, Plimsoll had joined the Militia (a forerunner to the Army Reserve) and went to a training camp as a humble gunner in the First Medium Brigade, Royal Australian Artillery. The camp lasted a month, "not a bad life", which he described as a good rest without any responsibility. Service in the ranks "removes any intellectual arrogance; the university graduate finds that he can get on very well with the labourer and the shop-assistant, and that these men can do some things much better than he can". But he was not enthusiastic about the army. After a month "there is a danger that you will stagnate, and acquiesce in becoming a vegetable". Reading was important "in maintaining flexibility of mind and in counteracting the dulling influences around you".[87]

On the outbreak of war in Europe Sir Alfred Davidson had contacted the Commonwealth Manpower Planning Authority and arranged that a select number of his staff in the Economics Department would be exempt from being called up. Plimsoll was one of these, as well as Tange.[88]

After Japan's entry into the war in December 1941, measures instituted at the university included air raid precautions. As union president, Plimsoll took his turn in duty shifts, sleeping in the union one night a week.

Despite the war, life in many ways continued normally. Plimsoll enjoyed a family holiday at Katoomba in the Blue Mountains over Christmas 1941, evidently taking some mild pleasure in bucking a government admonition not to go on holidays, and "did not feel guilty about defying the Prime Minister's ban". It was his first holiday since 1938, characteristically spent catching up on his reading. It was "very easy to forget the war when you leave Sydney; nobody seemed particularly interested, and it made me see quite clearly the difficulties of the Government in arousing popular enthusiasm".[89]

Plimsoll was concerned about his brother John, who had joined up late in 1939, as well as others known to him who were serving overseas in the forces. In his research work in the bank, the war became a constant factor to be taken into account. For many years he had followed the deteriorating situation in Europe closely through the press. He frequently participated in Union Night debates about the political and economic situation leading to war in Europe.

By April 1942, when he turned 25, Plimsoll had been absorbed in the university for nearly eight years. Later he wrote that "at the University . . . there is a danger to all of us lest we become the eternal undergraduate and never grow up".[90] He had to move on. Fortuitously, that month, everything changed quite suddenly for Plimsoll.

At the Union Night debate of 15 April, a message from Plimsoll was read out, submitting an apology for absence from his accustomed place in the Chair. That evening he would be travelling to Melbourne to join the army. He noted that over the years he had attended 150 meetings and wished them well. Later that night a motion was carried, congratulating

Plimsoll on his army appointment as recognition of those qualities which had made him an outstanding union president.[91]

The army appointment marked a considerable change in his rank. From being in the militia as a lowly gunner, Plimsoll, on enlisting in the army, immediately became a captain. The future was uncertain, but his upbringing, education and experience had unwittingly prepared him well for what lay ahead.

Endnotes

1 *Australian Institute of Industrial Psychology Report on Plimsoll*, 11/5/1934. MS 8048/10/1. JP papers, National Library of Australia (NLA).

2 Curate of St Matthew's Church, Bondi. JP papers, 8048/10/1 NLA.

3 "Sydney's first Anzac Day", *Sydney Morning Herald*, 25-27/4/1908.

4 George H. Peters, *The Plimsoll Line*, Barry Rose (Publishers) Ltd, Chichester and London, 1975, 92.

5 *Reminiscential Conversations between Hon Clyde Cameron and Sir James Plimsoll 1984*. TRC 1967, i, 96. NLA. Hereafter cited as Cam/Plim.

6 *Encyclopaedia of Fiji, Samoa, Tonga, Tahiti and the Cook Islands*, McCarron Stewart and Co, Sydney, 1907, 259-60.

7 I am indebted to Professor Phillipa Weeks and her father, John Weeks, for finding this information.

8 Marriage certificate, Registrar-General's Office, Suva, Fiji.

9 Harold Groves, conversation, 16/12/1998. Hereafter Groves.

10 Lionel Kentwell, conversation, 1/9/2000. Hereafter Kentwell.

11 K. Farnham, conversation, 18/5/1998.

12 Patricia Plimsoll, conversation, 13/7/1996. Hereafter Plimsoll.

13 Groves; Plimsoll.

14 Plimsoll.

15 Frank Murray, conversation, 30/12/97.

16 Cam/Plim, i, 96.

17 Cam/Plim, i, 101.
18 Plimsoll.
19 Margaret Whitlam, conversation, 1997.
20 Kentwell.
21 JP Papers, 8048/10/1 NLA.
22 Sir Roden Cutler, conversation, July 1996, hereafter Cutler.
23 Professor John Passmore described his time at the school in *Memoirs of a Semi-detached Australian*, MUP, 1997.
24 Cam/Plim, i, 93.
25 Basil Dickinson, conversation, 8/5/1998.
26 Mervyn Wood, conversation, 19/5/1998.
27 R.E. Johns, conversation, 8/9/2000.
28 Sir Richard Kingsland, conversation, 30/8/2000.
29 *The Record. The Magazine of the Sydney Boys High School.* xxiv, No. 2, December 1932, 68 and 73-5.
30 An excellent English teacher, Jennings was keen on debates in class. Kentwell.
31 Sir John Cornforth, letter, 7/11/1997.
32 Cutler.
33 Kentwell.
34 Cam/Plim, i, 100, Kentwell and Michael McGeorge, conversation, 16/3/2000.
35 C. Mathews-Drew, letter, 5/6/1934, ANZ Group Archives; R.E. Johns.
36 Ruth Dobson to John Plimsoll, 27/5/1987. Privately held.
37 *The Record,* xxv, June 1933, No. 1, 8 & 10.
38 Cornforth, op. cit.
39 JP papers, 8048/10/1 NLA.
40 JP papers, 8048/10/1 NLA.
41 Kentwell.
42 Psychological report on Plimsoll, op. cit.
43 D.J. Bradford to the Inspector, Bank of Australasia, 6/6/1934. From letter of 23/2/1998 and enclosures of Tony Miller, ANZ Group Archives.

44 The Bank of Australasia later merged with the Union Bank to form the ANZ Bank.

45 Letter, 23/2/1998, ANZ Group Archives.

46 H.W. Bullock, conversation, 1996.

47 JP papers, 8048/10/1 NLA.

48 Letter, 23/2/1998, ANZ Group Archive.

49 Cam/Plim, i, 93.

50 Letter, 23/2/1998, ANZ Group Archive.

51 His salary rose to £340 by early 1942. Julie Gleaves, Westpac Historical Services, letter, 6/2/1998.

52 It was a "sort of post-graduate school where raw graduates could be trained by more experienced staff to help in the solution of problems of a non-academic, practical kind". A.J. Hagger, *Torleiv Hytten 1890-1980 Norwegian immigrant Australian economist*, UTAS Hobart, 2007, 47.

53 R.F. Holder, conversation, 18/9/1999.

54 In 1935 Hytten had travelled to the UK, Europe and USA at Bank expense, during which he attended an inter-dominion conference in London as an adviser to Prime Minister J.A. Lyons, stood in for the absent NSW Agent-General at an international wool conference in Berlin, and attended the League of Nations Assembly as an adviser to S.M. Bruce. In 1937 he made a similar journey. He had also been extensively involved on behalf of the Bank in preparing material for the 1936 Royal Commission into banking and monetary systems in Australia. Hagger, op cit, 35-6, 43-6.

55 Westpac Archives, letter, 6/2/1998.

56 Walter Ives, later Secretary Federal Department of Primary Industry, conversation, 20/3/2001.

57 Cam/Plim, ii, 13.

58 "Unique era in Australian Banking," *Australian Financial Review*, 5/2/1965.

59 Brian Fleming, letter, 2/7/1997.

60 "An Australian anticipation of Mr Keynes." *Economic Record*, June 1939, 108-10. Copy located in JP papers, M2203/5, Box 1, Item 1, NAA.

61 Bruce Allen, conversation, 28/6/1997.
62 Peter Edwards, *Arthur Tange. Last of the Mandarins*. Allen and Unwin, Sydney, 2006, 25-6.
63 Betty Burke, letter, 20/7/1997.
64 Vesta Davies, conversation, 29/6/1997. Hereafter Davies. Kathleen Plimsoll, conversation, 26/3/2004.
65 Sir Arthur Tange, conversation, 6/1/1998.
66 Tange, conversation, 6/1/1998.
67 Ronald Mendelsohn, conversation, 30/3/1998. Hereafter Mendelsohn.
68 Davies, conversation, 29/6/1997.
69 Clifford Tunny, Ursula Bygott, and Peter Chippendale, *Australia's First. A History of the University of Sydney*. vol 1, 1850-1939. Hale and Iremonger, 1991, Sydney, 168.
70 Tange remembered Plimsoll in the Economics Department library of the Bank practising a speech for a Union Night. Eulogy, Memorial Service, St John the Baptist, Canberra, 21/5/1987.
71 Owen Davis, conversation, 19/4/1997.
72 Robson, conversation, 24/1/1998.
73 *Union Recorder*, 1941, xxi 179, 195, 208. Sydney University Archives.
74 Robson; and Rev John Garrett, letter to Plimsoll, 17/10/1953, JP papers, DFAT.
75 Gilchrist, conversation, 1/9/1997.
76 JP to Horne, 3/6/42. *Donald Horne Papers*, Box MLK 2132 Mitchell Library, Sydney, courtesy Donald Horne.
77 Gilchrist; Mendelsohn.
78 Gordon Jockel, conversation, 19/9/1997.
79 Mendelsohn.
80 *Union Recorder*, 1941, xxi, 16/10/1941, 220.
81 It was a "new world when, after a lunch-hour recital of Handel in the Union Hall, we can stroll past the new reproductions of Matisse in the Union ante-

room and then sit in the refectory and order, as a first course, that novelty of novelties, chilled soup". Donald Horne, *The Education of Young Donald*, Angus and Robertson, Sydney, 1967, 294.

82 Cutler.

83 Horne, *Education of Young Donald*, 294-6 and 320.

84 *Union Recorder*, xxi, 30/10/1941, 235.

85 Lt Simon Schiwy, ADC to Plimsoll as Governor of Tasmania. Conversation, 18/2/2000.

86 J.D.B. Miller, conversation, 6/3/1997.

87 JP to Horne, 8/1/1942. *Donald Horne Papers*.

88 Walter Ives recalled that Davidson wanted to exert his authority with the Army. "No one was going to tell him who he could and could not have." Another theory held in some quarters was that he expected to become Governor of the Commonwealth Bank, and wanted to keep people to take with him, but it all fell through as he was not offered enough pay. Walter Ives, conversation, 20/3/2001. Edwards, *Tange*, 23-4.

89 JP to Horne, 8/1/42. *Donald Horne Papers*.

90 JP to Horne, 11/6/44. *Donald Horne Papers*.

91 *Union Recorder*, No. 4, 23/4/42, 39.

2

Alf's Army, 1942-47

Ah, but what a life-changer [Alf Conlon] was! If it hadn't been for Alf [Jim Plimsoll] still would be an economist at the Bank of New South Wales.[1]

An academic untidiness but it was combined with a razor-sharp mind. [Plimsoll] did look as if he had slept in his uniform.[2]

Like many of his contemporaries the Second World War was a turning point for Plimsoll. While his life had been centred around banking and Sydney University, his time in the army led him in a completely different direction. Without any basic military training, overnight he had enlisted and been commissioned as a captain.[3] This transformation came about through a fellow student politician, Alfred Conlon. About 10 years older than Plimsoll, an Arts graduate who had returned to study medicine, Conlon served with Plimsoll on the Sydney University SRC, and on the union board as vice-president when Plimsoll was president. Earlier, in July 1939, Conlon was also elected as student representative on the University Senate. This appointment led to him becoming the unofficial university manpower officer. Early in 1942 the Prime Minister's Committee on National Morale was established with Conlon as the inaugural chairman.[4]

The Directorate of Research and Civil Affairs

For some time Conlon had felt there was a need for a think tank in the army to examine wider political and economic issues. In April 1942 Conlon enlisted and, with the approval of his friend, Major-General

Victor Stantke, the army's Adjutant-General,[5] he set up a Research Section (later Directorate of Research) of 25-30 people to work in Land Headquarters at Victoria Barracks, Melbourne.

Few were from the regular army. According to Peter Ryan, they were "all oddballs, working to a script by Evelyn Waugh" but it was "a mindblowing experience".[6] Mostly aged in their 20s and 30s and from academic posts at Sydney University, intellectual attainment was a hallmark of many of the Directorate members who were "an exceptional group of talented people".[7] Among these were Sydney anthropologists like Bill Stanner, H.I.P. Hogbin and Camilla Wedgwood. Another was John Andrews, senior lecturer in Geography. Plimsoll had known both Andrews and Hogbin through their involvement in student politics. There were James McAuley and Harold Stewart, later prominent poets. Some professors were recruited on a part-time basis, like Julius Stone and "Panzee" Wright (from Melbourne). Most did not undergo the normal induction into the army such as the medical examination, which a number might have failed.[8]

Some were recruited by people whose judgment Conlon trusted. For example, Eric Willis, later Premier of NSW, who had topped his year in Geography at Sydney University, was recruited by Andrews, his former lecturer.[9] While Conlon decided the army rank for each person, formal rank counted for little. Conlon himself started as a Major but had no problems about giving orders to some whom he had recruited as colonels. Promotions were handled in a similarly unorthodox way.[10]

Plimsoll was one of the most awkward, unmilitary-looking officers. He had no idea of how to wear his cap; his uniform was grubby and frayed around the edges. There was no vertical crease in the trousers, and his shoes were unpolished. Most army officers, including non-career, bought their uniforms from a military tailor, whereas Plimsoll was content with the version from the government clothing factory. A principal advocate of the view that it was not appearance that counted was Conlon himself.[11]

Conlon's outwardly easy manner – "Call me Alf" – and his encouragement of a spirit of free inquiry and discussion among his officers, contrasted with the secretive, controlling, even Machiavellian way in which he operated. The Directorate "had some of the elements of a Renaissance Court, with Alf as the Medici Prince".[12] He disseminated and delegated very little; almost everyone reported directly to him.[13]

The apparent humbleness of the Directorate's location in a vast weatherboard single storey barn contrasted with the access that Conlon achieved in the main bluestone building at Victoria Barracks. This was especially after General Sir Thomas Blamey, Land Forces Commander in Chief, announced in a Note of 6 October 1943 that he was taking personal charge of the Directorate. Major Conlon thus had direct access to the General. The Note, a masterpiece of brevity, gave no details of the advisory functions of the Directorate or of the nature of its research.[14] This gave Conlon, as well as Blamey, considerable room to manoeuvre. The Directorate had its period of greatest productivity and influence under Blamey.[15] Conlon continued to see Curtin occasionally.[16]

Conlon's basic proposition was that an Australian commander-in-chief needed a political dimension to his thinking: "He could not afford to be politically naive or uninformed in dealing either with his own Government or with Australia's allies."[17] Blamey, accustomed to dealing with politicians,[18] was responsive to the kind of advice he received from Conlon and his team. Plimsoll later asserted that during the War, partly because Blamey listened to Conlon, "the Australian Army was better attuned to civilian needs than probably any other army in the world".[19]

Conlon "could make people of the highest seniority see themselves and their role in a new light, giving stimulus to their thinking. He could also operate politically with daring, adroitness and aplomb". At his height, he was "a prestidigitator with remarkable skills".[20]

Plimsoll found Conlon full of ideas and projects, both good and bad. The atmosphere around him "could sometimes be very annoying, but it was always very stimulating". With Conlon, "there was a ferment of ideas, a certain amount of chaos – and out of all this came something that was worthwhile, something that was new". Plimsoll admired two particular qualities in Conlon, "a great capacity to discern some idea or trend in the world that was relevant to conditions in Australia", and the "capacity to influence persons in authority so that they did something about the problems that he thought they could contribute to".[21]

The small and secretive world of the Directorate attracted some resentment and criticism among public servants and army officers, particularly that few Directorate members had ever served in a front line, a notable exception being Peter Ryan, who joined in February 1944.[22] In the House of Representatives later that year a member requested "details of a unit of 24 members of whom nine are colonels, two majors, two captains and the remainder lieutenants", and why the Directorate "which many believe to be an excrescence, was established".[23]

The work of the Directorate

Presciently, the post-war administration and development of Papua New Guinea (PNG) was a major preoccupation of the Directorate.[24] Blamey, Conlon and others were determined to see that Australia played a role in the post-war settlement of the region, especially in relation to PNG.[25] Conlon foresaw that PNG would have to be under military administration for some time, so Blamey needed broad advice in drawing up directives for army units there. A huge relief map of PNG, 18 feet by 14 feet, was brought in by Professor E.S. Hills of Melbourne University's Department of Geography.[26]

PNG was a major part of Plimsoll's work. He shared an office with the geographer, John Andrews, who worked consistently on PNG, including on military terrain studies, and on possibilities for development. Plimsoll, who had been taken on as a research economist, wrote a study of the economy, "dealing with questions such as the restoration of production".[27] Their office adjoined that of John Kerr, who concentrated on post-war planning for PNG as well as other colonial territories. Kerr talked to Plimsoll frequently, especially before accompanying Blamey on a visit to London.[28] Plimsoll's involvement in New Guinea led to a lifelong interest in the Territory, as was also the case with others such as Kerr, McAuley, Ryan and Legge.

Plimsoll's other work in the Directorate included "a close study of US current affairs" in collaboration with McAuley, as a possible briefing for General Blamey,[29] as well as studying aspects of India and the USSR.[30] He wrote an extensive report about the wartime Chinese economy at the request of Conlon, who was interested in Australia's relations with post-war China.[31] Other tasks included contingency planning in the event that Japan established a foothold in some part of Australia, and of the civil administration of Australia, then divided into 32 parts. This included drawing up a series of regulations to enable appointment of a civil administration to work with the army in an area,[32] and confidential weekly briefing to civil authorities of the location of armed forces within Australia to ensure sufficient food supplies for the forces and civilians, especially in Queensland.[33]

Plimsoll reinforced the good impression that Conlon had of him from Sydney University. Although not one of Conlon's inner circle,[34] Conlon respected Plimsoll's views and saw him frequently – Plimsoll contributing to putting "some commonsense into Alf's numerous ideas".[35] Conlon was impressed by Plimsoll's capacity for analysis and for brief exposition, and by his ability to argue a view tenaciously. Conlon was an oral operator, an anti-bureaucrat. Plimsoll was in some measure a kindred spirit, sharing Conlon's reluctance to commit too much to paper.[36]

Plimsoll found working in the Directorate stimulating, increasing his knowledge of countries of future importance for Australia. As with the Economics Department of the Wales, Plimsoll was working with an interesting group of people, with many of whom, notably Conlon and Kerr, he would stay in touch. He was not, however, particularly extended;

there was rarely need for anyone to work evenings or weekends. Though he found the work interesting, after his hectic years in Sydney of working by day, and study and student affairs by night, it was comparatively quiet.[37]

Outside activities

Plimsoll wrote letters regularly to his parents. He managed to go home at least annually while he was in Melbourne. In 1944 he managed 32 days in Sydney. He also maintained contact with Sydney University, and at least once participated in union debates; Gough Whitlam recalled seeing him chair one in 1944 in which his father-in-law, Bill Dovey, participated.[38] Plimsoll's only other official travel away from Melbourne was one day in Canberra in 1943 and again in 1944, and three days in the Mt Lofty ranges in South Australia in 1944. Otherwise he was deskbound.[39]

As a colleague in the Directorate, Plimsoll was regarded as quieter and less extrovert than most. Cultivated, scholarly and amusing, he seemed older than his late 20s; mature, grave, dignified, discreet and already balding. He was awkward and socially inept.[40] Tall, slightly stooped, thin, with a "greyish, indoor look" about his complexion, he was "so gentlemanly and courteous, that it was hard to believe he would have ever pitched a fight with anyone". He had no capacity for small talk with people he did not know well; he just asked questions.[41] Despite his perceived social shortcomings, Peter Ryan thought Plimsoll had a sympathetic way of listening and was good at presenting ideas.[42] Of the Melbourne people in the Directorate, Plimsoll saw most of Sam Cohen, in later life an ALP Federal Senator for Victoria.[43]

As at the bank in Sydney, he did not spend much time socially with other members of the Directorate, being "more inclined to bend over books;"[44] nor did he join in after-work drinks.[45] He read extensively while in Melbourne, more than he did in the previous three years in Sydney. In 1942, his first year there, he recorded that he read 83 books, followed by 60 in 1943. In 1944, he read 81. Half of these were classic novels of

English literature. He read some books by Harold Nicolson, including *Diplomacy*.⁴⁶ At night and during weekends Plimsoll was busy on other matters, although he said nothing about these to his work colleagues. He was in contact with colleagues at the Wales in Sydney, especially Professor Tor Hytten. When Dr Howard Mowll, Anglican Archbishop of Sydney, approached Davidson about a sermon he was to make in which he wanted to refer to the future of university education, Davidson in turn approached Plimsoll who, instead of producing notes, offered a text. He also wrote an article about the problems of post-war reintegration of ex-servicemen.⁴⁷

In 1943, working at night and during weekends, he wrote a manuscript of some 80,000 words entitled *Bureaucracy and Democracy*. He was moved to do this by what he regarded as repressive, anti-democratic impulses in the Curtin Government, and tendencies to plan post-war Australia. Somewhat naively, he wanted the text to be acceptable to both the Government and the Opposition in Canberra. There is no evidence that he sought Conlon's permission. He sent the manuscript to Hytten in Sydney, asking whether he thought it worth publishing; if so, would that be all right by the bank (to which he expected to return eventually), and could he arrange for a publisher. Hytten approved the text after some changes. After checking with Davidson, he said the book was all right by the bank. But publication proved impossible with wartime shortage of paper and priority given to government requirements.⁴⁸

In letters, Plimsoll commented on the importance of maintaining civil liberties in wartime as far as possible, and on the shortcomings of local bureaucracy in Melbourne. Outside the Directorate, he was "surrounded by Sydney friends, who are busy organising industry, rationing, clothing, or educating the Army". He noted that the Department of War Organisation of Industry was "filled with Sydney economists, Walker, Butlin, Butler and Swan".⁴⁹ Apart from work colleagues and other transplanted Sydney people, he would have known few in a city in which he was a stranger.

With some other members of the Directorate, he joined a group of around 80 people who met monthly to share an interest in China, especially its art. The group was convened by Dr J. Hanson-Lowe, an eminent English geologist who had been recruited to the Directorate.[50]

In January 1943 Plimsoll found time to represent the NSW Branch at a meeting in Melbourne of the Central Council of the Economic Society of Australia, at the Athenaeum Club. He was considered to have been quite outspoken, raising matters relating to editorial policy and life membership. Most of his proposals did not find favour. But "it was a new development in the conduct of the Society's business to have such matters raised formally in open debate and pursued so strongly".[51]

Directorate members received a small accommodation allowance. Plimsoll was the only one to choose a hotel, The George in St Kilda, which at that time was one of the premier hotels in Melbourne, respectable, old-fashioned and medium-priced. In a curious parallel with his family home in Bondi, the George was situated about the same distance from the beach – although there was no surf on Port Phillip Bay. It was convenient to work – door to door it was a 15-minute tram ride to Victoria Barracks. From this experience there dated a penchant for living in hotels.

In 1944 the Department of External Affairs in Canberra recruited diplomatic cadets for the first time. In the Directorate Cohen and Legge both unsuccessfully sat the exam. Plimsoll, who did not apply,[52] wrote to Donald Horne congratulating him on his selection. Plimsoll gave no indication that he aspired to follow in Horne's footsteps. Although Plimsoll had not spent more than two days in Canberra,[53] that did not deter him from offering his views about the national capital.

The main problem was not the cold, but Canberra's "cloistered seclusion". On that account, he wrote, "the less time you have to spend in Canberra the better". Plimsoll disapproved of the concept of a separate national capital:

The bureaucrats think they represent the true passions of the people. That is one reason why so much Australian government is a ghastly flop, and why the Commonwealth Parliament in some of its decisions and actions shows itself to be so completely out of touch with popular feeling.

He thought the life of a diplomat should be "pleasant and useful".[54]

Plimsoll's comments reflect how little, at that stage, he was attracted to a career as a Canberra public servant, or a diplomat.

Extended visit to the USA

Plimsoll once wrote that he thought that Melbourne had been "jolted" very little by the War.[55] Perhaps the same could have been said about him, although his time in the Directorate reinforced his analytical ability, and stimulated his knowledge and interest in Australia's future role in the region to the north. He had now worked for six years in two remarkable research organisations.

Early in 1945 Conlon selected Captain Plimsoll to go to the USA, along with four other army officers. The visit, expected to last six weeks, was to attend the School of Military Government at Charlottesville, Virginia. This School had been preparing American, British and Canadian officers for the post-war military occupation and administration of Japan, Germany and Italy. Conlon wanted to ensure that Australia was involved in these areas and in others which had been liberated from Japanese control, such as Borneo and New Guinea. It was essential that Australian officers "be well trained in American practice". Armed with what they had absorbed, the officers would put it to instant use elsewhere.[56]

After the War Cabinet's approval on 9 February, the five Australian officers departed on 15 February from Sydney in a converted RAF Liberator bomber.[57] The 14 passengers sat on metal bench seats along the sides of the plane. Personal luggage was restricted to one kitbag each. All flying was at night, by astro-navigation, with the passengers and crew resting by day at a succession of stops. They hopscotched across the Pacific via Auckland, Nadi, Canton Island, and Honolulu. Shortly after takeoff from Honolulu, passengers smelt petrol in the cabin. The pilot returned immediately, concerned about the possibility of fuel leaking from the extra tanks being carried for the next stage of the journey. Fortunately no one had been smoking.[58]

The plane travelled via San Francisco, San Diego and El Paso to Dallas where it became weatherbound for 40 hours on account of rain. Finally they disembarked in Washington DC, and took a two-hour train journey to Charlottesville. They arrived on 23 February, four days after the course had started.[59]

Plimsoll decided to keep a diary of what was expected to be a brief sojourn abroad. This became a lifelong habit, a consistently discreet, bleakly factual record of who and what he saw and where he went.

The intensive six-week course in Military Government included restoration of civil government, and maximising use of the former civil infrastructure of an occupied area to restore administration. The syllabus covered operations (integration of civil affairs with combat forces), supply, legal, general administration (duties of civil affairs officers); specialised subjects including public safety and control of finances in occupied territories, and intelligence. The course was mostly about Japan. Students were "provided with an essential minimum of instruction on Japan and its people, sufficient to enable them to apply their general military government instruction in relation to the peculiarities of that country and its inhabitants".[60]

Plimsoll doubtless worked hard, the pressure probably contributing to his fainting one day near the end of the course. He also found time for discussions with academics at the university in the field of rural sociology, managed to fit in a few film shows and made a number of American and British friends among the students.[61] He seemed to know more American history than American students, politely putting some US officers right about details of the Battle of Gettysburg during the

American Civil War. He became known as the Professor. Ray Reynolds, one of the Australian officers, was impressed with how Plimsoll would remember and evaluate everything of interest after reading the huge Sunday edition of the *New York Times*.[62]

That Plimsoll had had a limited exposure to basic matters military was brought home to Reynolds, who shared lodgings with him in a nearby house. Each day they walked through the university campus, invariably passing a group of young US navy officers who would smartly salute the Australians. Reynolds noticed that Captain Plimsoll did not seem to know how to salute. He gave him some belated instruction.[63]

On the course there was no set doctrine on the military government of Japan[64] so Plimsoll's lack of military experience may not have been a drawback. He was graded superior (over 90%), and finished second overall.[65] Other Australian officers went home or to Borneo to assist with military government.

Plimsoll had a different assignment. He had a meeting at Pennsylvania Railroad Station in New York with John Kerr, who was passing through. Kerr proposed that instead of going to Borneo Plimsoll should stay in Washington with the Australian Military Mission. With promotion to Major, he would be the Civil Affairs Representative, keeping the Directorate in Melbourne "informed of what's going on here in America in the military government field, get ready to play a role with the Americans who will be dominant in the military government side of the Japanese operation and occupation". Plimsoll readily agreed. The background to the proposal was the distrust and dissatisfaction that General Blamey increasingly felt towards General MacArthur, that Australia might be marginalised and unable to project its own post-war requirements into the peace settlement with Japan. Kerr felt that the Directorate needed someone trustworthy in Washington.[66] Plimsoll must have seemed a suitable choice, given his performance at Charlottesville.

Nearly three months passed before the proposal was formally approved. Plimsoll spent the time seeing as much as he could of the

USA. It was the longest period that he was away from formal work. He travelled by train and bus through New England and the Midwest: to Providence, Rhode Island; Martha's Vineyard; and Nantucket, where he was shown over the Whaling Museum, and became a Sustaining Member of the Nantucket Historical Association.[67] He went to Boston, Portland in Maine, to Burlington, Vermont, and to Cape Cod. In the Midwest he went to Chicago, Ann Arbor, Detroit, and Cincinnati – where he was taken by ambulance to the US Air Force Hospital in Fort Thomas, Kentucky, with suspected appendicitis.[68] After three days under observation he proceeded to Indianapolis, St Louis, Kansas City in Missouri, Des Moines, Ames, Omaha, Sioux Falls, Minneapolis and Milwaukee.

Assuming that he would be returning to banking in post-war Australia, Plimsoll set out to learn about banking and the US economy. He called on representatives of the Federal Reserve and local commercial banks, farm credit administrators, university professors of economics and of business, and visited stockyards and farms. He reported his impressions to the Bank in Sydney.[69] He looked in on the further training that his colleagues at Charlottesville were undertaking, mainly in the Japanese language, and which the Australian army at that stage had declined, at US Army Civil Affairs Training Schools at Harvard, Yale and Northwestern universities.[70]

He called on newspapers and, in Sioux Falls, South Dakota, he was interviewed on local radio. He visited local British consuls, who were often helpful and hospitable.[71] He interested himself in American views on international affairs, visiting the Council on Foreign Relations in New York and the President of the Foreign Policy Association in Minneapolis. Wherever possible he went to art galleries, and to the theatre, including musicals.

Plimsoll enjoyed his travels and warmed to Americans, as he sought "to get the feel of the country. I like Americans just as much as Australians and feel in no sense a foreigner among them".[72] He derived a valuable insight into USA away from Washington DC and New York – two cities in which he was later to spend 11 years of his time as a diplomat. It was the beginning of a lifelong determination to travel widely.

Plimsoll found himself in Chicago on VE Day, observing that there was "a certain amount of excitement but no unruliness". He was not tempted out on to the streets, but assured his parents that he had spent his time "quietly", visiting the Director of Research for the Committee of Economic Development, lunching with the local Vice-President of the Federal Reserve Bank, and in discussion with specialists in public administration.[73]

While appreciating the "real flavour of America" that he encountered in the Midwest, he found Chicago a "very ugly city," very windy, and the people "much more isolationist" than those of New England and Virginia.

He was enthusiastic about New England:

> If I were choosing a home to live in permanently, I would go to New England without hesitation. It may be because I have lived most of my life beside the sea, and do not like to be too far from it. But I think it is more because of the atmosphere of New England, which is quiet and cultured without being decadent or unprogressive.[74]

Australian Military Mission, Washington DC

On 5 June his appointment as Staff Officer in the Australian Military Mission, Washington DC, responsible for civil affairs, was confirmed. But he could not start work without greater precision as to his duties, including his relations with the US Department of War and with the British Joint Staff Mission in Washington.[75] He spent his time mostly in New York, going to the theatre every evening, "because we have so little of it in Australia".[76] He visited more bankers and art galleries. He stood in the streets and watched the ticker tape welcome home for General Eisenhower.

Major Plimsoll's ID Card for Australian Joint Staff Mission, Washington DC, June 1945 (Plimsoll family)

On 27 June he finally received his duty statement about liaison with the US on military government, with a view to the occupation of Japan.[77] He began work the next day. Plimsoll found Washington very hot, with a shortage of accommodation. He shared a room with a succession of Australian, British and Canadian army officers.[78] Despite these "not very pleasant quarters," he still considered America "as agreeable as ever, and I hope to see a lot more of it before I go back".[79] Only weeks into his job the War suddenly ended following the dropping of the atom bombs on Japan. On 14 August, Plimsoll was among the crowds outside the White House, celebrating Japan's cessation of hostilities.[80]

Soon many at the Military Mission were ordered home[81] and Plimsoll expected that he would probably be among them. He kept in close touch with Conlon and Kerr by cable and letter.[82] A posting to Tokyo or to the Allied Control Commission in Germany was possible but in October it was decided that he would return home early in December.[83]

The Far Eastern Commission

At the beginning of November 1945 Plimsoll's situation was transformed. From being an army officer awaiting repatriation, he suddenly assumed a diplomatic role, plunging into an international conference to discuss high policy relating to Japan. He stayed in Washington for two more years. It was a turning point in his life.

Under the Potsdam Agreement in August 1945 the Far Eastern Commission (FEC) was to be established in Washington to coordinate post-war Allied policy towards Japan. Dr H.V. Evatt, the Minister for External Affairs, wanted Australia to be involved in the FEC, and also wanted to be involved personally.[84] Australia had to "get in and make our mark at the very outset of the postwar settlement processes or be left behind and virtually ignored". His overriding objective was to secure "an effective role for Australia" in the final peace settlement with Japan. Evatt unsuccessfully sought to become chairman.[85]

Bill Forsyth, a senior officer from External Affairs, Canberra, was assigned to prepare the way for Evatt at the inaugural meeting of the FEC. Forsyth soon found himself "overloaded with the paperwork our Boss's impetuosity required". He looked around for some help. This was not forthcoming from the understaffed Australian Legation in Washington. Alan Watt, the Counsellor, who was about to leave, had recently received a courtesy call from Major Plimsoll.[86] It was probably Watt who suggested to Forsyth that he approach Plimsoll as someone "whose recent training had versed him well in matters Japanese".

As it happened, while visiting Melbourne, Forsyth had previously met Plimsoll through his friend, John Andrews of the Directorate of Research. He also knew Conlon, who "had a knack of handpicking able and well qualified" people for the Directorate. Conlon had told him of Plimsoll's attendance at the course at Charlottesville. On 31 October Forsyth dined with Plimsoll and Ralph Harry of the Legation, and felt reasonably confident that he could satisfy Evatt of Plimsoll's credentials.[87]

Plimsoll teamed up with Forsyth, worked non-stop through the weekend and Monday 5 November, and through to 3:00am on the Tuesday, preparing a speech for Evatt to deliver at the Conference when it opened that day.[88] Forsyth spent long hours with Plimsoll: "It certainly was a hectic time, and Plimsoll's fund of information about Japan, his ability, his gift of ingratiation and his monkish dedication, made him very useful indeed to the Doc and earned him the confidence of that demanding and suspicious master". Forsyth also came to know Plimsoll's "unfailing good temper" and "mild" humour. They worked well enough together although Plimsoll was not a drinking companion for him. "It was thus that Jim Plimsoll was inducted into External Affairs work".[89] Forsyth later described Plimsoll as "brilliant".[90] Within ten days Plimsoll was elected chairman of an FEC subcommittee on the structure of the Japanese economy.[91]

After four years as minister, with limited travel abroad in wartime, Dr Evatt had had limited exposure to diplomats and their work. But he was sufficiently impressed with what he saw of Plimsoll's ability as a novitiate, and his industry, to want to retain him.

After three weeks Dr Evatt "felt he had set policy-making for occupied Japan on the right course". Before returning home Evatt put his seal of approval on Plimsoll, announcing that he would travel to Japan on a visit there by FEC delegations early in 1946. Plimsoll became the "de facto Australian representative on FEC".[92] Things were squared with the Australian army. Plimsoll would be "temporarily on loan when required to Dr Evatt's staff, particularly for military government and economic matters". And, as the UK and US delegations to FEC included officers at the rank of colonel, a "military member would be invaluable at present since Japan is under military control and contact is needed with the US War Department".[93] Major Plimsoll had access to reports from General MacArthur's headquarters in Tokyo, sent on the US army signals network, ahead of US State Department officials at the FEC.[94] He increasingly did less and less work for the military mission.

Dr Evatt's achievements as Minister for External Affairs are well known. A controversial figure, he was intensely disliked by most who worked closely with him for the way he treated people. Among Americans in Washington he had gained a reputation for creating "a tempest wherever he came" and "for dressing down everybody he came into contact with".[95] For years after Evatt had left the portfolio, External Affairs officers used to compete with each other in telling anti-Evatt stories. There was resentment that Evatt ran the department like a personal fiefdom, interfering in personnel matters in ways inappropriate for a minister and contrary to the Public Service Act.

It was Evatt who took over from Conlon as Plimsoll's patron. As Forsyth later recalled, "the opportunity to make himself useful to Evatt at the outset gave him a flying start" in his career as a diplomat.[96] During the next two years, 1946-47, Evatt dealt with Plimsoll directly as much as possible, and encouraged him in his work. Plimsoll for his part gave Evatt high quality service but avoided becoming too close to the minister. Plimsoll felt that "Evatt's ability was outpaced by his complete lack of principle – he saw everything in terms of his own interests. Thus, when he fought for something 'for Australia' in this or that organisation, he lost interest after he had won".[97]

On Boxing Day 1945, Plimsoll and other FEC member delegations flew to Honolulu where they boarded USS *Mount McKinley* on 28 December. The 12-day voyage gave delegates to this new international organisation an opportunity to know each other better. In addition to FEC meetings on board, Plimsoll spent time talking to the leader of the British delegation, Sir George Samson, who had had 30 years service in different parts of Japan, and was "recognised as an expert on the Far East".[98] Plimsoll talked to the ship's crew and watched the daily screening of "moving pictures".

In Japan he attended FEC meetings as delegates travelled to Senadai, Yokohama, Tokyo, Kyoto, Nara, Hiroshima and Osaka, sometimes for briefings from US experts, and sometimes for general discussions. These covered disarmament, rationing and price control, labour, war criminals, and export and import programmes.[99] Plimsoll recalled a journey by car from Yokohama to Tokyo where, for miles, not a building had been left standing after conventional bombing including incendiaries.[100] The visit to Hiroshima on 27 January 1946, some six months after the atomic bomb, made a deep impression: "Everyone came away very subdued, and we were all noticeably quiet that afternoon, so big was the impression created by this first glimpse of the shape of things to come." Kyoto, the former capital, was completely intact, not having been bombed. He walked with another official in little market streets crowded with Japanese, with no other foreigner around: "We were unarmed and yet felt no sense of insecurity whatever. It is a good example of the extent to which the occupation of Japan is effective."[101] At Yokosuka they embarked again on the *Mount McKinley*, and on 1 February they sailed for the US.

A week after his return to Washington, he sent Canberra a major report (54 pages) on the Japanese economy.[102] Exceeding his brief by going into political implications, Plimsoll stressed the importance of not "starting from scratch" in Japan. Dispensing with the old order would be unwise; the least likely to emerge from resulting chaos "would be democracy: it would be authoritarianism from the left or the right". It would be better to have a Japanese government and administration to work with as soon as possible, including retaining the Emperor and not putting him on trial as a war criminal (which Evatt wanted). Otherwise the costs of occupation would be much greater and it would be much less effective.[103] Dr H.C. Coombs thought the report had a significant influence on thinking at the highest level of the Australian Government, including the Prime Minister, J.B. Chifley.[104]

Plimsoll was pleased with the visit: "Japan was a very great experience to me in a new type of work and in an entirely new country". FEC work was interesting and worthwhile.[105]

Plimsoll moved his office out of the AMM as he was doing less and less army work. When the opportunity presented itself he set up a separate Australian delegation office, conveniently in the same building as the FEC, which had occupied the former Japanese Embassy. Increasingly well-established in the job, the Legation had confidence in him. He briefed Sir Frederic Eggleston, the head of mission, whenever the latter had to attend an FEC meeting, as he also did Eggleston's successor, Norman Makin, former Minister for the Navy.

It was surely Canberra's initiative rather than a request from Plimsoll which led to his being sent an assistant. This was Harry Bullock, newly inducted into External Affairs in Canberra after navy war service. Bullock found Plimsoll "nice but awesome. Very knowledgeable. Very hardworking, got to work at 7am". Plimsoll had read all the cables, the *New York Times*, and the London *Times* by the time Bullock arrived at 9. "Anxious to do everything himself. So it took time to get used to him."[106] Plimsoll had become accustomed to working on his own.

The FEC was a worthy endeavour, yet bound to be of limited practical value. Its 15 member-nations found it frustrating dealing with the USA, and especially with General MacArthur. He, as Supremo in Japan, went his own way, taking little notice of the FEC view, or of the Supreme Council of Allied Powers in Japan, which was on his own doorstep, or of the views of US agencies in Washington. When the FEC sent MacArthur a polite message, merely seeking information, "his imperious reply tended to be patronising, sometimes even slightly disdainful".[107]

For Plimsoll, the FEC proved to be excellent experience in multilateral diplomacy, including work with delegations of countries of importance to Australia, especially the US, UK, India, USSR and the Philippines.

In this period in Washington Plimsoll adopted a pattern of living that he maintained throughout his career, at home and abroad. The job at hand absorbed most of his waking hours, including opportunities provided by social functions for informal discussion of current issues with FEC counterparts. He rarely ate lunch or dinner alone. Occasionally he attended working breakfasts. He also got to know diplomats at the Australian Legation, notably L.R. "Jim" McIntyre, with whom he frequently lunched and who became a lifelong friend. He shared meals with others in the Legation, representatives of other departments from Canberra, and locally engaged staff members, one of whom was Tom Lewis, later Premier of NSW (1975-76).

He spent time with Australians visiting on business, such as Roland Wilson, and mixed with many within the Australian expatriate community in Washington. One was Betty Squire, social secretary to a succession of heads of the Australian Legation starting with Richard Casey. Plimsoll frequently went to dinners at her house and she helped him to organise his first cocktail party.[108] Her daughter, Rosemary, a university student, recalled Plimsoll as "already slightly stooped and with a sober rather middle-aged air". "His face lit with twinkling eyes that screwed up as he smiled, which he did slowly but readily". Although teetotal, he was "far from being a killjoy and had the endearing ability to pick up the atmosphere of a party and join right in, sometimes almost to the point of rowdiness!" Plimsoll said that he "liked moving countries, i.e., to the US, because you could shed reputations and start again, be whoever you wanted to be, take on a new personality". However Jim "was so consistently and inevitably Jim". Her mother once produced a broken bit of furniture in the hope that Plimsoll could fix it: "But no, Jim was willing but unable. Practical handyman was not his forte."

Rosemary also recalled an example of Plimsoll's "grasp and total recall of the history of international affairs". Struggling with a university thesis on the foreign policy of Anthony Eden, British Foreign Secretary between 1935 and 1938, she sought Plimsoll's help on a certain point:

> [I] was about to explain its context when, then and there, he pulled all the facts of the matter straight out of his head, together with the various viewpoints, reactions and nuances, and set them out as clearly as if he had actually taken part in the events, or had boned up on them just the day before. Even better, he never made me feel inferior in discussion, or in suggesting points that hadn't occurred to me.[109]

Occasionally he would stay with friends at weekends. Twice he stayed with Bob Barnett, an American colleague at the FEC, helping with terracing and building a garden wall. Mrs Barnett recalled that "two more unlikely people to engage in such work I can hardly imagine". However, they finished the job, while discussing FEC matters.[110] On Sundays, if not otherwise occupied, he would walk along the canals to the Arlington Cemetery, to the Washington Zoo, or to art galleries. He also went to the occasional film. Otherwise he was happy to find a corner of his hotel (the Shoreham) and read a book.

Money was not a problem nor of great interest. He had no time to scan the stock exchange – he decided to buy BHP shares whenever he could.[111]

Despite Evatt's interest, there were no guarantees as to how long this "temporarily on loan" work with the FEC would last. Plimsoll, like many others, sought suitable secure employment on demobilisation. He asked friends at home to alert him to jobs. He would have been able to return to the Bank of NSW, but after an absence of four years he wanted to consider other possibilities.

During 1947 three opportunities arose. Conlon suggested he apply for the post of registrar at the new "National University" in Canberra. Professor Hytten suggested he apply for a vacancy as Professor of Economics at the University of Tasmania. He applied for both, but without success.[112] Meanwhile Brigden, the Treasury representative in the Legation in Washington, told him that on his own initiative, he had informed his home office that he thought Plimsoll was "underemployed". Fred Wheeler from Canberra offered Plimsoll a job in the Treasury at 800 pounds a year, which he declined.

Fate intervened when Plimsoll underwent a personal crisis in his work when much involved in the FEC Committee on Reparations. In midApril 1947, at a critical point in negotiations, he reported to Canberra, which replied that reparations was not an appropriate subject for the FEC to handle.[113] This came as a shock. It was Plimsoll's first encounter with getting an instruction from home which seemed to make no sense to the diplomat on the spot. His feelings no doubt were exacerbated by his lack of experience at the Canberra end.

During the next week he consulted a number of close colleagues in other delegations, especially Sanson (UK) and Powles (NZ). Almost daily he saw the Australian head of mission, Norman Makin, repeatedly seeking permission to resign from the Australian delegation at the FEC. Each time Makin persuaded him to defer such drastic action. Finally Makin agreed to cable Dr Evatt. Meanwhile, Plimsoll wrote a speech for Makin for the next Council meeting, about Australia's stance on reparations, which was that the FEC had no jurisdiction to determine the shares of reparations of the interested countries.[114] Only later did Plimsoll hear that Australia's lone stand on reparations at the FEC reflected Evatt's continuing concern to ensure Australia's interests were taken care of in negotiations about a peace settlement with Japan; and that reparations should be part of such negotiations.

Evatt summoned Plimsoll home in July to accompany him on a visit to Japan which he was making at the invitation of General MacArthur. Plimsoll's explanation as to why an army major would be brought halfway round the world, because of his knowledge of "the American thinking on military occupation",[115] was perhaps true only up to a point. Evatt was also concerned about Plimsoll's threats to resign, as he wanted Plimsoll to join External Affairs in Canberra.

Evatt, who disliked flying, arranged to travel, accompanied by his wife, on a Royal Australian Navy ship. For Plimsoll it was another long naval sea voyage to Japan, during which he had many discussions with Evatt about the question of a peace treaty with Japan, and about the cables which Evatt received via the ship's communications. The disadvantage was that it was Plimsoll himself who had the laborious job of coding and decoding messages. Evatt also talked to Plimsoll about his joining the department. When Plimsoll told Evatt that his politics were directly opposite to his own, Evatt replied that he had realised

Plimsoll's political views, but that he would have every confidence in him as an adviser.[116]

For a minister to involve himself in public service recruitment was unusual. But Evatt "used to regard his department as his own possession and to expect his department to be the instrument of his will".[117] Evatt instructed Burton, Secretary of the Department, to arrange Plimsoll's appointment. Burton, although he had seen little of Plimsoll first hand, had seen his written work. He informed the Public Service Board that Plimsoll's work on the FEC had been "most valuable" to External Affairs, that his "background on Japanese economic matters is unequalled," and that "the loss of his services would be a serious drawback in our work on Japan".[118]

On return from Japan, Evatt arranged for Plimsoll to be secretary-general of a Commonwealth conference in Canberra on Japan, attended by the UK, Canada and New Zealand. At Evatt's behest Plimsoll carried out daily background media briefings on conference developments. He reported to Evatt late each evening with a copy of the proceedings of the day as soon as this had been produced by the secretariat. The sight of Major Plimsoll in army uniform at the conference was the first that many of his future colleagues in External Affairs would have had of him. Evatt then instructed Plimsoll to accompany him to the United Nations General Assembly in New York, in September 1947, as part of the Australian delegation.

Plimsoll's period of service in the army was a backroom, modest contribution to the war effort, while his two years of postwar service had little to do with the army. But the experience stood him in good stead in the future. In taking him in the direction of diplomacy, it changed the course of his life.

Endnotes

1 Ida Leeson in *Alfred Conlon. A Memorial by some of His Friends*, Benevolent Society of NSW, Sydney, 1963, 13. Hereafter: Conlon Memorial.

2 Laurie Baragwanath, letter, 2/10/2000.

3 Officer's Record of Service NX137303 James Plimsoll. Letter of 10/9/96 from Soldier Career Management Agency, Melbourne.

4 Tunny, Bygott and Chippendale, *Australia's First. A History of the University of Sydney*, vol ii, Hale and Iremonger, 1991, Sydney, 194-90.

5 According to H.W. Bullock, Plimsoll's version was that the Directorate's origins sprang from a conversation in Canberra that Conlon had with Prime Minister Curtin. This chapter benefits from comments by Graeme Sligo, author of *The Backroom Boys: Conlon and Army's Directorate of Research and Civil Affairs, 1942-46.* Big Sky Publishing. Sydney, 2013.

6 Peter Ryan, conversation, 9/4/1997. Hereafter Ryan.

7 Ryan entry on Conlon, *Australian Dictionary of Biography*, vol 13, 1993.

8 Dorothy Higgins, a Directorate member; conversation 9/7/97; and letter to author, 16/7/97.

9 J.D. Legge, conversation, 9/4/1997.

10 John Kerr, *Matters for Judgement – An Autobiography*, Macmillan, Melbourne, 1978, 100: Ryan conversation, 9/4/1997.

11 Ryan, conversation, 9/4/1997; Higgins, letter 28/3/99.

12 James McAuley in *Conlon Memorial*, 25.

13 Ryan. I. Butchart, a Directorate secretary, conversation, 1997.

14 Accession MP 742, file 240/1/880 NAA Melbourne.

15 David Horner, *Blamey, The Commander in Chief*, Allen and Unwin, Sydney, 1998, 281.

16 J.D.B. Miller, conversation.

17 James McAuley, "The John Kerr I knew", *Quadrant*, vol XX. (1), Jan 1976, 25.

18 Horner, op. cit.

19 *Reminiscential Conversations between Hon Clyde Cameron and Sir James Plimsoll 1984.* TRC 1967, i, 102. NLA. Hereafter cited as Cam/Plim.

20 McAuley *Conlon Memorial*, 25.

21 Plimsoll, *Conlon Memorial*, 15-16; Cam/Plim, i, 102.

22 Ryan believed that his experience (recounted in *Fear Drive My Feet*, MUP, 1959) was a factor in his recruitment, following such questions in the House. Ryan, conversation, 9/4/1997.

23 Question to the Minister for the Army from the Hon T.W. White, MP, 21/9/44, file GP121/779, NAA Melbourne.

24 Gavin Long, *The Final Campaigns. Official History of Australia in the War of 1939-45*, vol vii, 1963, AWM, 397-98; Sylvia Martin, *Ida Leeson – a Life*, Allen and Unwin, Sydney, 2006, 154.

25 Horner, *Blamey*, 438.

26 D. Higgins, conversation, 9/7/97.

27 Dr J.W. Burton, Secretary, Department of External Affairs, memo, 18 August 1947, to Public Service Board, Canberra. Plimsoll's Personnel file DFAT.

28 Ryan, conversation, 9/4/1997.

29 James McAuley, op. cit., 25.

30 Higgins, letter, op. cit.

31 Gilchrist, conversation, 1/9/1997.

32 Cam/Plim, i, 135.

33 Cam/Plim, ii, 375.

34 Legge, conversation, August 1997.

35 Higgins, conversation of 9/7/97, and letters of 16/7/97 and 28/3/99.

36 Gilchrist, conversation, 1/9/1997.

37 Plimsoll to Horne, 11/10/42, 8/11/42, 29/8/43. *Donald Horne Papers*.

38 E.G. Whitlam, conversation, 1996.

39 Plimsoll's summary of his travel records, JP papers 8048/4/2 NLA; JP to Horne 20/12/42, and 30/1/44. *Donald Horne Papers*.

40 Ryan, conversation 9/4/97; Legge, conversation, 9/4/97.

41 I. Butchart; D. Higgins.

42 Ryan.

43 Plimsoll to Horne 3/6/42. *Donald Horne Papers*.

44 Higgins.

45 Legge, conversation, August 1996.

46 In his previous three years in Sydney he had read 52 books in 1939, 59 in 1940 and 58 in 1941. JP papers 8048/10/1 NLA.

47 Davidson to Archbishop Mowll 17/6/1943. GM201/140. Hytten to Plimsoll 1/6/43. Economic Adviser files Box "P" General. Draft sermon is at W1.13. The Bank of NSW published "Demobilisation of servicemen" in its *Monthly Summary of General Economic Conditions* No. 5/44 dated 8/6/44. Westpac Archives, Sydney.

48 Plimsoll and Hytten corresponded extensively about this proposed book. P to H 25/9/43, H to P28/9/43, P to H 30/9/43 and 30/11/43, H to P 3/12/43 and 1/3/44, p to H 26/5/43, H to P2/6/44,, and P to H 20/8/44. Economic Adviser Files Box 37 "P" General. Westpac Archives, Sydney.

49 Plimsoll to Horne 3/6/42. *Donald Horne Papers*.

50 Higgins, letter, op. cit.

51 RH Scott *The Economic Society of Australia, Its History: 1925-1985*. Economic Society of Australia, 1990, pp. 24-5

52 Legge, conversation, 9/4/97.

53 JP, Personal travel records, JP papers, 8048/4/3, NLA.

54 JP to Horne, 11/6/44, *Donald Horne Papers*.

55 JP to Horne, 11/10/42, *Donald Horne Papers*.

56 War Cabinet, CRS A2670, Item 5/1945, NAA, Canberra.

57 Judge Ray Reynolds, conversation, 8/11/97.

58 Reynolds, and JP diary 17/2/45. JP papers, 8048/3 NLA.

59 Reynolds.

60 Report by Lt Col J.V.M. Shields about the 10th course 20/11/44, para 10, 881/32/4 54, Australian War Memorial (AWM).

61 JP diary 28/3/45. Reynolds.

62 Reynolds.

63 Reynolds.

64 Report by Shields.

65 JP diary 31/3/45, Reynolds.

66 Years later Kerr felt proud at "having played a small part at the outset of Sir James Plimsoll's long and distinguished diplomatic career". John Kerr, *Matters for Judgement*, 104-5; JP diary 21/4/45 and Reynolds, who was also present.

67 JP diary, 7/4/45.

68 JP diary 17/5/45 and letter home, 17/5/45. Privately held.

69 Plimsoll to Hytten, 1/5/45, 1/7/45, Economic Adviser files Box 37 "P" General. Westpac Archives.

70 Plimsoll to Capt DC Whitaker USMC, 16/6/45; JP papers, Box 1, Item 3, NAA.

71 In St Louis the British Consul arranged a lunch for him to meet bankers and economists; in Chicago the Consul-General took Plimsoll to dinner, then on to hear the Consul-General speak at a hospital nursing graduation ceremony, then back to his house for a party, and finally to a nightclub called Yar, run by a White Russian Army Colonel. JP diary, 1/6/45.

72 Plimsoll to Whitaker, op. cit.

73 Letter home, 10/5/45.

74 Bramall, letter home, 5/5/45.

75 JP to Major Hull, 29/6/45, Box 1, Item 3, JP papers, NAA.

76 Letter home, 16/6/45. Privately held.

77 Cam/Plim, i , 104. JP diary, 27/6/45.

78 JP diary, and letter home 30/6/45. Privately held.

79 JP to Herb Caen, at Harvard, 4/7/45, Box 1, Item 3, JP papers, NAA.

80 JP diary, 14/8/45.

81 JP diary, 4/10/45.

82 On 9/9/45 he received an "important letter" from Kerr. JP diary.

83 JP to Chapman, 22/9/45. Box 1, Item 3, JP papers, NAA; Land Headquarters Melbourne cables of 3/10, and 25/10/45; and Australian Military Mission, Washington cables of 3/10, 10/10 and 23/10/45. 54 881/32/4, AWM.

84 In a statement of 30/9/45 welcoming establishment of the FEC, Evatt noted that Australia had long advocated such a body "to enable countries who have taken a prominent part in the defeat of Japan to participate at the highest level in the consideration and formulation of a post-armistice policy". Cable I 31381 Overseas trips 1945 cables, London. *HV Evatt Papers*, Flinders University, Adelaide.

85 W.D. Forsyth, *Recollections*, Chapter on the Far Eastern Commission, unpublished MSS in DFAT, 4-5.

86 JP diary, 18/10/45. At the time the Australian Legation and the Military Mission each operated from different locations in Washington.

87 Forsyth, 9-10; and JP diary 31/10/45.
88 JP diary 1-6/11/45. Plimsoll approached the task with the advantage of some prior knowledge of the FEC, on which he had been reporting to Conlon. Sligo, letter, October 2013.
89 Forsyth, *Recollections*, 11.
90 Bullock, conversation, 15/1/98.
91 JP diary, 10/11/45.
92 Forsyth, op. cit., 11
93 Australian Military Mission messages of 6/11 & 29/11/45. 54 881/32/4 AWM. Also Cam/Plim i. 104.
94 John E. Ryan, diary 2/2/70. Privately held.
95 Plimsoll retained a typed copy of this extract from Forrest C. Pogue, *George C. Marshall*, vol ii, *Ordeal and Hope 1939-42*, 372. JP papers, DFAT.
96 Forsyth.
97 *Papers of Sir Walter Crocker*. Journal, xvi, 3764, 1/4/67. Barr-Smith Library, Adelaide University. Hereafter cited as WRC Jnl.
98 A.S. Watt to W.R. Hodgson, 22/1/44. EA miscellaneous correspondence, *Evatt Papers*, Flinders University.
99 JP diary, 16/1/46, 18/1/46.
100 Cam/Plim, ii, 240.
101 Letter home, 24/2/46.
102 Letters home, 15/2/46, 24/2/46. JP diary, 1/3/46.
103 Cam/Plim ii, 193-196, 452-3. Plimsoll's Report on visit to Japan with the Far Eastern Advisory Commission January 1946. A1067, ER 46/13/1, NAA.
104 H.C. Coombs, *Trial Balance*, Melbourne, Macmillan, 1981, 89; and Alan Rix, *Coming to Terms – the Politics of Australia's Trade with Japan 1945-57*. Sydney, Allen and Unwin, 1986, 42-3.
105 Letters home, 16 and 24/2/46.
106 Bullock, conversation, 1996.
107 Bullock, *My Time in Korea 1950-52, a Personal Memoir*, unpublished, 2000, 12.
108 JP diary, 1/4 & 10/4/46.
109 Rosemary Viret, letter, 19/10/97.

110 Mrs Patricia G. Barnett-Brubaker, letter, 18/8/98.
111 Bullock, conversation, 15/1/98.
112 Registrar, University of Tasmania to Sir Alfred Davidson 7/3/47 N2/51 Westpac Archives.
113 JP diary, 24/4/47.
114 JP diary, 26/4-5/5/47; and same dates in Diary of Alfred Stirling, Makin's deputy in the embassy, DFAT.
115 Cam/Plim i, 104.
116 Plimsoll told Kentwell this. Kentwell, conversation, 1/9/2000.
117 Paul Hasluck *Diplomatic Witness: Australian Foreign Affairs 1941-1947*, MUP, 1980, 293.
118 Burton memo of 18/8/47 to Secretary, Public Service Board. JP Personnel file DFAT.

3

The United Nations and Korea
1948-52

In this era a diplomatic career was one of movement, usually at intervals of two to three years. In Plimsoll's case, however, in the first five years as an officer of The Department of External Affairs he moved every few months, mostly abroad, and altogether had only some twelve months at home. The longest he was in one place was nine months, the shortest a matter of weeks. It was a question of where he would be most useful. Plimsoll's work mostly focused on the United Nations, then in its formative years. He was prepared to move at short intervals because he was without family responsibilities, he was used to traveling light, and it was interesting, often working directly to the minister. He became expert on the UN, and achieved rapid promotion and prominence.

Starting in the Department in Canberra

Plimsoll's start in External Affairs in Canberra early in 1948 was as unorthodox as was his recruitment. Normal graduate induction was a two-year diploma course at the Canberra University College (now a part of the ANU). Given his previous experience he was exempted; indeed, he found himself giving lectures to new arrivals. He began as a First Secretary (temporary), a good starting level at a time when seniority counted for a great deal. Evatt had requested he begin at the level of assistant secretary,[1] but the public service authorities evidently baulked at this. Evatt's main concern in any case was that Plimsoll be available to work closely to him.

After nearly three years away Plimsoll took some leave at the family home in Bondi. This was interrupted by a telephone call from Burton in Canberra requesting that he fly to Melbourne for a meeting the next day with Evatt. There Plimsoll found that he would contribute to a "review of foreign policy" which Evatt wanted.[2] Issues covered during the next six months were Japan, including reparations and a peace treaty, Korea, the UN, USSR, the Marshall Plan, Western Union, and Western Europe. Plimsoll wrote drafts and reports, while also contributing material for Evatt's speeches in the House of Representatives.[3] This included one for delivery in his electorate on "the employment position in Australia".[4] As this did not directly relate to foreign affairs, it was a questionable use of a public servant.

Plimsoll worked closely with Evatt, but as a member of the department, not as a member of the minister's staff. During the next two years Evatt grew to regard him as even more indispensable. The two consulted frequently, sometimes several times daily, both with others and alone, especially late at night and during weekends. Evatt lived in Canberra, not in his Sydney electorate. Plimsoll was always available. Besides drafting policy papers, Plimsoll also found himself writing speeches for the minister; along with Evatt and Burton, Plimsoll attended a meeting with the Prime Minister, Ben Chifley, to discuss the forthcoming meeting of the UN Economic and Social Council (ECOSOC).[5]

Plimsoll adjusted to work, and lodging at the Hotel Canberra, easily enough. He already knew many people in the department and outside, either as fellow students or from having met them while he was in the USA. Among lodgers whom he came to know were Paul Hasluck,[6] then working on the official war history, and W. McMahon Ball, a lecturer in political science at the Canberra University College. When McMahon Ball had to visit South-East Asia at short notice, in his absence Plimsoll took over his weekly lectures, covering American institutions of government and the UN, while continuing his normal work.[7] Plimsoll found time to address public groups in Canberra and Geelong about international affairs.

Plimsoll did not remain in Australia long. Evatt spoke to him about continuing his work on Japan; at different times Evatt spoke of his being posted to Washington or attending a conference in Washington about Japan; or accompanying a parliamentary delegation on a visit to Japan. At the same time Burton foreshadowed attendance at conferences in Geneva and then the UN General Assembly in Paris.[8] Plimsoll was in demand.

He was soon confirmed as a First Secretary. He was demobilised in November 1947; he now resigned from the Bank of New South Wales.

No fixed address

In July 1948 Plimsoll went to Geneva for an ECOSOC meeting, in a delegation led by Dr Ronald Walker, his former economics lecturer. Evatt attended for part of the conference, and was otherwise in London, though keeping in close touch with Geneva. Plimsoll's main task was writing his speeches. Evatt held delegation meetings at all hours. Plimsoll as a consequence ate some meals with Evatt and his wife.

Next Evatt decided that Plimsoll should be in the delegation for the United Nations General Assembly, which was held that year in Paris. Evatt was elected President,[9] thanks to strong lobbying on his behalf by the Australian delegation. Plimsoll found that the pace was busier than Geneva. There were more frequent meetings with Evatt who, as President, demanded more briefings and speeches to be written, as well as articles for newspapers and journals. He also had a project for a book. As he had in Geneva, Evatt went back and forth to London. Being also Attorney-General, Evatt had to appear before the Judicial Committee of the Privy Council in London after the High Court of Australia had found the Chifley Government's legislation to nationalise the banks invalid. Plimsoll was "the anchor man and voice of reason of a somewhat manic team".[10]

Plimsoll's work included Korea, in the course of which he came to know well two significant figures: Chang Myun, South Korean Ambassador in Washington and soon to be that country's prime minister; and a senior US State Department official, John Foster Dulles, later Secretary of State under President Eisenhower. Nearly 30 years older than Plimsoll, Dulles had considerable international experience.

At the end of the session, Plimsoll accompanied Evatt and his family on their sea voyage back to Australia, allowing Jack Walshe, Evatt's private secretary, seconded from External Affairs, to fly home to spend Christmas with his family.[11] Plimsoll had long periods on the six weeks journey coding and decoding cables between the minister and the department. It was perhaps some compensation for a young officer to have the opportunity to be the minister's only sounding board as he wrote his cables. Plimsoll drafted press releases and speeches for Evatt's progress home, which included stops in Durban, Perth and Melbourne before finally reaching Sydney. At all of these places Evatt went ashore, held press conferences and delivered speeches.[12]

Ghostwriting for Evatt

During the voyage Plimsoll had begun dictating drafts of the book which Evatt had undertaken to write. Upon return to Canberra, in nine days and nights of herculean effort, Plimsoll completed the draft of the whole book for Evatt to consider.[13] Besides his duties in New York, to which he returned for the next session of ECOSOC, Evatt still expected him to work on the book. The minister was constantly on the phone from Australia. On his behalf Plimsoll negotiated with the publisher and in his spare time finalised the text, checked the galley and page proofs, and prepared the index.[14]

The urgency was the desirability for the book to be published before the end of Evatt's year-long term as President of the UN General Assembly. The book, *The Task of Nations*, focused on current major UN issues, Greece, Berlin, Indonesia and Palestine. More space was devoted to Palestine than to any other subject, in order to incorporate a detailed account of Dr Evatt's chairmanship in 1947 of the Ad Hoc Committee for Palestine.[15] Plimsoll would probably have seen value in such a book about the UN, at that time still something of a novelty on the international scene, while writing it from an Australian perspective was a special opportunity. In the index that Plimsoll prepared, it is notable that references to Australia were as numerous as those to the United States and the United Kingdom. Evatt ensured the final text reflected pride in his role as President of the General Assembly and in the founding of the UN. If the only way for the book to be finished properly was for Plimsoll to carry out the final tasks, then he was prepared to assist.

With his own full-time UN duties, and not being one of the minister's personal staff, his role involved stepping into some questionable areas such as negotiations about the book's price. The book did not carry any acknowledgement of Plimsoll's help.[16] On the other hand, he may have taken some pleasure in sentences (which probably were his) like:

> There is no group of men and women in the world today who are more hard-worked than diplomatic representatives attending international conferences. It is a tribute to the ideals and practical possibilities of the UN that so many people are prepared to devote so much of their lives to wearying but vital work.[17]

Work in New York

What little time Plimsoll devoted to social life he spent in the company of the two other single members of the office in New York: Dick Heyward, later Deputy Director of the United Nations International Children's Emergency Fund, and Joyce Chivers, a locally engaged Australian who later married Sir Roland Wilson. The three enjoyed time together, including exploring second hand bookshops and seeing foreign films. Plimsoll thought nothing of asking Chivers personal questions, but without revealing anything about himself or his family, even where he lived in New York. She once met Plimsoll's father when he visited New York. At one point she commented critically to Plimsoll senior about his son's lack of attention to his appearance. He agreed, saying that Plimsoll was unworldly, and needed a wife. "Why don't you marry him?" he suggested. Chivers nearly fell off her chair.[18]

During April and May Dr Evatt presided over the resumed General Assembly. He also made a number of speeches, for which he relied on Plimsoll's assistance. From New York Plimsoll proceeded to Rome for a meeting of the World Health Assembly, then to Geneva again for ECOSOC. He was sounded out about taking a senior post in the Secretariat of the UN in New York, either as Head of the New York office of UNESCO, and three times about Director of the Social Activities Division. He declined them all.[19] The "question of his being considered" for Director of Palestine Refugee Relief was later raised with him.[20]

He then went to Washington DC to attend talks on sterling and the US dollar, a watching brief on behalf of the department; then to New York for the UN General Assembly. Evatt did not attend as federal elections loomed in Australia.

At the elections in December 1949 Labor was defeated and power passed to the Menzies Coalition Government. Evatt was succeeded as minister by another former Sydney barrister, Percy Spender. In mid-1950 Watt succeeded Burton as Secretary of the Department.

Plimsoll had found it stimulating to work for Evatt, and acknowledged his great strengths and achievements, especially in the evolution of the UN, and in getting across in the wider world that, more quickly than would otherwise have been the case, Australia now had an independent foreign policy.[21] But he found much of which to be critical in Evatt, such as his preference to be surrounded by chaos and disorder to facilitate playing people off against each other. Evatt had no concept of the orderly use of staff: people would be asked to do things that were "not in their province" – early in 1948 Plimsoll found himself helping Evatt, who was also Attorney-General, to settle a tram strike in Hobart. Evatt was contradictory, and his unreasonable behaviour frightened and flustered people. Plimsoll said he was not frightened by Evatt, although there were some stormy sessions with him when Plimsoll thought he was going to be dismissed.[22] Many of his colleagues retained memories of a difficult minister. But Plimsoll benefited enormously from the work opportunities that Evatt gave him including, at that early stage in his career, a special understanding of the needs of a minister.

Still without any formal posting or base, in 1950 Plimsoll found himself working for two Missions, UN in New York and the Embassy in Washington, dividing his time appropriately. Accommodation continued to be hotels in each city, although at one stage in Washington he stayed for a while with David McNicol, a first secretary, and his wife.

Sir Owen Dixon

In May 1950 Plimsoll was appointed liaison officer to Sir Owen Dixon, since 1929 a justice of the High Court of Australia. He had agreed to be UN Mediator on the Kashmir dispute between India and Pakistan.

Plimsoll was 30 years Dixon's junior, and had no special expertise on the Indian subcontinent. Yet he soon became a sounding board for Dixon during the weeks he was in the US. Plimsoll spent much time in Dixon's company, frequently sharing a meal, going for walks and visiting art galleries.[23] The experience was stimulating, both in further developing his interest in India, and for exposure to one of the great legal minds of the English-speaking world, with whom he became a life-long friend.

The letters which Dixon later wrote to Plimsoll from India and Pakistan were full and frank, and as if addressing an equal. On 7 August, from Karachi, he told Plimsoll of his planned return to New York, "where I imagine I shall call on you for moral support and a contribution of ideas. I do hope the Ambassador can spare you".[24]

Plimsoll was again promoted but through his old boss at the Bank of NSW, Professor Hytten, he received an offer to work for the Commercial Banking Company of Sydney (CBS) at £2,000 per annum, double his current salary. Plimsoll wrote to Watt "about my future in the organisation". Evidently he received a satisfactory response, as he declined the CBS offer.[25]

Spender, the new minister, accompanied by Tange, now the head of the UN Branch of the department, visited the UN for the 1950 General Assembly. Spender had decided to run for election for the vice-presidency of the General Assembly, and "for that purpose" Plimsoll was brought up from Washington "at once to assist".[26] This gave Spender an opportunity to observe Plimsoll at first hand.

Korea

The Korean War (1950-53) led to Plimsoll's first major responsibility. This was the one conflict during the Cold War in which forces of the two super powers, USSR and USA, actually engaged in combat against each other. It was also one of only two major conflicts since the Second World War in which a multinational force combined to fight under UN auspices – the 1991 Gulf War being the other. Plimsoll later recalled:

> The North Korean invasion of South Korea was seen at the time as the first major test of the collective security provisions of the Charter, and it was widely believed that, if the United Nations failed to respond to the act of aggression by North Korea, the United Nations would collapse and, with it, the structure of post-war peace.[27]

When North Korea attacked the South across the 38th parallel in June 1950 Korea became a major preoccupation of the UN and a focus of world attention as a flashpoint in the Cold War. Plimsoll had been in the thick of meetings and negotiations on the Korea question at the UN since 1948.

Korea had been divided into two at the end of the War, the north becoming communist. The UN wrestled with what to do about this. Western countries favoured reunification under free elections. Plimsoll had worked closely with the US delegate, John Foster Dulles, on the UN Resolution of 12 December 1948 which recognised the elections in South Korea in August that year, and which established the UN Commission for Korea (UNCOK).[28] In 1950 Plimsoll was involved in establishing its successor, the UN Commission for the Unification and Rehabilitation of Korea (UNCURK). The General Assembly also decided that UNCURK would be located in Korea, and that its committee members should be of ambassadorial rank. Australia was a member of UNCURK, as it had been of UNCOK.

Spender, in New York at the time, told Watt in Canberra that he wanted the best person available "for important job on new Commission". Spender seemed tempted to make an outside appointment. Two of the

UNCURK *meeting in Pusan, c 1951. Plimsoll is at lower right (Lady Currie)*

three names he wanted considered were Sir Bertram Stevens, a former Premier of NSW, and L.J. Hartnett, of General Motors Holden. The third was Colonel Hodgson, former secretary of the department, and currently Head of Mission in Tokyo.

It would be a difficult posting. Korea had a harsh climate, it was a war zone and it was remote. Australia's delegate would be out on a limb, sometimes needing to act without time to consult Canberra. Watt firmly advised against all of the minister's suggestions, on account of age, health and lack of suitable experience. The task required "someone younger with specialised knowledge of the Far East and the UN". Watt recommended Plimsoll. He had a "high opinion of Plimsoll's judgment. He has a special knowledge of the Pacific area. I know that he stands high in the estimation of the UN Secretariat and has turned down at least one important appointment there. His combination of political and economic training and experience seem to me to point to his selection". While Plimsoll was not well known publicly, "this should not be regarded as a determining factor. If he is appointed he should be given the necessary status";[29] in other words, perhaps given temporary promotion.

A few days later Watt cabled Spender again suggesting "immediate action". He had already talked to the Prime Minister, Menzies, who regarded Plimsoll as "suitable". In New York, Spender who had already had some opportunity to see and hear about Plimsoll, talked to him,[30] agreed to his appointment, and later issued a statement announcing it. He also agreed that Plimsoll should be upgraded to level of minister (diplomatic rank equivalent to junior head of mission). Spender encouraged Plimsoll to make decisions whenever there was no time to consult Canberra first: "Things may move very fast and difficult decisions have to be taken quickly. Whatever you do, the Australian Government will support you."[31]

Plimsoll was busy on UNCURK matters until he left New York. He squeezed in time for one or two personal preparations at the insistence of concerned friends. This included purchase of a heavy overcoat for the harsh Korean winter. Normal prior consultations went by the board: he knew the UN background; and he had had the benefit of a timely personal talk with Spender. Otherwise he was entering a totally new situation. Plimsoll left on 12 November 1950.[32]

In Korea itself there had been military successes. After being driven right to the south, UN forces under General MacArthur had successfully counter-attacked, and driven the communist forces back into the north.

Before leaving Plimsoll had issued a press statement, a brave act for a relatively junior officer. It stated that given progress on the military front, the end of the war was on the horizon. UNCURK could play a "big part in promoting peaceful relations in this vital region of the world" and contribute towards the UN's declared objective of "a united, independent and democratic Korea". It read that "the existence of this UN body and the declared objectives of the UN make resort to force wholly unwarranted and unnecessary". UNCURK could play an important role in the region as a whole and would "be available at all times to consult with the authorities of all neighbouring countries on all problems of common concern to them and to Korea". Evidently this was an invitation to China: "We shall devote ourselves wholeheartedly to bringing about the establishment of a united and democratic Korea which will be able to pursue its own way peacefully and independently, and which will not be a threat to the security of any other nation."[33]

With UNCURK in Korea

It took three days to fly from New York to Tokyo. Plimsoll arrived five days before the first meeting of UNCURK, scheduled for 20 November. One of UNCURK's first engagements in Tokyo was an invitation to lunch from General MacArthur, the Supreme Commander of UN forces in Korea.

Plimsoll later reported to Canberra that MacArthur had "created a good impression" on UNCURK members. MacArthur said that that morning US forces had reached the border of Manchuria. If the weather held, he forecast an end to all major military operations in Korea within a month. As for the possible entry into the war by Communist Chinese forces, he stated that their operations in North Korea had stopped, "as a result of heavy air bombardment".[34] Within days MacArthur's assessment, especially with regard to China, proved to be wrong.

UNCURK delegates received a warm welcome upon arrival in Seoul. As they drove into the largely devastated city they were greeted with a display of UN and Korean flags, and huge banners indicating local expectations of UNCURK with such hyperbole as "Welcome UNCURK – Apostles of Peace and Justice".[35] They stayed at the Chosen Hotel, also the venue for their meetings.

Plimsoll's UNCURK colleagues were something of a mixed bag. From Philippines, Thailand, Pakistan, Netherlands, Turkey and Chile, all but one were much older than he was. On the other hand, unlike Plimsoll, most had little or no previous diplomatic experience or background in the UN. One shining exception in this company was the Thai representative, Pote Sarasin. In his early 40s he had recently been foreign minister. He spoke impressively and was generally effective. He and Plimsoll got on well together.[36]

UNCURK was supposed to oversee the reunification and rehabilitation of the two Koreas, a formidable task, even at the best of times. At its first meeting on Korean soil, UNCURK was confronted with a dramatic development: contrary to what they had heard from MacArthur, Chinese forces had entered in strength; UN forces were being driven back. The war was unlikely to end soon, meaning UNCURK would be unable to carry out its mission to rehabilitate the country as a whole, let alone unify it.

The hotel meeting was held by candle-light as the city electricity supply had just failed. "There was noise going on around us, with the US Army in retreat". Ziauddin, Pakistan's Representative, quickly argued there was no point in remaining; that UNCURK should withdraw from

Korea as it was not possible to carry out their mission. For some the comparative safety, comforts and bright lights of Tokyo would also have beckoned. Apart from the Chilean representative, who abstained, only Plimsoll held out for staying put in Korea. While he agreed that it was doubtful whether UNCURK could carry out its designated functions, he made the critical point: the UN should not be seen to be turning its back on South Korea. It was not a question of what UNCURK could achieve so much as the interpretation that would be put on a decision by UNCURK to depart. It was a fierce debate. Plimsoll's arguments made no impact on his colleagues.[37]

Plimsoll promptly reported to Canberra. He also spoke with Muccio, the US Ambassador to Korea, who in turn reported to Washington. The State Department was anxious for a continuing UNCURK presence in Korea, and fully supported Plimsoll. It instructed US ambassadors in the capitals of all the UNCURK member states immediately to ask these governments to instruct their delegates to vote for UNCURK to remain in Korea. Australia similarly instructed its representatives abroad. The upshot was that UNCURK stayed. Plimsoll had played a key part in this achievement. Plimsoll later wrote: "In the darkest days at the beginning of 1951, I often wondered how I could face the Koreans if the decision were made to pull the United Nations out and abandon the Koreans to their fate."[38]

Given the military situation, with UN forces in retreat, there was a steady evacuation of Seoul to the southern port city of Pusan. There was considerable confusion, with roads and railways choked with refugees "pouring south in conditions of almost unbelievable hardship".[39] In the middle of one night at this time, President Syngman Rhee had gone to the airport intending to flee the country. Upon hearing this, Plimsoll, clad only in his pyjamas, pursued him to the airport and persuaded him to remain.[40] The now bedraggled banners of UNCURK's welcome were still displayed, but someone had altered one to read, "Welcome to

DUNCURK".[41] Most of UNCURK left by air after Christmas. Plimsoll, by contrast, remained in Seoul, along with Stavropulos of the UN Secretariat. Plimsoll later recalled on New Year's Day 1951:

> going along to see Syngman Rhee in Seoul and wishing him and the Republic of Korea a good year. At that time the normal rather conventional words took on a new meaning and sincerity because the Chinese forces at that stage were about thirteen miles from the capital and there was nothing between.

Few officials, Korean or foreign, remained in Seoul: "The atmosphere was very gloomy and the Koreans were only too glad to have people who were telling them that the forthcoming year might be a better one".[42] As the last of UNCURK remaining, Plimsoll and Stavropoulos finally left on 3 January when General Ridgway, US force commander, informed them he was closing a key bridge out of Seoul to civilian traffic at 6pm.[43]

Plimsoll returned to Canberra for two weeks of consultations at the end of February 1951. He did not lack high level attention. Although this was a busy time in parliament, immediately before a double dissolution, Plimsoll saw Spender three times, and lunched with Watt three times.[44]

Plimsoll returned to Pusan, at the time a "small, grubby port city" now swollen by the arrival of the Government of Korea as well as thousands of refugees. Accommodation arrangements for the all-male foreign representatives were makeshift, and UNCURK representatives, like others, had to slum it. "Everyone lived very hugger–mugger."[45]

The Australian mission was housed in a US Army compound, Hileah, named after a race track in Florida, and built during the earlier US forces occupation at the end of the War. The housing was "basic to say the least". Plimsoll and his two diplomatic staff, Bullock and Smyth, lived cheek by jowl in a grey concrete hut, consisting of two bedrooms, kitchen and bathroom and a combined living/dining area, in which there was a large oil heater, "ugly but welcome", which was on for nearly nine months of the year. Part of the living area was partitioned to make a small bedroom for Smyth.[46] They usually ate meals in the officers' mess of the nearby

US Army commissary unless they dined out or had guests to their own house. They had some domestic help; a cook, house boy and house girl.[47] They entertained, even in such basic surroundings. There was no garden, but Plimsoll started a small flower bed at the front steps.

Their modest hut doubled as an office. All three typed their own reports, Plimsoll in his room, the other two on the dining table. The usual confidential secretarial assistance was not possible in a war zone. A male stenographer from the Australian Defence Department "did not work out," and Plimsoll sent him back.[48] As there was no secure place to keep materials for coded communications with Canberra, these were stored with a rear echelon detachment of the New Zealand Army located in Pusan. This involved a 30-minute round trip by car when needed. Normally Bullock and Smyth would do the laborious work associated with sending and receiving cables but, characteristically, Plimsoll also took his turn.[49] He kept himself informed about wider international developments principally through BBC shortwave radio broadcasts and by reading the London *Times*.

Plimsoll, with his normally spartan way of living, had no difficulty with the austere living conditions. Having space for a minimum number of possessions was something he had become used to, with constant movement between hotel rooms during the past five years in the USA. To Korea he had travelled light, with just his old Army cylindrical kit bag, and overcoat. He did not accumulate much in the way of possessions, although browsing one day in an arcade in Tokyo, en route to Korea, the economist as well as the aesthete in him led to his buying some woodcuts, which he muttered would be a "good hedge against inflation".[50] Plimsoll was fortunate in his colleagues: both war veterans who had been through difficult situations, they adapted well.

Visit of Casey

In August 1951 Richard Casey, who had succeeded Spender as Minister for External Affairs earlier in the year, visited Korea as part of a first

R.G. Casey on his visit to Korea in 1951 pictured with President Syngman Rhee, Plimsoll and Prime Minister Chang Myun to his right, and with Pote Sarasin (Thailand Representative on UNCURK) and Alan Watt to his left (Australian War Memorial)

tour of the region. As a former diplomat, and no stranger to Asia, his eyes were opened to the difficult living conditions of many Australian diplomats. Casey, who breakfasted with Plimsoll and his colleagues in their hut, considered that "no diplomatic officer should live in" this accommodation. Max Loveday, Casey's private secretary, recalled that after an interesting day in Korea, including flying along the 38th parallel in a RAAF plane, Casey had seemed genuinely struck by the difficult living conditions, and said as much to Plimsoll. Was there anything he could do to improve their circumstances? Plimsoll's reply had been along the lines of, "what do you mean? This is wonderful". Thinking he had been misunderstood, Casey said he was referring to Plimsoll's living conditions. Plimsoll replied that these were "very good".[51] Casey was not convinced. On return home he told Tange that their living conditions resembled "a cowshed in the Mallee," and suggested that something ought to be done about it.[52] Plimsoll had instructed the other two not to complain about their living conditions. Watt, however, took Bullock aside to talk. As a result they were allowed to use the RAAF courier plane to go to Japan occasionally for a few days, although Plimsoll himself rarely availed himself of this.[53] As for accommodation, it was some years before any improvement was possible.

UNCURK redefined

During the next few months, Plimsoll established himself as *primus inter pares* among his UNCURK colleagues. His earlier work in New York on Korea gave him a certain standing with Prime Minister Chang and other ministers, and he was seen as a friend of Korea. No other member of UNCURK had anything like the same profile locally.[54]

UNCURK, a small, civilian UN presence in a war-torn South Korea swollen by the thousands of UN military personnel, mainly American, started to define a new role for itself. It maintained contact with the senior military commanders, notably the top US commanders, as well as with ministers and officials of the Korean Government, and with members of the fledgling National Assembly of the Republic of Korea.

Plimsoll was heavily involved in compiling reports on developments for New York. Pote Sarasin recalled that Plimsoll also would be called on to make a final editorial check in order "to be sure nothing was left out or unnecessary words were added".[55] In December 1950 UNCURK had reported on the extent of Chinese intervention in Korea. Although the substance was similar to views stated by MacArthur, UNCURK's "was distinguished by its calm, dispassionate tone, which enhanced its credibility," while UNCURK's avoidance, "through Plimsoll's efforts, of declamatory statements about Chinese aggression", was helpful.[56] With no direct access to the north during the war, most of UNCURK's work focused on the south. Plimsoll undertook most of the travel to accessible parts of the south, showing the flag. When it was his turn in the chair, he encouraged other delegations to travel the country instead of going to Tokyo, "making the idle in UNCURK work".[57]

In July 1951 Canberra learnt that Trygve Lie, UN Secretary-General, wanted UNCURK replaced by a single mediator. Plimsoll felt that a mediator would have no real function because there was no scope for bargaining between the two sides. Korea would be unified neither by force nor by diplomacy. He accurately foresaw that the only outcome of a ceasefire would be continued existence of two separate states, each supported by its allies. He believed UNCURK could continue to play an important role in sustaining South Korean morale, military capacity and economic growth, in fostering moderate political leaders, and in observing events on the cease-fire line. Plimsoll's views were supported by the department in Canberra, which urged rejection of Lie's proposal; in the event, it came to nothing.[58]

UNCURK's most significant and difficult role, in which Plimsoll was prominent, was as a means of communication with President Syngman Rhee on behalf of the UN General Assembly, and UN Force contributors in particular. Rhee was "a devious old Methodist", according to the British Chargé. The US Ambassador Muccio sarcastically referred to him as "the Princetonian" – Rhee had a doctorate from Princeton University. Aged in his late 70s, it was best to see him in the morning.[59]

MacArthur, at the lunch with UNCURK, said he had known Rhee for more than 37 years. He described Rhee as "a most reasonable man, and always willing to compromise". Sensing that problems might lie ahead, MacArthur warned that, in Korea:

> Western forms of political institutions and conduct could not be expected. All Koreans were opposed to foreign domination. They had suffered long from Japanese, Russian and American occupation. They were determined to run their own affairs. UNCURK should be chary of coming to decisions which the Koreans would refuse to carry out and which the UN could not enforce.[60]

During his visit in August Casey noted that Plimsoll was "obviously on good terms with Rhee".[61] Plimsoll, who won wide respect for the way he dealt with Rhee, recalled that "it was quite a dramatic period. I had quite a big influence on things, on both Americans and the South Koreans". He came to know Syngman Rhee well, and saw him frequently, sometimes with other UNCURK representatives, but more often on his own – sometimes at Rhee's request, and sometimes on behalf of the US, "to help persuade him to be reasonable". Sometimes Rhee would have his wife, an Austrian, invite Plimsoll to come over and discuss a proposed public statement: "Mr Plimsoll would not let me get into any trouble". Plimsoll likewise restrained Rhee from statements that could embarrass the UN in Korea.[62] Once Plimsoll was shown the draft of a Korean cabinet decision, and invited to amend it, being assured that this was accepted by the cabinet. He was expected to "make it more logical" and concise. Once he was invited to talk to Rhee when the latter was ill in bed.[63]

Rhee often wanted UN forces to go further than authorised. In January 1951 Rhee became agitated at news of ceasefire proposals at the UN General Assembly. Muccio asked Plimsoll to calm Rhee, which he did.[64] In June Jacob Malik, Soviet Ambassador to the UN, in a radio broadcast, called for truce talks. Plimsoll was awakened early in the morning by a call from President Rhee's wife. She told him of the broadcast, and sought advice as to how Rhee should react. Plimsoll urged that Rhee should not make any comment before consulting allied governments. Rhee himself was very agitated, seeing that if negotiations resulted in agreement, he would not achieve his aim of unifying Korea by military means.[65] But the US had realised that unification of Korea by military means was no longer feasible.[66]

Rhee was greatly troubled by the agreement at Kaesong on 26 July for ceasefire negotiations to begin. Again at Muccio's request Plimsoll called on Rhee and listened to his complaints but gave him little comfort. Plimsoll told Rhee that he would have to accept a settlement on the basis of a divided Korea.[67]

It was a matter of trying to restrain Rhee not only from undesirable words but also actions. The main aim of the UN was to defend a state which had been invaded, and to hold back communism. Many of the major nations contributing to the UN force held dear such principles as regard for human rights. While allowing for wartime conditions, Rhee was "manifestly undemocratic," often seeming as tyrannical as his communist enemy, and he showed scant regard for human rights. Plimsoll generally led the way in safeguarding those unjustly accused of collaboration.[68] He exercised a moderating influence on Rhee, carefully "striking a balance between excessive tolerance of abuses on the one hand and pressing him to the point of complete alienation on the other".[69]

Plimsoll cultivated a wide network of Koreans and foreigners. Circumstances dictated, however, that it was the Americans, especially Ambassador Muccio, with whom he was most frequently in touch. Occasionally he learned from Muccio of intended changes in US policy before Canberra did and was able to give the Australian Government advance warning: "Frequently Muccio consulted Plimsoll when asked by the State Department for advice on future policy developments. Muccio valued his assistance, particularly in helping to moderate impulsive reactions in Washington."[70]

Return to Canberra

Casey's visit to Korea had been his first opportunity to observe Plimsoll. He was "a useful fellow with brains and judgement". Yet Casey considered that from an Australian perspective UNCURK was "relatively unimportant"– and that it "could not be fulfilling much useful purpose". There was more important work elsewhere for Plimsoll. Casey noted: "We must find some place to employ him to greater effect, which won't be hard."[71] As Spender had observed a year earlier: "We are at the moment very weak in career officers to fill top appointments."[72] There were many such unfilled positions both in Canberra and abroad, especially in South-East Asia. This was a critical problem.

Casey and Watt also would have had in mind Plimsoll's high standing at the UN. Earlier in the year Trygve Lie had requested Australia to allow Plimsoll to take up a post in the UN Secretariat as Director, Social Affairs, which had been vacated by the previous incumbent, the distinguished Swedish anthropologist, Gunnar Myrdal.[73] With Plimsoll's agreement the request was declined. It was an interesting reflection of Plimsoll's preference to work for Australia that he was not overly impressed by a direct approach from the UN Secretary-General, nor tempted by the much higher pay being offered. In November Lie buttonholed Casey in New York about letting the Secretariat have Plimsoll or Dr Walker. Casey told him there would be the greatest difficulty in releasing either.[74]

In October, two months after Casey's visit, Plimsoll left Korea. At first there had been a letter (of 27 September) from Watt about a possible future appointment for him as minister (head of mission) in Burma to which Plimsoll had responded enthusiastically.[75] Then, on 4 October, Watt cabled asking him to return home "immediately".[76] Plimsoll left a week later. The Korean Foreign Minister, Y.T. Pyun, wrote to Casey about Plimsoll's "distinguished service" in Korea, "particularly the manner and spirit in which it was done".[77]

During December 1951 the allies considered how specific a warning statement should be given to China in case of violation of the Korean armistice, once it was achieved. Plimsoll warned against specifying any type of retaliatory action against the Chinese and that no time limit should be set on its validity. Consistent with his earlier expression of views, he doubted that any Korean settlement would proceed beyond a military armistice. The Republic might have to be defended indefinitely, and the allies would have to consider how to obtain a "responsible and non-provocative attitude" on the part of the Korean Government.[78]

Return to Korea

Five months later, having settled into Canberra, Plimsoll was reassigned to Korea. It is very rare for a diplomat to return to a post so soon after departure.[79] This arose following continuing difficulties with Syngman Rhee, whose term as President was due to end in June 1952. To be reelected he required the vote of a majority of the National Assembly. Doubtful about securing that support, he proposed that the Assembly vote for a change in the Constitution to have the presidency subject to popular franchise. In January 1952 the Assembly overwhelmingly rejected this proposal. Rhee then applied various forms of pressure; for example, using the police and youth corps to influence attitudes towards this end at grassroots level.

The Americans were concerned about how to deal with Rhee. A message went out to capitals of member states of UNCURK asking that they enhance their representation. In the case of Australia the State Department specifically requested that Plimsoll return to Korea. Spender, now ambassador in Washington, cabled that State Department officials "would regard Plimsoll's return to Korea for perhaps six months as an important factor in rallying UNCURK and exercising influence on ROK especially Rhee". In Canberra the American request was considered inconvenient but Casey reluctantly agreed. Australia only recently had secured the ANZUS security alliance, so, as Spender commented, doubtless thinking more broadly: "any assistance we can give [the US] in respect of UNCURK would I am sure, pay dividends".[80]

The request constituted a compliment to Australia, as well as to Plimsoll personally. It reflected problems that the US perceived with Rhee including his lifelong hatred of the Japanese, "which almost equalled his hatred of the communist aggressors". A more harmonious Korean approach to Japan would have suited the US in their role as post-war occupiers of that country.[81]

On return, Plimsoll was quickly brought up to date on developments. On 25 May Rhee declared martial law in Pusan, the temporary capital, and arrested many Assembly members. Profoundly concerned, like many others, Plimsoll arranged an UNCURK meeting with Rhee. Plimsoll was the only one at the meeting to criticise Rhee openly, saying that the arrest of Assembly members would have a negative effect on Australia's continuing support of the UN action. Rhee asked what he wished him to do, to which Plimsoll replied that he should free them. Although taken aback, Rhee released many but not all the Assembly members.[82] Plimsoll was advised by Canberra not to agree to any request for sanctuary for a Legislative Assembly member (Plimsoll had received one such request), so that he might preserve influence with Rhee. Henceforward, however, Plimsoll's influence with Rhee became "very limited" and personal relations "strained".[83]

Plimsoll and Lightener, the US Chargé d'Affaires, explored the possibility of "regime change" in Pusan with their capitals. However, it emerged that while there was revulsion and embarrassment about Rhee's acts, no one wanted to be part of an effort involving foreigners to be rid of him. A few months later Plimsoll, looking back, thought Rhee "not indispensable, but an alternative leader was unlikely to emerge until after Rhee had disappeared from the scene".[84]

Jim McIntyre, a friend in the department, wrote privately to Plimsoll on Canberra's caution about getting rid of Rhee. He understood Plimsoll's strong feelings about Rhee's abuse of human rights:

> I sense that your well-known conscience about Korea has been outraged, and that you feel that something decisive ought to be done to get rid of Rhee and preserve democracy. We agree with you in spirit, but we are somewhat hesitant about supporting anything in the way of drastic action.

He feared "unpredictable consequences on Asian and world opinion"; and getting saddled with "responsibilities that could later embarrass us". Further, a satisfactory replacement for Rhee "in addition to finding himself labeled as a UN stooge, might need a lot of propping up".[85]

For Australia Korea had become less important than concerns closer to home in South-East Asia. Domestically, communism was now a major issue, and unswerving anti-communism an article of faith in the Coalition Government. Whatever Rhee's faults (and both Casey and Evatt spoke of them in the House of Representatives), he was still fiercely anti-communist. Plimsoll was struck by the reluctance of the Asian members of UNCURK – Thailand, Philippines and Pakistan – to countenance any outside interference in an Asian neighbour. Looking back some years later, he believed that "their instinct was that whatever the rights or wrongs of what was being done, it was a matter for Koreans and not outsiders".[86]

Throughout this tense period Plimsoll consulted senior US Embassy and military leaders, including General Mark Clark, the new Supreme Commander of UN Forces. Despite their best efforts Plimsoll and Lightener found that, at that stage, Clark was reluctant to use his authority and influence with Rhee. Unfamiliar with Korean politics, his main concern was keeping his forces totally engaged fighting the enemy to the north. Provided Rhee could continue to ensure UN Command supply lines through the port of Pusan, Clark did not want to move against him. Later Clark told Plimsoll that he regretted not being able to "take a stronger line" with Rhee at the time, but militarily it would have been very difficult.[87]

A number of countries, including Australia, sent protests to Rhee, but to no avail. After releasing the detained Assembly members in July, Rhee confined the whole chamber until it amended the Constitution to his liking.[88] Later Rhee had 12 alleged communist sympathisers arrested. A military court was set up, but the evidence looked flimsy. Plimsoll saw the need for UNCURK to be represented daily in the court where for a while there was a UN interpreter,[89] until the Korean authorities put an end to it.

Plimsoll later recalled that his main preoccupation on return to Korea in 1952, "apart from trying to preserve some respect for constitutional government, was to prevent the President liquidating the Opposition". As to the former, he knew that, like others, he had had very limited success. Regarding the latter, however, "I think I probably saved some lives, and in any case maintained some of the Opposition as a political force".[90] In

1960 Plimsoll received a letter from Suh Minho, by then Deputy Speaker of the Korean House of Representatives in the National Assembly. He had survived eight years of detention, instead of being summarily executed – a fate from which he was saved only after Plimsoll's direct appeal to Rhee. Minho's memory of Plimsoll, "a friendly figure", had contributed to sustaining him during his imprisonment:

> You tried so hard to save my life from the bloody hands of dictatorship. I would not forget through all my days the endeavour and goodwill you displayed for me on the basis of genuine humanity and justice.[91]

Final departure from Korea

Casey was anxious to withdraw Plimsoll from Korea as soon as possible, but not at the cost of antagonising the Americans. In May Casey asked him when was the earliest he could leave.[92] Casey was also in touch with the Americans, but there was no response until the ANZUS Council meeting in August 1952 in Honolulu. There Casey noted that during discussion of Korea, Allison, Assistant Secretary of State for the Far East, said "it was recognised that [Australia] wanted to send Plimsoll elsewhere, but that they hoped very much we'd replace him with someone adequate".[93] Dean Acheson, the Secretary of State, however, told Casey that he preferred that Plimsoll remain with UNCURK. In September Casey once again sought to withdraw him, and announced his next appointment, as head of mission in Jakarta. Again the US Administration, anxious to preserve a minimum of credibility for UNCURK, urged that Plimsoll remain in Korea. Acheson was concerned about the future of UNCURK, as Trygve Lie's doubts had resurfaced about its continued value. The US attached importance to UNCURK's work, but only if it had high calibre people; there was concern that Plimsoll's departure could directly jeopardise UNCURK's continued existence. Despite Casey's other plans for Plimsoll, no Australian interest would be served "by causing the termination of UNCURK".[94]

Plimsoll's transfer to Jakarta was scheduled for late 1952. Tom Critchley, one of the department's most seasoned Asia hands, arrived in time for a handover. Critchley recalled finding Plimsoll a fount of knowledge about Korea, but somewhat awkward in his social graces. Plimsoll expressed regret about having to choose a tie to wear daily, after having worn a black tie continuously during court mourning for the death of King George VI earlier in the year. He also recalled that, although Plimsoll was knowledgeable about current popular music, he was "quite disturbed" about pressure for him to dance at a farewell party.[95]

Given the standing and access Plimsoll now had, as his departure drew near, Canberra instructed Plimsoll to remain longer, to report on a potentially important American initiative. This was the visit to Korea in December 1952 of US President-elect, General Eisenhower, to look personally into ending the war. Plimsoll later was privately scathing about that visit, which lasted only two days. Eisenhower had confined his discussions entirely to US commanders and had no private talk with Rhee. General Clark later confessed to Plimsoll that he had done all he could to ensure that Rhee was "frustrated" in his objective of trying to get all the political advantage he could from Eisenhower's visit.[96] Plimsoll was asked to report personally in Canberra before proceeding to Jakarta.

Plimsoll felt that for Australia there was "a lot that can be done unobtrusively and behind the scenes in encouraging and stimulating the Koreans and influencing and helping the Americans in the form of assistance they are giving the country".[97] He "confessed to leaving Korea with considerable regret. He had liked the Koreans and he had thoroughly enjoyed his frequent and often arduous journeys" there. Following his intellectual curiosity, as well as his interests as a diplomat, he had taken a particular interest in the buildings of an ancient civilisation.[98] Although his posting in Korea was "very strenuous" he "enjoyed every minute of it".[99]

Plimsoll's time in Korea enhanced his reputation among ministers and colleagues at home, and abroad especially in the US State Department and at the UN.[100] Korea remained a country where his experiences as a diplomat made a special impression on him, like the United States, and later India and the Soviet Union. Yet in none of these other countries did he acquire quite the same personal standing as he did in Korea. He returned on two short visits in subsequent years and received a special welcome. He had acquired an aura among Koreans that meant that wherever he was stationed, senior Korean officials and ministers made an effort to call on him, partly courtesy, but often in order to seek his advice, for instance on matters such as their relations with the USA, or the handling of the Korean question at the UN. At the UN General Assembly in 1974 Gordon Bilney recalled the "awe in which Plimsoll was held for his encyclopedic knowledge of the Korean question". When he "pronounced" in informal, private gatherings of senior delegates of various countries, "people would nod and change their views" more than 20 years after his time there.[101]

Endnotes

1 Kentwell, conversation, 1/9/2000.
2 JP diary, 2-4/2/1948.
3 JP diary, February to May 1948, passim.
4 JP diary, 23/6/1948.
5 Also present were Dedman, Minister of Post-War Reconstruction, and Dr HC Coombs, Director-General of Post-War Reconstruction. JP diary, 30/6/1948.
6 JP diary, 21/1/1948, 31/3/1948.
7 JP diary, 11/5/1948. The five lectures, during June, covered the US Presidency and the electoral system; the US Cabinet; the US judicial system; and state and municipal government; and the UN General Assembly and the Security Council. There is no mention in his diary of time spent preparing the lectures.
8 JP diary, 9/4 and 13/4, 5/5, and 17/6/1948.
9 A position which he had missed by only three votes in 1947.
10 Sir Brian Urquhart, letter, 20/10/1998.
11 Jack Walshe, conversation, 7/6/1998.

12 JP diary, 17-31/12/1948, and 1-21/1/1949.

13 JP diary, 26/1-3/2/1949. Others in the department contributed, possibly Alan Renouf, although he was in the UN Secretariat in New York at the time. Lady Wilson, conversation, 4/6/1999.

14 JP diary entries for 9/2, 13/2, 15/2, 19/2, 24/2, 1/3, 5/3, 6/3/, 7/3, 13/4, 17/4, 19/4, 20/4, 1/5, 15/5, 22/5, 23/5, 24/5, 27/5, 29/5, 31/5, 1/6, 2/6, and 6/6/1949.

15 Herbert V. Evatt, *The Task of Nations*, Duell, Sloan and Pearce, New York, 1949.

16 Plimsoll later told Crocker that Evatt "gave him no thanks" for his work on this book. Sir Walter Crocker, Journal. Barr-Smith Library, University of Adelaide, 8/3/1970, xx, 4572. Hereafter WRC Jnl.

17 *The Task of Nations*, 20. Tange described Plimsoll, also Shann, as "young men in the Department who were loaded with responsibilities in the UN without commensurate rank or emoluments". Tange, Personal memoir of Shann, *Australian Foreign Affairs Record*, vol 59, August 1988, DFAT, 330-2.

18 Lady Wilson, conversation, 4/6/1999.

19 JP diary, 12/8 and 19/12/1949; 18/1, 27/1, and 14/2/1950.

20 JP diary, 23/2/50.

21 *Reminiscential Conversations between Hon Clyde Cameron and Sir James Plimsoll 1984*. TRC 1967, i, 280-1, NLA. Hereafter cited as Cam/Plim.

22 Cam/Plim, i, 119, 156-7, 232, 254, 265, 270, 280, and ii, 231-2.

23 During three weeks from Dixon's arrival in the US on 26/4/1950 Plimsoll spent time with him almost every day. JP diary. Dixon was "a brilliant man" with wide cultural interests. "A very good classical scholar". Cam/Plim, i, 86.

24 Sir Owen Dixon papers – courtesy JD Merralls.

25 JP diary, 5/7, 8/7, 18/7, 25/7, 27/7/1950.

26 Cables I.13866 and I.13902 of 7/9/50. Spender-Watt messages, 1950, Watt papers, DFAT. Spender was elected 20/9/1950. JP diary, 8/9/50.

27 Washington Memo 642 of 6/3/72 by Plimsoll. JP papers, DFAT.

28 Cam/Plim, ii, 90-1.

29 Canberra 468 to UN of 7/10/1950, JP papers, Box 1, Item 7, NAA.

30 Canberra cable O.14671 of 12/10/1950. Watt papers, DFAT. JP papers, Box 1, Item 7, NAA. JP diary, 9/10/1950.

31 Robert O'Neill, *Australia in the Korean War 1950-53, Vol 1 Strategy and Diplomacy.* AWM and AGPS, Canberra, 1981, footnote 4, 128. Cam/Plim, ii, 425.

32 JP diary, 12/11/1950. He had had typhoid, typhus, tetanus and cholera injections on 12/10 and 18/10/1950.

33 JP papers, Box 1, Item 7, NAA.

34 Plimsoll Despatch 1/50, "Views of General MacArthur on Korea and the Far East", 21/11/1950. JP papers, Box 1, Item 10, NAA.

35 Bullock, unpublished memoir, 14.

36 Bullock, conversation, 15/1/1998.

37 Bullock, conversation, 15/1/1998.

38 JP to RH Gardner, 27/7/54, JP papers, DFAT.

39 JP to H Marshall, 21/12/1955, JP papers, DFAT.

40 Max Loveday and Ken Ward each recalled hearing this from Plimsoll.

41 Bullock, unpublished memoir, 19.

42 JP to JR Rowland, 22/12/1954, JP papers, DFAT.

43 JP diary, 3/1/1951.

44 He also called on Dr Evatt. JP diary, 28/2, 5/3, 12/3 and 13/3/1951.

45 Alec Adams, UK Chargé d'Affaires. Conversation with Dr Rosalind Hearder, London, 1998.

46 Bullock, unpublished memoir, 20.

47 JP diary, 17/5/1951.

48 Bullock, conversation, 1996.

49 Bullock, conversation, 15/1/1998.

50 Bullock, conversation, 15/1/1998.

51 Loveday, conversation, 30/9/1997.

52 Tange, conversation, 1996.

53 Loveday, conversation, 30/9/97. Bullock 15/1/98.

54 Bullock, 15/1/98.

55 Pote Sarasin, letter, 12/9/1996.

56 O'Neill, op. cit., 152-3.

57 Adams, conversation, 1998.

58 O'Neill, op. cit., 240-1.
59 Adams, conversation, 1998.
60 Despatch 1/1950, quoted above.
61 Casey diary, 9/8/1951. Casey papers, MS6150, NLA.
62 Bullock, conversation, 15/1/98. JP diary 29/3/1951 and 26/7/1951.
63 Cam/Plim, ii, 11, 255-6.
64 O'Neill, op. cit., 178.
65 O'Neill, op. cit., 237-8.
66 O'Neill, op. cit., 245.
67 O'Neill, op. cit., 243-4.
68 Adams, conversation, 1998.
69 O'Neill, op. cit., 259.
70 O'Neill , op. cit., 260.
71 Casey, diary, 9/8/1951.
72 Spender to Menzies, I. 15326 of 1/10/1950 from London, folder of Watt/ Spender cables 1950, Watt papers, DFAT.
73 Bullock, conversation, 4/6/1998.
74 Casey, diary, 19-20/11/1951.
75 JP diary, 3/10/1951; JP to Watt, 3/10/1951, JP papers, DFAT.
76 This request coincided with confirmation of Plimsoll's promotion to Counsellor. *Gazette* extract quoted in JP diary, 4/10/1951.
77 Letter of 9/10/1951, JP papers, DFAT.
78 O'Neill, op. cit., 275 and 277.
79 Another case approximating this is that of Sir Harold Beeley, UK Ambassador in Cairo, 1961-64, who three years later was reappointed at the express personal request of President Nasser, it being Beeley's last post before retirement in 1970. This information courtesy of the UK Foreign and Commonwealth Office Historical Section, which referred to his obituary in *The Times* of 1/8/2001.
80 I.2523 of 16/2/1952 from Spender, in Washington. JP papers Box 1 Item 10 NAA. On 16/2/1952 Watt "raised with me the possibility of my returning to Korea, in response to a Washington cable expressing State Department's wish to that effect". On 28/2/1952 Casey, in his office, "asked me to return to Korea". JP diary.

81 Robert Murphy, *Diplomat Among Warriors,* Greenwood Publishing Group, New York, 1965, 389.

82 O'Neill, op. cit., 302.

83 Cam/Plim, ii, 256.

84 B. Cockram, Deputy UK High Commissioner, Canberra, conversation with Plimsoll, 8/1/1953. DO 35/5821, PRO London. Courtesy Dr R. Hearder

85 McIntyre letter of 27/6/1952 to JP. JP papers, DFAT. See also Garry Woodard, "The politics of intervention: James Plimsoll in the South Korean constitutional crisis of 1952," *Australian Journal of International Affairs,* vol 56, 3, 2002, 478 ff.

86 Plimsoll address, "Australia and Asia," 10/9/1965 at Sydney University (unpublished), JP papers, DFAT.

87 Plimsoll, conversation with General Clark, 19/12/1952. A5954/1, NAA. Also Plimsoll "knew that Rhee was confident that the UN Command forces would never act against him or allow him to be overthrown". O'Neill, op. cit., 304.

88 O'Neill, op. cit., 300-6.

89 From 19/6 to 31/7/1952 Plimsoll attended trials several times a week. JP diary.

90 Plimsoll to H.Marshall, 21/12/1955, JP papers, DFAT.

91 Suh Minho to Plimsoll, 10/9/1960, JP papers, Box 5, Item 53, NAA. See also Nick Evers, "Plim," in *40 Degrees South,* Lindisfarne, Tas, Issue 25, Winter 2005, 11.

92 Casey diary, 7/5/1952.

93 Casey diary, 6/8/1952.

94 O'Neill, op. cit., 307.

95 Critchley, conversation, 10/6/1996.

96 Plimsoll conversations with General Clark, 19/12/1952 in Tokyo, A5954/1; and in Canberra with Cockram, 8/1/1953, DO 35/5821, PRO.

97 Plimsoll to Marshall, 21/12/1955. JP papers, DFAT.

98 Adams, conversation 1998. Cockram conversation, 8/1/1953, DO 35/5821, PRO.

99 Cam/Plim, ii, 359.

100 "Plimsoll achieved distinction in wider international circles for his leadership, his thoughtful and positive approach to his duties, which were arduous both physically and mentally, and his rare capacity to influence Rhee. It is not surprising that the United States Government exerted itself strenuously against his reposting from UNCURK." O'Neill, op. cit., 403-4.

101 Bilney, conversation, 4/2/1998.

4
"A Tiger for Work"
Canberra, 1953-59

Plimsoll's stay in Canberra came about unexpectedly. He was supposed to have brief consultations before going to Jakarta, which was becoming one of Australia's most important posts. But his return home in December 1952 coincided with an exodus of two out of four of the department's most senior staff: McIntyre had gone on an overseas posting, and Tange was about to do likewise.[1] As Secretary, Watt had become concerned about the effect of these departures on the department. He recommended to Casey that, although Plimsoll's appointment in Jakarta had been announced, it should be cancelled and that he should take Tange's place in Canberra. Casey agreed.

During Plimsoll's six years in Canberra from 1953 his main responsibilities were Asia and national security, matters of the greatest interest to Casey, with whom he formed close ties.[2] His work impressed Casey, but more importantly the Prime Minister, Robert Menzies – which led to his further rise in the next few years.

Plimsoll had seen little of his family since 1945. Occasionally he spent a few days at the family home in Bondi taking things quietly, including surfing and walks with his father. In December 1956 the latter retired from David Jones. Plimsoll was home for the last years of his mother's life; she died in May 1957. And his brother John was married in October 1957 – with his older brother as best man.

Plimsoll settled into an unusual way of life in Canberra. Partly this was instinctive, partly it was by deliberate choice. Previously he had only lived there for a few months. Canberra did not become a home to him. He put down none of the usual roots, buying neither property nor a car.

His way of living was not unlike a diplomat in a post, spending time with foreign diplomats, academics, bishops, journalists and politicians.

He lived in the Hotel Canberra, five minutes walk from the department, just across the road at the southern end of West Block, one of the earliest Federal office buildings. He "shuttled between an organised living space to an organised work space, and took them as ambiences that were given".[3] His board, lodging, and laundry were all taken care of. His hotel costs were deducted from his fortnightly pay. He hardly ever went to a bank. The hotel, with its size, central location and elegant public areas, was the best in Canberra. Over coffee in the hotel lounge he talked to senior government officials visiting from Melbourne like Charles Spry and Fred Chilton, occasionally ministers, most of whom stayed there,[4] and to business people and other visitors. This contact gave him perhaps a broader insight into opinion and developments in Australia than most other Canberrans in the small, isolated national capital of the 1950s. Australian heads of mission abroad, when visiting Canberra on periodic leave and consultations, also stayed there. Plimsoll's talks with them supplemented those he had in the office. Among them was Walter Crocker, with whom he continued to keep in close touch.

The hotel was not luxurious. No stationery was provided in the rooms. Plimsoll lived in a modest bedroom, lino floor, single bed, cupboard and chest of drawers with no personal furnishings or decorations.[5] When away on lengthy visits, he had to vacate his room but, as the hotel's sole "permanent" resident, he seemed to get it back on return without difficulty.

For Plimsoll, Canberra meant a very small area: hotel, West Block and Parliament House, outside of which he ventured little. Official social functions were often at Parliament House, or at the hotel itself. Dinners with foreign diplomats, and in homes of colleagues in the department or friends at the ANU, were all in suburbs close by. He once walked to Civic, the city centre, to stand in the crowd and greet the Queen as she drove past during the Royal Visit of 1954.[6] Otherwise he visited

Civic only to get inoculations before going abroad. Occasionally he took a Sunday walk to the Australian-American War Memorial at Russell Hill, or to Government House in Yarralumla to sign the book the next day after dining there. A journalist friend once took him on a drive to Queanbeyan. On another occasion Archbishop Eris O'Brien drove him around to show him some Catholic schools under construction.[7] Sometimes he went to the local repertory theatre, in which the cast often included members of the department, and occasionally to one of the few art galleries. He suggested to Casey that there should be an Asian art gallery.[8]

He spent time with old friends from Sydney who were also living in Canberra, or who visited, such as John Kerr. He went to meetings of the Royal Institute of Public Administration. He arranged for meetings of the Canberra Branch of the Australian Institute of International Affairs, of which he was a member, to be held in a room in the department, and for one of his junior staff to act as branch secretary.[9]

Reading was his main diversion: mainly classical novels of English literature, also American, Russian and French. He read more than 80 in 1955 and in 1958. The number decreased to 70 and 61 respectively in 1956 and 1957,[10] perhaps reflecting greater work pressures.

Not concerned with practical matters such as housing and schooling like most of his colleagues, his outlook sometimes reflected a certain otherworldliness. At a colleague's suburban home, looking at the back garden, he asked what were those "round metal frame things" he kept seeing in people's backyards. "They are rotary hoists for drying clothes". "Oh," he said in wonderment.[11] He advised children of a colleague not to pass the time on a drive to Sydney by playing games, but by learning the kings and queens of England.[12]

He did not attend church, but his generous donation (intended to be anonymous) of £600 over three years to a building appeal for St John's Church in Reid,[13] his attendance at the opening ceremony of St Mark's Library,[14] and friendships with both the Anglican Bishop, Ernest

Burgmann, and the Roman Catholic Archbishop, O'Brien, suggested at least that he saw value in organised religion in society.

His more elevated status caused no change in his demeanour; on the other hand, he always looked older than he was. Both in Canberra and elsewhere he found that people often asked him for directions, even when he himself was a complete stranger. Perhaps "in times of uncertainty people tended to turn to conservative-looking older figures of authority". He had one dark blue suit that he wore constantly, along with white shirt, plain dark tie and black shoes. This "mode of dress took him everywhere, it was fit for all occasions, it made packing for travel simple and his luggage light, and he never had to worry about matching up his shirts".[15]

Jane Austen, one of Plimsoll's favourite authors, wrote that a single man, who was well off, needed a wife.[16] A bachelor in his mid-30s, a senior public servant who spent little and invested well – thanks to the help of his father and later his brother – must in many respects have seemed "a good catch". Plimsoll enjoyed company and had many friends, both men and women; but none very close. Perhaps the right person did not cross his path. He remained single, despite some well-meaning attempts to "marry him off". Even the Menzies invited him to a dinner party with this in mind. But in his life up to that point there is no evidence that he sought the company of single females. During his six years in Canberra this did not change. Very private, a loner, "he led a rather monastic life, sufficient unto himself".[17] As Hugh Gilchrist, a colleague who had also been a contemporary at Sydney University, put it, "Plimsoll was married to Sydney University and bigamously married to the department."

Plimsoll was once described by the Melbourne *Herald* as "a tiger for work" – "Besides a normal working week he regularly spends most of Saturday, a good deal of many Sundays and many nights at his office desk".[18] In May 1954, departmental records show that Plimsoll was working up to 116 hours a week, not including work done outside, such as after-hours meetings in Parliament House, official functions, or outside phone conversations.[19]

Why did Plimsoll work so hard? Throughout his career he was absorbed in the fascination and importance of the work. Colleagues observed that he was "passionate about his work",[20] constantly looking "for situations in which to absorb himself and worry about" and that he had a "genuine concern for the nation".[21] A further factor in the 1950s was an acute staff shortage in Canberra,[22] while pressures to increase staff at posts abroad meant little staffing improvement in Canberra, "especially at the middle level" where good people were "terribly short".[23]

Plimsoll did not expect others to work as hard as he did. He recalled that John Quinn, who worked for him, would often "work late at night on a draft which was needed next day, rather than shuffle off on someone else what he regarded as his own duty and rather than let something shoddy go forward".[24] This was also a self-description for Plimsoll.

Well meaning advice of friends not to work too hard made him once admit that, "it probably does one good to have a bit of a break"; yet throughout his life he took few holidays. The idea of a beach holiday horrified him.[25] He was disinclined to plan a real holiday for himself.

When Plimsoll started work in Canberra in January 1953, few knew him. Apart from Casey, only one other minister had met him.[26] In a small national capital, this quickly changed. A more personal relationship than today existed between senior public servants and ministers, who had no policy staff, and would normally receive them alone. Plimsoll quickly made an impression. Although new to the public service in Canberra, his years in the USA and at the UN had given him some insights into governance as well as confidence and poise. Besides international issues he could discuss in depth a wide variety of subjects from cricket to literature, although lacking in small talk. He impressed members of the small diplomatic corps in Canberra, one of whom was Lord Carrington, later to be UK Foreign Secretary. Carrington recalled that when he had been in Canberra, "Plimsoll seemed to be the intellectual force behind the policies pursued by the department. He was quite clearly the most thoughtful and perceptive of those whom I recollect".[27]

In a time before television and the internet it was essential to read airmail copies of the London *Times*, *The Economist*, the *New York Times* and *Le Monde* in order to supplement information in official reports. Plimsoll was always well informed about subjects that were not directly his responsibility, vital for whenever he was acting head of department and liable to have to recommend on current issues, or to "transform a draft" – he was "the cleverest man with a pen," and an intuitive mind.[28] He had a photographic memory and an ability to explain complex matters quickly and clearly both on paper and face to face.[29] When Casey once asked him to produce urgently something about the value of SEATO he dictated a page off the top of his head without changing a word.[30] Casey was impressed that the US Secretary of State, Foster Dulles, called Plimsoll by his first name.[31] Plimsoll was "one of few diplomats who had real understanding of the motives, and environment in which politicians operated. He was fascinated by politics – loved to get to know politicians: collected them like art works".[32]

He came to know all future prime ministers up to 1972: Holt, McEwen, Gorton and McMahon,[33] as well as many key public servants. Whenever standing in for Tange, however, he did not take the opportunity to learn in any depth about the complex management of the department.

Plimsoll's preference was to be working abroad. He tolerated six years in Canberra, forming no attachment to it. Nevertheless, he would have thought this long period one of the most stable and satisfying of his career because of his regard for Menzies, his affection for Casey (shared by Plimsoll's close colleagues, despite Casey's shortcomings as minister[34]), and his close relationship with Tange, who became Secretary in 1954. It was a period of great interest, pioneering Australia's diplomatic involvement in Asia. Plimsoll liked working in the very small department that External Affairs then was. He did not object to the greater process and organisation which Tange as Secretary strove to inculcate, but he was more comfortable with the greater flexibility and reduced process that it replaced. As regards policy, he once wrote, emphasising flexibility:

> We have our policy more clearly defined now. We seem to progress by a series of spurts, stopping periodically to take breath and survey where we are, and then plunging forward again. Most foreign policy gets worked out that way, and it is much more effective than a doctrinaire line rigidly adhered to.[35]

Asia and Security

Plimsoll's main responsibility was for the Asian region and Australia's security relationships. These matters were intertwined. Although development of relations with Asia was a major objective in itself, Cold War aspects were much to the fore. The Petrov affair in 1954 reinforced concern about communism within Australia as well as without.

An important policy question was what approach should Australia take towards China after the communists took control in 1949. The possibility of recognition of Communist China had been politically sensitive – communism had been an issue in the 1949 election; Menzies was scornful of a suggestion for early recognition. Plimsoll, however, believed that Menzies had been "intellectually convinced" that Australia should recognise China some time in 1950, but the Korean War had put paid to that.[36] In 1954 Plimsoll had noted that it was not realistic to consider the question of recognition "purely on its merits as far as China itself is concerned". Relations with the US and the US attitude to the UN were also important. China's admission to the UN would not help "if the US were simultaneously to withdraw in consequence".[37] Cabinet rejected Casey's submission in June 1955 recommending recognition of Communist China.[38] In 1957 Plimsoll spoke privately of the desirability of diplomatic relations with China, as with the restoration of relations with USSR, although in both cases "most of the Cabinet was opposed".[39]

Plimsoll was not in the vanguard of efforts to develop relations with China: his experience in Korea may have contributed to this.

As for the new regional security arrangements to which Australia was a party – ANZUS, ANZAM and SEATO – the relationship with the US was paramount. Plimsoll thought that Australia's basic interest was to keep the active presence of both the major power blocs "as far from Australia as possible", which meant striking "a delicate balance so that we have an effective US guarantee to us, plus their capacity to deliver the goods, but at the same time we should aim to keep communist power as far away as possible from our shores". Americans generally had "done remarkably well" as a new great power, although "they have not yet learnt to accept emotionally the obligations and odium". He approved of their self-belief, despite the "rather self-righteous confidence" of Dulles.[40] US support was vital, but ANZUS was "no blank cheque"; the US attitude to it was something that had to be watched and kept "under review, day to day, year to year".[41]

The US guarantee was the crucial ingredient in SEATO. In the early stages Plimsoll had advocated avoiding setting up an organisation; but other counsels prevailed.[42] SEATO was not to be regarded "as itself being an instrument for effective practical action". It had its deficiencies, but it provided "legal cover – a treaty relationship – for possible action by the US to combat some act of communist aggression".[43] A continuing British military involvement was also important. For example, following a SEATO military planners discussion in 1956 about the level of threat presented to the Treaty area by China, the British appeared to think the threat had been exaggerated in order to facilitate passage through the US Congress of a large defence programme. But Britain's own approach betrayed a desire to find arguments to support reducing its own overall defence expenditure.[44]

Plimsoll was concerned at the level of Australian military capability. Following the surrender of French forces at Dien Bien Phu in Indochina in 1954, he thought that "Australia will have to make up its mind to spend more money on defence than it is doing at present".[45] Early in 1956, as Malayan independence approached, he commented privately at the "peculiar position we were getting in of telling the British that they should not get out of Malaya but at the same time being unable or unwilling to provide further Australian forces to handle the subsequent unrest".[46]

Indonesia was a major preoccupation, not least in relation to West New Guinea, where Australia was supporting the continued Dutch presence. Australian public opinion would have opposed an Indonesian takeover and all major political parties favoured the Dutch remaining. Calwell, then Deputy Leader of the Opposition, used to phone Plimsoll "quite often", to "stiffen" him, and "to ensure there would be no weakening on the part of the Government".[47] In the event of an Indonesian attack, however, the "big question", Plimsoll noted, was "whether or not Australia should make any military commitments to the Dutch".[48] US intervention in support of Australia "might not occur immediately". Australia needed the means to "look after itself until its allies make up their minds to come to our assistance".[49] But the Government preferred to give priority to economic development rather than increase defence expenditure.

In this connection establishment of close working arrangements between External Affairs and Defence was a priority. This was not easy as Defence was still located in Melbourne and given the history of suspicion and strained relations in the wake of the Evatt and Burton years.[50] Nevertheless, Watt, and later Tange and Plimsoll, successfully built up a close working relationship, portraying External Affairs as "a department that was trustworthy and had something to offer. External Affairs officers had to show that we had a contribution to make to Defence thinking and operations that was worthwhile and, indeed, essential".[51] At meetings in Melbourne of the Defence Committee, which was attended by the Defence Secretary and the service chiefs, Tange, or Plimsoll if deputising for him, were able to inject External Affairs views.

Plimsoll's responsibilities also included the South Pacific, for which he could find little time, and had few staff. He regularly attended the annual Canberra Summer School of the Australian Institute of Political Science, and an old friend, Arthur Lowndes, the chairman, accepted his suggestion that New Guinea should be the subject for 1958.[52] Plimsoll, who attended throughout, thought it was very successful, especially in stimulating public interest in the topic. Plimsoll was aware of how pressures for decolonisation at the UN could intensify, and of constraints on how long Australia could continue to retain responsibility for PNG. The Summer School discussions deepened his conviction that Paul Hasluck, the Minister for Territories, was wrong in his cautious approach to self-government: UN pressures would cause movement "much more quickly than would be desirable in a logical world, and self-government may come to New Guinea whether they are ready or not or else we will be faced with a colonial war or Asian intervention". Plimsoll also considered Hasluck's educational policy, aimed at avoiding creation of an elite, unrealistic.[53]

Plimsoll sometimes found himself involved in issues outside his direct responsibilities, partly when acting secretary and partly because of his previous UN experience. Tange sought his help in interesting Menzies to see the UN Secretary-General, Dag Hammarskjold, when he visited Canberra early in 1956.[54] The sole officer working on disarmament in the department once was told to take a cable draft to Plimsoll, then acting secretary. Plimsoll rewrote it, showing "surprising detailed knowledge of developments, and more grasp of the subject" than those responsible.[55]

Plimsoll's experience abroad made him acutely aware of the value of the department communicating well with posts: "We really do need to know something about who is thinking what, and why, and in general what lies behind this or that decision", wrote his friend McIntyre from London.[56] In this spirit Plimsoll regularly wrote personally to McIntyre, Crocker (New Delhi), Waller (Bangkok), Walker (Tokyo), and Watt (Singapore), all people in key posts.[57] Plimsoll would also send Australian newspaper cuttings. Watt once thanked him, saying he valued this, but "it is fantastic that you should have to waste your time" on it.[58] Plimsoll's help was also sought on various personal or sensitive matters; Waller once "traced your fine Italian hand" in a manoeuvre Plimsoll successfully executed for him in Canberra.[59]

Watt once criticised Plimsoll, as a former Secretary "and as a friend", about reports that Plimsoll compiled of his conversations while on a tour of several Asian countries in 1956. Watt was surprised "at the range of topics you initiated" with interlocutors. "We can only operate within the general lines of policy laid down, listening and explaining and countering invalid arguments, but scarcely going beyond that".[60] But Casey had read these reports and agreed with the approach Plimsoll had taken. Plimsoll agreed with Watt about the importance of keeping within government policy and of taking account of the views of other Australian representatives. But he stressed the importance of "instinct", and "playing it by ear" during opportunities that open up in conversation. Plimsoll noted that, during his visit to Cambodia, meetings had been at an unexpectedly high level, with Sihanouk involved. He had been "skating on very thin ice, but I do not think I fell through".[61] Plimsoll had a rare feel for how far he could push the boundaries of conversations into areas of potential policy sensitivity.

Working with Casey

Casey's favourable impression of Plimsoll in Korea was quickly reinforced in Canberra. After seven months Casey told him that he was recommending him for an honour at a higher level than the normal OBE.[62] Two years later the award of CBE for Plimsoll was announced in the 1956 New Year's Honours List.[63]

A number of Plimsoll's contemporaries, like Tange, Waller and Shann, also developed close ties with Casey. But Plimsoll's collaboration continued for almost seven years, longer than Casey's with any other member of the department except Tange. Close trust and understanding developed between two very different people: the one smartly dressed, interested in anything mechanical or to do with engineering, and passionate about flying; and the other, who had little interest in clothes, who did not even drive a car, could not change a light bulb, and was devoted to the arts and literature. For his part, Plimsoll enjoyed Casey's hospitality, occasionally sandwiches while working with him in Parliament House in Canberra; and meals at Casey's club in Melbourne and visits to stay at his country house near Berwick.

Plimsoll admitted to frustrations in working with Casey: "Work which is urgent is not normally important and work which is important is not normally urgent. What is urgent and what takes up [Plimsoll's] time is some side-show or toy or enthusiasm of the Minister".[64] Plimsoll and Tange frequently found themselves advising Casey against his ill-judged proposals for press releases; and Casey usually took their advice. It was a "disadvantage" that Casey spent so much time in Melbourne.[65] Casey often would arrive at the Hotel Canberra from Melbourne on the latest plane possible the night before Cabinet meetings, after 9.30pm, and Plimsoll would then brief him.[66] Casey on average was abroad for three months a year, often for more than four weeks at a time. He returned home after long visits without stopping in Canberra. Tange or Plimsoll would fly to Kingsford Smith Airport to have quick contact with him before his onward journey to Melbourne.[67] All this meant that, at a time of primitive communications, much of the daily business of foreign affairs in Canberra was handled without the minister being present or having an input. This included matters where the Prime Minister was involved and wanted advice urgently.

When Casey did come to Canberra, contact was considerable. He would often meet Plimsoll two or more times a day. That Casey frequently spent time in the department Plimsoll warmly approved of; most ministers had not, while "others never ever set foot in it".[68] Sometimes Casey addressed the department's policy officers – they all fitted into the small library.

Plimsoll admired the way that Casey, and Maie Casey, in their Asian travels, "desired good relations, not simply out of intellectual conviction, but from instinctive understanding and rapport with the people of the region".[69]

Plimsoll, who occasionally attended cabinet committee meetings, noted that sometimes "relatively minor things would panic members of cabinet, whereas Casey would take things in his stride". He attributed this to Casey's wide experience and perspective, for example having had to deal with a famine facing 60 million people when he was governor of Bengal: "Casey had great common sense, which often led him instinctively to the right decision".[70]

However, Plimsoll sometimes despaired of Casey's casual attitude to preparing for meetings: "There were always dangers in his urge to go into talks without any clear idea of what he wanted to get out of them or what he was going to say himself". It seemed that, to Casey, "a process of constant touring and talk must have some inherent value almost irrespective of what was discussed and with whom".[71] Having talked to Chou En-Lai during the Geneva Conference on Indochina in 1954, Casey later wanted to propose to Chou that they have talks somewhere in China. Plimsoll recalled that he "had difficulty in dissuading him until it was clear what he could say. I thought that Chou would certainly have expected something other than inconsequential chatter, and that such a meeting would do harm all round"[72] at a time when Casey's cabinet colleagues were flatly opposed to relations with China. The talks did not happen.

Casey's performance in cabinet was disappointing. Plimsoll thought that one factor was that Casey "would act more by instinct and could be very fuzzy in his presentation. He often tended to assume that his propositions were self-evident and therefore he did not argue them. Casey was not able to explain himself, particularly in abstract or sophisticated terms".[73] A senior cabinet colleague, John McEwen, thought that Casey had "great talents but not judgment".[74] He encountered considerable difficulties, as has been commented on elsewhere.[75] He was up against ignorance, even bigotry, among cabinet colleagues, as well as a lack of interest.[76] There was also suspicion "that a new department like EA is encroaching on the functions of other departments when it merely attempts to exercise the functions which a foreign office in an older country carries out as a matter of course".[77] And there was a "lack of belief that all this opening up of relations with Asia was important".[78] Australian political leaders of the time were "deeply conditioned by the view that the people who one had to look to ultimately were to be found predominantly in London and Washington".[79]

Given these attitudes, and the importance which Casey assigned to "doing what I can to create an Australian awareness of the movements going on in Asia and of the importance to us of the relations which we may develop with our neighbours"[80] Plimsoll rendered invaluable assistance to Casey in public relations.

Plimsoll had a significant role in drafting Casey's major speeches, especially a periodic statement to parliament about international affairs, leading into a debate. Although an experienced speaker, Casey "dreaded" this task.[81] Good speech drafts would have bolstered his confidence. In an era when ministers did not have their own speechwriters, such assistance was a particularly important function for senior officials.

Casey's book, *Friends and Neighbours*, was published in 1954. It drew attention to the importance of Asia to Australia. It was a notable pioneering effort at a time when there was little public knowledge or understanding of Asia, little contact with the region, and little information available.[82] The book was more explanation of policy than detailed description and was kept to a suitable length for a mass readership. The first edition sold out. Michigan State University in the US published a paperback edition,[83] which was also significant given the importance attached to trying "to interest the Americans in South-East Asia, an area of the world in which they had not had any interest" except in relation to the Philippines.[84]

Plimsoll had a major role in drafting the book, a considerable effort in addition to his normal responsibilities. He managed to devote most of a day to drafting the first chapter,[85] but from then on the task had to be squeezed in among other tasks. To finish he had to defer leave and be relocated to the room in the department normally reserved for the minister. This took him away from normal work. Yet he still had to be available for two matters in Parliament that week – a debate on SEATO and the Cocos Bill.[86] As had been the case with Evatt's book, there was no public acknowledgment of Plimsoll's assistance. Plimsoll, being very discreet, "would not have let on that he wrote or had a major hand in writing something that came out over Casey's name". But in the department it was "general knowledge around the place that Plimsoll had drafted all or most of the book".[87]

Once, when Casey was to speak at Sydney University, Plimsoll was informed by a friend that it had been decided to close down the School of Oriental Studies. Given the importance Casey attached to Asia Plimsoll had no difficulty persuading Casey to include in his speech a plea to keep the School going. As a result the decision was reversed.[88]

Casey was active with the Australian media, then predominantly print and radio.[89] It was unusual at that time for public servants to talk to journalists. But Plimsoll was alive to the importance of working with the media, and confident after earlier experience with journalists in the US and then in Korea.[90] In 1953 he did a background briefing about an Australian wheat gift to Pakistan.[91] The SEATO Council meeting in Canberra in 1957 was a major international conference, "big time" for the Australian press, with John Foster Dulles, and foreign ministers of other member states attending. A journalist recalled that Plimsoll "went out of his way to see that we were properly informed" by organising press briefings, standard practice now but a "bold initiative for EA then". That the press coverage was "excellent" owed a lot to Plimsoll, "who was always approachable".[92] In 1957 he briefed the press on the transfer of Christmas Island from Singapore;[93] and in 1958 at the SEATO Council meeting in Manila.[94]

Plimsoll was prepared to be available on background to journalists of the parliamentary press gallery. Much of this flowed from acquaintance over meals at the Hotel Canberra where a number of journalists stayed. It was not possible to escape company at meals which were only served in the dining room. Michael McGeorge of *The Age* recalled that, although courteous, Plimsoll did not take a turn at bringing a bottle of wine to the table. "He was extremely well-read, genial, helpful and kind, able to talk engagingly about any subject that arose. He was, however, basically a quiet and serious man, dedicated to his work," and careful in what he said. Once, when McGeorge showed special interest in something Plimsoll was saying about Australian aid, Plimsoll left the table and later returned with several paragraphs written out for him. The report made the front page of *The Age* next morning.[95] E.H. Cox of the Melbourne *Herald*, doyen of the press gallery, was often in touch with Plimsoll, sometimes over drinks, or at meals at his house.[96] Creighton Burns, a member of the Radio Australia panel of international affairs commentators who visited Canberra for occasional briefings, recalled that Plimsoll was "very good at explaining current foreign policy", and that he would mention alternative policy options, not only the official policy.[97]

Plimsoll exerted influence in other ways. He encouraged Australian ambassadors in the region to be helpful in talking to visitors like Professor McMahon Ball or Norman Harper, both of Melbourne University, who were also respected commentators on international affairs, personally known to Plimsoll.[98] In 1957 Plimsoll encouraged Jim McIntyre, newly arrived ambassador in Jakarta, to make contact with local US, UK and Australian press representatives, something of which his predecessor, Crocker, had done little.[99] At the request of Norman Cowper, National President of the Australian Institute of Political Science (AIPS), Plimsoll drew up a plan for five lectures for the 1959 Summer School, together with notes on the issues each should cover. He also suggested suitable speakers, mentioning that he had sounded out Casey about his willingness in principle to speak.[100]

Plimsoll did some public speaking, also a role that public servants rarely embarked on. He spoke whenever opportunities offered: several times to the Parliamentary Committee on Foreign Affairs on various subjects, and to annual courses of Australian industry representatives that the Defence Department convened. He spoke in public to various groups in Canberra and Melbourne, especially on Korea during 1953 when the issue was prominent with developments leading to the ceasefire. He also spoke about more general topics such as foreign policy and Australia and the UN.

In 1958 Casey confided in Plimsoll about a sensitive matter for a senior minister, his forthcoming retirement. In about August Casey had told Menzies he would like to retire at the end of 1959. Menzies told Casey that he could remain minister for as long as he wanted; he raised with Casey the recent British innovation of a life peerage. Casey responded with interest. Some weeks later Casey conveyed the foregoing to Plimsoll when they were travelling abroad together. He asked Plimsoll what he knew about life peerages, which, being the omniscient Plimsoll, "was quite a lot". Plimsoll then made further enquiries on Casey's behalf in London. A friend had said to Plimsoll: "I trust you are not being, in the kindness of your heart, Dick's private secretary."[101] But he was, and much more, as helping Casey in this way showed. Late in 1959 Casey told Plimsoll he planned to retire at the end of the year, and would be created a life peer.[102]

Following his actual retirement in February 1960, Plimsoll sent him a handwritten letter:

> I shall miss you enormously. As far as I have been personally concerned, our relationship could not have been more satisfying, and I owe an immense amount to you in so many ways since you became Minister ... It is not easy for one who is naturally reticent, to put in cold words on paper all that I should like to say. I think we understand one another. The Department will miss you, as a human being ... your impetus, and imagination and courage, and you've given our foreign policy a wrench that put Australia into a

new posture, facing the second part of the twentieth century and our Pacific environment.[103]

In Casey's equally warm handwritten reply, he agreed that they did, indeed, understand each other:

> There is no one in a fairly full and long life, who has given me such intelligent, farseeing and thoughtful help – for which I am infinitely grateful. You are probably the most dedicated human being that I've ever known. In a not too easy world you've been a solid rock of character and friendship.[104]

Working with Menzies

Casey and Plimsoll's collaboration did not take place in a vacuum. In Canberra of the 1950s, both for ministers and senior public servants, the Prime Minister, Robert Menzies, was pre-eminent. Relations between Casey and Menzies were sometimes difficult, both at the personal level and in terms of policy. Plimsoll and others had to navigate possible shoals.

An unintended service that Casey did for Plimsoll in his lengthy time in Canberra was bringing Plimsoll into frequent contact with Menzies. Plimsoll saw Menzies about subjects in which he was interested and for which Plimsoll was responsible, notably Japan. Developing a better relationship with Japan was a fundamental objective and the Prime Minister was conscious of its sensitivity in the post-war years.[105] One issue was the Japanese request to resume their pre-war pearl fishing in north-western Australian waters. Plimsoll represented External Affairs in considerable inter-departmental consultation. In October 1953 Plimsoll saw Menzies alone about Japanese pearling and about Japanese membership of the UN – although the main topic was a forthcoming visit by Richard Nixon, the US Vice-President.[106]

Plimsoll admired Menzies's handling of the Japan issue. There remained much bitterness among Australians about Japanese atrocities during the War, and the perceived threat of Japanese invasion. It was widely feared that Japan would become an aggressor again. Looking back, in 1964, Plimsoll wrote:

> The constructive politician will not take public opinion as a fixed fact but will regard it as a variable factor which he can himself try to influence, and he will on occasion run risks to do so.

Australian relations with Japan, "which are now extremely good", was an example of "what can be done to give a lead to public opinion". The government's programme of settling every one of the differences with Japan remaining from the War was accomplished remarkably quickly.[107] Japan probably was an example of the Prime Minister's capacity to think "8-9 months ahead", which Plimsoll also admired.[108]

For his part, Menzies "praised Plimsoll's mind and integrity". He was also impressed with how well read Plimsoll was.[109]

Plimsoll was impressed with Menzies's approach to economic matters, which he knew he could not neglect.[110] He was also impressed that at the 1957 Commonwealth Prime Ministers' Conference, which Plimsoll attended, Kwame Nkrumah of Ghana, the first independent African leader to attend, had later said he felt closest to Menzies of all those there, because the latter had treated him "just like anyone else".[111]

Plimsoll was not uncritical, however. Privately he had disliked Menzies' attempt to ban communists through the Communist Party Dissolution Bill. It was "not a proper exercise in democracy to eliminate a political party" in peacetime.[112] Like other colleagues, Plimsoll was irritated by the Prime Minister's tendency not to inform External Affairs of the substance of his conversations with other heads of government, or to arrange for advance warning to posts of his statements of policy:

> Unfortunately our PM does not record or report very fully on what is being done, particularly at the formative stages, and we often have to rely upon what we pick up from him when he returns.[113]

As recorded elsewhere, like Tange and Casey, Plimsoll had private reservations about the Government's focus on national development at the expense of defence, but there is no evidence that he discussed this with Menzies.

Sir Alan Watt recalled Menzies' "quickness of apprehension and decision"; and his disinclination to read material "unless this was unavoidable". He preferred to have an adviser "tell him what the problem was, in clear and simple terms", then "ask singularly pertinent questions", and then decide on the matter.[114] Plimsoll, when acting secretary, developed confidence in dealing with the Prime Minister in this way.

Early in 1954 Australian officials thought that the United Kingdom, in arranging for the independence of Malaya, could detach Christmas Island and transfer it to Australia. Plimsoll talked to Menzies, who at first was "rather hostile, that Australia should not be going around trying to pick up new territories". He was persuaded, however, by the argument that "this would be a major source of phosphates needed for Australian agriculture".[115]

In 1956 the Middle East took centre stage following nationalisation of the Suez Canal by President Nasser. Suez was more the day-to-day responsibility of others but, in the latter part of the year, Plimsoll found that the Suez crisis "dominated my working life",[116] because of long periods as acting secretary while Tange was abroad, either accompanying Casey or Menzies.[117] Suez contributed to the development of Plimsoll's confidence in understanding Menzies and in dealing with him. When British and French military intervention took place Australia announced its support. Plimsoll, who had not expected the invasion, told the Prime Minister that he considered this a mistake. This was not only on moral grounds, but because he could not see what would happen if the invasion was successful – no Egyptian government would have agreed to work with the invaders.[118] This frankness did not alter Menzies' attitude towards him. By contrast, Tange, in London, temporarily fell out with the Prime Minister, being as opposed as was Casey to the approach Menzies took.[119]

Australia and Egypt broke off diplomatic relations. Qantas, then government-owned, thought the government would no longer permit it to fly through Cairo, which at the time was an important hub – and Qantas would lose some £1 million weekly. As Menzies felt so strongly about Suez, it was thought impossible to broach this with him, and that, in any case, he would never agree to Australia trying to resume such flights. Plimsoll, however, felt that he could always get a hearing from Menzies. That evening he saw him about a number of matters, and raised the question of the cost to Qantas if it was not allowed into Cairo. "I think we ought to try to approach the Egyptians to allow it". Menzies had no objections. The Department of Civil Aviation was "rather surprised".[120]

A year later, in 1957, Plimsoll saw a possible opening towards eventual restoration of relations with Egypt. It had become customary for the anniversary of the start of the Second World War battle of El Alamein on 23 October 1942 to be observed on the spot by representatives from the former combatants, the UK, Australia, New Zealand and India. The Indian Ambassador in Cairo, without consulting anyone, had proposed to the Egyptian authorities that the other three countries each be allowed to send a representative to the ceremony, although diplomatic relations with them had been severed. Egypt had agreed. The UK and New Zealand rejected the proposal, which the Australian Defence Department thought Menzies would too. As acting secretary, Plimsoll saw Menzies who was also acting minister. He suggested Australia should be represented. Australia would not want to rebuff India which, although it had not consulted Australia first, thought it was being helpful. Further, it would be useful to have someone visit who could also make contact with the Egyptians and inspect Australian diplomatic properties in Cairo. Menzies asked if he had in mind sending someone "all the way from Australia?" Plimsoll replied that he suggested sending Owen Davis, then senior external affairs representative in London. He was a Second World War veteran and a former prisoner of war of the Japanese. Menzies said he had no objection. The visit by Davis led to contacts in Cairo, which in turn led to an Australian being seconded as second secretary in the Canadian Embassy to attend to Australian interests.[121]

Three years later, in 1960, Plimsoll was based in New York when Menzies visited at short notice.[122] Relations had not yet been restored with Egypt, partly out of concern about the "strong feelings" of Menzies, which led to diffidence in Canberra about approaching him. Accompanying Menzies to a dinner, Plimsoll told him that the Egyptian Foreign Minister, Fauzi, would be attending, that he, Plimsoll, thought it was time to restore relations, and that Menzies might have an opportunity "to say a word about it". Menzies agreed. He later told Plimsoll that Fauzi had agreed, and that relations would be resumed. Plimsoll commented: "One of Menzies' strengths was that he could be persuaded to do things he didn't like . . . that this was what he ought to do".[123]

1957 brought further contact with the Prime Minister. In April Plimsoll had responsibility for the SEATO Council meeting to be held in Canberra, as mentioned earlier. It was the first time a major diplomatic conference had been held since the Commonwealth conference on Japan in 1947. Menzies was closely involved, along with Casey.[124] In April Plimsoll accompanied Menzies on a visit to Japan, the first by an Australian prime minister since the War; and afterwards to Hong Kong, Thailand, Philippines and Papua New Guinea. The visit went "very well":

> The PM fitted in better in his contacts with the Asians than I expected. He got on very well indeed with them all and I think he left an impression of his very powerful personality and this in turn no doubt enhanced Australia's standing.[125]

In mid-year Plimsoll accompanied Menzies to London for the Commonwealth Prime Ministers' meeting.[126] In December came the visit to Australia of Mr Nobusuke Kishi, the first by a Prime Minister of Japan.

Menzies travelled overseas with a small party, with few accompanying policy advisers and no media. On his visit to Japan and other countries, apart from Plimsoll, there was only one other policy adviser.[127] There was considerable opportunity for real exchanges between the prime minister and accompanying officials, and to learn about his *modus operandi*.[128] Like some other senior officials who had dealings with the prime minister, Plimsoll was invited to the Lodge for meals from time to time, often at a weekend. With the Tanges he was among guests at a dinner to celebrate Menzies' 64th birthday.[129]

In a survey of senior federal public servants a commentator reported early in 1959 that in External Affairs "the power behind the scenes is the number two man, Mr James Plimsoll, a dedicated Father Joseph, who certainly has the PM's ear and has been chosen to accompany him on several overseas trips".[130] Menzies regarded public servants "fundamentally as human beings". He also regarded them as experts. He came to regard External Affairs people as having a greater degree of expertise than any other department except perhaps Treasury.[131]

Working with Tange

Tange, as secretary, and Plimsoll, his deputy, were two very different people yet with much in common. Both were loners who had had friendly acquaintance, and mutual respect, going back to their common pre-war experience as economists at the Bank of New South Wales.[132] Working closely together over six years in Canberra forged a closer bond. There was "a sort of chemistry" between them.[133] Although work was what they talked about most, there was a mutual interest in cricket.[134]

Neither had had as much first hand experience in External Affairs as had a number of their contemporaries. Tange's career had been largely that of a Canberra public servant, while Plimsoll's much shorter career had been mainly based abroad. Both had risen to the top rapidly, partly through their performances in multilateral diplomacy. Each worked hard,

Tange with a more balanced approach. He took time off and spent it with his family, and always took his leave. Plimsoll would have agreed in principle about the importance of balance; he had many outside interests, but in practice he mainly worked.

Tange remained secretary despite at least one rumour that Plimsoll was to succeed him, which reached UK officials in London in 1957.[135] Tange's priority was building the department at home and abroad. Except on the most important issues, such as Indonesia, he left much day-to-day policy-making to his Assistant Secretaries (effectively deputies).[136] Tange regarded Plimsoll as his "first lieutenant", with " more political nous than others", and trusted him greatly, especially on policy matters.[137]

Sir Leslie Melville thought "Tange always looked a very determined man".[138] A former rugby player, he could be confrontational, both within the department and outside, especially in his approach to the Treasury and the Public Service Board. These consistently obstructed his efforts to achieve better conditions for staff serving at posts. Achievement of status was important to Tange.[139] Plimsoll looked serious but calm, and was little interested in status. He favoured more subtle approaches; getting to know key people and influencing them, if necessary seeking consensus. In contrast to Tange, Plimsoll maintained personal friendships with Sir Roland Wilson, Secretary to the Treasury – Casey had urged him to keep in touch with Wilson[140] – and Len Hewitt who, as a very senior official, was the Dr No of the Treasury insofar as External Affairs was concerned.

Tange was a remote, authoritarian figure, insisting on discipline and the right tone in the place.[141] Respected not least for his ultimate power as secretary, he was feared by many for his temper and cutting remarks. Few apart from the most senior saw him. Plimsoll, on the other hand, was accessible and on speaking terms with people at all levels, remembered their names and often something about them, without getting familiar or revealing much about himself. One recalled that Plimsoll "enjoyed something of a halo of perfect professional performance".[142] He was involved most years in the graduate recruitment process for the department, interviewing personally every applicant who reached the final stage of selection in Canberra. Later he invited each of those chosen to come and see him after starting work.

Appointment to New York

A possible posting for Plimsoll was considered but not pursued at least twice. Tange had intended to recommend him for Jakarta in 1957, and there was a plan to send him to Washington in October 1958 as number two in the embassy to Sir Howard Beale. Indications in August that year were another two years in Canberra.[143] But six weeks later Tange told him privately he would be going to the UN in New York as Australia's permanent representative.[144] The appointment was not announced until March 1959. Tange recalled that Plimsoll was "a logical choice". It was a time of increasing anti-colonialism, which the USSR was exploiting. Australia needed a strong advocate who understood Australian policies. Casey had high regard for Plimsoll as being reliable, someone who saw the issues clearly, a good negotiator, someone prepared to go to the top, and able to make excellent contacts.[145]

His appointment probably had some connection with the Suez Canal crisis, and the reaction at the UN, where Australia's stance put it at odds with Asian neighbours and with other countries. As Percy Spender wrote to Plimsoll from Washington: "We really had a beating at the Assembly this year".[146] The UN was by no means central to the Menzies Government's foreign policy, in contrast to the approach of the previous Labor Government. But, during the crisis, Menzies, as he confessed to President Eisenhower, was struck by the significant role played by the UN General Assembly, which he had hitherto "wrongly regarded as no more than a debating forum. The whole conception of the UN has sustained a most dramatic change".[147]

Suez underlined the need to be well represented in New York. Plimsoll had become highly regarded by both Casey and Menzies, including for his expertise on the UN. An example of this was an eight-page paper, "The Middle East in the United Nations", which Plimsoll wrote after a number of high level conversations during a short visit to New York with Casey in November 1956. In that paper he analysed the situation of the US, the changes in the UN since he had seen it six years before, and the effect of Suez on UK prestige.[148]

At 42, he was (and remains today) the youngest appointment as permanent representative,[149] although his age partly reflected the relative youth of the Australian diplomatic service at the time.

There is no evidence that Plimsoll had sought the position. His personal preference would have been an Asian posting, as a follow-up to the work he had been doing in Canberra. Waller thought that he would "do in New York admirably", but that his appointment was "a waste". He was well suited for Asia where he "could have made a real contribution".[150] Crocker, by contrast, noted Plimsoll as saying he would have preferred Moscow,[151] perhaps because of the special challenge of reopening there after a five-year break.

There were many farewell functions for Plimsoll. In Canberra, among many dinners, was one by Lord Carrington, British High Commissioner. In Sydney, Sir Garfield Barwick, then Attorney-General and Acting Minister during Casey's absence for a month, had him to lunch; as did Dr and Mrs Evatt. In Melbourne Casey had a small dinner, where the guests included Sir Owen Dixon, Chief Justice of the High Court of Australia, Sir Edmund Herring, Chief Justice of the Supreme Court of Victoria, and the Chairman of BHP, Sir Colin Syme.[152] Plimsoll made a point of making farewell calls on Hasluck and Calwell and on Sir Roland Wilson and Len Hewitt in the Treasury.[153]

Before leaving Canberra Plimsoll wrote a valedictory report for Casey. This used to be common practice among departing ambassadors, but rarely after completing a term at home. "Some observations on leaving Canberra" was a wide-ranging look into the future. Besides Cold War considerations, his forthcoming UN preoccupations influenced much of what he wrote about India, Africa, Latin America and, especially, PNG. He felt the South Pacific was deserving of increased attention by Canberra. The same applied to Africa, which earlier he had prophetically described as "this emerging part of the world which will become increasingly important in international affairs".[154] Crocker, to whom Plimsoll passed a copy on a personal basis, gave it to Menzies to read when the Prime Minister passed through Ottawa, where Crocker was then assigned, and he told Plimsoll of the Prime Minister's interest.[155]

Plimsoll's health

In Canberra Plimsoll's work regime began to affect his health. There was no attempt to deal with insufficient days off, inadequate leave and exercise, and too many meals out and constant hotel fare. In August 1958 Tange expressed concern "about Plimsoll's need of recreation leave",[156] before Plimsoll was to accompany Casey on a strenuous nine weeks journey abroad. In London Alfred Stirling, who encountered him there, thought he looked tired and unwell. Two specialists examined Plimsoll at Westminster Hospital, but found nothing wrong.[157] In Ottawa, a few days later, however, Crocker thought Plimsoll "looked worn out, almost ill, overwork, strain of Casey's cat-on-hot-bricks-ism and not enough fresh air".[158] Later, in November, Plimsoll took his father on a walking holiday in the Blue Mountains. In any event, his compulsory medical examination, before proceeding to New York, found nothing amiss.

Despite lack of interest in clothing, before leaving Plimsoll bought three lounge suits, a dinner suit and an overcoat, loyally patronising David Jones in Sydney.[159]

He left for New York on 17 June 1959 as planned.

Endnotes

1 McIntyre's departure "left a substantial gap in the department"; and that of Tange "was another blow ... to the effective work of the department". A.S. Watt, *Australian Diplomat. Memoirs of Sir Alan Watt*. Angus and Robertson, in association with the AIIA, Sydney 1972, 194.

2 See Peter Edwards, *Arthur Tange. Last of the Mandarins*, Allen and Unwin, Sydney, 2006, 66-114, for invaluable background to this chapter. An earlier version of part of this chapter first appeared in proceedings of an AIIA Forum in Canberra on 9 February 2010. See "Casey and Plimsoll: a close working relationship" in Melissa Conley Tyler, John Robbins, and Adrian March (eds), *R.G. Casey: Minister for External Affairs 1951-60*, AIIA, Canberra, 2012, 61-80.

3 A.D. Campbell, conversation, 5/4/1997.

4 Opposition MPs mostly stayed at the Hotel Kurrajong.

5 T.R. Zouch, conversation, 2009.

6 JP diary, 13/2/1954.

7 JP diary, 15/1/1956; 15/7/1956.

8 Casey diary, 29/10/1958.

9 JP diary.

10 At the back of each diary Plimsoll listed the books he had read that year.

11 P.G.F. Henderson, letter, 27/2/2003.

12 H.D. Anderson, conversation, 7/2/1997.

13 Letter from St John's Appeal Office, 23/9/1955, JP papers, DFAT; and JP diary, 21/9/1955.

14 JP diary, 24/2/1957.

15 A.F. Dingle, letter of 4/8/1998, noting a conversation with Plimsoll in about 1974.

16 *Pride and Prejudice*, first sentence.

17 Tange, conversation, 1996.

18 Melbourne *Herald*, 19/3/1959. "25 hours a day" according to a colleague. B.C. Hill to Plimsoll, 30/1/1954. JP papers, DFAT.

19 Tange memo to J.E. Collings, PSB, M340,1 Item 1, Administration, July 1953 to September 1954, NAA.

20 Tange, conversation, 1996.

21 L.H. Border to Tange 21/6/1987. Tange papers, DFAT.

22 Casey noted in his diary on 22/5/1956 that there were 66 "diplomatic" (policy) officers at home, and 103 overseas. See also Casey diary, 26/3/1956. Plimsoll to J.C.G. Kevin, 21/4/1954; to D.W. McNicol, 25/9/1955; and to D.O. Hay, 11/1/57, JP papers, DFAT.

23 Waller to Plimsoll, 7/9/1957, and Plimsoll to Watt, 30/9/1957, JP papers, DFAT. "A department struggling inefficiently with too few people, especially too few competent people, to meet the demands placed upon it". Edwards, op. cit., 81.

24 Plimsoll, "In Canberra as new policies emerged 1954-60" in *John Paul Quinn – recalled by some of his friends for his children*, 1968, privately printed. Quinn had died in an air crash in the Middle East in 1961.

25 *Reminiscential Conversations between Hon Clyde Cameron and Sir James Plimsoll 1984*. TRC 1967, ii, 78-9, NLA. Hereafter cited as Cam/Plim.

26 This was W. McMahon, who had met him while on a visit to Korea as Minister for Navy and Air. JP diary, 28-30/11/52.

27 Lord Carrington, letter, 26/6/1996. See also reference to Plimsoll as the department's "grey eminence" in Geoffrey Sawer and W.J. Hudson in "The United Nations", in N.D. Harper and G. Greenwood (eds), *Australia in World Affairs 1956-60*, FW Cheshire, Melbourne, 1963, 166.

28 G.A. Jockel, conversation, 19/9/1997.

29 Casey preferred policy proposals that were "more concrete" and less intellectual. Sir Arthur Tange (ed Peter Edwards), *Defence Policy-Making. A Close-up View*, 1950-1980. Strategic and Defence Studies Centre, Canberra Papers on Strategy and Defence No. 169. ANU E-Press, Canberra, 2008, 133.

30 R.W. Furlonger, conversation, 15/10/1996.

31 R.R. Fernandez, conversation, 19/3/1997. Plimsoll had worked closely with Dulles on the Korean issue at the UN from 1948 to 1950. See chapter 3.

32 Alexander Downer, Third Secretary in Brussels in Plimsoll's time, and later Foreign Minister of Australia, 1996-2007. Conversation, 30/3/1998.

33 He had no contact during this period with E.G. Whitlam, Prime Minister from the end of 1972. He already knew Whitlam and Margaret Whitlam from Sydney days, and he knew his father, Fred Whitlam, in Attorney-General's Department, who was also a fellow committee member of the Canberra Branch of the Australian Institute of International Affairs.

34 See pp. 97ff.

35 Plimsoll to G.J. Price in Saigon, 5/10/1955. Plimsoll papers, DFAT.

36 Cam/Plim, ii, 285. See also Crocker Journal extract quoted in Edwards, op. cit., 76

37 Plimsoll to Watt, Singapore, 8/7/1954. JP papers, DFAT.

38 Edwards, op. cit., 76. For the submission, see *Australia and Recognition of the People's Republic of China 1949-72*, David Lee and Stuart Doran (eds), *Documents on Australian Foreign Policy*, DFAT, Canberra, 2002, 110-24.

39 Crocker in conversation with Hay and Plimsoll, WRC, Jnl, 18/2/1958, vii, 1479.

40 Plimsoll to Crocker, 7/8/1958. JP papers, DFAT.

41 Cam/Plim, i, 445; Plimsoll "Some observations on leaving Canberra", 17/6/1959, 8-9, Plimsoll papers, DFAT.

42 Waller to Plimsoll, 13/2/1958. A1838/269, TS 688/27, Pt 1, NAA.

43 Plimsoll, "Some observations," 9.

44 Plimsoll to McIntyre, 9/7/1956. JP papers, DFAT.

45 "There is opposition from all ministers except Mr Casey to an increase in the defence vote". Plimsoll to Watt 1/6/1954, and 29/7/1954. JP papers DFAT.

46 Plimsoll to McIntyre, 19/1/1956, JP papers, DFAT.

47 Cam/Plim, i, 437; ii 396. At a meeting of senior departmental officers with Casey, Crocker noted Casey's "obvious concern and inhibition was whether Australian public opinion (which means, I argued, mostly Australian newspapers) would stand a change in policy". WRC, Jnl, v, 9/4/56, 938.

48 Moodie to Plimsoll, "Joint Planning Committee," 25/6/1958; Plimsoll to the Secretary, 2/1/1958. A1838/269 TS696/3/1, NAA.

49 Plimsoll note on "General Australian Defence Policy," 24/7/1958. Unclear to whom it was addressed. JP papers, DFAT.

50 Burton once told Plimsoll that the Department of Defence "has no part in a forward-looking foreign policy". Cam/Plim, i, 139.

51 Plimsoll, "In Canberrra as new policies emerged 1954-60" in *Quinn* op. cit., 25. Moodie recalled that Burton "was paranoid on defence matters" and referred to the Joint Intelligence Committee in defence as a "little fascist group in Melbourne". C.T. Moodie, unpublished memoirs, 1992, 25.

52 Lowndes to Plimsoll, 23/5/1957. JP papers, DFAT. Proceedings published as John Wilkes (ed), *New Guinea and Australia*, AIPS 24th Summer School, Canberra.

53 JP to H. Gilchrist in Pretoria, 20/2/1958. JP papers, DFAT.
54 JP diary, 13-14/2/1956.
55 K.H. Rogers, conversation, 12/11/1999.
56 McIntyre to Quinn 28/1/1955. JP papers DFAT.
57 Crocker, who valued Plimsoll's explanations of what lay behind various policy statements, later complained that, after Plimsoll's eventual departure from Canberra, "I got no intellectual response at all – like addressing oneself to a wall". Crocker to Plimsoll, 2/7/1964. JP papers, Box 5, Item 53, NAA.
58 Watt to Plimsoll, 27/7/1954. JP papers, DFAT.
59 This was to persuade the Defence Department of the desirability that General Sir Henry Wells, Chairman of the Chiefs of Staff Committee, should arrive for a SEATO meeting in Bangkok aboard an RAAF plane, rather than an RAF one. Waller to Plimsoll, 6/8/1958. JP papers, DFAT.
60 Watt to Plimsoll, 4/5/1956. JP papers, DFAT.
61 Plimsoll to Watt, 9/5/1956. JP papers DFAT. Casey noted reading Plimsoll's reports without critical comment. Casey diary 15/4/1956. Sir Douglas Copland in Ottawa wrote that he could not imagine "anything more illuminating than [Plimsoll's] reports on the current problems of the whole of the area". Copland to Plimsoll, 7/5/1956. JP papers, DFAT.
62 JP diary, 26/8/1953.
63 He received 93 congratulatory messages. JP to parents, 8/1/1956. JP papers, DFAT.
64 Crocker, conversation with Plimsoll. WRC Jnl, May 1955, Series 1, vol iv, 539.
65 Cam/Plim, i, 233.
66 E.g., JP diary, 12/7/1954.
67 JP diary, passim for the period. Sydney was then the only international airport in Australia.
68 Cam/Plim, i, 233.
69 JP obituary note about Lady Casey, submitted to *The Times* (London), 21/1/1983. JP papers, 8048/21/82, NLA.
70 JP to Hudson, 13/1/1987. JP papers, 8048/21/97, NLA.
71 W.J. Hudson, *Casey*, Oxford University Press, Melbourne, 1986, 27.
72 JP to W.J. Hudson, 13/1/1987. JP papers, 8048/21/97, NLA. Hudson, *Casey*, 251-2.

73 JP to Hudson, 17/12/86. JP papers, 8048/21/95, NLA.

74 Menzies recalled this to Stirling in 1972. Stirling diary, 30/4/1972, DFAT.

75 "He lost out on many occasions in Cabinet, which was clinging to the past and containing some racial prejudices". Tange, *Defence Policy-making*, 131; Hudson, *Casey*, 233-5, 245-7.

76 Casey felt most of the cabinet was "hostile to the UN, hostile to the Colombo Plan, and unsympathetic with Asia". In cabinet budget discussions he commented: "The gap in thinking is so great that it is useless to argue. It is no pleasant thing to be one among 22. Ignorance, prejudice and dead-certainty." Casey diary, 2 & 28/7/1958. In 1955 Menzies told the New Zealand High Commissioner, Alderton, that the majority of cabinet was opposed to the Colombo Plan, and that he himself thought Australia got little value out of it, except for the impact it created in Washington. Alderton to McIntosh, 27/7/1955, NZ Archives, courtesy of Garry Woodard.

77 Watt, "Australian Foreign Policy, and the Department of External Affairs," Valedictory, 29/1/1954. JP papers, DFAT

78 Tange, Oral History, TRC 1023, 1981, 90, NLA.

79 Tange, ibid., 113.

80 Casey statement on retirement as minister, 23/1/1960, *Current Notes on International Affairs*, vol 31, 1960, DFAT, Canberra, 46-7.

81 Peter Boyce, who entered External Affairs in 1957, and served briefly in Casey's office. Conversation, 12/5/2007.

82 *Friends and Neighbours. Australia and the World*, FW Cheshire, Melbourne 1954. Tange recalled "there was very little to read about those countries – we had very little information about what moved people in South East Asian countries or Asian countries generally". Tange, Oral History, TRC 2482 1989 and 1992, NLA, 4.

83 A second edition was prepared in the department at Casey's request, but did not see the light of day after Casey's retirement in 1960. Malcolm Morris, conversation, 15/3/2010.

84 Tange, Oral History, TRC 1023, 1981.

85 JP diary, 4/12/1953.

86 Tange to Casey, undated, on JP's personnel file, probably late October 1954, DFAT.

87 F.R. Dalrymple letter 9/3/2009; G.J. Price, conversation, 1997.

88 Dr Marjorie Jacobs, conversation, 6/7/1998. Casey spoke on 7/4/1953 about "The new Asia in world affairs". Later Plimsoll himself gave a personal donation of £100 to the School library. Acting Vice-Chancellor, Sydney University to Plimsoll 28/6/1956. JP papers, DFAT.

89 Tange later commented that, as a department, "I doubt that we did enough to persuade him of the need to carry public opinion with him in his endeavours in Asia". Tange, *Defence Policy-making*, 132.

90 JP diary, passim.

91 JP diary, 12/4/1953.

92 John Malone of *Sydney Morning Herald*, letter, 10/6/1997. John Bennetts approached Plimsoll about press arrangements in advance of the Council meeting – JP diary, 23/1 and 12/3/1957.

93 JP diary, 6/6/1957.

94 JP diary, 11 and 12/3/1958.

95 Michael McGeorge, *The Age*, letters 20 & 28/3/2000.

96 JP diary. Others mentioned in the diary in this period included Bruce Grant (*The Age*), John Bennetts (Melbourne *Herald*), Ken Schapel (*Daily Telegraph*), Ian Fitchett (*The Age*), Hal Myers (*Sydney Morning Herald*) and Alan Reid (*Sydney Daily Telegraph*).

97 C.L. Burns, conversation, 1997.

98 JP to Dr E.R. Walker, Tokyo, 8/1/1954. JP papers, DFAT.

99 JP to McIntyre, 31/1/1957. JP papers, DFAT.

100 JP to Norman Cowper, 23/4/1958. JP papers, DFAT.

101 Hay to JP, 22/9/1958. JP papers, DFAT.

102 JP to Hudson, 13/1/1987. JP papers, 8048/21/97 NLA.

103 JP to Casey 25/1/1960. JP papers, 8048/1/37 NLA.

104 Casey to JP 11/2/1960. JP papers 8048/1/37 NLA.

105 A time of particular sensitivity was before the Federal elections of 1954. See JP to Walker, 29/1/1954, 4 and 19/2/1954, 15/4/, 2/7, and 24/8/1954. JP papers, DFAT. See also, "We can't be soft with Jap butchers," by A.A. Calwell, *Truth*, 12/2/54, and Cam/Plim, i, 427-429.

106 JP diary, 19/10/1953, 6/4/1954. JP to Watt, 18/4/1956. JP papers, DFAT.

107 Plimsoll, "Towards a wider conception of our common humanity", in

The Emerging World. Jawaharlal Nehru Memorial Volume, Asia Publishing House, Bombay, 1964, 160-2.

108 Cam/Plim, i, 69.

109 WRC, Jnl, 20/2/1958, vii, 1486.

110 Menzies told Coombs, Governor of the Commonwealth Bank (1949-60) and then of the RBA (1961-68), to telephone him personally if there was an issue to which Menzies should be applying himself. Plimsoll thought it was a "major defect" in both Evatt and Whitlam that they were not really interested in economics. Cam/Plim, i, 440.

111 Cam/Plim, ii, 115. JP to PR Heydon, 15/8/1957. JP papers, DFAT.

112 "Though in War it might be different, if you knew a party was actively engaged in subversion". Cam/Plim, i, 112.

113 JP to Watt, 22/6/1956. Other examples: "The PM made no record of his conversation nor has he mentioned it to anyone". JP to McIntyre, 4/1/1956; and "The PM took the letter and put it away without saying anything to anybody". JP to McIntyre 9/5/1956. JP papers DFAT.

114 Watt, *Australian Diplomat*, 169.

115 Cam/Plim, i, 435. See also in handwritten note by JP, in his letter to Watt of 20/10/1954, that he saw the PM on that day, not in 1956 as he later told Cameron.

116 JP to Price, Saigon, 11/10/1956. JP papers, DFAT.

117 Plimsoll was Acting Secretary for seven weeks from 12/8 to 3/10/1956. See also Casey diary 4, 7, 8, 9, and 11/9/1956.

118 Cam/Plim, ii, 390. JP diary 31/10/1956. He also called on Menzies on Sunday 4/11/1956.

119 Tange to JP, handwritten, 14/9/1956. "The PM saw me as a 'Casey man' – once he had heard my views once or twice I found him considerably less receptive to anything I had to say". See also Edwards, *Tange*, 116-22.

120 Cam/Plim, ii, 391.

121 Cam/Plim, ii, 387-93.

122 See chapter 5, 127ff.

123 Cam/Plim, ii, 394.

124 JP diary, 10-13/3/1957.

125 JP to McIntyre, 9/5/1957. JP papers, DFAT.

126 Along with Bunting, Sir Roland Wilson and Edwin Hicks. JP diary 22/6-11/7/1957.

127 This was Sir Allen Brown, then Secretary of Prime Minister's Department. *Current Notes*, April 1957, vol 28, 303-4.

128 Plimsoll learned that Menzies was disinclined to do anything before 10am, but "if you gave him papers as late as 11:30pm he would read them before going to bed". Cam/Plim, i, 69.

129 JP diary, 20/12/1958. He also attended a small dinner Sunday 17/4/1955, and afternoon tea Sunday, 24/4/1955 after a discussion with Menzies about Formosa; and dinner Monday 6/4/1958. JP diary.

130 "'Jindivik.' A not so bland outlook", *Nation*, no. 10, 31/1/1959, 6.

131 Henderson conversation.

132 Later, after Tange had stayed with him in Brussels, Plimsoll told someone of what a "pleasant, relaxing time" they had had. "You're the first man I've ever met who said that being with Arthur Tange was relaxing," was the reply. Cam/Plim, ii, 27.

133 Price conversation, 30/6/1997.

134 Once in Melbourne, after briefing Menzies before an overseas visit, they went together to watch the last hours of a day's play in a Test at the MCG. JP diary, 4/1/1955.

135 Ben Cockram, Director of Information at the Commonwealth Relations Office, and former UK Deputy High Commissioner in Canberra, told Stirling "of Tange's reported succession to Spender in Washington and of Plimsoll's to Tange". Stirling diary, 7/10/1957, DFAT.

136 Neil Currie, quoted in Stirling diary, 9/10/1954. Tange told Crocker that he was resigned to not normally being the principal adviser on foreign policy. "He spends most of his time on personal details (e.g., an officer getting into trouble) and on 'emergencies' – this or that fancy of the Minister or of Cabinet". WRC Jnl, 24/4/1956, vol v, 956.

137 Tange, conversation, 6/1/98.

138 Sir Leslie Melville, conversation, 12/11/1997.

139 Edwards, *Tange*, 111-3. Plimsoll, perhaps understanding this side of Tange, once tried to get him listed in the British *Who's Who*. JP to O.L. Davis, then Senior External Affairs Representative in London, 28/7/1958 A1832/2 936/5 Pt 6, NAA. After Tange was knighted in 1959, his entry was automatic.

140 Casey diary, 3/7/1953.

141 In a talk to the graduate entry in 1957, Tange told them to be sure to have their jackets on when they stepped out of their offices and into the corridor; and not to park their bicycles near the front door. Boyce conversation.

142 Campbell conversation. "Even at that time, Plimsoll was somewhat of an icon, and very good with young officers. He got to know them by their first names, and came and talked to them". Fernandez conversation.

143 WRC Jnl, 30/4/1956, vol v, 965; JP to his father, 6/4 and 23/4/1958; JP to Waller, 13/7/1958. JP papers DFAT.

144 Tange to JP, 1/10/1958, JP papers. DFAT.

145 Tange, conversation, 1996.

146 Spender to JP 27/2/1957. JP papers, DFAT.

147 R.G. Menzies to President Eisenhower, 18/11/1956. Cable 999 to Washington TS 175/11/20/7A Pt 2, NAA.

148 3/12/1956, JP papers, DFAT.

149 Hasluck was younger at 40, but not given the rank. M.J. Costello was also younger at 40 but served temporarily in the position for four months in 1988.

150 Waller to JP, 1/7/1958; JP to Waller, 1/7/1958; JP to Waller, 13/8/1958; Waller to Shann, 23/6/1959. Waller papers, DFAT.

151 WRC Jnl, 22/6/1959, vol ix, 1883.

152 JP diary, 1959. 11/6/, 5/6. 15/5, 16/6 and 30/5.

153 JP diary, 15/5 and 3 and 10/6, 1959.

154 JP to S.A. Jamieson, 22/9/1958. JP papers, DFAT.

155 "I showed it to the PM and he kept it for two days (his programme here was vey light)". Crocker to JP, undated (probably mid-1959). JP papers DFAT.

156 Tange to Casey, 5/8/1958. Plimsoll personnel file, DFAT.

157 Stirling diary and JP diary, 26-28/8/1958. Plimsoll was seen by Dr R.I. Bayliss, a physician specialising in endocrine, metabolic and cardiac diseases, and by Dr P.J. Kerley CVO, CBE, Radiologist (see their entries in the British *Who's Who*); Casey diary, 27/8/1958.

158 WRC Jnl, vol viii, 1611 and 1614. 6/9/58 and 7/9/58.

159 JP diary, 4/6/1959 and 16/6/1959.

Plimsoll with UN Secretary-General, Dag Hammarskjold, after presenting credentials, June 1959 (UN photo)

5
The Highlight of His Career:
the United Nations, 1959-63

Sir James Plimsoll was so soft-spoken, straightforward, and courtly. There was an aura of distinction about him. He was one of my favourite people.[1]

The Australian permanent representative at the UN in New York holds one of the most sensitive and demanding diplomatic appointments, responsible for ensuring that, in the process of discussions, debates, resolutions and votes at this major diplomatic centre, Australia's views are accurately and cogently presented. An issue of sensitivity at home could be difficult to handle, particularly when having to speak or vote without time to consult Canberra. In Plimsoll's time that was often the case with the prevailing state of communications in the late 1950s and early 1960s. The permanent representative needed to be constantly abreast of any developments around the world that could arise at the UN, and always be ready to express a view, either privately or in public in one of the forums of the UN, and thus through the media to the wider world. In this sense, there has always been a high level of personal accountability involved.

The UN in New York is very much a permanent representatives' world. They are at the centre of affairs. Plimsoll was assiduous in getting to know his counterparts from elsewhere as foremost among people who could be helpful to him. He had "a remarkable capacity for talking to people in their own terms, freely encouraging them to explain their viewpoints and problems. This was not a contrivance, but part of his nature and feeling for people".[2]

A key element in Plimsoll's effectiveness at the UN was that he possessed, to an unusual degree, knowledge and understanding of how the UN worked as well as of Australian policies; and the talents and personal qualities required at the UN. The personal standing of a permanent representative among the others is an important element in that country's day-to-day influence. A permanent representative must be competent enough to operate alone in the informal, continuous discussions among counterparts. Sir David Hay, Plimsoll's successor in 1963, recalled that the task "is really different from any other ambassadorial job. It's a highly professional assignment, you're dealing with a body of treaties and of doctrine, and unless you know your stuff you're not in the race in your discussions with colleagues or even with the well-informed UN press corps". Hay thought that Plimsoll's advantage was "his knowledge of the UN Charter, of the precedents, and his ability to find his way in a kind of labyrinth of resolutions and cross-references".[3]

With the advantage of previous UN experience Plimsoll quickly settled into the job. When the General Assembly was not in session he would arrive at the office before anyone else, personally open the diplomatic bag from Canberra and distribute the mail, functions normally carried out by a junior officer.[4] It was part of his management of staff. He was not keen on meetings.[5] He preferred a small team: when presented with an easy opportunity to acquire an additional staff member, he did not pursue it.[6] He had a close relationship with younger officers and their families, once dropping everything to help the wife of a junior officer with last minute packing when the officer left suddenly after a family tragedy in Australia. This included sitting on a suitcase to help close it.[7]

Plimsoll virtually "carried" his deputy, John Hood, an additional burden.[8] Thirteen years older, Hood had been Plimsoll's head of mission in New York in 1949-50. He was a very senior diplomat, who once had seemed "destined to go far," and who at times had been a "formative influence in Australian diplomacy".[9] Unfortunately he was not in his best form, but Plimsoll did not seek his withdrawal, displaying "humanity and understanding".[10]

Pressure on the mission in New York builds up considerably in the last four months of each year when the General Assembly meets. In Plimsoll's time the Australian mission in New York trebled in size to cover all the committees, with the addition of officers from Canberra and from other posts, as well as two members from the Commonwealth Parliament. As permanent representative, Plimsoll had to lead this diverse group. The delegation often included Sir Howard Beale, a former Coalition minister now ambassador in Washington.[11] Last but not least, there was the Minister for External Affairs, who normally attended the Assembly, often staying for up to three weeks. No other post had such regular and extended ministerial attention.

After the General Assembly in 1959, Plimsoll observed to Tange that the delegation came under special strain when Casey took three of them to Washington for the concurrent Antarctic Treaty negotiations. Tange replied that getting through the General Assembly with such a "slim team" was "a remarkable achievement".[12]

Plimsoll kept a close eye on the work of Australian delegates in all the committees, and sometimes intervened.[13] In the evenings he was often at the office checking all reporting cables with their authors. There was "not a fraction of the overall work in which he was not involved".[14]

In 1960 Plimsoll had problems with one of the MPs on the delegation, the outspoken Liberal backbencher, W.C. Wentworth.[15] Plimsoll had warned Tange that he foresaw "clear storm signals ahead".[16] His concerns proved well founded; Wentworth represented a "waste of time, exasperation, and some embarrassment" and Plimsoll had to "spend hours in reasoning with Wentworth to dissuade him from impetuous or ill-advised courses". He allowed him "more latitude" than other delegation members, although concerned about "what Wentworth would say once he got going".[17] The UN Sixth Committee was normally "very stodgy". But once, when the delegation lawyer was away, Wentworth took the opportunity to go "out of control," attacking the USSR for its colonialist record. The speech, which produced headlines in the *New York Times* next day, had been right up to a point, but ill-timed, out of place, and unauthorised.[18] At one stage Plimsoll showed Wentworth a draft cable, addressed personal to Menzies, requesting his immediate withdrawal. It was a good technique: Wentworth was shaken and chastened.[19] Plimsoll felt, however, he could not forbid Wentworth outright from making impromptu interventions.[20]

Menzies takes the External Affairs portfolio

Following Casey's resignation in February 1960, Menzies himself took the External Affairs portfolio for nearly two years. Generally he had little affection for the UN. His attitude was one of "resigned tolerance".[21] He found "the posturing, exhortation, moralising and occasional vituperation of some of its members offensive to pragmatic commonsense".[22] This could have made life difficult for Plimsoll, but, after his long sojourn in Canberra, Plimsoll felt he had some understanding of the Prime Minister's mind. He foresaw that there would be an even greater problem for the department "to secure a big enough share of the Prime Minister's time and attention in view of all the other pressures upon him".[23] It reinforced in him an inclination to seek guidance from Canberra as little as possible.

Plimsoll proceeded with the confidence to know what Canberra would and would not worry about. He was prepared to sail very close to the wind in order to "push policy forward".[24] If asked by another permanent representative about Australian policy on an issue peripheral to Australian interests, he would reply that he was not sure that the Australian Government had considered it recently. "But my personal view is . . ." invariably became the Australian position.[25]

Once, when Plimsoll spoke out on such a matter on which there had been no guidance from Canberra, one of his staff asked him about this. Plimsoll replied that in Canberra there would be a "few gulps in the throat", but now he had voiced an opinion, no one would chastise him – whereas, if he had asked first, he "probably would have received a no". Few were prepared to trust their own judgment, especially at a time when Menzies was also the minister.[26] This innate self-confidence in his understanding of Menzies was a key ingredient in Plimsoll's performance at the UN.

Menzies visited New York on 6 June 1960, where he saw the Secretary-General, Dag Hammarskjold.[27] Months earlier Tange had written to Plimsoll to "help me on this at the right time by using your persuasive powers".[28] Plimsoll had agreed:

> Some day we may want Hammarskjold's support on the question of Dutch New Guinea, and for that reason, if for no other, it is in our interests to give him the impression that we are a progressive and constructively-minded people and government.

He felt unsure of how Hammarskjold and Menzies would get on, "but they are both men of great intellectual capacity, and I hope there can be a meeting of minds".[29] In fact, they developed close personal cooperation on some matters,[30] which contrasted with Menzies' general reservations about the UN.

The General Assembly 1960: "The greatest circus in the history of the UN"

Although Sir Garfield Barwick had already arrived to lead the delegation, at the last minute Menzies decided to attend the 1960 General Assembly, after an exchange of messages with the Prime Minister of Britain, Harold Macmillan. This 15th session has been called "perhaps the greatest circus in the history of the UN".[31] Among those attending were Khrushchev, Castro and various leading figures in the non-aligned movement: Nehru (India), Tito (Yugoslavia), Sukarno (Indonesia), Nasser (Egypt), Nkrumah (Ghana) and Sekou Toure (Senegal); as well as Macmillan and Eisenhower.

A few days after arrival in New York, Menzies disappeared to Washington for weekend discussions with Eisenhower, Macmillan,

Christian Herter, US Secretary of State, and Lord Home, British Foreign Secretary. They discussed Khrushchev's speech at the UN in which he had called for immediate freedom for all colonial territories, and Nehru's resolution calling for renewed "contact" between Eisenhower and Khrushchev. Menzies found his colleagues agreed to his proposal to move an amendment to Nehru's resolution, so that the meeting should be a reconvening of the summit of four nations (including UK and France), not two.[32]

However, as Barwick recalled, "these worthies had no professional officer with them at all". As a matter involving the UN, Plimsoll should have been there to give his advice, "even if he [Menzies] decided to disregard it".[33] Tange was in Washington at the time, but he was not consulted either. Beale, as Ambassador to the US, was with Menzies, but, according to Tange, he "knew nothing whatsoever about world affairs".[34]

Plimsoll was unaware of all this. On the following Monday, Menzies returned with the proposed amendment to Nehru's resolution and asked Barwick to lodge it. The latter replied, supported by Brian Hill, another Australian delegate, that they would need time to cultivate support. Plimsoll's view was that the proposed amendment was "probably right but it's too late". Menzies told them to lodge it.[35] Plimsoll tried to talk him out of it. Menzies replied: "Well Jim, you're probably right, but it's too late now".[36]

Menzies's short speech introducing the amendment went down like "a lead balloon" with the General Assembly.[37] Nehru made a vitriolic speech, tearing strips off Australia. Tito did likewise. Menzies wanted a "right of reply," something not possible under the UN rules of procedure. Plimsoll had to restrain him physically from doing so, and told Parkinson to take Menzies into a side room and give him a martini. Plimsoll "handled the PM magnificently, saving him from even greater humiliation". Meanwhile, Plimsoll was being bombarded, but also was trying to muster votes. When he heard that Herter was hesitant about supporting the amendment, Plimsoll reminded him that

The Highlight of His Career: the United Nations, 1959-63

Visit of Australian Prime Minister, Robert Menzies, to the UN in October 1960. With Frederick H. Boland (Ireland), President of the UN General Assembly, and Plimsoll (UN photo)

Menzies had moved it at US instigation, and if the US did not support it, the consequences for US-Australian relations would be "incalculable". Herter would have to face a "breach" between Australia and the US.[38] Only the US, Britain, Canada, Spain and Portugal gave support.[39]

Things later worked out better for Menzies: his speech to the General Assembly in the afternoon was nationally televised and well received in the US, Nehru withdrew his resolution, and the PM had a good meeting with Khrushchev. Several days later, Menzies, very "cheesed off" with the UN, told Plimsoll that he was wasted there and that they had to get him out.[40] Nothing happened, however, and he remained in New York.

Africa, anti-colonialism and PNG

In October 1961 the general debate of the Assembly brought another example of Plimsoll's understanding of Menzies's views. It also illustrated Plimsoll's strong sense of principle and his understanding of the UN. The Foreign Minister of South Africa, Eric Louw, criticised a number of African governments for poor treatment of their peoples in contrast to that received by Africans in South Africa. This was not well received: the Representative of Liberia moved that the whole of Louw's speech be deleted from the record.

Plimsoll sensed that the mood was such that this motion could succeed unless something was done quickly, setting a dangerous precedent for the future working of the UN. Without time to seek instructions, he spoke on a point of order. He expressed understanding that Louw's views were "not merely fundamentally opposed by most representatives here but offend their consciences". Australia, too, could not condone many of the basic elements of South African apartheid policy. But, firstly, such a motion to "expunge a statement by a sovereign government", if passed, would create a bad precedent. Instead, he proposed that "a much more effective way of expressing an opinion" would be to debate "the substance of these matters", for which there would be ample opportunity during the session.

Secondly, for the UN to discuss something, it needed to have before it the position of the parties to whatever is raised. It would not be possible to attack a statement if it was not on the record. Further, as many delegation leaders were not present, the time being well into the lunch hour, a decision might best be postponed. If it was put to the vote at once, Australia could not support it, because "it is a fundamental decision on the whole working of this Organisation, not related only to South Africa".

Later the same day Liberia withdrew its motion. Plimsoll had turned the debate. A Brazilian delegate wrote to Plimsoll that he felt "very sad and discouraged that out of 95 delegates" Plimsoll had been the only one to "say something intelligent, sensible, and logic[al]".[41] A few days later in Canberra, Menzies took the opportunity of a question from the Opposition front-bencher, Dr Jim Cairns, to praise Plimsoll's handling of the matter. Menzies said: 'I was proud of him. I thought it was an admirable attitude and an admirable speech on his part, particularly as he had no opportunity to consult us at all." He added that "Mr Plimsoll represented this country with great dignity and immense commonsense and courage".[42]

The South African incident typified a new element in the UN agenda, an emphasis on concerns of African nations, who predominated among the numerous newly independent nations that had recently joined the UN. Since Evatt's time, Australia had believed that, given the domestic jurisdiction clause of the UN Charter, apartheid was a domestic matter, and should not be discussed at the UN. But earlier, in April 1961, Australia had changed its vote on an apartheid resolution at the 11th hour. Tange told Plimsoll later that his report of the estimated voting intentions of other countries was a major factor in the final decision. It enabled advice to the Prime Minister that, if a resolution criticising apartheid was supported by all except Australia, there would be "serious misunderstanding world-wide about Australia".[43]

Africa in this era was the unknown continent. Plimsoll visited it three times during his New York posting. This was not much, but more than most other diplomats, and it gave him a better understanding of some of the impulses and problems, and stimulated his thinking about the implications for Australia and for the UN.

His first journey was in June 1959. Casey asked Plimsoll to proceed to New York the long way round, via Cairo, to discuss the possible resumption of normal diplomatic relations with Egypt. A second task was to visit Nigeria, Britain's largest African colony, about to become independent, and recommend whether Australia should open a diplomatic post. Another objective was to visit Accra, Ghana, Australia's first post in newly-independent Africa.[44]

Crocker, who saw Plimsoll as he passed through New Delhi, noted "how tired and worn he looked, how much older":

> Not only is he making this trip at the worst time of the year in all the countries covered, including West Africa, but much though he needs a holiday and a sea voyage, he is being made to fly to New York.

Crocker, who earlier had spent some years in Africa, felt this was a reflection of "Casey at his least attractive".[45] Plimsoll's actual itinerary, which made him more tired than normal, was, however, self-inflicted. In nine days, between Perth and Cairo, Plimsoll stopped in six places: Jakarta, Singapore, Kuala Lumpur, Bangkok and Karachi, besides Delhi.[46] Discussions and meals with colleagues and others in each gave Plimsoll a quick, on-the-spot update on Asia as he passed through. On reaching New York he found that "more than one Afro-Asian representative has shown signs of satisfaction at learning that an Australian diplomat would feel it worthwhile to come to the UN through Asia and Africa without stopping off in Europe or England".[47]

Plimsoll told Casey about the value of the visit to Africa: "I was able to get a general impression of the movements under way in that part of the world."[48] Australia "should take some cognisance" of

African developments.⁴⁹ He recommended restoration of relations with Egypt, and was told that his report "helped in the long process of getting [resumption of relations] cleared through the PM".⁵⁰ Plimsoll recommended opening a post in Nigeria:

> . . . it would make it easy for us to differentiate ourselves from South Africa and avoid being identified with the policies of South Africa. Such a step would also have benefits in our relations with Asia.

Casey expressed "congratulations" for "readable and useful reporting," and said he was persuaded about Lagos.⁵¹

Six months later the independence celebrations of the Cameroons took place on 1 January 1960. As the timing cut across the traditional Australian holiday season, no minister was keen to attend. At short notice, Plimsoll, although tired at the end of the General Assembly, agreed to represent Australia.⁵² Just before departure, while returning to New York by train on 27 December after spending Christmas in Washington, he broke his nose when the train came to a sudden stop. Though bloodied he was unbowed, and after seeing his doctor, the next day he stoically flew to the Cameroons via Paris.⁵³

This visit to Africa seemed "timely," the Sydney *Daily Mirror* commented: "A pilgrimage to Africa is now on the 'must' list for every important political leader."⁵⁴ Hammarskjold currently was visiting, Macmillan would go shortly, US Vice-President Nixon and President De Gaulle had each been there recently, and Khrushchev was planning to go. Plimsoll's visit was, on the surface, a "goodwill gesture", but his real purpose was "to establish vital diplomatic links with new African leaders as Canberra somewhat belatedly acknowledges the awakening of the dark continent". Plimsoll himself wrote to a colleague that "Canberra can have no excuse for not being aware that Africa is on the move and is important".⁵⁵

While attending the celebrations in Cameroon, he talked to a number of foreign consuls-general based in the Belgian Congo about conditions there. Three weeks later came the sudden announcement that the Congo would become independent in six months. Following his talks, Plimsoll presciently reported his "rather gloomy forebodings" about the situation in the Congo, with the possibility of anarchy, and the implications for the UN.[56]

The Congo crisis, which developed after independence, occupied much time in the Security Council. Although Australia was not a member at the time, and had no direct interest, Plimsoll was frequently invited to private meetings of a number of European permanent representatives to discuss a difficult situation.[57] The crisis constituted the UN's first major foray into multinational peacekeeping. Its handling of this, under Secretary-General Hammarskjold, led to fierce criticism of the operation's financing from the USSR in particular. During his visit to the Congo, Hammarskjold tragically was killed in a plane crash over nearby Northern Rhodesia (later Zambia). In turn the need to agree on a new Secretary-General led to a period of dispute about how the UN should be run, with Moscow suggesting a "troika" system of management, until U Thant, the permanent representative of Burma, was finally installed as Secretary-General.

Of concern to Australia, and to other administering powers such as the UK, was increasingly strident anti-colonialism in the UN. The new African states, feeling their power in the General Assembly, made aggressive demands for immediate independence for all remaining colonies. As Sir Brian Urquhart, at the time assistant to the Secretary-General, put it, this was:

> a constituency which had little direct interest in European affairs, disarmament, or in the East-West relationship. It was a radical, angry constituency which strongly resented the established, profitably industrialised, dominant Old World. Neither the West nor the Soviet Union was comfortable in this new environment.[58]

All this carried implications for Australia's administration of Papua New Guinea, a major Australian interest at the UN. In 1961 Plimsoll was not looking forward to the General Assembly, where he would deliver the Australian statement in the general debate because imminent Australian elections meant no minister would attend. It was "going to be very sticky and unpleasant", with an agenda "filled with items that will be difficult and embarrassing for Australia". There was a Soviet agenda item calling for "practical measures" to implement the Declaration on the Granting of Independence to Colonial Countries and People, which was passed in the General Assembly in 1960,[59] that is, granting immediate independence. At that time Plimsoll had deliberately voiced understanding of the Declaration to be "a general statement of agreed aspirations rather than as a binding document".[60]

The Committee of 17 (later 24) had been set up as a consequence of the Declaration, to push for accelerated independence for colonies. Tange considered the Committee of sufficient concern to ask Plimsoll to attend its meetings personally and "not put anyone else in the seat".[61] Earlier, in March 1961, Barwick, as acting minister, had reflected similar concerns in Canberra about defence of PNG in the UN Fourth Committee. He asked Plimsoll himself to "handle the main items" there, while appreciating this would "impose additional burdens on you".[62]

PNG comprised both a colony and a UN Trust Territory, which Australia wanted to develop properly and unhurriedly, to a stage when its people could make their own decisions about the future. It was also a near neighbour, of major strategic interest. In 1961 Australia was concerned about implications for PNG if Indonesia under Sukarno were to get control of Dutch New Guinea. The UN anticolonial focus was mainly on Africa but, as Plimsoll recognised, regionally "we too will soon face our difficulties".[63]

Plimsoll firmly supported the view of colonial powers that across-the-board grants of immediate independence were unrealistic, and that the situation of colonies should be examined individually. This applied especially to PNG. It was also a matter of "trying to explain and defend the necessary compromises and delays and safeguards that have to be insisted upon by those who bear responsibility, when it is so much easier for representatives of other countries to put forward simple unqualified propositions, demanding for example immediate independence".[64]

He remained on good personal terms with a number of African permanent representatives, for example, the Ghanaian, Alex Quaison-Sackey, who would be the first African to be President of UN General Assembly in 1964-65. There was from 1960 "a finesse and moderation not evident in the 1950s" in Australian diplomacy on colonial issues. Plimsoll's speeches were much "more conciliatory and his activities much more flexible than those of his predecessors. Anti-colonial delegations noted a change and commented favourably on it". Similarly, "it was characteristic of Plimsoll's diplomatic style that he was able to convey sympathy with the causes of self-determination and Africans' rights and, at the same time, argue some of Britain's cause"[65] in relation to Southern Rhodesia.

In a comment in 1961 on what policy Australia should adopt on the Portuguese territory of Angola, Plimsoll noted that such a decision would have implications for policy on other Portuguese overseas territories, "not least Portuguese Timor, of most direct concern to Australia". Anticipating a later Australian government's stance, he doubted that "Australian interests would suffer greatly by Portuguese Timor becoming part of Indonesia, provided that the transfer was made in an orderly and peaceful manner".[66] Early in 1962 Plimsoll spoke critically in the UN about Portugal's overseas empire, which "greatly annoyed the Portuguese".[67]

The emerging problem of Rhodesia

By 1962, with the looming break-up of the Central African Federation, Southern Rhodesia "was becoming very hot indeed". Plimsoll had to make several speeches in the UN "on which I got virtually no instructions".

He advocated that Rhodesia be brought towards independence, in a multi-racial society with a black majority. There was need for a period of education of both the blacks and the whites, so that all "will fit in with this concept". He received no criticism from Canberra, and assumed that this view also "was helpful to the British, but at the same time liberal and pushing them".[68]

A number of leading Southern Rhodesians visited the UN, but most were "unrealistic" about the situation. In April Plimsoll was a guest at a dinner for the Australian business magnate, Lord Baillieu. Another guest was Sir Donald McIntyre, a senior minister in the Cabinet of the Central African Federation. When Plimsoll unexpectedly was asked to propose a toast to McIntyre, whom he had not met before, he spoke in measured but deliberate terms. He said that the special problems of Rhodesia were appreciated, but Australia had PNG, with its problems, and was bringing it to independence. The Australian view on Rhodesia was that the processes of transfer to an African majority must be speeded up. "It would be impossible for us to defend countries for not doing what we were doing ourselves and committed to do". McIntyre obviously did not like it. After the dinner he approached Plimsoll, saying: "They are giving you a bad time at the UN are they?" To which Plimsoll replied: "They are not giving me a bad time, they're giving you a bad time." McIntyre's response was: "Don't worry. All this talk in the UN will blow over. Now that they've had their say, we won't hear any more about it."[69]

In May Plimsoll visited London briefly en route to Africa. To his surprise Duncan Sandys, UK Secretary of State for the Commonwealth (and for Colonies as from July that year), wanted to see him. He had met Sandys before, but did not know him well. Sandys saw him alone. Plimsoll raised Southern Rhodesia during the conversation, seeking confirmation that the UK was not going to grant independence until there was majority rule. To which Sandys "literally rose out of his chair about nine inches" and sat down again. He confirmed that they were going to make Rhodesia independent soon. Plimsoll responded that, although speaking without instructions, "I don't think we'd agree." Under the UN Charter the UK was obliged to bring independence to the people as a whole. "Oh but this is terrible," replied Sandys. Canada had been consulted and agreed with the UK approach, "we did not think Australia would have any objections".[70] Returning from Africa in June, Plimsoll found that Barwick had agreed to his cabled report and given instructions that the British be told that Australia did not support independence with a white minority government.

Shortly after returning to New York, Plimsoll became aware that an item on Southern Rhodesia had been listed for early debate in the General Assembly. Canberra advised him to consult the Prime Minister, who would be passing through New York for three days. On what was a "very successful" visit, Menzies had a good meeting with U Thant, as well as handing him a well-timed cheque for $US4 million, as Australia's contribution to UN bonds, which "averted the UN having to borrow that weekend". The cheque was banked in 20 minutes.[71] Try as he might, however, Plimsoll found Menzies unwilling to focus on Southern Rhodesia. Finally, at the airport, at the foot of the aircraft steps, Plimsoll tried once again for guidance for his speech. Menzies slapped him on the shoulder and said: "My boy, I'm glad you're making it, not me."[72]

Plimsoll sought to draw out the implications for Australian interests in what would become of Southern Rhodesia (which in 1980 became Zimbabwe). In June 1962 Plimsoll noted:

> As a means of gaining understanding in the UN for Australian policies on PNG and time for these policies to take effect, it is in our interests to create a picture of ourselves as a liberal and enlightened country whose objectives for dependent peoples are self-government and independence as quickly as possible on a basis of racial equality.

That was one way in which Australia had a direct interest in the way Southern Rhodesia was handled. If the situation deteriorated into fighting, "the exacerbation of relations between the Afro-Asian countries and the British would certainly affect attitudes to Australia as fellow Anglo-Saxons". Further, if Southern Rhodesia was declared independent, Australia would have to decide whether to recognise it, and support its admission to the Commonwealth and the UN. He foresaw great problems if independence was granted in 1962 on the break up of the Central African Federation.[73]

At home for consultations in August 1962, Plimsoll had no fewer than six meetings with Barwick, now the minister. Southern Rhodesia was among issues discussed. In September Barwick sent a message to Duncan Sandys. Unusually his cable noted that Sandys (when Plimsoll was in London in May) and Barwick had each discussed Southern Rhodesia with Plimsoll. The message bore many similarities to an earlier one from Plimsoll, with the same object of persuading the British not to grant independence prematurely, that is, under a white minority government.[74]

In May 1962 Plimsoll had made the third of his visits to Africa, this time as part of the UN Committee of 17 delegation. He was the only ambassador of a Western country on the delegation; the others, given their countries' involvement on the continent, preferred a lower profile. The Committee held meetings in Rabat, Casablanca, Marrakesh, Addis Ababa, Nairobi and Dar es Salaam. The possible sensitivity of his presence on this journey did not worry Plimsoll. He socialised easily with his African colleagues, even accompanying them to a night club in Tangier.[75] Not noted for frequenting night clubs, it showed his adaptability in the line of duty. He also took opportunities for sightseeing.

The British delegation's report noted that Plimsoll "stood head and shoulders above the other members of the Committee and was an extremely valuable ally ... His natural modesty prevented him from playing a leading role in the Committee but his interventions were always well considered and had considerable influence with the more reasonable members of the Committee".[76] Modesty perhaps, but probably it was a desire to avoid prominence on the Africans' home ground, when Australian interests were less directly involved than those of European countries.

A Permanent Representative's World

Plimsoll had more contact with the British permanent representative than any other, especially because of intense consultation about colonialism and Africa. For most of Plimsoll's posting this was Sir Patrick Dean. Although a very senior member of the UK Foreign Office, Dean had had only one previous posting abroad. At one point, during Security Council consideration of Angola, Dean told Plimsoll that he had been instructed that "great importance" was attached to his "keeping in constant touch with Plimsoll".[77]

Contact with the United States was less intense but still important. Plimsoll and others at the UN would have felt a special bond with the presidential campaign of 1960, when the US permanent representative since 1953, Henry Cabot Lodge, was nominated as Nixon's vice-presidential running mate on the Republican ticket. Plimsoll wrote a despatch about Lodge, which Menzies found valuable,[78] and he forwarded separately his personal views of Vice-President Nixon and Senator John F. Kennedy, which "the Prime Minister was pleased to have".[79]

The Kennedy victory brought Governor Adlai Stevenson to New York as Lodge's replacement. Although not close to Kennedy, Stevenson's involvement in the select circle that convened to advise the President during the Cuban missile crisis underlined his influence. During that period Plimsoll's reports of conversations with Stevenson were a useful supplement to reporting from elsewhere.[80] An indication of Plimsoll's standing among the Americans was the approach to him early in 1962 by Richard N. Goodwin, a senior State Department official, closely connected to President Kennedy, about "breaking the ice" with Cuba.[81] Plimsoll had declined a US invitation early in 1960 to allow his name to go forward for the post of UN High Commissioner for Refugees.[82]

Plimsoll "collected permanent representatives" widely, regardless of political orientation. His contact with them (and often with their visiting foreign ministers and officials from home) was of wider significance than only UN matters. At the time of his arrival in New York, Australia had only 33 overseas posts, and so had limited direct communication with many important governments. Plimsoll was able to exert some influence on representatives of those countries and report useful information that would not otherwise have been gained. For example, Australia had no embassy in Sweden until 1963; and Plimsoll was in frequent contact with Agda Rossel, the Swedish permanent representative, who was the first woman to hold such rank in New York.

Plimsoll with UN Secretary-General U Thant, Australian Foreign Minister Sir Garfield Barwick, and US Permanent Representative Adlai Stevenson, September 1962 (UN photo)

In relation to the communist world, Australia had no posts except Moscow, which only reopened in 1959, five years after the Petrov affair. Communication with communist permanent representatives was not easy, but Plimsoll persisted. With his capacity to win people's confidence quickly, and encourage them to open up, he was able to have interesting talks with counterparts from many of the communist bloc countries.[83]

At the end of his introductory call on the Albanian permanent representative, for example, the latter said that although they were on opposite sides of the fence, if there was anything he could do for Plimsoll personally, Plimsoll should let him know. When Plimsoll was slightly taken aback, the Albanian broke down and cried: "You are the first permanent representative to call on me".[84] Some time later, in the General Assembly, a vote was brought on for which it appeared from his nervousness that the Albanian had yet to receive instructions. As often happened in moments of pressure, the Soviet team had not yet told him how to vote. Seeing the man's distress, Plimsoll told him which way he should be voting – which was, of course, the opposite of the way Australia was itself about to vote.[85]

Plimsoll was well-informed on many different countries. On return to Manila from the General Assembly of 1960, Senator (later President) Ferdinand Marcos spoke of his impressions of Khrushchev, of Castro, and of Plimsoll and his "amazing knowledge of the Philippines political machine".[86] His knowledge of all the important current UN issues was partly through his energy in personally tapping the expertise of people in other missions. Plimsoll did not restrict himself to other PRs: he liked to talk to diplomats and officials of all ranks. Gough Whitlam, visiting the UN in 1962, noted how delegates of all levels would come up and greet Plimsoll in the corridors.[87]

Plimsoll realised that in other missions, especially in the big ones like the UK and the US, or in the Secretariat, it was often less senior people who understood best the detail of often complex current issues. He included in his lunches and dinners those whom he considered exercised particular influence in their missions. This delighted them, and doubtless influenced their attitude towards Australia.[88] He talked easily with younger officers and "wasn't the least pretentious, or self-promoting". A junior US delegate recalled Plimsoll was "always trying to understand underlying issues, not just carry out the instructions of the moment". In this he was "more rigorous and energetic than all but a few at the UN".[89] A junior New Zealand diplomat, later head of the New Zealand Defence Department, recalled being at the UN as a "humble Third Secretary" when he encountered Plimsoll as they both walked to a meeting of the Trusteeship Council. Plimsoll was hailed by the President of the General Assembly:

> In the presence of the great I stood respectfully apart, but Jim drew me in smoothly and said "I'd like you to meet a colleague of mine, Gerald Hensley." Entirely trivial, but a mark of Jim's deep courtesy, even to the insignificant, and I never forgot it. For the rest of my working life I introduced members of my Department, however junior, as "my colleague", in a permanent tribute to Jim's influence.[90]

For Plimsoll a sensitive aspect of his role lay in ensuring the effective presentation of Australian policies at the UN, in the sometimes highly charged atmosphere of debates, for example, when questions of race or relative wealth were involved. Policies should be presented:

> in a way that makes them emotionally understandable to representatives of other countries. We cannot always convince other countries of our policies, but it should be possible to word our policies, and to explain our policies, in such a way that other countries can understand them and that, though they may disagree with them, they will not resent them.[91]

Sometimes this was difficult to achieve. Joshua Nkomo, a leading Zimbabwean political figure, was "highly displeased" with Plimsoll's speech on Rhodesia in July 1962; Plimsoll felt that "the difficulty for any outsider at present is that we are expected to line up firmly behind one or the other, and any one who tries to edge the parties closer together on a middle ground is regarded with hostility on all sides".[92]

Plimsoll's ability to speak with just a few notes, even on complex subjects, enabled him to choose his words to take account of the atmosphere. He seemed to be the only one who did this. Even at a time when most states sent their best as permanent representative in New York, they feared being misunderstood or misreported, and usually read from a text, either prepared in New York or in the home capital.[93] Plimsoll's approach could give the impression of little time spent in preparation; in fact, the reverse was the case. When he had to speak off-the-cuff he relied on his understanding of the issue, his memory for detail, and his confidence about reflecting the views of Canberra.

This way of speaking attracted unusual attention: "Instead of a boring diatribe, geared to get every word of the capital's brief into the text, Plimsoll made a speech into something interesting."[94] A New Zealand colleague recalled Plimsoll "leaning over the podium, looking fixedly down into the eyes of the delegates, speaking apparently without notes and with the sort of conviction that suggested he really believed he could swing delegates' votes in favour of his cause. His style was a refreshing change from the perfunctoriness of most of our colleagues".[95]

While there was no lack of confidence in him at home, for domestically hot issues, notably the Middle East, once or twice Canberra resorted to sending him prepared texts for delivery without alteration. Plimsoll was a little hurt and mildly resentful of this.[96]

Life in New York

"I just don't think you are capable of leaving your dear, beloved office for a day, even on a Sunday," Menzies's secretary, Hazel Craig, told Plimsoll.[97] His time in New York was among the most busy and pressured of any of his postings; even his book-reading declined. In

Canberra, his annual average had been some 80 full-length novels and other books; in New York he managed 30. TV, then still a novelty in Australia, and non-existent in Canberra, did not attract him much in New York. In 1960 he only watched Princess Margaret's wedding in London, the US Democratic Convention and Kennedy's debates with Nixon; and, in 1962, President Kennedy's national address during the Cuban missile crisis.

Apart from ministers and leading Opposition figures, there was a flow of visitors from Australia. These included trade union representatives, young academics, two Miss Australia winners and their chaperones, and others, including Plimsoll's father, and some friends.

At weekends he was happy enough to visit an art gallery alone. He attended opera and theatre. Others sometimes arranged for him to get away from his normal round. Sir Josiah Francis, Consul-General in New York, and his wife, included him in outings that he enjoyed, like the US tennis championships or Davis Cup Challenge Round ties.

There were "busman's holidays," like a month-long Law of the Sea conference in Geneva in 1960 and the three visits to the African continent. Plimsoll was usually uninterested in taking recreational leave but, while in New York, friends and colleagues pleaded with him not to work so hard and to take some time off. In 1961 Tange told Hay in Ottawa that Menzies agreed with him about the importance of Plimsoll's taking some leave. By this point Plimsoll actually admitted that he needed "some break now".[98] A friend, the Canadian permanent representative, Charles Ritchie, persuaded him that after a few days consultations in Ottawa he should take a fortnight's walking holiday in the Canadian Maritimes, on his own. Tange, writing just before Plimsoll assumed his "heavy responsibilities" at the 1961 General Assembly, intoned that "each one of us should regard our good health, and capacity to cope, as an asset to the Government as well as to ourselves, and that we should, if only for that reason, not wear ourselves out on things that seem highly important at the moment".[99] The next year, while home on leave and consultations, Plimsoll also spent two weeks in the Blue Mountains with his father, probably on his father's initiative.

There was another development which doubtless was a great tonic.

Arise, Sir James

On 24 May 1962, while in Morocco on his third African safari, Plimsoll was handed a telegram. A letter from Government House, Canberra, had arrived for him in New York after he had left for Africa. Marked "Personal In Confidence," no one else could open it. After two weeks without any response, Government House enquired and discovered where Plimsoll was. As Australia had no resident representation in Morocco, and the message was urgent, the British Consul-General was asked to convey it to Plimsoll.[100]

Ten days later, in Addis Ababa, another telegram was a considerable interruption to the business in hand. It conveyed congratulations from his staff in New York, his first intimation that his knighthood had been announced. Plimsoll was "beaming with pleasure and being (for him) quite elated, but he didn't go on about it, nor celebrate in any particular way. Nor did he suddenly become pompous or take himself more seriously. (Nor buy himself a new suit!)".[101]

Menzies, visiting London, on being informed of the precise time of the announcement in Australia, said, with evident satisfaction, "he is now Sir James Plimsoll".[102] Menzies felt strongly about "the dreadful work" at the UN that Plimsoll had had to do, and about "the impeccable way" in which he had done it.[103] If anything, he felt that Plimsoll should have been knighted earlier.[104] Plimsoll's award was unusual as normally public service recipients were already heads of departments.[105] He was relatively young at 45.

In New York, messages of congratulation poured in, including from the UN Secretary-General, Menzies and 16 of his ministers and two recently retired ones, two British cabinet ministers (Lord Carrington and Duncan Sandys), and his US counterpart at the UN, Adlai Stevenson. There were many other messages from senior officials in Australia and the UK, as well as from colleagues and friends in many walks of life in Australia, including the public service, the armed forces, members of parliament, and academics. Among journalists was a joint message from Donald Horne and Peter Hastings (of *The Bulletin*): "Congratulations to a parfait gentil knyght."[106] A friend of many years, Archbishop Eris O'Brien of Canberra, wrote: "You have been a most devoted servant to the human race."[107]

A common theme of many messages was genuine delight. From the Tanges: "This recognition will bring the greatest pleasure throughout the service."[108] Allan Eastman, another colleague, told Plimsoll: "It is good to see that the Government can make a break from the routine time-rank rationing system and confer a very high honour in cases of exceptional merit". He added that his wife was "convinced that you have no hope of escaping matrimony now".[109]

During his time at the UN, his speeches were often reported by the Australian media. Many people were more aware of him than would have been the case with an award for a public servant based in Canberra. As Sir Frederick Shedden noted, "Your press reports have been good, and many people who do not know you have spoken to me expressing an admiration for your representation of Australia."[110]

At the end of 1962, Plimsoll could look back on a year of considerable achievement. He had received widespread public acclaim, both in Australia and at the UN. He was elected a Vice-President of the General Assembly, no doubt in part due to his personal standing, and chaired meetings three times in the absence of the President.[111] The future was bright and Sir James was looking forward to at least another year in New York where he was now deeply involved and respected.

From New York to New Delhi

Towards the end of 1962 there was some Australian media speculation that Plimsoll would become Secretary of the Department or the first career ambassador in Washington.[112] A move was afoot, but to neither of those places. Early in February 1963, Tange, who was visiting Washington, asked Plimsoll to join him there.[113] Barwick had asked Tange to sound out Plimsoll about going to Delhi as High Commissioner. Tange explained the reasoning that lay behind the proposal, with which the Prime Minister was "fully in accord".[114] Barwick recalled later that Plimsoll was "very angry," having wanted to stay at the UN.[115] But as a dutiful public servant he agreed to go. The Indian Government gave its agreement and the appointment was announced on 21 February.

Farewell functions included those by U Thant, the UN Secretary-General, Sir Patrick Dean, and Adlai Stevenson. The UN Correspondents Association had a lunch in his honour at which he spoke and answered questions. Sir John Bunting told Plimsoll of his "great admiration" of his performance on that occasion, especially his handling of some "very loaded" questions. "Some of our Ministers would envy your capacity to reply at respectable length without going in deeper than you wished."[116] His sudden departure meant he had had to withdraw an offer to Dame Joan Sutherland to host a dinner for her. She wrote back understandingly: "Perhaps I shall sing in Delhi!"[117]

Plimsoll left New York on 9 March, within a month of first being approached about Delhi. He wrote to a friend that he would "miss the UN, which has become very much part of me, but it is not something that I will shed completely".[118]

A British delegate considered that Plimsoll "exercised an influence on the UN quite disproportionate to Australia's standing in the world".[119] This personal impact was especially important at a time when the UN was a more important means of projecting a country's image than now, when many other means of communication are available. He was widely consulted even on matters not of direct concern to Australia: his advice generally was "eminent commonsense, rather than great wisdom or vision; sensible, studied, moderate input that gained acceptance".[120] He had become perhaps the most successful permanent representative "because of a good sense of balance, and because he could easily win the confidence of people".[121] He was admired for this ease, including among the developing nations.

In a changing and difficult situation at the UN, Plimsoll held the line on Australian interests, especially in relation to PNG. Speaking in 1965, he considered that it remained the case that "Australia has been treated relatively gently on colonial questions," while the Committee of 17 had focused on Africa.[122] However, his skill, as well as the good personal standing that he enjoyed, doubtless helped while he was there.[123]

Above all, Plimsoll had impressed three cabinet ministers who were to have an important influence on his future. These were Barwick, Hasluck and, especially, Menzies.

As Plimsoll's departure for India drew near, Barwick, who regarded Plimsoll as "a very good human being", praised him for "the reputation which you have acquired for Australia as well as for yourself in United Nations circles" and for his "handling of controversial public matters".[124]

Tange once counselled Plimsoll to be careful about his reporting on UN matters relevant to PNG, about which Hasluck, as Minister for Territories, was touchy and had "grumbled". Plimsoll took the point but felt "it was my duty" to be frank.[125] Hasluck's regard for Plimsoll, however, was shown in August 1962, when he offered him the post of Secretary of the Department of Territories, which was becoming vacant. Plimsoll declined, although if the offer had been to be Administrator of PNG, "I think I would have accepted it."[126]

Last but not least, Menzies already had it in mind that Plimsoll should assume higher responsibilities in the not too distant future.

Endnotes

1 C.V. Narasimhan, former Under-Secretary General of the UN, letter, 18/11/2002.
2 Tange, conversation, 1996.
3 Sir David Hay, Oral History, TRC 121/65-1, 2:2/3 NLA.
4 R.H. Robertson, conversation, 11/10/96.
5 Peter Curtis, conversation, 21/10/96.
6 John Starey, conversation, 9/8/98.
7 R.H. Robertson, conversation, 11/10/1996.
8 After the 1962 UNGA Sir Laurence McIntyre commented to Tange of Plimsoll: "He of course operates in his own idiosyncratic and lone-wolf fashion, and I am not sure that he organizes his forces as efficiently as he might; but this is partly a reflection of his not having a really adequate deputy." McIntyre to Tange, 21/2/63. Secretary's correspondence with Ambassador, Tokyo, 1959-64, Tange papers, DFAT.
9 A.S. Watt, *Australian Diplomat: Memoirs of Sir Alan Watt*, Angus and Robertson, in association with the AIIA, Sydney, 1972, 26. See also Ralph Harry, *No Man is a Hero: Pioneers of Australian Diplomacy*, Arts Management Sydney, 1997, 21-9.
10 Loveday, conversation, 10/6/2004. Loveday attended a number of UNGAs from Washington where he was based. H. Gilchrist, conversation, 5/11/05. Curtis, conversation, 21/10/1996.
11 Casey informed Plimsoll that he had told Beale before UNGA 1959 that when he (Casey) left New York, Plimsoll "will lead". Casey to JP 4/8/1959, JP papers, Box 2, Item 21, NAA.
12 Tange to JP, 1/12/1959. Tange papers, DFAT.
13 H.A. Dunn, conversation, 26/10/1999.
14 Sir Nicholas Parkinson, conversation, 20/6/1996.
15 Tange to JP, 2/9/1960, Tange papers, DFAT.
16 JP to Tange 22/8/1960, (handwritten), Tange papers, DFAT.
17 JP to Tange, 1/12/1960, Tange papers, DFAT.
18 Parkinson, conversation, 20/06/1996.
19 Parkinson, conversation, 20/06/1996.
20 Parkinson, conversation, 20/06/1996.

21 A.W. Martin, interview with Tange, 7/8/1987; courtesy of A.W. Martin.
22 Watt, *Australian diplomat*, 171.
23 JP to Tange, 15/2/1960. JP papers, Box 2, Item 26, NAA. RA Woolcott, conversation, 12/12/1997.
24 M.J. Cook, conversation, 28/3/2000.
25 A.R. Parsons, conversation, 6/5/1997.
26 Cook, conversation, 28/3/2000.
27 JP diary, 6/6/1960.
28 Tange to JP, 4/3/1960, JP papers, DFAT.
29 JP to Tange, 28/3/1960, JP papers, DFAT.
30 *Reminiscential Conversations between Hon Clyde Cameron and Sir James Plimsoll 1984*. TRC 1967, ii, 133-4, hereafter: Can/Plim.
31 Sir Brian Urquhart, *A Life in Peace and War*, Harper and Row, New York, 1987, 172.
32 An earlier summit between Eisenhower and Khrushchev had been cancelled following the U2 affair.
33 Sir Garfield Barwick, conversation, 2/11/1996.
34 A.W. Martin, interview with Tange, 7/8/1987. Courtesy of A.W. Martin.
35 Barwick conversation, 2/11/1996; Parkinson, conversation, 20/6/1996.
36 Parkinson, conversation, 29/11/2000; Cam/Plim, ii, 145.
37 Dunn, conversation, 26/10/1999.
38 Cam/Plim, ii, 146.
39 Parkinson, conversation, 20/6/1996.
40 Parkinson, conversation, 20/6/1996. See also A.W. Martin *Robert Menzies. A Life. vol. ii 1944-1978*, Melbourne University Press, Melbourne, 1999, 418-23, and Sir Robert Menzies, *Letters to my Daughter 1955-75*, Heather Henderson (ed), Pier 9, Sydney, 2011, 45-7.
41 Eventeano to JP, 13/10/1961. JP papers, Box 3, Item 30, NAA.
42 *Current Notes on International Affairs*, DFAT, vol 32, no. 10, October 1961, 54-7. Menzies was replying to a question in the House of Representatives on 17/10/1961.
43 Tange to JP, 11/4/1961, Tange papers, DFAT.
44 Opened in 1957; no senior officer from Canberra had yet visited it.

45 WRC, Jnl, 22/6/1959, vol ix, 1883.
46 Waller to Shann (then based in London), 23/6/1959, Waller papers, DFAT.
47 JP to PR Heydon 20/8/1959. JP papers, Box 2, Item 21, NAA.
48 JP to Casey, 21/7/1959. Tange papers, DFAT.
49 JP to Tange, 14/7/1959. JP papers, DFAT.
50 B.C. Hill to JP, 17/7/1959. JP papers, Box 2, Item 21, NAA. The embassy in Cairo reopened in January 1960.
51 New York Memo 603 of 14/7/1959. The Lagos post opened on 1/10/1960, immediately after independence. Casey to JP, 5/8/1959. JP papers Box 2, Item 21, NAA.
52 JP diary, 11/12/1959.
53 He was diagnosed as "having a fractured nose but no displacement". He did not pursue an invitation to claim for damages against the railroad company. JP papers, 8048/1/2 NLA.
54 Probably after talking to Plimsoll at a function that A.D. Rothman held for Australian journalists in New York. JP diary, 22/12/1959.
55 JP to S.A. Jamieson in Accra, 8/2/1960. JP papers, Box 2, Item 26, NAA.
56 JP to J. Quinn, 4/2/1960. JP papers, Box 2, Item 26, NAA. Cable UNE59, 28/1/1960, JP papers, DFAT.
57 Plimsoll recalled later that "during the height of the Congo troubles, we had a saying about events in the Congo: 'If you're not confused, you don't understand the situation'". A.N. Smith Lecture, Melbourne, 1965, 3.
58 Urquhart, *A Life in Peace and War*, 171.
59 Letters to J.M. McMillan, 10/8/1961, A.P. Renouf, 15/8/1961 and Crocker, 30/8/1961, respectively. JP papers, Box 3, Item 30, NAA.
60 JP to Watt, 13/2/1962. JP papers, Box 3, Item 31, NAA.
61 JP to C.T. Moodie, 17/3/1962. A1838/1 1290/1/12/2 Pt 1, NAA.
62 Canberra cable, EUN 619 of 29/2/61. JP papers, DFAT.
63 JP to R.N. Hamilton in London, 3/3/1962. JP Papers, Box 3, Item 31, NAA.
64 JP to Lord Caradon (formerly Sir Hugh Foot). UK PR from 1964, 19/11/1964. JP papers Box 5, Item 53, NAA.
65 Geoffrey Sawer and W.J. Hudson, chapter on "The United Nations" in *Australia in World Affairs 1961-65*, Gordon Greenwood and Norman Harper

(eds), FW Cheshire, Melbourne, 1968, 244-6.

66 UN New York Memo 494 of 18/5/1961, A4359/13 File 221/5/19, NAA.

67 JP to Chester Bowles, US Ambassador to India, 24/12/1964. JP papers, Box 5, item 53, NAA. Plimsoll speech to UN General Assembly, 18/1/1962.

68 Cam/Plim, ii, 3-4.

69 Cam/Plim ii , 4-5; JP to Caradon 19/11/1964. JP papers, Box 5, Item 53, NAA.

70 Cam/Plim ii, 5-6.

71 JP to George Ivan Smith, 13/7/1962. JP papers, Box 2, Item 21, NAA.

72 JP conversation with author, 1986; also Fernandez, conversation, 1997, and Cam/Plim ii, 7.

73 Cable I.16074 of 29/6/1962, A1838/371 Pt 1, NAA.

74 Barwick to Sandys, 0.15478 of 3/9/1962, JP papers, DFAT.

75 JP diary, 21/5/1962.

76 Para 3 of UK Report of 12/06/1962 by John Sankey. JP papers, DFAT.

77 Cable I.14462 of 8/6/1961 A1838 935/17 Pt 1, NAA.

78 "Menzies urged me to read Plimsoll's despatch on Lodge. He spoke very approvingly of Plimsoll." Alfred Stirling diary, 4/8/1960, DFAT.

79 Hazel Craig, personal secretary to Prime Minister, to JP, 1/11/1960. JP papers, Box 2, Item 26, NAA.

80 See, for example, I.31887 from UN New York of 17/12/1962 A11536/1-14, and CRS A1838 262/12/8/1 Pts 1-3 NAA; and Cam/Plim, ii, 147-8.

81 Canberra said no to Plimsoll getting involved in talking to the Cuban permanent representative about opening up negotiations to secure release of prisoners taken in the Cuban Bay of Pigs affair. Tange to JP, 4/4/1962. Tange papers, DFAT. I.I7721 from UNNY 30/3/1962 A11536/1 Pt14, NAA.

82 JP diary and Cam/Plim, ii, 158.

83 Cook, conversation, 28/3/2000.

84 Whitlam, conversation; 1996; also Parsons, conversation, 6/5/1997: he heard this from Ralph Harry.

85 Similarly, on another occasion, when the PR of Belarus was faced with a sudden roll call vote, he asked Plimsoll how he should vote. Robertson, conversation, 11/10/1996. Cam/Plim, ii,112.

86 Stirling, diary, 22/2/1961.
87 Whitlam, conversation, 1996.
88 Cook, letter, 24/08/2006.
89 Dr Tom Bartlett, letter, 29/04/2003.
90 Gerald Hensley, letter, 14/8/2004.
91 Plimsoll, address to Parliamentary Joint Committee on Foreign Affairs, Canberra, 11/5/1965. 561/1/1 All Post Memo 40. JP papers DFAT.
92 JP to George Ivan Smith, 13/7/1962. JP paper, Box 3, Item 31, NAA.
93 Cook, conversation, 28/3/2000.
94 Parsons, conversation, 6/5/1997.
95 Merv Norrish, NZ Deputy Permanent Representative, letter, 3/8/2004.
96 H.D. Anderson, conversation, 7/2/1997.
97 Hazel Craig to JP, 1/11/1960. JP papers, Box 2, Item 26, NAA.
98 Tange to Menzies, 9/6/1961, Tange to Hay, 13/6/1961, JP to Tange, 5/6/1961, JP Personnel File DFAT.
99 Tange to JP, 29/9/1961, Tange papers DFAT.
100 JP diary, 24/5/1962.
101 Warwick Mayne Wilson, letter 26/5/2004. JP diary 2/6/1962.
102 R.W. Furlonger, conversation, 15/10/1996.
103 WRC, Jnl, 3/6/1962, vol xi, 2716.
104 As Menzies told Roden (later Sir Roden) Cutler shortly after the announcement. Cutler, conversation, July 1996.
105 In the years that followed a number of Plimsoll's contemporaries as diplomats were knighted, who were not at that stage heads of department: E.R. Walker, L.R. McIntyre, J.K. Waller, and P. Shaw. Others, K.C.O. Shann, D.O. Hay, A.R. Cutler and W.R. Crocker were also knighted for services that included tenure of other positions(including departmental head) after extensive periods as Australian diplomats. See also, Edwards, *Tange*, 111-2.
106 JP papers, 8048/1/5-8, NLA.
107 O'Brien to Plimsoll, 8/8/1962, JP papers, DFAT.
108 Tange cable, 3/6/1962. JP papers, Box 3, Item 31, NAA.
109 A.J. Eastman, letter, 3/6/1962. JP papers, 8048/1/5-8 NLA.

The Highlight of His Career: the United Nations, 1959-63   155

110 Shedden, letter, 6/6/1962, 8048/1/5-8, JP papers, NLA.
111 JP diary, 22/10/1962, 18/12/1962, 20/12/1962.
112 See media cuttings in 8048/13/3, JP papers NLA.
113 JP diary, 9-10/2/1963.
114 See chapter 6.
115 Barwick, conversation, 2/11/1996.
116 JP diary 5/3/1963. Bunting to JP 25/3/1963. JP papers, Box 4, Item 36, NAA.
117 Sutherland to JP, 29/3/1963. JP papers, Box 4, Item 36, NAA.
118 JP to Ivan Smith, 18/2/1963. JP papers, Box 4, Item 38, NAA.
119 James Scott, UK Delegation, letter, 28/11/1997.
120 Curtis, conversation, 21/10/1996.
121 Barwick heard this opinion from the British permanent representative, Sir Patrick Dean. Barwick, conversation, 2/11/1996.
122 Plimsoll address to the Parliamentary Joint Committee on Foreign Affairs, Canberra 11/5/1965.
123 In the event, the Committee of 17 caused a resolution directed at PNG to go through the General Assembly in December 1966.
124 Barwick to JP, 22/2/1963. A9749/1, NAA. Barwick conversation, 2/11/1996.
125 Tange, conversation, 1996; also Tange to JP, 16/2/60, JP to Tange 26/2/60, Tange papers, DFAT.
126 The offer came when Plimsoll called on Hasluck in Canberra, while on consultations. The proposal was to be Deputy Secretary, and then Secretary in a year's time when C.R. Lambert retired. Cam/Plim, ii, 249; Plim diary, 9/8/1962.

6

Indian Indulgence, 1963-65

Everyone tells me that you are practically running the sub-continent of India. This is what I would have expected.[1]
Barwick simply hasn't enough Plimsolls to go round.[2]

New Delhi was a major diplomatic centre, with India a leading country in the Non-Aligned Movement, and increasingly powerful within its own region: there was always much of interest to analyse and discuss. With the great variety of people and conditions, making up a massive population in a huge territory, India was, and is, like a world unto itself (much like China, Russia and the USA). It continued to hold to parliamentary democracy, and administrative and legal systems inherited from the Raj.

Australia had long wanted a closer relationship with India, but longstanding diplomatic relations had produced little substance. There were many obstacles. Australia was firmly Western; India was non-aligned. There was the cool atmosphere between the two respective long-serving prime ministers, Nehru and Menzies. India was primarily concerned with its own considerable developmental problems. Small to medium countries like Australia, which could provide only limited amounts of assistance, struggled to make much of an impact.

At about the same time as the Cuban missile crisis of 1962, across the world in the Himalayas there was the clash of Chinese and Indian forces along their common border. India suffered military reverses, and its attitude towards the West changed with recognition of its need of military aid. The Chinese incursions "had brought about a sudden understanding in India of the strategic vulnerability of the country in the face of air attack from the north".[3] It seemed an opportunity to see if India and Pakistan might settle their long-standing dispute over Kashmir. China "injected continuous poison into the Indo-Pakistani relationship. It was already easy to foresee that a generous arms aid programme for India would arouse suspicion among Pakistanis that, if the Chinese did not return, the arms could be turned in their direction".[4]

Sir Garfield Barwick, Australia's Minister for External Affairs, visited Pakistan and India in December 1962. Waller, who accompanied him, told Plimsoll that he and Barwick "were both very much struck by the rather confused state of thinking in New Delhi and the willingness which ministers and senior officials showed to turn to other people for advice and ideas". Australia could play a role: "The old days when India was right and the rest of the world wrong, have gone. They will be less 'non-aligned' and we shall I hope be less bellicose" in public.[5] Waller recalled "walking up and down the High Commissioner's Residence in Delhi, discussing with Barwick what he could do". At which time Barwick first thought of assigning Plimsoll, as "a man who was uniquely suited to giving a feeling of confidence to Australian-Indian relations".[6] The High Commissioner post had been vacant for nine months.

Before Plimsoll left New York, Barwick told him that the prospects of a settlement of the Kashmir dispute "are not good", but it was worth trying. "Success would mean a major addition to the strength of the Western world against Communism, and avoidance of a disastrous religious war." He added: "I have sufficient regard for your capacities and great sense of purpose to believe that you might be able to help Indians to the point of making some reasonable concessions, assuming Pakistan does its part." He thanked Plimsoll for agreeing to go at short notice.[7]

Waller later told Plimsoll that there had been a period of just a few days when it might have been possible to settle the Kashmir question.

"Barwick thought that if we could get you there before Christmas you might play a major role." However, when Plimsoll arrived in March, "some of the feeling we had noted had evaporated; the Indians had recovered their confidence".[8]

Plimsoll had left New York "very precipitately," only four weeks after being asked to go, with no time to make the customary farewells, or to have briefings. His doubt of the need for such haste was confirmed on arrival in Delhi early in March. The British and the Americans had each sent special envoys to talk to the Indians: Duncan Sandys, Secretary of State for Commonwealth Relations, and Averell Harriman, Assistant Secretary of State for Far Eastern Affairs, respectively. With these efforts to get India and Pakistan to come to an agreement, there was little in the short term that Australia could contribute. On 27 March Plimsoll cabled Canberra about Kashmir, expressing "some caution on my part" about rushing in when he was "insufficiently abreast of the problem", and cautioning against Australia putting forward a "plan". Australia might be able to contribute, but given the potential leverage that the US and UK had because Pakistan and India "each want something substantial from these countries", it was important that Australia "not overestimate our capacity" to help.[9]

Plimsoll had been aware in New York of the problems between India and China. In November 1962 he had noted a report from London which quoted a UK official as saying that "we are now playing for very high stakes, the abandonment by India of non-alignment". Plimsoll had suggested that "this objective needs some examination". It might be better "to allow matters to take their course", and for the West not to try to push things. Closer Indian alignment with the West might happen anyway. Further, "there would be more advantage to us in having India remain non-aligned while exercising its judgment on specific matters in a way more sympathetic to the West". Canberra agreed.[10]

Visit to Australia

Soon after arriving in Delhi Plimsoll returned to Australia, accompanying T.T. Krishnamachari, Minister of Defence Production in India. Ranked number three in the Cabinet and "a very powerful figure in India", Krishnamachari was interested to see Australia, having "not taken us particularly seriously" in the past. Plimsoll, who arrived home in advance of Krishnamachari, was concerned to find that the programme arranged for the minister was "very low level" and told Menzies it was not good enough. At Menzies's invitation he made some suggestions. Menzies was "more than cooperative" and involved himself and other ministers in the programme, which was rapidly transformed.[11]

On arrival in Sydney Krishnamachari stayed at Kirribilli House, at that time the official guest house for VIP visitors. Barwick had him to lunch and dinner with prominent guests. Next day he spent a morning with Fairhall, Minister for Supply, and his staff, leading to agreement for an Australian team to visit Indian ammunition factories and recommend any improvements needed. He lunched with the Board of the Reserve Bank of Australia. In Canberra, although a public holiday, Menzies had Krishnamachari to a small, informal lunch at the Lodge, and afterwards had a private talk in his library for an hour. Next morning he had discussions with cabinet ministers and then lunched with them. After another 30 minutes in cabinet he met the Indian community.[12]

Krishnamachari was impressed, all the more when on a subsequent visit to Canada, he saw "almost nobody". A year later another Indian minister told Plimsoll that cabinet became bored with the number of times that Krishnamachari "keeps telling us how much better they do things in Australia than we do them here".[13] Krishnamachari's visit illustrated Plimsoll's view that his own relations with Menzies were such that he was "able to persuade him, perhaps more than anyone else could, to take an interest in India and be sympathetic", despite past clashes with Nehru.[14]

While in Australia Krishnamchari had talked with Gough Whitlam, then Deputy Leader of the Labor Opposition, including about the controversial question of the US communications installation at North West Cape. Krishnamachari told Plimsoll that he had said to Whitlam that if Australia opposes North West Cape, "it's mad":

> The presence of that installation there will be of value to the whole of us in the region. We cannot have it in India. But if it's in Australia, then the American capacity is there in support of our defence if we ever need it.[15]

In May another high level joint UK/US mediation in India, involving Sandys and Dean Rusk, the US Secretary of State, was to no avail. At the end of 1963, after visiting India (where he stayed with Plimsoll) and Pakistan, Casey felt that relations between the two countries seemed to be "as bad as they have ever been".[16]

Plimsoll followed the Kashmir dispute closely, but not from any hope of a settlement. Shortly after arrival in Delhi Sir Owen Dixon, whom he had assisted in an attempt to mediate on the question in 1950, wrote to express sorrow "that you should be plagued by the Kashmir affair". He added "I can't help thinking that it is a trouble which does not belong to Australia".[17] Writing to Dixon ten months later, Plimsoll said he was "impressed by the ingenuity of human beings in devising plausible arguments to put forward for not doing what they have no intention of doing". He concluded, "I believe, and have always believed, that Kashmir is not worth it all for either country, and that it would not have mattered who gained the Valley so long as it was settled."[18]

Offer to be secretary of the department

Barwick's letter to Plimsoll of February 1963 had been about the importance of his being in India. But within two months Barwick had changed his mind: he wanted Plimsoll to be secretary of the department in Canberra.

This idea had had a long gestation. In 1954, when Tange was

appointed secretary at the age of 39, cabinet's intention had been a three to five year tenure, with "periodic succession to the position".[19] After Casey's retirement in 1960, Menzies increasingly considered that Tange had been too long in the post.

Menzies's favourable impression of Plimsoll as a professional in Canberra in the 1950s was reinforced by Plimsoll's performance at the UN in New York. Menzies was also well disposed towards Plimsoll as a person, partly because Plimsoll was not one of those who tried to impress or who "had tickets on themselves".[20] In 1958 Menzies told Crocker that he was "not satisfied with Tange as head of External Affairs. He praised Plimsoll's mind and integrity," and he was "astonished" at the breadth of his reading.[21] In late 1960, Peter Heydon was number two in the department, and one of its most senior and experienced officers. Having long aspired to becoming secretary, he took an opportunity privately to sound out Menzies, whom he had known for many years, about the possibility of his succeeding Tange at some stage. Menzies replied by asking Heydon whether he really thought that he, Menzies, could give him the job over Plimsoll.[22]

In June 1962 Crocker took the opportunity to say to Menzies that "Plimsoll, with his experience, intellect and character, was now needed in Canberra." Menzies agreed, and recalled that Tange had originally been appointed on the basis that he would only be three to five years in the job. In 1961 Menzies had "asked Tange about his taking a post overseas, and let him know that he thought he ought to go, reminding him that he had never been an ambassador". But, Menzies told Crocker, "Tange wants to stay on."[23]

In March 1963 Crocker visited Canberra from The Hague.[24] Menzies told him that in spite of having made two "brutal suggestions" to Tange that he take a post overseas, he was sticking in Canberra. Tange had to be "removed". Crocker observed that Tange seemed more firmly in the saddle than ever. Menzies replied: "No he is going." Crocker later noted that the reason why no one had yet been appointed to New York in place of Plimsoll and why Hay was being made to hold the fort for the time being was that the Prime Minister wanted Tange sent there. Menzies implied that this would happen, but it did not.[25]

Barwick also felt that Plimsoll should become secretary. When Menzies had appointed Barwick as minister at the end of 1961, he had hinted strongly to him that Tange should go. Barwick had disagreed.[26] However, after 15 months in the portfolio he had reached the same view, while also having a suitable successor in mind.[27]

Barwick talked to Plimsoll, when the latter was in Australia with Krishnamachari. On Sunday 21 April 1963 Plimsoll visited Barwick at his home in Sydney; the next day Barwick had Plimsoll to lunch at the Australian Club, and then went with him to the airport to greet Krishnamachari on arrival.[28] For a minister to engage in such extended private talks with a visiting head of mission is unusual. Barwick enjoyed Plimsoll's company, and would have discussed the UN, especially Rhodesia; and perhaps India.[29] But he particularly wanted to propose to Plimsoll that he become secretary of the department at the end of the year.

To his surprise Barwick found Plimsoll reluctant. Plimsoll would have realised that Barwick was speaking to him at an early stage in a process. If cabinet had already decided, including a decision about Tange's next appointment, Plimsoll would have found it difficult to decline. Next day, on 23 April, at the External Affairs offices in Sydney, in an interval between official talks with Krishnamachari, Plimsoll met Crocker unexpectedly. He was one of very few people in whom Plimsoll would have confided about such a matter. Plimsoll told Crocker, "in great confidence", that Barwick had offered him the "headship of the Department and would like him to take over at Canberra at the end of the year!" Crocker was delighted. Plimsoll, however, had pleaded he felt obliged to stay in India for longer than that "for the sake of Indian amour-propre". Crocker strongly disagreed. Having twice been High Commissioner in Delhi, Crocker told Plimsoll that Delhi did not compare in importance with being secretary, and urged him to accept Barwick's offer. Later, at

Barwick's dinner for Krishnamachari at Kirribilli House, Crocker repeated his view to Plimsoll. "Ministers, like governments, change and he should seize the opportunity before it evaporated," especially given the political uncertainties in Canberra, where the Government had a majority of only one in the House of Representatives. Plimsoll might not get a similar offer again.[30]

On return to The Hague, Crocker wrote to Plimsoll: "The Department needs you – and so does the Minister. Go and do your duty!"[31] But Plimsoll could not be budged. Hitherto Plimsoll had always gone wherever he was asked, without question and often without much notice. This was the first time that he had baulked.

By the end of 1963 Barwick had persuaded Tange that he should "spend some time in the paddock". Tange had chosen Delhi as his posting.[32] The matter had not been formalised before Barwick's resignation, in April 1964, on becoming Chief Justice of the High Court of Australia. Paul Hasluck, who replaced Barwick, was told by Menzies that Tange had to go, without giving any reason except that Tange had "been there too long" and would benefit from some overseas experience.[33]

There now came a second time of asking. Hasluck informed Plimsoll that it was the wish of cabinet that he become secretary. Tange would replace him in India.[34] Plimsoll could not refuse this formal request, but sought to delay taking up the job. He wrote a "very unenthusiastic" reply,[35] expressing appreciation of the "confidence" shown in him, and that he would accept "if that is the Government's wish". He explained that he "would have been content to continue [in New Delhi] for several years". Seizing on an opening in Hasluck's letter to the effect that Tange himself was in no hurry to make the change, which Tange had also mentioned in a separate letter to Plimsoll, he asked to be allowed to complete two years in Delhi:

> I have been greatly interested in India, politically, culturally and in other ways – and I have, I believe, been able to do something to

develop cooperation between our two countries. But I have been here too short a while to do more than scratch the surface.[36]

But fascination with India was only one factor in Plimsoll's reluctance to be secretary. Months later, with modesty and self-awareness, Plimsoll unburdened himself to his close friend, Jim McIntyre, who was returning to Canberra to be deputy secretary. "If I had a determining voice, I would have liked to see you become Secretary and me remain here"[in Delhi]. There were his shortcomings in management: "Unlike Arthur [Tange] I am not interested in administration as such." He realised his "own deficiencies in this respect".

"Another cause of hesitancy" was "a feeling that the Secretaryship should come near the close of one's career in the Service instead of in midpassage",[37] as in normal UK practice where becoming permanent under-secretary of the FCO is invariably the final assignment before retirement. But, as Plimsoll well knew, a different situation applied in the young Australian service. Of his three closest predecessors, two had been even younger than he was (48) on appointment.[38]

Further, the death at the end of 1963 of Athol Townley, the former Minister for Defence, who was to have replaced Sir Howard Beale as ambassador in Washington, led to Plimsoll hoping he might be chosen in Townley's place; his name had appeared in domestic media speculation.[39] A posting to Washington would have been attractive. At that time it commonly lasted six years; and if he had been offered it at that time, he probably would have accepted it over Delhi. But Keith Waller was chosen in mid-1964. Waller's reply to Plimsoll's message of congratulations was ironic. Confessing to some "dread" about Washington, Waller wrote he "had hoped that they would send you and that I might succeed you in Delhi which as you know I have always coveted and for which I have been offering myself for years".[40] Waller had been unaware that Plimsoll was designated to become secretary.

Menzies agreed to Plimsoll's request to remain longer in Delhi,[41] perhaps because Tange had finally agreed to go and Menzies may have felt unconcerned about the precise timing of the changeover. In retrospect, the agreement represented an extraordinary indulgence.

Another development, at the UN, could have shortened Plimsoll's time in India. Early in 1964 the UN was seeking a suitable mediator for the conflict in Cyprus. Listening to Radio Australia news one morning, Plimsoll heard his name mentioned as a candidate.[42] He later discovered he was on a short list for this "extremely delicate and difficult" task,[43] and, furthermore, heard that he was "the leading candidate" from a friend at senior level in the UN Secretariat.[44] In the event, being the first preference of the British,[45] the former colonial power, may not have endeared him to the Cypriots and someone else was chosen. A member of the US Mission in New York commented to an Australian diplomat that Plimsoll would have been a most suitable choice, but "we value him too highly to send him to Cyprus", given the likely dangers in the assignment.[46]

Indian indulgence

Just after Plimsoll's arrival in Delhi John Bunting wrote to him: "There is scope for developing our relations with India. In fact I would think that it could be made into a key Asian post."[47] Plimsoll was realistic about how far relations might develop in the short term. It would take "hard work and use of imagination" and depend on "the policies one can project". He accurately foresaw that it was something that "cannot be left to government unaided by itself".[48]

During 1963 and 1964 Canberra's interest in India declined as the situation in South-East Asia became the overriding focus.[49] Late in 1962 in New York he had received a copy of a cable to Menzies, visiting London, following cabinet discussion of the annual Strategic Basis of Defence Policy paper:

> Our strategic situation has changed for the worse over the past three years in the light of the increased Communist (especially

mainland Chinese) potential, the present open situation in Laos, the failure to keep pace with insurgency in South Vietnam, the possibility of a potential threat from Indonesia, and a decline in confidence in SEATO.[50]

Towards the end of 1962 the first 20 Australian Army training team went to Vietnam, a precursor of Australia's military commitment there for ten years. Early in 1963 had come Indonesia's decision to "confront" the newly-formed Malaysia.

In Delhi, Nehru's funeral in May 1964 was attended by Dean Rusk representing the United States. He took the opportunity to talk to the Foreign Minister of Japan, also in attendance, about the seriousness of the situation in Laos and Vietnam. Plimsoll reported that Rusk said that "the US was prepared to react in whatever way necessary to meet a threat", not excluding bombing Peking itself. Although there would be a presidential election in November, the Administration would "not lose any votes" if it took up a stronger position in South-East Asia this year. Rusk wanted the Japanese to know that the United States took a most serious view of the situation, and asked that they use their channels to inform the Chinese of this.[51]

For Menzies, Nehru's death presented an opening to establish a better personal relationship with his new Indian counterpart, Lal Bahadur Shastri. But a possible visit by Menzies late in 1964 did not eventuate. Menzies had not been well and was advised not to overdo things;[52] moreover, he had, unusually, to fight a half-Senate election as well. Nor did Barwick, or later Hasluck, visit. Only one cabinet minister came: Allen Fairhall, Minister for Supply, about Australian military assistance, while Doug Anthony, then a junior minister, led a visiting parliamentary delegation. Tange visited once.[53] Bunting visited to help with setting up an agency in India similar to the Prime Minister's Department, which arose from Tange's visit.[54]

Diplomats stationed abroad can feel isolated, even forgotten, by their home capital. This would have been the first time that Plimsoll experienced such a feeling.[55] He was under less day-to-day pressure than he had ever been. There were no particularly difficult current issues. Bill Pritchett, who had been acting high commissioner, had already set in train Australia's relatively modest military assistance to India, while specialist personnel in the High Commission oversaw the civil aid programme. Australia's aid shipments of grain were of a token nature: only the US had the capacity to make a significant contribution to India's grain shortfall. The perennial problem of the India-Pakistan relationship was tense but relatively dormant.[56]

Being Plimsoll, however, he took no leave and worked hard, but in ways of his own choosing, rather than responding to requests from Canberra. He was fortunate with his health, apart from a brief early bout of gastroenteritis.[57] By contrast, ill-health caused the premature departure of three of his staff.[58]

Being high commissioner in Delhi has long been one of the most sought after postings in the Australian service.[59] For Plimsoll it opened up new professional dimensions: all his other postings had been multilateral;[60] this was his first bilateral. Marshall Johnston, the deputy for most of his time in Delhi, recalled that Plimsoll took to India "in an extraordinary way". He loved the place: they could do no wrong. He had very good contacts with people, and seemed so sympathetic. The Indians he met returned the affection, and with admiration. Plimsoll took full advantage of a vibrant, open society offering to a high commissioner good access to people in all walks of life. Many of the leading civil servants were of a high calibre. Plimsoll had great regard for those with British training, with "ICS" after their names, perfect English, articulate, and impressive, who were spread throughout the top layer of the various ministries. Plimsoll also came to know a number of Indian ministers, including Mrs Indira Gandhi.[61]

There was enormous interest to be had in India's centuries of history, fascinating architecture, art and dance, and a virtual continent to tour.

Indian art and culture were of particular fascination for Plimsoll. A tireless visitor to art galleries and temples, he would slip out at short notice to have a quick look at a new art exhibition. He bought many Indian paintings and sculptures and, later, he would always have some on display wherever he was based. Plimsoll also revelled in the other sensations of India, the heat, dust, colour, and its people. He loved being in crowds and in market places – he even did not want air conditioning in his official car because it would make him feel separate from the people.[62]

Also interested in Indian literature, Plimsoll wanted regular two-way visits between literature academics of the two countries. Professor C.D. Narasimhaiah of the English Department at the University of Mysore, who had recently visited Australia, arranged for *The Literary Criterion*, his university's periodical, to devote an entire issue to Australian literature; Plimsoll wrote the foreword.[63] With his avid interest in literature, he went beyond a short formal introduction, and offered some comparisons between Australian and Indian literature, particularly fiction. He discussed the question, "why Indians might have an interest in Australian writing and be moved to read some of it," arguing:

> Indians will find some Australian novels grappling with themes which Indians too are conscious of and which they will not find, or not in the same way, in English and American writings. There is the battle against the elements of nature – fire, flood, drought – and the opening up of a new country beating against the hazards of nature to establish the foothold of a farm.

But, citing Patrick White's novel, *The Tree of Man*, he added that it would be a mistake to take this analogy too far, not only because the conditions of Australian and Indian farmers differed so much, but because the Indian farmer most likely to find a counterpart in that novel "is unlikely to be reading a novel in English at all".[64]

Improving the relationship

Given that Canberra's foreign policy priorities lay elsewhere, Plimsoll set out to see what he could achieve personally to develop the Indian relationship. He began with the advantage of Indian appreciation for Australia's sympathetic and practical response to Indian feelers for military assistance after the Chinese incursions. And there was the mutual obsession with cricket.

A major problem was the negative image of Australia created by its restricted immigration policy. Plimsoll could hardly have failed to recognise the folly of taking Anglo-Indians of limited capacity and rejecting Indians who could have substantially contributed to Australia. It was also barely concealed racism. Some junior External Affairs officers at Australian posts in Asia, whose responsibilities at the time included immigration, became increasingly disenchanted with the policy and did their best to find ways around it. One of these was Dick Smith, a third secretary in New Delhi on his first posting. Smith sought to be more flexible in applying the policy, putting greater emphasis on whether the applicant would or would not make a good migrant. Plimsoll, probably aware of the way the policy was being applied, did not question it.[65] Such discreetly taken decisions would, however, have had little effect at the time on this negative perception. Attitudes changed only gradually, especially after alterations to the policy in 1966.

One matter Plimsoll raised with Canberra was the practice of sending to Asian posts official films about Australia intended for attracting migrants from Europe. Such films were unsuitable for Asian viewers, "indeed an embarrassment in countries where we are turning them away". An attempt ought to be made to produce some films "with Asian audiences specifically in mind".[66]

Personal impact

In his short time in India Plimsoll made a considerable personal impact, not only among ministers and officials, but in wider circles, especially educational and cultural. He pursued effective development aid, including in the scientific field. He had limited success; for example, Canberra was unmoved by his support for a project for a cyclotron. T.N. Kaul, a leading Indian diplomat of the time, recalled over 30 years later, with perhaps a measure of overstatement:

> Plimsoll was an ideal diplomat and an example on how to conduct bilateral relations in a manner most conducive and beneficial. His contribution, in particular, to bringing India and Australia closer in mutual understanding and esteem and developing cooperation in the economic, political and scientific and technological fields was second to none.[67]

Indian External Affairs officials sought his advice and help over their relations with Burma, Nepal, Bhutan and Sikkim.[68] With regard to the Himalayan states, "India believes that Australia can be trusted to exercise an influence . . . in a way that is friendly to India and directed against the common threat of Chinese expansion" while India felt that the great powers "might have interests of their own to advance", while "Afro-Asians . . . might try to help Peking".[69]

In April 1964 a group of leading Indians, including Vice President Zakir Husain and Lal Bahadur Shastri, decided to publish a book of essays which would be presented to Nehru on his 75th birthday in November. When Nehru died in May it was decided to publish the volume in his memory: it would consist of "reflections by some of the eminent thinkers of our times on the present outlook in human knowledge and achievement".[70] The essayists included a number of internationally well-known figures of the period: Earls Attlee and Mountbatten, Willy Brandt, Pierre Mendes-France, Gunnar Myrdal, Arnold Toynbee, Carlos Romulo, Professor J.K. Galbraith, Linus Pauling, as well as several leading Indians including President Radhakrishnan. Plimsoll was the only foreign diplomat then serving in Delhi to be invited to contribute; he was also the only Australian.

Plimsoll's essay, "Towards a common conception of our humanity", had a strong emphasis on human rights, and drew on his experiences as an official in Canberra, and as a diplomat at the UN in New York, as well as his time in India. He had, he wrote to Tange:

> tried to write something that will give a good picture of Australia as a country with a liberal outlook; and also to make by implication two points which I feel quite strongly about in regard to India, namely that action has to be taken to prevent Hindu-Moslem tension intensifying and broadening until it gets out of control, and that such action needs to be taken continually and not simply when explosions start to occur. But this is done very indirectly.[71]

Today his text seems unremarkable. The book received little attention in Australia.

Plimsoll travelled around India as much as he could. This was important for a diplomat, especially in such a large and diverse country. He would have applauded that part of President Kennedy's 1961 exhortation to US ambassadors to travel extensively away from capital cities. "Only in this way can you develop the close, personal associations that go beyond official diplomatic circles and maintain a sympathetic and accurate understanding of all segments of the country".[72] In fact, 20 years earlier, Plimsoll had written that "the secret of a good diplomat nowadays is his ability to get away from the narrow official circle and feel something of the pulse of life in the more active and battling sections of the community".[73] Plimsoll took great personal delight in travel, wanting to see things for their own sake. He was not only open to new experiences, but anxious for them.[74] Unlike some of his diplomatic colleagues in Delhi, he had no interest in shooting expeditions, or riding on elephants.

He was able to plan travel away from the capital sometimes for two weeks at a stretch, in one case three, relying on an able deputy to hold the fort, and confident that there was nothing requiring his constant presence in Delhi. He called on local officials, viewed various forms of economic activity and Australian aid projects, and visited schools and universities, art exhibitions and historical monuments. He addressed local groups about Australia, and about the UN – a subject of local interest – and was frequently interviewed by local media. He liked to be accompanied by one of his staff, not only on account of the periodical need for assistance, but also because he did not like eating alone and preferred company.[75]

His extensive travels included visits to Sikkim, Bhutan, and the North East Frontier Agency, as well as to the Kingdom of Nepal, to which he was also accredited. He travelled to the south and spoke to the Indian Army Staff College at Wellington. He had frequent contact with Indian defence officials. Much of this was about Australia's military assistance, and involvement in joint air force exercises. In a rare gesture towards a Western diplomat, he was invited to lecture at India's National Defence College.

Early in 1965 the Indian army allowed Plimsoll to visit their most forward formations facing Chinese military units in the Himalayas, and to talk to Indian commanders and their officers. Not wanting to encourage other diplomats to seek the same opportunity, Plimsoll was asked not to mention where he had been.[76] The consensus from a number of frank discussions with army officers of various levels was that US involvement in Vietnam was beneficial for India by diverting China and reducing Chinese military pressure on India. Plimsoll told Averell Harriman, US Under-Secretary of State, who was visiting from Washington, that he had found "senior officers all of the view that Americans must not get out of Vietnam," but that "a stable political regime had to be found quickly or there would be no base to support and build on: repeated coups were doing immense harm" internationally.[77]

In May 1964 he made a mildly daring visit to Goa, the Portuguese enclave which India had wrested by force in December 1961. Afterwards he issued a statement about "my first visit to this part of India", which constituted a public reference to Australia's recognition. In doing so Plimsoll made possibly the first visit to Goa by a foreign head of mission. There might have been some sensitivity about this in Canberra as Australia, along with many others, had been critical of the invasion. His visit established recognition of the fact – a typical example of taking a pro-India position.[78] Plimsoll may not have sought Canberra's permission first, but probably felt safe in acting as he did. He was disappointed at the lack of reaction from Canberra to his report on the visit.[79]

The Portuguese protested in Canberra that the statement said "Goa was part of India; it gave the impression that the Portuguese had neglected the churches; and it gave the impression that economic conditions in Goa today were better than under the Portuguese". Plimsoll readily acknowledged that the Portuguese were right on all three counts.[80] This was Plimsoll being mischievous; he probably took some secret pleasure in annoying the Portuguese, with whom he had had the odd brush in New York over their colonial policies. He also did it to please the Indians – who instantly publicised the statement. Generally, however, Plimsoll's enthusiasm for India did not cause him to push Australia in any direction that Canberra did not want to go.[81]

Visit to Korea

On 17 December 1963 Plimsoll attended the inauguration of the democratically-elected President of the Republic of Korea. Given that federal elections at home on 30 November would make it difficult to spare a suitable senior minister, and that there was then no Australian ambassador in place in Seoul, Plimsoll with his "past distinguished connection with Korea" represented the Government. Further, it was felt that en route it would be "timely and fruitful" for him to have talks with the Japanese on developing contacts between Japan and India, given Canberra's wish to foster such relations.[82]

Departure

When the announcement came of Plimsoll's appointment as secretary, the decision had been successfully kept under wraps for nearly nine months. Hasluck had expressed concern to Plimsoll about maintaining secrecy about the appointment so as not to spoil the smooth working of the department in Canberra. Plimsoll, who typed his reply himself, said that he had his own reasons for keeping things under wraps. "I would find any leakage, or too early an announcement, an impediment to my own work here;" he worried about becoming a lame duck in Delhi.[83]

Plimsoll was deeply sorry to leave India: after only two years, he still felt he had barely "scratched the surface". In a speech shortly before departure, he expressed "regret that I am leaving at this stage. It is not my own choice that I am leaving. I have been very happy in India". He concluded by saying that he would "remain a friend of India. The problems of India will continue to concern me".[84] These words went beyond normal politeness: in an earlier letter to Tange he said he was leaving "with great pangs. For the past year I have been conscious of 'Time's winged chariot hurrying near' and that I am living on borrowed time. I could happily have lived in India for many years to come". In his later roles, especially as secretary, Plimsoll continued to try to foster Australia's relationship with India.

Compared to his predecessors, Plimsoll's time in Delhi saw "the greatest progress made in building a relationship of understanding, partly because the circumstances were more propitious and partly because of his sensitive appreciation of Indian culture, his understanding of the Asian mind, and the skill and dedication which he brought to the diplomatic task".[85] In the event, it was to be more than 30 years before the relationship broadened significantly, and that came about mainly as business in both countries became stronger and more outward-looking. But Plimsoll, and then Tange after him,[86] laid the foundations for an effective dialogue between two governments of a very different nature and often with divergent international outlooks.

Endnotes

1 Sir Hugh Foot (later Lord Caradon), UK Permanent Representative in New York to JP, 16/12/1964. JP papers. Box 5, Item 53, NAA.

2 Alan Reid, "Barwick and the Plimsoll line. A shortage of diplomats", *The Bulletin*, 16/3/1963, 6-7.

3 Paul Gore Booth, *With Great Truth and Respect*, Constable, London, 1974, 306. He was UK High Commissioner in New Delhi at the same time as Plimsoll.

4 Ibid., 299.

5 Waller to JP, 8/3/1963, JP papers, Box 4, Item 39, NAA.

6 Sir Keith Waller, *A Diplomatic Life – Some Memories, Australians in Asia*, Griffith University, 1990, 32-3.

7 Barwick to JP, 22/2/1963, A9749/1, NAA.

8 Waller to JP, 8/3/1963; *A Diplomatic Life*, 32-3.

9 JP to McNicol (High Commissioner to Pakistan,) 28/3/1963. JP papers, Box 4, Item 45, NAA.

10 UN 1578 of 2/11/1962, and EUN 3470 of 5/11/1962. JP papers, DFAT.

11 *Reminiscential Conversations between Hon Clyde Cameron and Sir James Plimsoll 1984*. TRC 1967, ii, 383.

12 Cam/Plim, ii, 384.

13 Cam/Plim, ii, 382-4.

14 Cam/Plim, ii, 382.

15 Cam/Plim, ii, 172.

16 Casey added that "one of the most certain ways to get shot would be to offer to mediate in this impossible situation". Casey diary, 3/12/1963 – attaching letter of 23/12/1963, which he copied to Plimsoll. JP papers, Box 4, Item 47, NAA.

17 Sir Owen Dixon to JP, 18/6/1963. JP papers, Box 4, Item 42, NAA.

18 JP to Dixon, 1/4/1964. Dixon Papers, courtesy JD Merralls.

19 Bunting to JP, JP papers, DFAT.

20 Hazel Craig, conversation, 14/9/1999.

21 WRC, Jnl, 18/2/1958, vii, 1486; and Crocker conversation, 4/11/1998.

22 B.C. Hill, conversation, 17/8/1997.

23 WRC, Jnl, 3/6/1962, xi, 2716.

24 The Dutch Ambassador in Canberra "tried unsuccessfully to interrogate me on why Plimsoll had not returned to Canberra, as everyone was expecting, to head the Department, and how Tange had managed to stay on. He said they all knew that Tange does not want to give up his post but they could not understand how he had succeeded". WRC, Jnl, 8/3/1963, xii, 2869.

25 WRC, Jnl, 26/3/1963, xii, 2886-7.

26 Barwick, conversation, 2/11/1996.

27 Peter Edwards, *Arthur Tange – Last of the Mandarins*, Allen and Unwin, Sydney, 2006, 141-2.

28 JP diary, April 1963.

29 Barwick, conversation, 2/11/1996.

30 WRC, Jnl, 23/4/1963, xii, 2916-7; JP diary, 21-23/4/63. Plimsoll had received a letter from Bunting shortly after arriving in Delhi, speculating that Menzies might call an election at the end of 1963, a year earlier than required. Bunting to JP, 25/3/1963, JP papers, Box 4, Item 36, NAA. In fact the elections were held on 30 November 1963.

31 Crocker to JP, 2/6/1963. JP papers, Box 4, Item 39, NAA.

32 Tange was pleased to be given a choice, and indicated that he would like New Delhi, having become fascinated by what he had observed during a visit while Plimsoll was there. Barwick, conversation, 2/11/1996. Edwards, *Tange*, 141-2. Tange had told McIntyre of his delight about New Delhi, "the post I sought and which will give me the kind of relief from tension, after something over 11 years". McIntyre to JP, 22/2/1965. JP papers, Box 5, Item 60, NAA.

33 Hasluck to A.W. Martin 13/1/1988 – copy courtesy Martin. As Menzies's daughter, Heather Henderson, recalls it, Menzies genuinely felt that 10 years in the job of secretary was too long for anyone. At a personal level Menzies liked, and was friends with, both Tange and his wife. H. Henderson, conversation, 20/2/05.

34 Hasluck to JP, 22/5/1964. JP papers, DFAT.

35 JP to McIntyre, 15/3/1965, JP papers, Box 5, Item 6, NAA.

36 JP to Hasluck, 16/6/1964. JP papers, DFAT.

37 JP to McIntyre, 15/3/1965. JP papers, Box 5, Item 6, NAA.

38 Burton was aged 31, Watt 49, and Tange 39, respectively, on becoming secretary.

39 Letter from Father, 9/6/1964. JP papers, DFAT.
40 Waller to JP, 25/6/1964. JP papers, Box 5, Item 53, NAA.
41 Hasluck to JP, 30/7/1964, JP papers, DFAT.
42 JP diary, 27/2/1964.
43 Tange to JP, cables 129 and 180 to Delhi of 27/2/1964, and 25/3/1964. JP papers, Box 4, Item 51, NAA.
44 C.V. Narasimhan to JP, 20/3/64. JP papers, Box 5, Item 53, NAA.
45 Hay to Tange, Ottawa cable 50 of 14/2/1964. JP personnel file, DFAT.
46 M.J. Cook, letter, 24/08/2006. He heard this from Dick Pedersen, No.3 in the US Mission in New York.
47 Bunting to JP, 25/3/1963. JP papers, Box 4, Item 36, NAA.
48 Plimsoll to Sir Guy Powles, a New Zealand colleague from FEC days, 27/3/1963. JP Papers, Box 4, Item 36, NAA.
49 "I am ever conscious of my own inability to come to grips with India and Pakistan." Jockel to JP, 26/8/1964. Waller (FAS) and Jockel (AS) were responsible for both South-East Asia and the Indian sub-continent. JP papers, Box 5, Item 53, NAA.
50 Cable 0.16057 of 11/9/1962. A1838/346 677/6/4, NAA.
51 JP memo of 3/8/1964. A1838 3107/40/114, NAA.
52 Bunting/Tange letter. JP to Crocker, 11/12/64. JP papers Box 5, Item 53, NAA. "I am extremely tired. Although the doctor had prescribed a month's complete break away from the office, this seems almost impossible". Menzies to Stirling, 11/12/1964. Stirling papers, DFAT.
53 JP diary. Tange to JP, 1/9/1964. JP papers, Box 5, Item 53, NAA.
54 JP to Bunting, 11/12/1964, Bunting to JP, 4/12/1964. JP papers, Box 5, Item 53 NAA.
55 He consoled Owen Davis, Ambassador in Rio de Janeiro, that "our first hand contact with the Department is no greater than yours in Rio". JP to Davis, 14/8/1964, JP papers, Box 5, Item 53, NAA.
56 It was Tange who was to be there for the India-Pakistan war late in 1965, six months after Plimsoll's departure.
57 Tange expressed concern lest Plimsoll try "to do too much in the hot season". Tange to JP, 1/7/1963. JP papers, Box 4, Item 40, NAA. JP diary, March/April 1963.

58 Pritchett, M.E. Lyon, First Secretary, and an aid official in the High Commission.

59 Cam/Plim, ii, 159, 382.

60 Apart from his periods of shuttling into Washington from New York during 1949-50.

61 M.L. Johnston, Deputy High Commissioner, Delhi, conversation, 7/2/1997.

62 R.J. Smith, conversation, 11/11/99.

63 Plimsoll also informed him that he had just bought a copy of the Professor's book on the English literary critic, F.R. Leavis. JP to Narasimhaiah, 17/6/64. JP papers, Box 4, Item 45, NAA.

64 C.D. Narasimhaiah (ed), University of Mysore, "An introduction to Australian Literature", *The Literary Criterion*, Jacaranda Press, Milton Qld, 1965. Foreword, v-x.

65 R.J. Smith, conversation.

66 Plimsoll, Memo 1028 29/6/64. JP papers, Box 5, Item 53, NAA.

67 T.N. Kaul, letter, 3/6/1998. Courtesy R.S. Laurie, High Commissioner.

68 Cam/Plim, i, 388-389.

69 Plimsoll, New Delhi Despatch No. 1, 27/3/1965.

70 Zakir Husein to JP, 6/4/1964. JP papers, Box 5, Item 53, NAA. The book was *The Emerging World – Jawaharlal Nehru Memorial Volume*, Asia Publishing House, Bombay 1964.

71 JP to Tange, 15/5/1964, and Inward cable 280 to New Delhi of 21/5/1964. JP papers, Box 5, Item 53, NAA.

72 Letter of 29/5/1961, quoted in *The Modern Ambassador – the Challenge and the Search*, Martin F. Herz (ed), Institute for the Study of Diplomacy, Georgetown University, Washington DC, 1983, 182-4.

73 JP to Horne, 11/6/1944, Donald Horne Papers.

74 R.J. Smith, conversation. He accompanied Plimsoll on some of his journeys.

75 R.J. Smith, conversation.

76 Crocker thought Plimsoll's visit represented "not only a change in [the Indians'] attitude but also what a remarkable standing you have managed to get with the people who matter". Crocker to JP, 2/4/1965. JP papers, Box 5, Item 60, NAA.

77 I.9106 of 5/3/1965, A1838/2, 250/9/1 Pt 6, NAA.
78 M.L. Johnston, conversation.
79 JP to Crocker, 19/6/1964, JP papers, Box 5, Item 53, NAA.
80 JP to Bowles, 24/12/1964, JP papers, Box 5, Item 53, NAA.
81 M.L. Johnston, conversation.
82 Loveday to Minister, 20/11/1963, JP Personnel file, DFAT.
83 JP to Hasluck, 16/6/1964, JP papers, DFAT.
84 Speech on "Australia and India" to India International Centre, New Delhi, 23/3/1965. JP papers, DFAT.
85 Gordon Greenwood, "Australian foreign policy in action", in *Australia in World Affairs 1961-65*, Gordon Greenwood and Norman Harper (eds), FW Cheshire, Melbourne, 1968, 73.
86 Edwards, *Tange*, 157-68.

Official portrait as Secretary (DFAT)

7

The Dutiful Secretary
Canberra, 1965-70

*His combination of modesty, almost humility, with courage
and intellect, is striking.*[1]

Plimsoll had not taken any leave for nearly three years and, although about to become Secretary, the most difficult task, he still did not. He returned from India on a weekend. After staying overnight at the family home in Bondi he flew to Canberra, resumed residence in the Hotel Canberra, and went straight into the job on Monday 5 April 1965.[2] He was driven by a sense of duty although reluctant and concerned about his suitability. His appointment, however, had been well-received on both sides of politics and in the media, while in the department there was an air of expectation about someone already widely known and respected. Without fanfare he took up occupation of the secretary's suite, complete with private secretary, personal assistant and a walk-in filing safe, and direct lines to the minister, the prime minister and the secretary, Prime Minister's Department.

In the six years since he had last worked there the growing department had relocated to the Administration Building, now the Sir John Gorton Building, which it shared with other agencies, notably Defence, Trade, and Attorney-General's. He was supported by one deputy secretary (Sir Laurence McIntyre), and four first assistant secretaries. Responsibilities included Australia's aid programme, and the Antarctic Division which was located in Melbourne. There were small offices in Sydney, Melbourne and Perth and, beyond that, 45 posts overseas.

As secretary, Plimsoll worked extremely hard, including weekends and evenings.[3] He hardly took any leave. He had a week's absence following the death of his father.

Having spent most of his career abroad Plimsoll's instincts were more those of a diplomat than of a Canberra-based public servant. Unlike others in the job, he spent much time with the diplomatic corps, attended their dinners and national day receptions, included them in his own dinners, attended their presentations of credentials at Government House and signed condolence books on the deaths of their leaders.

Prime Ministers

As secretary Plimsoll was confronted by a succession of prime ministers. Although the department's minister is the secretary's first concern, the prime minister looms large as well. For Plimsoll personally, one of the most positive aspects of becoming secretary was the prospect of working closely with Menzies again. But in January 1966, aged 71, Sir Robert retired. He told Plimsoll: "I just could not keep on going. I was too tired."[4]

After 16 years of Menzies, there were five successors in the next decade.[5] They came and went in unusual ways: Holt (1966-67) disappeared, presumed drowned; Gorton (1968-71) voted himself out of office; McMahon (1971-72) suffered electoral defeat (the only conventional departure); and Whitlam (1972-75), dismissed by the Governor General, who immediately commissioned the next one, Fraser (1975-83).

Holt's enthusiasm for foreign affairs was not always matched by understanding of the issues involved.[6] Plimsoll considered he was "the worst PM he had dealt with", as he "could not comprehend, let alone absorb, the detail of Australian foreign policy. Couldn't make head nor tail of his daily cables".[7] Hasluck recalled that Australia was "well served during this period by a triumvirate of very good top public servants in Plimsoll, Hicks (Secretary, Defence) and Bunting and they worked very closely together on the shaping and application of policy". With

Hasluck, these three "succeeded in avoiding many dangers and turning [Holt's] thoughts towards reality" and "the major issues".[8]

In 1965 Plimsoll had recommended postponing any decision to open an embassy in Taiwan: "We have gone as long as this without one, and I do not see any great disadvantage in continuing without one. Australia's support for Nationalist China has been demonstrated firmly and continually".[9] But new and unbriefed, Holt personally committed Australia to set up an embassy.[10] At the Commonwealth Prime Ministers' meeting in London in 1966, Plimsoll recalled that on Rhodesia, when Holt arrived, "he was completely pro-white government, and I had many goes at him to pull him more towards centre. But he was a very impressionable man, and within a few days he'd swung so much to the other extreme that I was working hard to bring him back to the middle".[11] In the end, "Australia came out of the meeting well". Holt said very little

With Paul Hasluck, Australian Minister for External Affairs, at talks in Tel Aviv in 1966 with Abba Eban (far right), Foreign Minister of Israel. To Plimsoll's right are Bill Landale, Ambassador to Israel, and Geoff Bentley, Acting P/A to Hasluck (Israel Foreign Ministry)

on Rhodesia, which, as Plimsoll told Crocker, was "the best thing he could have done".[12]

It was the affair of the VIP planes that "got out of hand because of Harold Holt's incompetence; he would not stop talking about it". This brought Gorton favourably into public view. Plimsoll recalled that dissatisfaction with Holt's leadership was building within the party.[13] In the evening of 17 December 1967, when Holt disappeared while swimming in the ocean, Plimsoll attended a small dinner, along with Hasluck and Senator and Mrs Gorton, at the New Zealand High Commissioner's residence. Over a game of scrabble Gorton and Hasluck agreed they would each be candidates to succeed Holt. Plimsoll then let them discuss the leadership in private.[14]

Plimsoll had first met Gorton as chairman of the Parliamentary Foreign Affairs Committee in the 1950s. During 1960-61, while Menzies was also Minister for External Affairs, Gorton was Minister Assisting. From July 1965 to December 1967 Gorton's service as Acting Minister at various times,[15] in regular contact with Plimsoll, helped towards a good working relationship as prime minister. Plimsoll recalled, however, that Gorton would go on "frolics of his own", without consulting ministers, made "off the cuff decisions," was "stubborn", sometimes did things simply to "shock people", and "tired easily". But he had "great qualities" and Plimsoll felt he always got on well with him. Although they had a number of disagreements, Gorton "never held it against me".[16] One example was when Gorton wanted the deputy in a post moved. Plimsoll refused, saying such a staffing matter was for the department. Gorton did not like it but Plimsoll "heard no more about it".[17]

For Gorton's first visit to Washington as prime minister in 1968, unusually Plimsoll as secretary was not included in the small accompanying party. After media reports of problems with Plimsoll and of Gorton's contempt for the department, Gorton contacted Plimsoll to say these reports were without foundation, that Washington would be a "brief visit, fairly definite subjects" and he could get all the necessary advice and assistance from Waller and the embassy. But in future, "if ever I go overseas and you would like to come, just let me know, and you can come". Plimsoll accompanied him on two subsequent journeys to Washington, and on other visits.[18]

In July 1968 a Russian prawn fishing vessel, the *Van Gogh*, was in the Gulf of Carpentaria. This led to concerns in Canberra for Australian fishing boats in the area. Gorton, a former Minister for the Navy, wanted the nearest RAN vessel to be authorised in certain circumstances to "put a shot across its bows". The Chief of Naval Staff, Vice-Admiral Victor Smith, told Gorton that this could be done, but that it would be recorded as contrary to the advice of himself and Plimsoll. Gorton eventually reconsidered.[19]

Hasluck

More challenging than prime ministers were the three ministers Plimsoll served in five years: Hasluck for nearly four years, Freeth for nine months and then McMahon for just over eight months.

Hasluck was relieved to find on becoming minister that Plimsoll would become secretary because, apart from knowing him well, he had hoped for someone other than a former working colleague in the department in his own time there, like Waller, McIntyre, or Tange.[20] This was one factor that underlay difficulties between Hasluck and Tange during the year until Plimsoll took over. Tange, after ten years as Secretary, had strong views about the department's role, whereas Hasluck considered it had limited functions: officers were not to volunteer policy advice. Tange fell out with Hasluck, and felt that he had little influence during the last six months.[21]

After Barwick's warm manner towards his officials, Hasluck was like an iceberg. Hasluck kept the department "as far beyond arm's length as possible",[22] seeming almost to disdain public servants; while most ministers felt they greatly depended on loyalty and service from their department, and sought close contact. He once said that his door was always open to ministerial colleagues, then to MPs, then the general public and last to the department.[23] His attitude was influenced by his earlier experience of Evatt's intrusive approach as minister.[24] Hasluck dispensed with the usual seconded junior officer to act as his private secretary, except during 1967.[25] He dispensed with briefings before receiving foreign ambassadors, and with having a departmental officer with him, dictating his own records of conversation.

Normally Hasluck communicated with the department in writing, through the secretary.[26] Some messages had a suspicious, almost venomous tone. In one, about proposed five-power consultations on the South Pacific in 1967, Hasluck said to Plimsoll: "I cannot avoid feeling that the Department in its handling of this matter has been more interested in getting a quick decision out of me than in helping me to make the right decision."[27] Being the principal channel of communication with the minister took up time that Plimsoll might have spent better. He found himself carrying out the role of a super personal assistant, personally checking on the department's arrangements for the minister's international travel and, when Hasluck was visiting his electorate in Perth, watching for interesting overseas media reports to forward. Such acts were second nature to Plimsoll, having previously worked closely with ministers, yet it was a diversion from what he might more properly have been doing.

When in Canberra Hasluck received Plimsoll in his office just once a week,[28] and never saw him for a meal or a drink by himself. Plimsoll, who earlier had been on first name terms with Hasluck, ceased this practice.[29]

There was a Jekyll and Hyde aspect to Hasluck. In contrast to the impressions of those in Canberra who saw him, or dealt with him by way of written submissions, officers in posts saw a positive, even charming, side to him.[30] Hasluck regularly presided over heads of mission meetings overseas, "with commendable lightness and urbanity" as one ambassador recorded of the 1965 European HOMs meeting in Rome.[31]

Earlier Casey, writing to Plimsoll, had alluded to possible problems: "I hope that you'll manage somehow or other to get along with Hasluck".[32]

Plimsoll and Hasluck with Australia's Heads of Mission in South East Asia, Manila 1968. From left to right: Plimsoll, Allan Eastman (Kuala Lumpur), John Ryan (Vientiane), Max Loveday (Jakarta), Lewis Border (Saigon), David McNicol (Bangkok), Alfred Parsons (Singapore), Hasluck, Francis Stuart (Manila), and Noel Deschamps (Phnom Penh (DEAT)

Plimsoll could not have appreciated Hasluck's curious, aloof approach, and disdain of his own department, yet the two of them seemed to accommodate one another. Plimsoll felt "very close" to Hasluck.[33] In later years Plimsoll kept in touch with him, and sprang to his defence at "even the most muted criticism".[34] As for Hasluck, the regard that he already had for Plimsoll[35] grew on closer acquaintance, noting that Plimsoll was one of a small number of senior public servants of whom Menzies had "a high opinion;" that Plimsoll exemplified officials "who pressed their own views strongly up to the point of Cabinet decision but kept discreet silence about official matters".[36] Hasluck described Plimsoll as "a dedicated, selfless, diligent, thoughtful, considerate and unassuming man deeply concerned about the effect, the final outcome of whatever he was doing". He "thought about what should be done and what could be done, he thought about what would serve the interests of Australia or best help in meeting the objectives of policy or establish a sound principle". He was "a great Australian".[37]

Despite his attitude towards the department at large, Hasluck respected and frequently sought Plimsoll's advice, often asking him not to discuss an issue with anyone else. For preparing his parliamentary statements Hasluck's "usual method" was to discuss with Plimsoll the matters to be covered, draft something himself from departmental briefing papers, then discuss it with Plimsoll, or send it to him.[38] They had in common that both were very upright, expecting the highest standards of conduct and behaviour,[39] and shared a special interest in Papua New Guinea.[40]

When Tange was secretary Hasluck had wanted to have a say in the selection of a new deputy in Washington. Tange refused, insisting that, as permanent head, appointment of staff overseas, other than heads of mission, was his responsibility. On becoming secretary Plimsoll told Hasluck he accepted that, given the importance of Washington, the minister should have a say – just as he would expect Hasluck to consult him about head of mission appointments, even though this was the minister's responsibility. Plimsoll suggested Furlonger: Hasluck talked to him and agreed.[41]

Hasluck liked Plimsoll to accompany him abroad. This was contrary to normal practice whereby the secretary accompanied the prime minister, while the appropriate senior officer in the department accompanied the minister. Plimsoll did some of both. Hasluck also had Plimsoll represent him at the UN in New York (see below under "McMahon"). Early in 1967 Tange expressed to Plimsoll his concern at the extent of the latter's absences abroad. "When the minister is abroad the secretary should be at home". Plimsoll was "going to have a dissatisfied department and a disorganised one – if the minister is allowed to use you like a private secretary, or personal envoy".[42]

Tange had a point but it was Plimsoll, not Tange, who had to work with Hasluck. The job of secretary varies according to the incumbent and the minister. There is much in the relationship between the two "which is essentially personal and which overlies the formal requirements of their relative positions".⁴³ Accompanying Hasluck internationally provided Plimsoll opportunity to talk to someone unreachable at home. Also, Plimsoll thrived when working overseas; he was abroad for nine weeks on two trips in 1965; for eight weeks (two trips) in 1966; for seven weeks (two) in 1967; for 10 weeks (five) in 1968; and 11 weeks in 1969 (five).⁴⁴

In his own way Plimsoll could be quietly devious. In 1966, Hasluck, frustrated that the department was unable to control the content of Radio Australia broadcasts, tried to have Radio Australia separated from the ABC, moved to Canberra and put under the department's control. He instructed Plimsoll to prepare a submission. But Plimsoll resisted. Whether he found this offensive to freedom of speech, or was concerned about the additional burden on the department is not clear. Plimsoll put the draft ministerial submission in his filing cabinet. "Inactivity can be a policy," he told a colleague. Hasluck did not raise the matter again.⁴⁵

Policy matters

After six years abroad, in New York and New Delhi, what view of the world did Plimsoll bring to the task? Relatively young at 48, perhaps more than any other incumbent he had been steeped in UN work;⁴⁶ bringing to bear expertise in the UN, while realistic about its limitations. His UN experience had led to understanding of the African scene and its implications; and to a realisation of how little time would remain before independence for PNG. With regard to India, at the 1967 officials talks in New Delhi, Plimsoll, as leader, monopolised the talking, while Tange, as high commissioner, sat back with "a tolerant smile". Plimsoll was eager, and felt at home.⁴⁷ Plimsoll's New Delhi posting cemented for him the "great importance" to Australia of India;⁴⁸ and, together with his experience in Korea, reinforced his cautious approach to China. A latent interest in the Soviet Union, and how it might be helpful in relation to China, also emerged. As he had at the UN, Plimsoll made it his business to keep abreast in detail of all current international issues. As a contemporary recalled, Plimsoll was the last secretary who could personally advise ministers on any current issue. He was almost "a self-sufficient foreign service in himself".[49]

In Australia the predominant issue was involvement in the Vietnam War. The decision to commit Australian combat forces was taken before Plimsoll returned, and Vietnam was not a subject in which, at his level, he was greatly engaged. Outwardly loyal and supportive, he kept his personal views to himself. In public speeches he spoke about China, the UN, or Australian foreign policy, but not Vietnam specifically. Crocker thought he detected reservations during private talks with Plimsoll as secretary. Plimsoll himself knew of Crocker's own reservations about the Government's policy. In a conversation in 1966, Crocker noted:

> In his praise of [President] Kennedy and his comparison with [President]Johnson, and especially his point that if Kennedy had stayed on as President there would probably not have been this war in Vietnam, I sensed that Plimsoll doesn't like the war. (We didn't discuss Vietnam. He knows my point of view).[50]

In another conversation in 1967: "By tacit consent we keep off Vietnam. He knows my attitude but naturally can't agree with it."[51] Plimsoll's view, if Crocker was right, was not surprising. Diplomats naturally prefer to achieve national objectives without resort to war. Plimsoll was protective of any officers who privately had reservations. Nor, at a time when officers normally went where they were sent, did he insist on anyone serving in Saigon against their will.[52]

He participated in discussions on Vietnam in meetings of the Defence Committee, with the Secretary of Defence (Sir Edwin Hicks, then Sir Henry Bland), the service chiefs, and the secretaries of Prime Minister's and Treasury. He knew them all from his earlier time in Canberra. One of these recalled Plimsoll's "moderating influence".[53] The

Committee was concerned about the broader picture: the deployment of Australia's limited forces in the region as a whole, given Australia's other continuing ADF involvements in Malaysia, and in the defence of Papua New Guinea.[54] This problem was exacerbated by the British decision in 1967 to withdraw its forces east of Suez, forcing "a reconsideration of the basis" of Australian foreign policy.[55] The intentions of the US in the region after Vietnam would be critical, but Plimsoll advised the Committee that the US would not express a view before the war's end.[56]

General Sir Michael Carver, UK Commander-in-Chief Far East, had dealings with both Plimsoll and Bland over the planned UK withdrawal. Carver found Bland "tough, aggressive and sometimes rude", whereas, while Plimsoll was "just as firm" as Bland in defending Australia's position, his approach was "always helpful, sympathetic and courteous", while also showing he was "a complete master of the subjects".[57]

Plimsoll's general approach was much influenced by a view of China as unpredictable and a potential threat to the region. Although such thinking was common, Plimsoll's views were perhaps more strongly held following personal experience in Korea and in India, given China's incursions in both. Nehru had told Plimsoll that the Chinese had said to him that "they could suffer hundreds of millions of casualties and deaths in a nuclear war and still survive, whereas other countries could not".[58] In October 1965, speaking at the UN General Assembly, Plimsoll said that the Chinese "flaunt" to the Asian region "their capacity and their willingness to contemplate nuclear war". They said "every country should have its own nuclear weapons".[59] In 1969 he said that China had long shown "aggressive tendencies". Finding a way to bring China into "the international community" was "not something that is going to be achieved in any single act. We do not believe that simply recognising Peking or admitting it to the UN would in itself bring an end to the problems posed by China".[60]

The China factor was among a number of reasons that Plimsoll adduced in advocating that Australia sign the Nuclear Non-proliferation

Treaty (NPT), at a time when some were advocating that Australia become a nuclear power itself. In the Defence Committee early in 1968 Plimsoll emphasised that it would be bad for relations with the US and for its impact on Australian public opinion if Australia seemed to be trying to prevent a treaty. An attempt to strengthen the ANZUS Treaty as a condition for Australia signing the NPT was a non-starter in the present mood of the US Congress, but, in any case, "the real basis of security was not simply a legal treaty, important though that was, but the development of mutual trust and cooperation between Australia and the US". He was concerned also about the effect that a decision to adopt a nuclear weapons programme would have on Australia's conventional force capability.[61] In a note to Hasluck, Plimsoll summarised the advantages of signing the NPT: prevention of proliferation, providing restraints not only on Australia but on others such as Indonesia, contribution to worldwide peaceful coexistence, and cooperation between the US and USSR in handling China.[62]

On the evening 15 April 1965 Menzies, in checking his speech to the House of Representatives announcing the committal of the first Australian infantry battalion to Vietnam, felt that it did not explain adequately why Australia was doing this. Plimsoll, who was with him, immediately wrote out a passage about the downward thrust of Chinese communism. Plimsoll was later criticised for this passage, although Menzies chose not to use Plimsoll's exact words in his speech.[63]

During the India-Pakistan war in 1965 over the Rann of Kutch dispute, Plimsoll informed Tange in Delhi that cabinet considered it "reasonable that India should want assurances that Kashmir is not going to be exposed to Chinese penetration or be defenceless against China". The close association between Pakistan and China "makes [cabinet] less sympathetic towards Pakistan gaining the Valley of Kashmir. But the same preoccupation about China makes them fear that, if Pakistan were to find itself losing, it might turn to Peking for assistance".[64]

Plimsoll shared the view that if North Vietnam took over the South, the regional consequences would be disastrous. He did not believe in the domino theory as such, but felt communism of the Chinese variety would be strengthened. If communism triumphed in Vietnam, it could tip the balance for the Communist Party in Indonesia. There were uncertainties about what the Cultural Revolution in China portended.[65]

The United Nations

At the UN several issues called for delicate handling: notably China, Australia's administration of PNG, and southern Africa. Hasluck was well versed in the UN, a consequence of his earlier experience in the department[66] and his long period with ministerial responsibility for PNG, but he had high regard for Plimsoll's UN virtuosity, and delegated much to him.

In 1965 Plimsoll led the Australian delegation at the UN General Assembly.[67] Hasluck cabled that Plimsoll's speech in the general debate had been "well received here and also expressed our views with strength and balance".[68] A year later, with Hasluck required at home for the elections, Plimsoll again led the delegation.[69] In other years Plimsoll accompanied Hasluck on short visits to the General Assembly and remained after Hasluck's departure.

On return from the UN General Assembly in 1965, in a note about Australia's position in the UN, Plimsoll said that given sensitivity to the charge that Australia was a "running dog" of the US, "while Australia's policies normally coincide with those of the US, they do not always come from the same reasons. We gain more support and understanding from other members in the UN if we can make them see that we are adopting positions as a result of our independent assessment of our own interests". Secondly, given the continuing need to defend Australia's administration of PNG, "Australia should look for issues where it can take positive and forward-looking stances" because on other issues it would "often be taking positions that can be represented as unduly restrictive or reactionary" such as on colonial questions.[70] Hasluck agreed about conclusions reached independently from the Americans; and that Australia should "try to help make American decisions as wise as human decision can be". He nevertheless conceded that "we have damaged our prospects of success along these lines by giving the impression that we have no critical discretion of our own".[71]

Plimsoll and the Australian permanent representative, Patrick Shaw, were on good terms, and Plimsoll, used to operating on his own, posed little burden to the mission. With his own standing at the UN, as well as being unofficially Hasluck's personal representative, he had access to the Secretary-General, the US Secretary of State, and the UK Foreign Secretary and other senior visitors to the General Assembly.[72] At the UN in October 1965, during the buildup to Rhodesia's Unilateral Declaration of Independence, Plimsoll talked on three occasions with the Foreign Secretary, Michael Stewart, with Dean Rusk participating in the last of these meetings.[73]

Plimsoll approached African issues from a different perspective from the Government. In October 1965 Plimsoll prophesied to Hasluck that Smith's UDI regime was "doomed". However long it took, "the Africans will never relax their pressures; subversion and terrorism will grow. Rhodesia will become another Algeria, if not another Congo". Since 1962 Australia had consistently said that the objective in Rhodesia should be a government and society with equal opportunities regardless of race and colour.[74] In a speech in Melbourne in November, Plimsoll spoke of "the strength of feeling that inevitably grips Africans when they see other Africans still under domination by Europeans and with little prospect of moving to independence or equality".[75] He could not always bring the Government along with him. Hasluck resisted his suggestion that Alex Quaison-Sackey, Foreign Minister of Ghana and earlier its permanent representative with Plimsoll in New York, be invited to visit Australia. Hasluck wanted to avoid inviting African politicians "until they have settled down a bit and learned a few more facts of life".[76]

In 1966, at the General Assembly, there was a proposal to declare that South Africa's mandate for South West Africa (later Namibia) no longer existed, and for the UN to take it over. Western countries were opposed; Hasluck cabled to Plimsoll that the Government also was against such a declaration. But, he qualified, "you have of course discretion to vote differently if you think you should," a discretion Plimsoll exercised. He explained Australia's vote by saying that, in contrast to PNG, which Australia was bringing to self-determination under the UN Charter, for over 50 years South Africa had failed to do this, and accepted no obligation to do so.[77]

Papua New Guinea

Plimsoll foresaw increasing UN pressure for early independence for PNG. Independence "would come sooner than many thought".[78] He favoured a more liberal approach to PNG's constitutional development than many in Canberra, for example in establishing indigenous ministerial authority in Port Moresby sooner rather than later: "If they are going to make some mistakes, it is well for them to do so while we are still there to help patch up again."[79] From 1965 Plimsoll was urging the Department of Territories in Canberra to increase the exposure overseas of PNG politicians and senior officials,[80] and to start training a PNG foreign service.[81]

In 1968 Plimsoll predicted to the Defence Committee that Australian defence aid to PNG "will probably still be needed" after independence. Its defence "should be seen as part of the defence of Australia".[82] In 1969, in a committee discussion about possible deployment of the Pacific Islands Regiment, following problems in Bougainville, Plimsoll warned of "incalculable" international reactions in response to police or army action by a colonial administration, especially in the event of deaths. There would also be repercussions in Australia. It would be undesirable for Bougainville to secede; and the UN would "not be sympathetic" to the idea of a "breakaway," as it had shown over Katanga and Biafra. But all this could change if a riot led to deaths.[83]

Explaining foreign policy

In Australia there was increased domestic interest in foreign policy, following decisions to introduce conscription at the end of 1964, and to deploy combat forces in Vietnam from 1965. Unlike many of his public service contemporaries, Plimsoll was active in public relations.

Hasluck realised the importance for the Government to promote "a more thoughtful approach to the public discussion of foreign policy". This was especially given his belief that "the media . . . are less trustworthy and academic discussion is less objective than ever before in recent Australian history".[84] Plimsoll was of similar view in relation to the media: "The average level of the Canberra press corps is low. Ill-educated and with no knowledge of history." But Plimsoll thought Hasluck was ineffective with the media and despised them to his detriment: "Because he will make no gesture to these arrogant people his political career is being ruined. They are out to kill him."[85]

Hasluck employed the department to compensate for his own shortcomings. Deluged with letters, mainly about Vietnam and Rhodesia, he insisted on individual answers to letters instead of pro forma replies.[86] He also directed the department to produce information pamphlets and volumes of documents about Vietnam. Plimsoll established production of historical documents volumes as a function of the department, in order to provide greater public access. For this task he chose Professor R.G. Neale, a well-regarded historian. An advisory body of independent historians was also appointed to ensure that "documents were being selected in a completely impartial way".[87]

Unlike Hasluck, Plimsoll throughout his career had been accessible and confident with the media although normally on background. Sir John Crawford thought that public explanation of policy was probably "the most tricky part of a Permanent Head's role", but it was necessary to "have contact with real life" by exposure "occasionally to semi and even public debate".[88] This was especially the case in a national capital as isolated as Canberra then was. Plimsoll was one of the few public servants willing to do so at that time.

Hasluck was sensitive to and critical of the role of the department's press relations office,[89] but he allowed Plimsoll considerable latitude. For example, in May 1965 Plimsoll addressed the Parliamentary Joint Committee on Foreign Affairs about the UN;[90] he touched on important issues of foreign policy in a speech about "Australia and Asia" at Sydney University on 10 September; and on 23 November he delivered the 28th A.N. Smith Memorial Lecture in journalism at Melbourne University, about "Asian issues in the Australian press", in which he encouraged a more serious effort by the media to report Asian developments, especially by stationing more Australian journalists in the region. This speech was widely praised, including by Prime Minister Menzies.[91] In the same month Plimsoll appeared in a television documentary about the department along with other officers.

Plimsoll liked informal contact between senior officers of the department and ANU academics interested in international affairs through the Third Monday Group. This was started by Professor Bruce Miller, a contemporary of Plimsoll's at Sydney University. Plimsoll enjoyed the discussions, and participated vigorously. He probed, asked many questions, but was not himself easy to question.[92] Sir Alan Watt praised Plimsoll's involvement since the information available to senior officers "makes it possible for them to influence views of others which are not soundly based".[93]

Plimsoll personally approved the manuscript of Crocker's book, *Australian Ambassador*, about his experiences over 20 years as a head of mission, provided that it was published after Crocker left the service, and did not implicate the department.[94] The book appeared in 1971.

Meals normally combined business and pleasure. He frequently lunched at the Commonwealth Club either with Sir John Bunting or Sir Frederick Wheeler, less often with others, such as Sir Henry Bland. With Len Hewitt, Secretary of the Prime Minister's Department under Gorton, who was not a member of the Commonwealth Club, he periodically had sandwiches in Hewitt's office. He often dined with ANU academics. Occasionally he would dine privately at Government House with the Caseys.[95] He became conscious of his weight, even though he walked to and from the office each day, the equivalent of two kilometres. He weighed himself regularly.[96] He saw visiting friends from university, banking and army days, especially John Kerr.

Like his previous time in Canberra, he did not seek a "private life" as such.[97] He derived relaxation from reading about 80 books a year, attending the theatre and opera, sometimes joining Justice Sir Richard Eggleston of the ACT Supreme Court, and Lady Eggleston. He constantly visited art galleries in Canberra, and in spare moments when interstate and abroad. For someone who spent almost nothing on things for himself, art was an exception. Once, while in New York for the UN General Assembly in 1969, he bought a small item of Indian art for $10,000.[98]

In 1968 Gorton included Plimsoll as the only public servant on the Interim Council of the Australian National Gallery to be established in Canberra.[99] Plimsoll threw himself into this, even when meetings lasted all day. James Mollison, the Gallery's first Director, recalled that Plimsoll was "a supporter of the Australian National Gallery project at a time when supporters were few".[100] His was a quiet, behind the scenes contribution.

He became president of the local Boy Scouts Area Committee for Canberra and Monaro District, succeeding Air Marshal Sir Frederick Scherger. Plimsoll "did an excellent job in that reserved, dry way of his", and performed tasks allotted to him "without hesitation".[101]

As a non-driver and daily walker, Plimsoll suggested some

improvements to Richard Kingsland, Secretary of the Department of the Interior, on behalf of the pedestrian who "is neglected to quite a degree in Canberra".[102]

Management

In 1967 Hasluck sent Plimsoll a 10-page essay on "The future of overseas representation", containing some prescient observations. Australia "today is much lonelier in foreign affairs and necessarily must be more independent than ever before". Hasluck noted the need for more skilled analysts, language specialists, conference delegates, and lawyers. There was "a steadily increasing need for the performance of consular functions overseas". Were present capabilities in all these matters up to the task? Would there be merit in a separate foreign service? He anticipated the need for the department to provide "common services" to all Commonwealth agencies represented at posts.[103]

There is no indication that Hasluck followed up this paper, perhaps hesitant about getting further involved in Plimsoll's responsibilities. Nor is there any indication that Plimsoll showed this paper to anyone else or did anything about it.

As already mentioned, Plimsoll was well aware of his defects in handling management tasks. Before leaving Delhi he had written to McIntyre: "If I am to make a success of my Secretaryship I shall have to try, not so much to run the Department, as to see that it runs."[104] There was no hint of a new broom wanting to reinvigorate an agency that had been under the lead of one person for 11 years. He once quoted approvingly to a colleague, British Prime Minister, Lord Salisbury, as having said that "the time for change is when you can no longer resist it".[105]

Plimsoll did not see himself spending half his time on administration, as had Tange,[106] yet he was conscientious about his obligations. Plimsoll found it difficult to delegate, even to his friend McIntyre, who later commented that it would have been better if Plimsoll had "let me run the routine administration of the Department, but his conscience wouldn't let him do this". He felt obliged to "maintain control over the administration as well as everything else".[107]

There is no indication that Tange consulted Plimsoll about appointing McIntyre as deputy secretary. The selection would have pleased Plimsoll personally, but it was made because Tange could not think where else to put McIntyre. Tange described McIntyre as strong in some respects, good overseas, but "indecisive and feeble on policy innovation and in inter-departmental hurly burly". Somewhat defensively Tange wrote that "I appointed him Deputy Secretary because he had been twelve years abroad and was so senior that I had to put him in that slot."[108] Knowing both Plimsoll and McIntyre as well as he did, was it wise to have two "non-managers" together at the top?

Plimsoll was not decisive enough. Gordon Bilney was temporary personal assistant to Plimsoll at the end of 1969. On his first day he examined four in-trays laden with papers from Plimsoll's walk-in strongroom. Many were marked "urgent" or "decision required in four days", going back years.[109] Plimsoll "was a master of benign neglect": others were not as canny in letting things go.[110] However, he tended to put aside difficult issues. David Anderson once called him "Quintus Fabius[111] Plimsoll" to his face over one instance of dilatoriness. Plimsoll was one for "decisions of gold," reached after mature reflection or agonising, instead of quick decisions or delegating.[112] Crocker thought Plimsoll's indecisiveness was partly a by-product of seeing "too many sides to a question".[113]

With his monastic way of living, and no family responsibilities, Plimsoll did not have the zeal of most of his colleagues for improving conditions of service overseas, although he was sympathetic. Others, accustomed to Tange's style, expected Plimsoll to fight directly for improvements with Sir Frederick Wheeler of the Public Service Board and Sir Richard Randall of Treasury. While he discussed and negotiated with them, it was not Plimsoll's way to be aggressive, especially with two who were friends.

Plimsoll "preferred the Department when it was small and personal", when it had been modestly located at the back end of West Block in Commonwealth Avenue. Now it was a more "layered bureaucracy",[114] a small part of the Administration Building,[115] which it shared with a number of other departments. Plimsoll had no particular enthusiasm for increasing the size of the service.[116] In 1965, when informed that embassy staff in Washington would grow "so large that it will need an additional building", he was appalled.[117] However, pressures for the service to respond to identification of wider Australian interests in Europe and elsewhere led him to accept the need for additional posts abroad, despite staffing constraints.[118] During his tenure as secretary posts opened in Nairobi (1965), Belgrade (1966), Mexico City (1966), Beirut (1967), Malta (1967), Tehran (1968), Lisbon (1970) and Berne (1970). Nearer to home, only Taiwan (1966), which he had opposed, and Bombay (1967) and Calcutta (1970), both of which he supported, were opened.

On the other hand, Plimsoll was more accessible than previous incumbents. He liked to walk about the corridors, especially in evenings or weekends, talking to people. He did not convey a sense of being under pressure. He asked for views and listened, although without indicating if he agreed.[119]

And he took a particular interest in personnel matters. It was in some ways admirable: he directed that if junior members of the department were conscripted for national service, the department should keep in touch with them. One who was injured during training was surprised to get a letter from the secretary.[120] He made time to see every departmental officer of diplomatic rank, including the most junior, on departure or return from postings.

As he had in Canberra in the 1950s, he took a personal interest in selections for graduate entry, interviewing final candidates who were invited to Canberra, and hosting a drinks party for them. Ensuring the best possible entry was important: "You are bringing someone in, a man or a woman, who could be with us for more than 30 years."[121] Of those recruited in 1968 and 1969 no less than five became heads of Commonwealth departments or agencies: W.J. Farmer (Immigration and Multicultural Affairs); R.C. Smith (Defence); D.J. Richardson (ASIO, later DFAT, and now Defence); G.C. Evans (Resources and Energy, then Primary Industries and Energy, later Transport); and D.A. Hollway (Industry, Science and Technology; then Employment, Education, Training and Youth), and, later, became CEO of the Sydney Olympic Games in 2000.

His view about recruiting female officers reflected the social conservatism of many of his generation. In 1966 amendments to the Public Service Act allowed married women to continue normal careers instead of having to resign. Plimsoll considered trying to have the department made an exception to the Act's provisions, but was persuaded wisely not to pursue this.[122] Penny Wensley, who joined in 1968, was one of many applicants who was personally interviewed by Plimsoll. She later became the first female to be permanent representative at the UN New York, and head of mission in New Delhi and in Paris. Subsequently she became Governor of Queensland.

He was not encouraged by increasing numbers of applicants. He was "shocked" at the decline in university standards: applicants with honours degrees "who can't write properly. Even some of the lecturers [providing references] can't write proper English". He saw this as part of a larger "cultural decline" affecting Australia and other countries.[123]

But, seeking perfection, his insistence on making final decisions on all diplomatic postings, including third secretaries, slowed decision-making.[124] Occasionally he responded decisively to direct approaches from officers about their posting preferences: one officer found himself third secretary in Mexico City three weeks after approaching Plimsoll at dinner at the Hotel Canberra and asking to be sent there. Another mid-level officer, working on UN affairs, took the opportunity of a chance meeting to tell Plimsoll that he would like a posting to the UN in New

York. He left in six weeks. Two years later, while in New York, Plimsoll listened to the same officer's wife complain about how little she saw of her husband as a consequence of work pressures. Six weeks later they were transferred to Belgrade.[125] Such interventions played havoc with carefully laid, integrated proposals for postings and placements of perhaps 30 officers at a time.[126] As for promotions, there was no schedule or time frame. It was a matter of "when you could get round to it". It was "not a very structured way of doing things".[127]

He had increased graduate entry recruiting, 20 or more being appointed in each of his first three years, but was cautious about appointing relatively young officers as ambassadors, curious considering that he himself had been one. He moaned to Tange about "the great shortage" of middle range officers: "I am at my wit's end to find officers to fill places." Compounding the problem was loss of some good people to other parts of the government,[128] while Defence was trying to entice External Affairs officers into its new Joint Intelligence Organisation.[129] Tange encouraged Plimsoll to let younger officers have their chance: "The corollary of the shortage of numbers of staff is that you will have to make a decision, and face the criticisms, to select relatively young" officers for senior positions. "There is nothing strange about this. The Trade Department, Defence Department and so forth are doing this every day."[130]

The department's management structure was "operating on a shoestring,"[131] urgently needing reorganisation and expansion; but this was not tackled in any meaningful way.

In 1969, its long-serving head, Keith Brennan, enumerated the problems: human resources were over-stretched as a result of "growth, new functions, the increasing complexity of some old functions, and inexperience"; and the department had grown by about 50 per cent in seven years and was "over-regulated"(mentioning the problems of dealing with the Public Service Board and the Treasury).[132]

Crocker later reflected on the department's growth:

> When I joined the Australian Foreign Service in 1952 there were only about 100 officers all told, Australia had only 20 missions overseas, and there were only 14 missions accredited to Canberra. When I retired [in 1971] the number of diplomatic officers had grown to 300 (plus about 1000 administrative and clerical personnel), our missions overseas to 68 and the missions accredited to Canberra to 53. It was thus a new service. Having grown so quickly, its foundations were neither fixed nor secure.[133]

Freeth

In February 1969, Hasluck resigned as Minister for External Affairs on appointment as Governor-General in succession to Casey. He was replaced by another Western Australian, Gordon Freeth, who had variously been Minister for the Interior, Shipping and Transport, and Air. Like Prime Minister Gorton, he had been an RAAF pilot during the War, but they had different personalities,[134] and were not close politically. Freeth "felt Gorton was erratic".[135]

Aware of speculation about Plimsoll's replacement as secretary,[136] Freeth made an early visit to the department and "rather brashly" assured Plimsoll that "I had no intention of replacing him".[137] Freeth's visit was refreshing after Hasluck's remoteness,[138] while Tange later noted from afar that Freeth allowed FAS's direct access to him: "He treated officers like adults."[139]

Freeth "liked Plimsoll and respected him", but became concerned about the department's administration. Visiting Washington, Freeth sounded Waller about taking the deputy secretary post in the department, although he would not have wanted Waller as Secretary.[140] Waller was not interested: "I said I liked and admired Jim but the Department was in a mess and I honestly did not believe that I could do what was needed to be done in the No 2 position. I could not conceive that Jim would give me the necessary authority and I did not relish the notion of a constant battle with the Permanent Head", who under the Public Service Act had the power in administrative matters. "I should find myself with responsibility and no power".[141]

Freeth is best remembered for a controversial passage in a speech in the House of Representatives on 14 August 1969, when introducing a periodic debate on international affairs. The passage was about the Soviet Navy and the Indian Ocean, which had been suggested by Plimsoll. This had followed a recent speech of Brezhnev making the first comment by the Soviet Union on the Indian Ocean – where there had been increased sightings of Soviet naval and commercial shipping.[142] Would it be worth trying to "test" Brezhnev a bit? Plimsoll, who wanted to "send them a signal," and respond in some exploratory way, asked that a speech be drafted for the minister.[143]

It was a daring idea: the 1968 Soviet invasion of Czechoslovakia had increased public suspicion of the USSR. But a few weeks earlier Plimsoll had noted that the Government, which continued to seek bilateral cooperation with the USSR, had tried to handle the Czechoslavakian issue "in a way that would not isolate the USSR and turn it from efforts towards world cooperation".[144]

Plimsoll had long been interested in the USSR despite not having been there. In September 1963, he had written privately to Crocker from Delhi, agreeing that "the Russians are thinking differently now". There were "possibilities of achieving something of a détente with the Soviet Union". The Sino-Soviet dispute, and "new trends of thought" in the USSR, "result in great opportunities for us to explore new lines of approach". Western countries still had to keep their guard up, and only relax it in response to appropriate Soviet moves: "But I have felt for some years that ways were beginning to open out, and many people in the West, including some Australians, were still thinking of the Soviet Union too much in terms of what it had been in the days of Stalin."[145]

Plimsoll advised Freeth to make the point "that it was natural for the USSR to be in the Indian Ocean". If this right were challenged, "we'd get policies based on the wrong premises and they'd collapse . . . We can query what they are doing, but we can't query their right to be there".[146] Freeth liked the idea of including something along these lines. The speech draft was carefully worded with appropriate qualifications.[147]

Freeth assumed that Plimsoll saw the final text before delivery. In any event the speech had been approved by Gorton.[148] Plimsoll later recalled that a factor in Gorton's support for saying something about the Indian Ocean was that in a speech about a week earlier, the Minister for Defence, Allen Fairhall, had implied that the defences of Western Australia were non-existent.[149]

Freeth's speech on 14 August covered several matters including Vietnam. On Soviet activity in Asia, Freeth referred to "the movement of ships of the Soviet Union in the Indian Ocean" as an illustration of "increasing interest and activity" by the USSR in the region: "Australia has to be watchful but need not panic whenever a Russian appears. It has to avoid both facile gullibility and automatic rejection of opportunities for cooperation. Practical and constructive dealings with the Soviet Union as with any other country" would be welcome.

That passage was prominently reported.[150] A Liberal Party backbencher at first thought that Freeth had made "an extremely good speech". But John McEwen, Deputy Prime Minister and Leader of the Country Party, thought the speech represented a major policy change, taken without cabinet consultation.[151] A few days later cabinet attempted to mollify McEwen by noting that the passage "made no change in policy but merely related it, in a realistic way, to Russian initiatives". Cabinet also commented that given that China had long been regarded as the main security threat in South-East Asia, "it was good sense" to examine Soviet suggestions for an Asian collective security system, especially given Australian support for "a policy of collective security in the area".[152]

James Killen, then another Liberal backbencher, later recalled that "Freeth's speech was not all that radical", but "certainly some parts of it would have been better left unsaid or at least modified". With an election looming by the end of the year there was "a savage reaction" from the Democratic Labor Party which contended that the speech indicated that "the Government was going soft on the communist question".[153] For the Government, the DLP's support was critical to retaining power. Freeth's speech made it difficult to fight an election with foreign affairs as a prominent issue.

During that time Plimsoll was at a dinner, attended by Gorton. Asked about his election prospects, Gorton replied that earlier he would have thought the Government might lose about four seats. "But now with this speech that Jim's written, I'm going to lose a few more." According to Plimsoll, Gorton said this in a "joking way, he didn't hold it against me".[154] At an ANZUS Council meeting in Canberra shortly afterwards, Freeth showed the passage to William Rogers, US Secretary of State in the Nixon Administration, who thought it was "a good thing".[155]

At the election of 25 October 1969, the Government's majority was cut from 39 to 7. The only minister to lose his seat was Freeth, the only time that this has happened to a serving Australian foreign minister. It was widely believed that this was due to the speech of 14 August, for which Plimsoll was blamed. Freeth later recalled, however, that there was "fairly conclusive evidence" the loss was not due to his speech:

> Most Western Australian voters couldn't care less about foreign policy issues. I had a majority of about 6000 votes in the previous election – there was a local political issue about fat lamb exports, plus the well known fact that Gorton was a Centralist – wanting more power for Canberra – whereas Western Australia was very strongly against that. Two Country Party seats – Canning and Moore – lost more voters than I did, but they had larger majorities and were able to absorb the losses.[156]

Plimsoll was upset by criticism of the speech,[157] but he did not resile from this approach to the USSR when later he spoke in the Defence Committee in December:

The Soviet Union's basic philosophy and course of action were contrary to Australia's, but we should take advantage of the Soviet Union's actions and policies whenever and wherever they might accord with ours, and we should also seek to influence the Soviet Union so that it would see in certain situations that its own interests to some extent accorded with ours.

For example, the USSR would not want to see Chinese hegemony over South-East Asia: "All this meant that Australia should adopt a policy of some discrimination and delicacy, admittedly it was not always easy to explain to the Australian people" – a barbed comment perhaps about the Government's incapacity to explain itself. As for the Indian Ocean, "it would be very bad to create publicly the impression that Australia was automatically ranged against the Soviet Union in that ocean and that we were trying to organise and rouse other countries against the Russians".[158]

McMahon

On 12 November 1969 Gorton reshuffled the ministry. In the wake of an unsuccessful challenge to Gorton's leadership, William McMahon was moved from the Treasury to External Affairs.[159] McMahon had been Deputy Leader of the Parliamentary Liberal Party for nearly four years, but few leading figures among his colleagues spoke well of him. McEwen's view of him had effectively put McMahon out of the running as successor when Holt disappeared. Gorton recalled a small ministerial meeting under Holt in which McEwen was "tearing hell out of this squirt".[160] Gorton knew that Menzies once had confronted McMahon about his leaking to the media, and made him sign a piece of paper acknowledging that he would have to resign if he was caught doing it again.[161]

Plimsoll himself had known McMahon slightly over the years,[162] and as secretary he formed an unfavourable impression that did not improve on closer acquaintance. In 1965 Hasluck had told him that Menzies wanted

Plimsoll to lead Australia's delegation to the UN General Assembly, because Hasluck had to remain at home as acting prime minister at a time when Menzies and other senior ministers would be abroad, and Menzies did not want to leave McMahon in charge.[163] Other things[164] meant Plimsoll's impression did not improve. After McMahon became minister, Plimsoll recalled that he "didn't get on particularly well" with him: "Partly because I found him so disorganised and he could never remember from one minute to another what he'd already decided;" and because "he was intriguing against his colleagues and telling them one thing and doing another, and I couldn't stand that".[165] The same negative impression of McMahon was formed by Plimsoll's departmental colleagues. To Nick Parkinson, he was "the stupidest foreign minister and prime minister we ever had". To Jim McIntyre he was "a rather vain and silly little man, not notable for integrity or truthfulness".[166] To Colin Moodie, "he was, along with Evatt, the most ambitious, unscrupulous minister I struck. But Evatt had a touch of genius and McMahon had not".[167] Alf Parsons felt that of all foreign ministers he had served, "McMahon was without doubt the least effective, least interested and least intelligent," someone who "would do almost anything for publicity", and who "had a unique ability to create chaos and misunderstanding".[168]

For his part McMahon soon decided that he wanted to be rid of his permanent head.[169] McMahon was "bearing down on him" but Plimsoll would not be bullied into giving advice that McMahon wanted to hear. McMahon felt uncomfortable with Plimsoll. Hewitt attributed this to the "acute sense of inferiority which McMahon suffered in comparison with Plimsoll's capacity and ability". McMahon also exploited criticism which he heard of Plimsoll's management of the department.[170]

Although initially reluctant to become secretary, after nearly five years Plimsoll thought carefully about quitting. He would have recalled Hasluck's 1964 letter offering him the appointment, with a note from Bunting about cabinet's view of the desirability of "periodic succession" in the post, which "should not be filled for long periods by one occupant", as well as Hasluck's interpretation that the "assumption is that after a period of years you yourself might well be considered for another overseas posting".[171] On the other hand, "permanent heads could not be removed unwillingly until they had reached retirement age".[172]

One day McMahon said to Plimsoll: "You are always telling me what I cannot do. I don't care about that. I care only what the electors of Lowe think". Plimsoll responded: "In that case I wish to resign immediately. This is no good."[173] Years later Plimsoll said that it had come down to this:

> If a Minister and a Permanent Head aren't getting on in a reasonable way, then the Permanent Head ought to go. There was no personal bitterness between us, but it just wasn't working out very well and he wanted Waller.[174]

After consulting Plimsoll, McMahon agreed to propose to cabinet that he be posted to Tokyo, and Freeth to Washington. After the cabinet meeting Plimsoll was surprised when McMahon told him that cabinet had "accepted my recommendation that you are to be Ambassador in Washington" and Freeth would instead go to Tokyo. Plimsoll later learned that most ministers, including Gorton, wanted him to stay as secretary while "McEwen said categorically that he would not agree to my moving unless to Washington".[175] Plimsoll "didn't think anyone in cabinet wanted me to go except McMahon". Gorton had asked him privately if he really wanted to go, and he replied that he felt he should not stay as McMahon did not want him. Hewitt thought that if it had not been for McMahon's determination to be rid of Plimsoll, Gorton would not have agreed to him being moved.[176]

Plimsoll was instructed to sound Waller in Washington about becoming secretary. Waller agreed, "rather reluctantly"; telling his wife the news, he added: "What a fool I am."[177] He was under no illusions about what lay ahead.[178]

The appointments of Plimsoll, Waller and Freeth were announced on 28 January 1970. Plimsoll would complete five years as secretary on 5 April. The *Sydney Morning Herald* commented that Plimsoll was "one of Australia's most respected public servants and certainly one of the best loved. He is by far the most devoted man in Canberra and literally lives for his job. Gentle in speech and courteous, he has a keen and whimsical sense of humour".[179]

Crocker, visiting Canberra in March, concluded that "whatever his disappointment might have been first on leaving the Secretaryship I sensed that now he is feeling relief".[180] McMahon leaked Waller's valedictory despatch[181] on the US to "buy press support" for his own political advancement.[182] Lord Casey and Plimsoll each talked to Crocker about it. Plimsoll said that contrary to McMahon's reputation for toughness, "he was very unsure and quite a weak man".[183] But later, as Plimsoll worked through his last days with McMahon, Crocker noted:

> Plimsoll now half regrets that he accepted or concurred with the government's wish that he go to Washington. Legally he said he could have refused and stayed on as head. He now half wishes that he did, as McMahon probably won't last, though he added that McMahon was a real difficulty for him; already sharp disagreements.[184]

But five years as secretary arguably is long enough. Since Tange, with only two exceptions,[185] no one has held down that most demanding job longer than Plimsoll. When he started he had not had leave for nearly three years, and he took none in the next five, all of which may have contributed to health problems. In August 1965 Plimsoll collapsed at a function in Sydney. He was taken to hospital, but discharged next morning. He had been addressing the annual meeting of the India League, some 200 people "in a small basement restaurant which was quite hot", as he tried to play it down in a letter to U Thant, UN Secretary-General, who was among many who sent messages of concern. "I think there was simply a shortage of oxygen."[186] Sir Harry Bland, and others, suggested that he "stay away from the office a little longer".[187] Characteristically,

Plimsoll disregarded this advice. In later years as secretary, there were other blackouts or fainting fits.[188] Shann recalled two of these, caused by Plimsoll being "overworked and overwrought by the need to deal with McMahon as Foreign Minister".[189]

McIntyre recalled that "during those five years External Affairs held its own and prospered. Plimsoll, while not a forceful Permanent Head, was widely respected among his colleagues for his intellectual quality".[190] Their friendship survived the time in Canberra. He considered Plimsoll of "very great intellectual calibre, a very logical mind, a quick mind, a capacious, remarkable memory, a dedicated worker".[191] Lenox Hewitt recalled that Plimsoll's advice was always "spot on; measured, well-considered, intelligent – like the man himself".[192] Plimsoll "was particularly strong in the way that he informed himself, analysed, debated with himself, considered what was put to him, listened to argument – then reached a decision and tendered advice". He "would not trim his sails to derive a result which the minister would wish to hear. He maintained his courage and steadfastness once having decided on what was the proper advice, whereas others bent with the wind".[193]

On the policy front Plimsoll did his best to draw attention to particular issues, with some success. But should Plimsoll have been allowed to complete two years in India? While his contribution in India was important in the long term, in hindsight it would have been more important to have had his involvement in Canberra dealing with urgent critical problems for Australia, especially those concerning Vietnam. 1964 was a difficult year given developments in South-East Asia. There was the delicate policy path taken by Australia over continuing Indonesian confrontation of Malaysia, with Australian troops in action against Indonesian "volunteers" while at the same time maintaining high level communication with the Indonesian Government. That was all being well handled. But, at the same time, there was the increasing dilemma about the appropriate Australian response to the deteriorating situation in South Vietnam. There were attempts through the UN and elsewhere to seek a peaceful resolution. During this period Tange, while still secretary, had a strained relationship with Hasluck, affecting the department's contribution to policy. If, instead of being allowed to stay in India another year, Plimsoll had been instructed to return and become secretary without delay, then given Plimsoll's rapport with Menzies, and Hasluck's respect for Plimsoll, would the outcome in relation to Vietnam have been any different?

Plimsoll did not "grow in the job" in the "incremental" way that Tange did.[194] Little seemed to change about him. He worked and lived his life very much as he had the last time he was in Canberra. Plimsoll had the misfortune to have his predecessor, Tange, looking over his shoulder. In New Delhi, observing from afar the department he had ruled over for eleven years, Tange found time to write lengthy criticisms of its management. Perhaps it was not without some guilt for what he might have done better while he had been secretary.[195]

To become secretary is normally regarded as the height of one's career, but it can engender unrealistic expectations. As Sir John Crawford once wrote: "The permanent head is the alleged possessor of a range of qualities which I personally do not expect to find in anyone this side of heaven." [196] In assessing levels of performance as secretary, personality, brains and character all play key parts. There are also the elements of luck: who the minister happens to be and what support is forthcoming from within the department itself, the state of one's health, and the general situation. Plimsoll held the job for five years and performed better than many, and he was among the best with regard to the policy advising role. But it was not his finest hour. Barwick, who had favoured making him secretary, later reflected that it had "turned out not to be his cup of tea. The routines of the Department and so on was not the way his mind worked. It did not fit him".[197] It was the least successful appointment in his career up to that time. But new and more suitable challenges lay ahead.

Endnotes

1 WRC, Jnl, 5/4/1966, xv, 3550.

2 His last holidays had been the two weeks he took in Canada in 1962. His leave credit was 15 weeks, the maximum accrued level, which led to him forfeiting eight weeks due to him for his two years in India. JP, personnel file, DFAT.

3 Most would take a day off, as then permitted.

4 J.A. Lavett, letter, 25/3/2002.

5 Holt, Gorton, McMahon, Whitlam and then Fraser (six if McEwen, December 1967-January 1968, is included).

6 Plimsoll thought that "Holt feels a glamour about foreign affairs and fancies himself in them – though pretty ignorant, his heart is generally in the right place". WRC, Jnl, 27/3/1967, xvi, 3760.

7 Lavett, letter, 25/3/2002. Hasluck commented to Plimsoll that "the Government is getting more and more into a flurry of purposeless activity in foreign affairs. We are making news but not making policy". Hasluck to JP, 4/8/1967, JP papers, DFAT.

8 Paul Hasluck *The Chance of Politics*. Nicholas Hasluck (ed), Text Publishing, Melbourne, 1997, 109 and 137.

9 JP to Hasluck, 2/6/1965, JP papers, DFAT.

10 "Holt, just after becoming PM, unbriefed and new to these things, allowed himself to be seen by the Chinese Ambassador [i.e., Formosa] and committed himself to it". WRC, Jnl, 18/9/1966, xvi, 3649.

11 *Reminiscential Conversations between Hon Clyde Cameron and Sir James Plimsoll 1984*. TRC 1967, ii, 366. NLA. Hereafter cited as Cam/Plim.

12 JP to Crocker, 27/9/1966, JP papers, Box 6, Item 69, NAA.

13 Hasluck told him: "Gorton has got great merit in the eyes of the public by getting up and freely confessing the faults of his colleagues." Cam/Plim, ii, 180-181, and 184. On the VIP planes affair, see Ian Hancock, "The VIP Affair, 1966-67", *Australasian Parliamentary Review*, vol 18(2), Spring 2003.

14 Cam/Plim, ii, 185-6. JP diary, 17/12/1967. Hasluck, *Chance of Politics*, 148-50.

15 Minister's overseas travel. JP papers, DFAT.

16 Cam/Plim, i, 191-2 and 195.

17 Cam/Plim, i , 356.

18 Cam/Plim, ii, 367.

19 JP to Hasluck, 15/7/1968. Russian prawning in the Gulf of Carpentaria, (two submissions), Plimsoll papers, DFAT.

20 Woolcott, conversation, 12/12/1997.

21 Tange, conversation, 6/1/1998. Edwards, *Tange*, chapter 8.

22 D.J. Kingsmill had served as private secretary to Barwick and, then, briefly, to Hasluck. Conversation, 19/8/2002.

23 Hay, conversation, 10/10/1996. Hay, then a division head in the department, discovered this when, having been appointed Administrator of PNG, he paid a call on Hasluck as a former Territories minister. See also, Joan Beaumont, "The Diplomat as Minister", in Joan Beaumont, Christopher Waters, David Lowe, with Garry Woodard, *Ministers, Mandarins and Diplomats: Australian foreign policy making 1941-1969*, Melbourne University Press, Melbourne, 2003, 130-53.

24 A.M. Morris, conversation, 9/12/2002. He learned this from Tange.

25 Hasluck asked Geoffrey White to be his private secretary after working with him at an ECAFE conference, which was White's responsibility in the department. The job involved long hours and extensive international travel. After a year White, who had a young family, was allowed to return to the department. White, conversation, 31/3/1998.

26 Tange, conversation, 6/1/1998. One exception was that on Vietnam and other South-East Asian matters Hasluck dealt directly with Jockel and, after him, H.D. Anderson.

27 Hasluck to JP, 16/6/1967, A1838/274 277/2/12 Pt. 4, NAA.

28 JP diary.

29 Cam/Plim, i, 158. Hasluck at short notice once had Renouf, who had been a close subordinate of his at the UN, to a meal at his flat. Renouf, Oral hist, TRC 2981/6, 83, NLA.

30 Waller noted that Hasluck overseas was "certainly a most agreeable person to travel with". Waller to JP, 25/6/1964, JP papers, Box 4, Item 53, NAA. Jockel, who accompanied Hasluck on a visit to Burma, recalled a cultural display featuring drums in which Hasluck got up and joined in – he had had some earlier experience in PNG with drums. Jockel, conversation, 25/5/2010.

31 At the 1965 Ambassadors meeting in Rome, "Hasluck did outstandingly well throughout – relaxed but mentally knife-edged and most alertly interested." Stirling diary, 8/5-14/5 1965. See also Crocker's comments on the 1968 HOMs meeting in London. WRC, Jnl, 6/11/1968, xix, 4268.

32 Casey to JP, 3/2/1965, shortly before becoming Governor-General. JP papers, Box 4, Item 47, NAA.

33 Cam/Plim, i, 244, 468.

34 Lavett, letter, 25/3/2002.

35 See chapters 5 and 6.

36 Hasluck to A.W. Martin, 13/1/1988. Courtesy A.W. Martin.

37 Hasluck to Crocker, 2/6/1987. Hasluck private papers. Courtesy Nicholas and Sally Hasluck.

38 Hasluck papers, MS 5274. *Foreign Affairs*, vol ii, 1964-68, Box 3, 17 NAA.

39 Crocker considered that both Hasluck and Plimsoll believed relentless discipline and standards of behaviour were vital for a diplomatic service. "In this sense Plimsoll was perfect with Hasluck – a puritan too." Crocker, conversation, 4/11/1998.

40 Cam/Plim, ii, 249.

41 Cam/Plim, i, 355-6.

42 Tange to JP, 1/2/1967. JP papers, DFAT.

43 J.G. Crawford, "The Role of the Permanent Head", *Public Administration* (Sydney), September 1954, 157.

44 Secretary's movements, JP papers, DFAT.

45 Errol Hodge, *Radio Wars. Truth, Propaganda and the Struggle for Radio Australia.* Cambridge University Press, 1995, 90; Woolcott, conversation, 24/7/2012.

46 Two other permanent representatives in New York, Woolcott (1982-88) and Wilenski (1989-91), and Costello (1988-89) who briefly acted in the position, all later became secretary; but without earlier having five years over two postings on UN matters as Plimsoll had.

47 Anderson, conversation, 7/2/1997.

48 Cam/Plm, ii, 360.

49 R.J. Greet, conversation, 5/11/1998.

50 WRC, Jnl, 5/4/1966, xv, 3550.

51 WRC, Jnl, 9/4/1967, xvi, 3770. For Crocker's view, see *Australian Ambassador*, Melbourne University Press, Melbourne, 1971, vi and 166.

52 Cam/Plim, i, 462; ii, 329.

53 Lt-General Sir Thomas Daly, Chief of the General Staff, conversation, 1999.

54 At a Defence Committee meeting on 20 April 1965, after the announcement of Australia's decision to commit a battalion to Vietnam, Plimsoll said that the United States should provide written assurance that if Australia's forces were needed elsewhere, they could be withdrawn, and the US would transport them. General Wilton replied that Plimsoll had exaggerated the likelihood of such a contingency: and such a request for assurance would "make a bad impression on the Americans". Plimsoll, notes of Defence Committee meeting, 20/4/65. Quoted by David Horner, *Strategic Command. General Sir John Wilton and Australia's Asian Wars*, Oxford University Press, Melbourne, 2005, 236.

55 Clifford-Taylor Mission. Notes of meeting at Prime Minister's Lodge, Canberra, 30/7/67. 1209/80 1967/7524, NAA.

56 In a Defence Committee discussion in September 1967 about the consequences of British withdrawal, Plimsoll noted that most of the Committee favoured continuation of Australia's forward defence posture. But if the US especially and the UK ceased to be involved, "Australia could not adopt the same forward defence strategy alone" or with only small military powers. Australia needed to know US intentions involving longer term commitment to the region. Plimsoll advised that the US "would not express a view" before the Vietnam war was over. The best thing to do was to make the US conscious of Australian priorities. Plimsoll, Note to Hasluck about Defence Committee meeting of 28 September 1967 discussing "Consequences of British withdrawal from east of Suez". A1838/346 Pt 1. TS 696/1/1/2, NAA.

57 Carver, letter, 30/9/2000.

58 Cam/Plim, ii, 124.

59 Quoted in *Times of India*, 28/10/1965. JP papers, DFAT.

60 Plimsoll at press conference, New Delhi, after joint officials talks with India, 15/3/69. JP papers, DFAT.

61 Non-Proliferation Treaty. Plimsoll's notes of Defence Committee meeting 21/3/68. JP papers, DFAT.

62 JP to Hasluck, Treaty on Nuclear Non-Proliferation, 29/4/68. JP papers, DFAT.

63 Tange considered that Plimsoll, in referring to a "direct" threat from China, "went beyond the formal position of the [Australian] advisory machine". Still, Hasluck and Menzies in earlier public statements had spoken of possible use of military means by China. "A Secretary is not just there to offer advice to Government as to best policy, but to find ways to justify policy (though not

necessarily agree with it)". So Plimsoll "was being quite ingenious in choosing words which were ambiguous but simply served back to the PM words which had already been used". Tange, conversation, 6/1/1998, and in note to me, 4/2/1998.

64 JP to Tange, 16/9/1965. JP papers, DFAT.

65 Anderson, conversation, 7/2/1997.

66 When, as minister, Hasluck visited the United Nations in 1964 he was recognised among senior Secretariat members who had known him earlier as a departmental officer "not only as Foreign Minister but as a technical and professional expert in the UN field". Hay, Oral Hist, TRC 121/65, .2/2/19, NLA.

67 See note 13 above.

68 Hasluck to JP, EUN 1604 of 1/10/65. JP papers, DFAT.

69 Following is an exerpt from a Hilaire Belloc-style verse circulating in the department at the time:

> The Minister as was his yen
> Snubbed all his very senior men
> Except the highly favoured Jim
> It seemed he had some trust in him
> And so with undisguised elation,
> Made him lead the Delegation.

70 26/11/1965. JP papers, DFAT.

71 Hasluck to JP, 18/7/1966. JP papers, DFAT. Plimsoll had a small success when Cabinet agreed to Australian recognition of the Mongolian People's Republic in 1967, something to which the US was opposed. Plimsoll to Tange, 27/1/1967. JP papers, DFAT.

72 During the 1965 UN General Assembly Plimsoll visited Washington to call on Dean Rusk the day before Plimsoll's speech in the General Debate. JP to Hasluck, UN.1356 from New York. JP papers, DFAT.

73 Cables I.41907 of 22/91965; I.43831 of 4/10/1965; I. 44755 of 8/10/1965; I.44828 from New York. JP papers, DFAT.

74 Secretary to Minister, A1838 190/10/2, part 23, 254-3, NAA.

75 A.N. Smith lecture, 23/11/1965, 6, 17.

76 McIntyre, acting secretary to JP in New York, 6/10/1965. JP papers, Box 5, Item 60, NAA.

77 Cam/Plim, ii, 251-2. JP to Tange, 4/11/1966. JP papers, DFAT.

78 In 1968 Plimsoll felt that "things were changing so rapidly and unpredictably in PNG", and that "independence would come sooner than many thought". Plimsoll, personal notes of Defence Committee meeting, 30/5/1968 (Agendum No. 19/68) on Size and Role of the Pacific Islands Regiment. A1838, 689/2, part 3, NAA.

79 Marginal note by Plimsoll on minute from M.R. Booker to Hasluck, 14/1/66, A1838 936/5 iv. NAA. Quoted in S.R. Doran (ed), *Australia and Papua New Guinea 1966-69*, Documents on Australian Foreign Policy, DFAT.

80 M.J. Hughes, conversation, 2000. 1964 had witnessed election of the first House of Assembly in PNG.

81 Hughes, conversation, 2000. See also JP to Warwick Smith, 13/10/69; Warwick Smith to JP, 24/10/69; and JP to Brennan 24/11/69, A1838 936/6/10 part 1, NAA: all quoted in SR Doran (ed), op. cit.

82 JP, personal notes of Defence Committee meeting, 30/5/1968 (Agendum No 19/68) on Size and Role of the Pacific Islands Regiment. A1838, 689/2 part 3, NAA.

83 Plimsoll, note of Defence Committee discussion of PNG – Use of the PIR in Bougainville, A1838 936/3/21, Pt 1, NAA.

84 Hasluck to Secretary, 25/10/1967, quoted from his enclosed essay on "The future of overseas representation".

85 WRC, Jnl. 28/3/1967, xvi, 3760. For Hasluck on McMahon, see *Chance of Politics*, especially 184-9. Also Hasluck, *Light That Time Has Made*, Canberra, 1995, 149-58.

86 The author worked in the section of the department dealing with this during 1964-66.

87 Cam/Plim, ii, 287. Plimsoll, together with the historian, Sir Keith Hancock, interviewed Neale; also DCS Sissons and Assoc Prof WJ Hudson. JP diary, 6/3/70.

88 Sir John Crawford "The Role of the Permanent Head", *Public Administration*, Sydney, vol. 13, no. 3, September 1954, 162.

89 Richard Woolcott, *The Hot Seat: Reflections on Diplomacy from Stalin's Death to the Bali Bombings*, Harper Collins, Sydney, 2003, 73, 87.

90 Renouf to JP, 10/6/1965: "One of the best explanations of the UN and what it can and cannot do that I have ever read." JP papers, Box 5, Item 60, NAA.

91 See Rohan Rivett to JP, 25/11/1965, Box 5, Item 60, and Prime Minister Menzies minuted "jolly good", 19/12/1965, Box 5, Item 62, JP papers, NAA.

92 J.D.B. Miller, conversation, 6/3/1997.

93 Watt, *The Evolution of Australian Foreign Policy 1938-1965*, Cambridge University Press, London, 1968.

94 Crocker noted that Plimsoll "made no criticism of the publishing of it or of its main theme, only some details (all his points good). My general impression is that he liked it – a little to my surprise". WRC, Jnl, 9/3/1970, xx, 4573.

95 Peter Howson, conversation, 27/8/1997: JP diary.

96 JP diary. The department was now located in the Administrative Building (now named the John Gorton Building).

97 In 1952 Watt approached Lord Strang, Permanent Under-Secretary, UK Foreign Office. "I want your advice on how to secure some private life while being head of a foreign office." Strang replied: "I can't help you in the least for I have none." Stirling, diary, 8/6/1952, DFAT.

98 JP diary, 10/1969.

99 Others included Dame Zara Holt (later Bate), James Fairfax, Professor Sir Joseph Burke of Melbourne University, Sir William Dargie and Kenneth Baillieu Myer.

100 James Mollison, letter, 6/8/1996.

101 John Deeble, Area Scouts Commissioner, conversation, 27/10/2000.

102 Kingsland, note of 28/4/1969.

103 Hasluck to JP, 25/10/1967, JP papers, DFAT.

104 JP to McIntyre, 15/3/1965, Plimsoll Papers, Box 5, Item 60, NAA.

105 R.W. Furlonger, conversation, 15/10/1996.

106 R.F. Osborn recalled Tange dicatating a letter to William Dunk at the Public Service Board, saying, "I am spending more than half my time on administration." Osborn, conversation, 4/11/1997. See also Peter Edwards, *Arthur Tange*, Allen and Unwin, Sydney, 2006, 84.

107 McIntyre, Oral history, TRC 121/67, 2:31, NLA.

108 Tange to McMahon, 16/12/1969. Tange papers, DFAT.

109 Bilney, conversation, 4/2/1998. Shann, when acting secretary, found promotions and postings recommendations for senior officers that went back

two years. Conversation with D.W. Evans, 11/3/2000, who had heard this from Shann.

110 For example, in relation to the submission requested by Hasluck on Radio Australia, mentioned above.

111 Quintus Fabius Maximus, nicknamed Cunctator (Delayer), was an ancient Roman politician and general.

112 Bilney, conversation, 4/2/1998. H.D. Anderson, conversation, 7/2/1997.

113 Crocker, conversations, 4/11/1998, and 20/10/2000.

114 P.J. Galvin, letter, 7/8/2002.

115 Now called the Gorton Building

116 "Plimsoll also agreed with me that [embassy] staffs everywhere are apt to be too big." WRC, Jnl, xvi, 31/3/1967, 3763.

117 JP to Brennan, 10/8/1965. JP papers, DFAT.

118 Hasluck to JP, 13/5/1965. JP papers, DFAT.

119 L.H. Border, conversation, 14/2/1998.

120 B.J. Blackburn, conversation, 1999.

121 Cam/Plim, i, 369.

122 P.G.F. Henderson, conversation, 1997.

123 WRC, Jnl, 5/4/1966, xv, 3550.

124 R.J. Greet, conversation, 5/11/1998.

125 Conversations with K. Baker, 2000; and D.W. Evans 11/3/2000.

126 Henderson, conversation, 18/2/2004.

127 Greet, conversation, 5/11/1998.

128 D.O. Hay became Administrator of PNG (1966), R.W. Furlonger became first Director-General of JIO (1968), and B.G. Dexter transferred to aboriginal affairs in Prime Minister's Department (1967). Also A.R. Cutler became Governor of NSW (1965).

129 JP to Tange, 17/10/1969. JP papers, DFAT.

130 Tange to JP, 21/10/1969. JP papers, DFAT.

131 Greet, conversation, 5/11/1998 .

132 Brennan to Secretary, 8/8/69. Tange papers, DFAT. See also entry on Brennan in the *Australian Dictionary of Biography*, vol. 17, MUP, 2007, by Peter Henderson.

133 W.R. Crocker, *Travelling Back*, Macmillan, Melbourne, 1981, 192.

134 "Gorton being flamboyant when in the mood and inclined at times to be rash and self-indulgent, Freeth was stolid, thoughtful and well-organised." ACC Farran, letter, 30/9/2002.

135 He had pleaded with Hasluck, his fellow West Australian, not to become Governor-General, but to stay and contest the leadership again. Freeth, letter, 2/3/1999.

136 An example of these had been by journalist Eric Walsh: "That Hasluck was a victim of 'Gortonism' is not even an arguing point. Any remaining doubts should be swiftly removed if he is followed out of the Department" by Plimsoll "and this is being confidently predicted as a further stage in Mr Gorton's bid to put his own stamp on foreign affairs and government generally". *Daily Mirror*, 22/2/1969; and on 25/2/1969 that Plimsoll "has only a shaky hold on his present position".

137 Freeth, letter, 3/12/1996.

138 Plimsoll noted in his diary (14/2/1969) that Freeth "spent most of the afternoon working in the Minister's office there". Plimsoll strongly approved that Freeth later worked there at least monthly. WRC, Jnl, 1/4/1967, xvi, 3764.

139 Tange to McMahon, 16/12/1969. Tange papers, DFAT.

140 Farran, letter, 30/9/2002.

141 Waller to Tange, 23/10/1969. Tange papers, DFAT.

142 The Soviet naval presence in the Indian Ocean was "more potential than actual ... It has not as yet formally stationed a squadron of any size there". EA memo of 8/8/1969. A1838/274 169/7/9, Pt 1, NAA.

143 D.M. Sadleir, conversation, 11/4/1997.

144 Plimsoll in Australia/India Officials Talks, 13/3/1969, New Delhi. 1838/272 169/10/1/1 Pt 4, NAA.

145 JP to Crocker, 19/9/1963, JP papers, Box 4, Item 38, NAA. See also chapter 4.

146 Cam/Plim, i, 275 and 277.

147 Sadleir, conversation, 11/4/1997.

148 Gorton "actually made some small amendments to the text in pencil in his own handwriting". Freeth letters, 3/12/1996 and 2/3/1999.

149 Cam/Plim, i, 276-277.

150 On the day that the speech was to be delivered, Plimsoll had asked

Pierre Hutton, the Department's Public Information Officer, to ensure the Parliamentary Press Gallery took note of the passage on the Indian Ocean. Hutton, letter, 8/10/2000.

151 McEwen was aggrieved at not being brought in on what he thought sounded like "a fundamental change of foreign policy". Peter Howson, *The Howson Diaries: The Life of Politics*, Don Aitkin (ed), Viking Press, Ringwood, 1984, 541.

152 Cabinet Minute, Decision No 1212 of 19 August 1969. JP papers, DFAT.

153 Howson, *Diary*, 544; and Sir James Killen, *Killen: Inside Australian Politics*, Mandarin, Melbourne, 1989, 144-5.

154 Cam/Plim, i, 277.

155 Cam/Plim, i, 275.

156 Freeth, letter, 2/3/1999. Senator Peter Sim, who campaigned for Freeth, similarly thought he lost because farmers in the electorate, who were undergoing a rural recession, "thought they'd teach him a bit of a lesson". John Farquharson, "Today", *The Age*, 5/12/2001.

157 Attending the UN General Assembly in New York two months afterwards, Plimsoll said he had been surprised at the reaction at home. "The speech seemed all right to me". Evans, conversation, 11/3/2000.

158 Defence Committee, 18/12/1969. JP's meeting notes about "Defence implications of the Indian Ocean," A1838/37 697/8, Pt 4, NAA.

159 McMahon's unsuccessful challenge to Gorton's leadership in the party room after the 1969 election probably contributed to his being moved from the Treasury.

160 Gorton, conversation, 19/1/1999.

161 Gorton, conversation. Gorton said that he did not see the piece of paper. Heather Henderson recalled that it was kept for years in Menzies' own safe.

162 Having first met in Korea, when McMahon visited as Minister for the Navy and Minister for Air, subsequently in the 1950s in Canberra he had a few meetings with McMahon as Primary Industry Minister in relation to Japanese pearling issues; they had not worked closely.

163 Cam/Plim, ii, 260.

164 Plimsoll told Crocker that McMahon was "secretly helping" journalists to destroy Hasluck. WRC Jnl, 28/3/67, xvi, 3760. In 1967 McMahon was "actively working against" Holt. On the evening of Holt's disappearance, Hasluck told

Gorton in Plimsoll's hearing that for the sake of the Coalition, following Holt's disappearance, "McMahon must be kept out" of the leadership. Cam/Plim, ii, 185.

165 His "continuing telephoning and wanting Plimsoll to see him. One urgent convoking turned out to be to show him two congratulatory telegrams that McMahon had received". WRC, Jnl, xx, 22/4/70.

166 McIntyre, Oral History, TRC 3:9, NLA; Parkinson, conversation, 20/6/1996.

167 Moodie, unpublished memoirs. Privately held, 92.

168 Alf Parsons, *South East Asian Days*, Australians in Asia paper No. 22, Griffith University, April 1998, 101-5.

169 McMahon was "obviously set on getting rid of Sir James Plimsoll". McIntyre Oral history, TRC 3:9 NLA.

170 Sir Lenox Hewitt, conversation, 1/7/1998.

171 Hasluck, letter, 22/5/64, JP papers, DFAT; and JP papers, Box 4, Item 50, NAA. Bunting to Plimsoll 4/6/1965, enclosing copy of Cabinet decision No. 244. JP papers, DFAT.

172 Edwards, *Tange*, 145.

173 Lavett, letter, 27/3/2002. Lavett said he heard this several times from Plimsoll, while serving with him in Washington.

174 Cam/Plim, i, 147 and 350.

175 Cam/Plim, i, 350-1. Plimsoll told Crocker that he would have preferred Moscow or Tokyo over Washington. WRC, Jnl, 8/3/1970, xx, 4572.

176 Gorton, conversation, 19/1/1999; Hewitt, conversation, 1/7/1998. Cam/Plim, ii, 328-329.

177 JP diary, Waller, *Diplomatic Life*, 42-3; conversation with Lady Waller, 1998.

178 Waller recalled Plimsoll as "a great human being but an appalling administrator; [as Secretary] I inherited a machine which had very nearly ground to a halt and in which everyone had grown extraordinarily slipshod". Waller, *Diplomatic Life*, 43.

179 *Sydney Morning Herald*, 29/1/1970. For another account of the top level appointments early in 1970, see Edwards, *Tange*, 171-5.

180 WRC, Jnl, 8/3/1970, xx, 4572.

181 A valedictory dispatch was a final report by an ambassador before leaving a post.

182 WRC, Jnl, 12/3/1970, xx, 4575, and 13/3/1970, xx, 4577.
183 WRC, Jnl, 14/3/1970, xx, 4577, 15/3/1970, 4580.
184 WRC, Jnl, 22/3/1970, xx, 4583.
185 Calvert (1998-2004) for over six years; Henderson (1979-84) for five.
186 Plimsoll to U Thant, 14/9/1965, JP papers, DFAT.
187 Bland to JP, 19/8/1965, JP papers, DFAT.
188 Gordon Jockel recalled Plimsoll collapsed early one night in Canberra – "a kind of paralysis – ceased functioning, though not a stroke". Jockel, with two or three colleagues, took him back to the Hotel Canberra, and called a doctor. "Unwisely perhaps," Plimsoll was back in the office next day. Jockel, conversation, 19/9/1997.
189 Shann to JR Burgess, 17/3/1975. Courtesy Burgess.
190 McIntyre, TRC 3:2, NLA.
191 McIntyre, TRC 2:31, NLA.
192 Hewitt, conversation, 19/1/1999.
193 Hewitt, conversation, 1/7/1998.
194 Jockel, conversation, 19/9/1997.
195 While in Delhi, Tange told a visiting officer: "If only I'd been a head of mission before I was head of the Department I would have run it differently, I would have known a great deal more about it." J.C. Ingram, Oral History, 30, NLA.
196 Sir John Crawford, "The Role of the Permanent Head", *Public Administration*, Sydney, vol. 13 no. 3, September 1954, 154.
197 Barwick, conversation.

With President Nixon at the White House after presenting credentials, June 1970 (Richard Nixon Library and Museum)

8
"A Precious Vase": Washington, 1970-74

He was the only Australian diplomat that I heard senior US diplomats praise lavishly – and that was years after he had retired.[1]

Because of the importance of relations with the United States Washington is Australia's most prestigious and demanding ambassadorial post. Since being raised to ambassadorial level in 1946, all incumbents had served for six years. Plimsoll, the second professional appointment, hoped for the same.

When Plimsoll presented credentials as ambassador, President Nixon told him: "You yourself are no stranger to our shores, your accomplishments have been many."[2] Plimsoll was, indeed, unusually qualified, and well-known in Washington. During the quarter century since he had first gone to the US as an army captain, he had worked there for more than eight years. In his two periods in Canberra, relations with the US had been a major focus. Ever since his performance in Korea, 20 years before, he had been regarded in Washington as one of Australia's most respected diplomats. After five years as secretary of the department he had an intimate knowledge of Australian policies, a broad knowledge of international issues, while Plimsoll's talents in public speaking and handling the media were invaluable attributes in the US. He did not take any leave before departing for Washington but spent nearly three months preparing, including extensive visits to remote areas of Australia in order to acquaint himself with industrial developments at first hand. He also visited Papua New Guinea. He insisted on the importance of doing this, despite Waller's protest to McMahon that Washington should not be without an ambassador for so long.[3]

He arrived in Washington at 6am early in June with minimum personal luggage. He went straight to the office to meet the numerous staff. He faced a number of difficulties. At head of government level relations were no longer as close personally as had been the case with Menzies and then Holt when Lyndon Johnson had been in the White House.[4] Richard Nixon, in office since January 1969, had been greatly impressed with Menzies, whom he had first met in 1953 as a young vice-president.[5] But Menzies's successors made no such impact. Further, for foreign ambassadors, the White House was virtually closed, while the State Department was excluded from involvement in major foreign policy decisions. Australia, a close ally, would receive only short notice of major US announcements. It was partly a reflection of personality. Nixon was "not an open person. He didn't much like meetings, and preferred to study the papers and decide".[6]

For Australia this relationship between two close but unequal partners and allies always required careful management. It was not as important to the US as to Australia. "A super power looks at things differently from a country the size of Australia."[7] US ambassadors in Canberra have nearly always been non-career appointments of varying quality. In 1972 Waller told Plimsoll that the current incumbent, Rice, had "no rapport with senior members of the Australian Government" and was "somewhat of a laughing stock".[8]

In Plimsoll's time there were certain special developments. There were unprecedented demonstrations and riots in major US cities and university campuses in opposition to the Vietnam war and the draft. In Washington, from 1973, the Watergate scandal reflected an unfolding crisis of governance. Meanwhile, in Canberra, there was unusual political turbulence: during the three-and-a-half years Plimsoll served four foreign ministers, and three prime ministers. Each prime minister insisted on the importance of the US relationship but did little about it. Gorton, and then his successor, McMahon, were concentrating on political survival, while the advent of the Whitlam Government brought a minor crisis in the relationship.

McMahon

In Canberra, rivalry between Gorton and McMahon continued.[9] In 1970 Waller once mentioned to Plimsoll that letters from Nixon to Gorton as prime minister, of legitimate interest to the foreign minister, were not being passed to McMahon. Plimsoll understood the department's problem, but also Gorton's reluctance to share sensitive material with a notorious leaker. When Waller urged that a solution be found at the Washington end, Plimsoll told Waller that it would need careful handling as "it could be harmful to give the White House the impression that things were being kept from the Minister and Department by the Prime Minister and that might make the White House even more circumspect".[10]

Plimsoll's opinion of McMahon did not improve. McMahon, as foreign minister, visited Washington for ANZUS Council talks in September 1970. At a dinner in his honour at the Residence, guests included William Rogers, Secretary of State, and Richard Helms, Director of the CIA. After dessert, while guests were still at table, McMahon quietly left. Plimsoll followed him out. He said to Plimsoll that he was tired and was going to bed. Plimsoll replied that the guests included a number of important, busy people who had come to meet him. McMahon replied: "Some other time." He had turned to go up the stairs, when Plimsoll seized him by the back of his coat. "All right I'll stay."[11]

He asked Plimsoll to arrange for him to see Nixon. The president would not normally see a foreign minister; on this occasion he agreed. McMahon saw him alone. Nixon briefed him on an imminent cross-border operation by US forces in Vietnam. Before leaving McMahon had not told even Plimsoll about the substance of his talk with the president.

On his return he gave the Sydney media "a rather garbled version of what the president had told him in confidence". As this was the first that Gorton had heard of the meeting with Nixon, he summoned McMahon to Canberra. McMahon "promptly telephoned Plimsoll and asked him not to report his conversation with Nixon, since he had forgotten what Nixon had told him". Plimsoll replied that he could hardly report the conversation since "this was the first he had heard of it".[12]

In March 1971 Plimsoll was alerted that Gorton was trying to phone him from Canberra about a matter concerning the National Gallery of Australia. Then Ainsley Gotto, principal private secretary to the prime minister, told Plimsoll that Gorton would be unable to speak to him, as he had to go to a meeting of the parliamentary party that was to discuss the leadership. On the telephone Plimsoll heard Gorton's voice from across the room: "Tell Jim that it will be all right, I've got the numbers." But later an embassy officer told him that McMahon had challenged Gorton and was now prime minister. Plimsoll replied: "Well, that's the end of the Coalition Government, because they won't last with him."[13] At first, however, Plimsoll was worried that McMahon might replace him with some minister whom he wanted to be rid of.[14]

Plimsoll travelled extensively around the United States. He promoted Australia and its policies, besides keeping in touch with wider thinking. He spoke to university and business gatherings, and local groups especially Rotary, and the English Speaking Union. As the only ambassador representing US allies in Vietnam who travelled frequently and spoke to local media, Nixon learnt of Plimsoll's defence of allied policy; he was pleased. This brought better access to the White House than other ambassadors enjoyed.[15] During regular visits to official functions in New York he kept in touch on developments at the UN with his old friend, Jim McIntyre, now the permanent representative. But except for longer visits, to Stockholm for the UN Human Environment Conference in 1972, to the West Indies (for which he was also responsible) and to a Commonwealth senior officials meeting in Ottawa, he was usually away from Washington for not more than two or three days at a time.

At lunches and dinners Plimsoll's guest lists reflected an emphasis on getting to know members of the Congress. Before arriving he already knew a number, including two congressmen from New York. Sam Stratton had been on the Far Eastern Commission 20 years before, while Jonathan Bingham had been on the US delegation at the UN in the 1960s. Guests for a lunch in 1970 for John McEwen, the Deputy Prime Minister, included Gerald Ford, Republican Minority Leader in the House of Representatives, who four years later became president.[16]

The Australian Residence had established a reputation for entertaining well, a matter in which there was intense competition among embassies.[17] Plimsoll's strategy was small groups of "people of some consequence who would get something out of the dinner and let us get something out of the dinner".[18] Plimsoll was a very active host, and vastly overspent out of his own pocket, perhaps by as much as $A15,000 per year.[19] Plimsoll continued the traditional practice of separating the men and women after dinner, with the men remaining at table for cigars and port before rejoining the women. This caused quiet murmurs of protest from some female guests. In the 1970s, "feminism was starting to walk confidently in the corridors of power in the US".[20]

Plimsoll's contact with the highest officials in the State Department partly reflected previous acquaintance, and partly his unusual standing. His closest contact was with Marshall Green, Assistant Secretary for East Asia, whose responsibilities included Vietnam and China. Green would invite Plimsoll's comments on draft US policy submissions.[21]

A Five Nations Nuclear Disarmament Conference had been an idea that the USSR and China, together and later singly, had promoted. The US and the British saw it as largely a propaganda exercise. In August 1971 the Canadian and Australian counsellors were called to a meeting at the State Department, and invited to bring their ambassadors. Plimsoll attended. The subject was not mentioned beforehand. At the meeting it was explained that, without upsetting their allies, the US wanted to give a positive signal to the Chinese, with whom the US had been having discreet talks through their ambassadors in Warsaw. There was some discussion and questions, and then Plimsoll, who had no detailed knowledge of the subject, indicated that if it were him, he would "do it this way". He reeled off the wording of a message to Moscow, one to Warsaw for passing to China, and then messages to other governments. The State Department later sent a message thanking the ambassador, and informing him that messages in the terms he had suggested had been sent.[22]

During the crisis of the "Yom Kippur" war in the Middle East in October 1973, although not directly involved, Australia was concerned about possible widening of the conflict. Australia, moreover, was presiding at the UN Security Council which was heavily involved. In any case, Canberra expected to be treated as "an ally": to be perceived as being kept well-informed, and as having some dialogue.[23] Plimsoll arranged with Joseph Sisco, Assistant Secretary of State responsible for the Middle East, that, given Sisco's preoccupations, Plimsoll would see him for only 10 minutes at a time.[24]

Vietnam and China

On the Vietnam war a most important task for the embassy was to try to predict what the Americans would do next. If US service personnel in Vietnam increased, a request for more from Australia could follow. If numbers decreased there could be domestic pressure in Australia to do likewise.[25] On one US withdrawal announcement, General Haig, Deputy Assistant for National Security Affairs in the White House, told Plimsoll that, while providing Australia with the details, the president wanted the prime minister to know that he had felt obliged to make his statement that afternoon at short notice because of a leakage. Also that he, Plimsoll, was the only person being informed at that stage. Haig asked that he guard the information closely and not inform anyone else (except McMahon), including the State Department.[26]

Washington was the "imperial capital of an empire at war, and at war at home".[27] With public demonstrations the National Guard was sometimes deployed in the streets. In May 1971 Plimsoll decided to sleep on his office couch one Sunday night, concerned that a planned demonstration might prevent him reaching the embassy next morning.[28]

For the McMahon Government the question of diplomatic relations with China was one in which domestic political considerations weighed heavily, frustrating senior officials in the department.[29] Waller gave high priority to having the Coalition Government achieve recognition, but without success.[30] Plimsoll, however, remained more cautious about China.[31] On the evening of 15 July 1971 Secretary Rogers phoned to give one hour's advance notice of Nixon's announcement that Kissinger had visited China from 9 to 11 July, and that Nixon himself would visit there by May 1972. Plimsoll estimated that he managed to have his message in Canberra about 20 minutes before McMahon was due to go into the House for Question Time, and be able to tell the House that he had been told in advance of Nixon's projected announcement.[32]

The announcement evoked some strong reactions in Canberra about the secrecy with which the US had changed policy.[33] In an internal handwritten note Mick Shann, deputy secretary in the department, noted a need to consider "where we are now". He was bitter and despairing.[34] Sadly, McMahon contacted Plimsoll in the middle of the night to complain that it was being said that "the President told me about the development of American policy on China. He didn't, did he?" Plimsoll replied: "I don't know. I wasn't there."[35] Plimsoll tended to downplay the significance of the China development. Basic differences between the US and China remained "and are likely to continue for a long time to come". Both countries were "still in the exploratory stage of relations", and relations with Japan would be "more important for the indefinite future". Plimsoll expressed some sympathy for the degree of US secrecy. It was "dangerous" that relevant US officials were not involved and unable to offer advice; Nixon, however, had no alternative. "Once he had begun consultation with even the closest of US allies, the risks of leakage would have become unbearably high".[36] Doubtless Plimsoll's unspoken thought was of the current Australian prime minister. As for Nixon's own administration, there had been significant leaks, notably publication of the Pentagon Papers.

Crisis on the Indian sub-continent

1971 also saw troubles in Pakistan, leading to eventual emergence of the new nation of Bangladesh. The US approach was influenced firstly by its relationship with Pakistan as an ally, and an often troubled relationship with India; and, secondly, by its relationship with the Soviet Union. The US was uneasy that the Soviets seemed to be getting closer to India. Kissinger commented: "We can't allow a friend of ours and China's to get screwed in a conflict with a friend of Russia's."[37] The situation produced a "watershed" in the relationship of the two super-powers.[38]

By December the United States was concerned that Indian forces, having overcome Pakistani forces in East Pakistan, would invade and conquer West Pakistan. The US, which felt it had no influence in New Delhi, looked to the USSR to "restrain the Indians". On 9 December Nixon warned Vorontsov, the Soviet Chargé in Washington, that "if India moves forces against West Pakistan, the US cannot stand by. We must inevitably look towards a confrontation between the USSR and the US". The next day Vorontsov told Moscow, after talking with Kissinger, that the US was "only interested in the situation on the western border between India and Pakistan," and the US "are turning a blind eye" to East Pakistan, where India had won.[39]

Plimsoll's sympathy for India was well known.[40] Similarly, Waller, on becoming secretary, had been determined, like Plimsoll before him, to do something about relations with India, "which had never been given the importance which I thought they merited".[41] Besides instructions from Canberra, Plimsoll told one of his counsellors that he received a personal message from the Prime Minister of India, Indira Gandhi, asking him to intercede with Dr Kissinger, so that Kissinger would have a more balanced view of the Indian position.[42]

Plimsoll later recalled that he thought the US, in their support for Pakistan, were "behaving in a very dangerous way". He saw Rogers and other officials, "to try to hold them back from any violent support of Pakistan". But, as he reported at the time, he could not be sure that his message was getting through to the White House, where "decisions are being made and closely held", and access for ambassadors was difficult. Two years later, however, at a White House dinner, Nixon greeted the Australian Ambassador and then turned to the guest of honour and said of Plimsoll: "He knows a great deal about the Far East, and he was of immense value to us in recent troubles in India and Bangladesh." Two months later Nixon saw Plimsoll at another function and repeated the sentiment: "I will never forget what you did for us on Pakistan, India and Bangladesh. I will always be grateful. We owe you a great debt." Plimsoll felt that, on hearing it a second time, it was "not just polite persiflage". But he was unsure what the president was referring to. Perhaps the US had been contemplating some sort of military intervention, probably naval, in support of Pakistan, and that "what I had been saying to people may have held them back".[43]

Plimsoll saw the emergence of Bangladesh as inevitable. After the cease-fire he urged that Australia recognise Bangladesh early, preferably before the USSR, to contribute to ensuring Western influence from an early stage. He later noted that the situation had been "the only issue on which Australian and US policies have diverged markedly".[44]

In an article comparing career and non-career ambassadors in the diplomatic corps in Washington, the *Christian Science Monitor* reported that Plimsoll and ambassador for Japan, Ushiba, were "among the most respected career men".[45] An embassy officer recalled his "prodigious knowledge" in the wide range of issues on which he had to be involved, including Vietnam and other defence matters, international trade and finance, and cultural questions, and his very wide range of contacts.[46] At the same time he was probably the worst dressed ambassador.[47]

Watergate

1973 proved a difficult year with the unfolding crisis of governance in Washington, as well as a crisis in Australia's relations with the US. In Washington, the Vice-President, Spiro Agnew, resigned in mid-year. The Watergate affair intensified with resignations and subsequent indictments of senior White House figures, Haldeman, Ehrlichman and Dean, the resignation of Attorney-General Elliot Richardson, and the President's firing of the Special Watergate Prosecutor, Archibald Cox. Yet there were also important foreign policy developments with the ending of the war in Vietnam, significant progress in the relationship with the USSR, the ushering in of détente, and further steps in restoration of contact with China.

Plimsoll later recalled realising that there had been a "diseased atmosphere" detectable in the White House after Nixon's re-election in November 1972, before Watergate "gathered steam". A lawyer who had attended a meeting with White House officials told Plimsoll that, when the constitutionality of a proposed measure was discussed, the response was, "If the President wants it, it's constitutional." Plimsoll, by no means an avid TV watcher, found himself often glued to the one TV set in the embassy as key witnesses testified before congressional Watergate hearings. The country became divided, and the conduct of normal business, especially in the White House, became increasingly difficult.[48] Nixon seemed to be "isolating himself" and "a lot of small but important decisions appear to have been left aside", not least in international affairs.[49]

Plimsoll later recalled finding it hard to believe that Nixon could have been "that stupid" to be personally involved in the Watergate burglary. If Nixon had admitted involvement early on, "he would probably have got away with it". Many members of Congress had their own skeletons in cupboards, and at first they were not "inclined to pursue him too far".[50]

In reports to Canberra about Watergate Plimsoll took a cautious approach, which did not always find favour with younger members of his staff. He instructed that "while we should report what was happening the embassy should not make any comment". Also, "if Nixon said he didn't do it", then "we had to accept that and shouldn't be putting our own opinion forward".[51] As ambassador, Plimsoll had contact with senior White House figures as well as members of the Administration. He knew Maurice Stans and Elliott Richardson, who in different ways both suffered over Watergate. Another he knew was Alexander Butterfield, who later revealed the existence of the tapes of Nixon's conversations. Any leakage of embassy comment on Watergate would have been disastrous for maintaining White House contact, and for achieving what became a major problem, a Whitlam visit to the White House.

The Whitlam Government

"A period in the doldrums" was how Plimsoll's successor, Sir Patrick Shaw, later described Australia/US relations in 1973. He said that the US was largely to blame for this. It had been "slow to understand the changes in style and substance which were introduced by the new Australian Government in December 1972".[52] But the new Australian Labor Government, raw and inexperienced after 23 years out of office, shared responsibility. The new Prime Minister, Gough Whitlam, also Foreign Minister for the first year, wanted to keep tight control of foreign policy but did not keep his colleagues informed. In his haste to use his new power to change Australian foreign policy towards a "more independent" stance, he tended to take the US for granted. Nixon, hypersensitive in the wake of the problems of Watergate, was deeply upset by Australia.

On 22 November 1972 Sir John Crawford, Vice-Chancellor of the Australian National University, telephoned Plimsoll, with the offer[53] of becoming Master of University House. Plimsoll did not reject it outright, but said he would think about it. On 2 December Whitlam's Labor Party won the elections; perhaps this influenced Plimsoll, like many relieved by the departure of McMahon, and hopeful about Whitlam. He declined Crawford's offer.[54]

Plimsoll hoped to establish a good working relationship with Whitlam. He had known Whitlam and his wife Margaret for many years, as well as Whitlam's father, a former Commonwealth Crown Solicitor. Whitlam had visited Plimsoll in New York, and in Delhi. In Washington the Whitlams stayed with him at the Residence in 1970 and 1972. [55] He and Whitlam were of a similar age and height, and with similar elephantine memories and enthusiasm for the arts and literature.[56]

When Plimsoll had seen Whitlam in Canberra during his consultations in August 1972, the latter had spoken frankly about the composition of his cabinet, assuming electoral success.[57] With the Whitlam Government installed, on 20 December Plimsoll came back on a shorter visit for consultations with the new government.

Before leaving Washington he had conveyed Whitlam's personal message to Nixon strongly opposing renewal of bombing of North Vietnam. Read today, the message seems balanced if intense, "a reasonably moderate statement of alarm, but Nixon was very annoyed by it because he had never been rebuked by an Australian".[58] Whitlam had expressed his "deep concern". Nixon's angry reaction was: "Doesn't he think I'm concerned?"[59] This "reflected a feeling that somehow the US was being let down by an old friend". Whitlam's message "contrasted with the lesser reactions of countries which had for long opposed US policies in Vietnam".[60] Unaware of Whitlam's message, three of his ministers, Cairns, Cameron and Uren, each issued statements which "intruded with mounting stridency about murderers and maniacs in the White House". Nixon's anger "turned to fury".[61] All this "took some explaining to the Americans, because they had never been subjected to public criticism by Australia; we had always been at great pains to keep our differences in private".[62]

Kissinger telephoned Roy Fernandez, Chargé d'Affaires in Plimsoll's absence, to register that the Administration was not amused by statements from Canberra. He asked Fernandez to get a message to Canberra without it being leaked. (A good proportion of the messages had been leaked to *Nation Review*, but not the cable reporting Kissinger's comments.) Fernandez replied that the Australian public were very friendly and well disposed: the Administration "should not let a few lefties screw it up".[63]

On 27 December 1972, Australia announced cancellation of all military aid to South Vietnam, and abandoned a plan to train Cambodian troops in Australia.[64]

Despite the traditional holiday season, a new government meant that many were at work in Canberra. Plimsoll saw some of the new ministers as well as key officials.[65] On 28 December, in Sydney, Plimsoll had a wide-ranging discussion with the new prime minister/foreign minister. Whitlam was critical of US policies on Vietnam. He took issue with Plimsoll's analysis of US attempts to get out of the war, but apart from the "intractable question" of Vietnam, he saw no other problems with the US. For his part, Plimsoll was concerned at Whitlam's apparent lack of interest in the possible economic consequences of "reckless" measures he was considering in relation to French nuclear testing in the South Pacific. Plimsoll warned that France's influence in the European Community could damage Australia's relations with Europe and cut off our trade "if we went about this the wrong way". Whitlam professed to be unconcerned. The testing issue was of primary importance to him "even if it meant losing all our trade with Europe".[66]

Plimsoll's home consultations were shortened as Whitlam asked him to return to represent the government at the funeral of former US President Harry Truman.

Soon after becoming Prime Minister Whitlam signalled a desire for "a more independent Australian stance in foreign affairs".[67] Earlier, in 1971, Plimsoll had warned about the dangers of such an "emotionally attractive" concept, as seen from Washington. He doubted that Australia would "achieve anything by announcing important decisions without first having genuine consultation with the United States". Although Australia and the US had "different roles to play, their "basic interests" were the same. Australia needed to work "in the greatest intimacy. Australia has a bigger interest in that than the US has".[68] But early 1973 were heady days in Canberra for the first Labor Government in 23 years. Changes in foreign policy by what Plimsoll called "dramatic gestures"[69] were easier to achieve than in domestic policies, and there was more to come.

Fernandez noticed that since his return from Canberra Plimsoll had "not looked very happy".[70] But Plimsoll steeled himself for being "the meat in the sandwich between an irate White House and the tempestuous new Labor Government in Australia".[71]

He saw Rogers on 8 January. In Australia, maritime trade unions had boycotted US shipping. Plimsoll felt that the Americans had not been well served by their embassy in Canberra. He told Rogers "some of the facts of the political situation in Australia, such elementary things as you can't expect a Labor Government as one of its first acts to come out and criticise the trade unions in Australia".[72] Plimsoll reported to Canberra that "the dominating question [from Rogers] was: where are Australian-American relations going", given the statements by the three Australian ministers, and the trade union boycott. Rogers had told him that the statements had "caused great resentment in the White House and in the Administration generally".[73] Plimsoll and Rogers, who knew each other well, had a "reasoned discussion". However, Rogers asked him to report to Canberra "that we feel very strongly about this. Don't send back a report that we are taking this in our stride because we are not".[74]

Plimsoll had conveyed to Rogers that Whitlam "wished to have good and close relations with the US and that he saw Vietnam questions as the only substantive matter of difference". The problem with that proposition was that, seen from Washington, Vietnam had long been a core part of bilateral cooperation. It was from this that Whitlam now was departing.

The Vietnam peace agreement came into effect on 27 January. Whitlam wanted Australia involved quickly in international relief and rehabilitation efforts throughout Indochina. Canberra felt that the agreement opened the way for establishment of diplomatic relations with

North Vietnam. Plimsoll reported "dismay" in the State Department at the speed of Australia's proposed action, as well as a lack of prior discussion with the US, such as the Americans had had with Canada and Japan. The US had hoped that friendly countries would hold back on such a step "to see whether North Vietnam was ready to give effect to the agreement". Plimsoll warned that a move towards diplomatic relations "would be bound to touch a raw nerve in the White House" and recommended moving slowly. Canberra agreed to delay until Kissinger visited Hanoi "so as not to appear discourteous to the Americans and to give them a chance for the consultations which they complained we had not undertaken".[75] However, on 26 February, Whitlam announced that Canberra and Hanoi had decided to establish diplomatic relations.[76]

Nixon retaliated. Australia was included in a list of countries to be treated in a discriminatory fashion. The ambassador was not to be received by the Administration or by senior officials. Embassy officers were to be received at no higher than desk level in the State Department. Marshall Green protested, but there was much angst in the White House.[77]

Plimsoll later recalled that it was a "difficult period". His contacts, however, continued "as much as ever". Rogers, who much later spoke to Plimsoll of this White House edict, said that he and Green were not going to stop talking to him. As they could not see him on the golf course, Plimsoll not being a golfer, they saw him at his residence.[78] Rogers "had a very high regard for Plimsoll as perhaps the best informed diplomat in Washington on several key United Nations issues and strategy".[79]

Of other members of the cabinet, Attorney-General Elliot Richardson "went out of his way to be helpful and cooperative". The Secretary for Health, Education and Welfare, Caspar Weinberger, with whom Plimsoll had become friendly, blatantly disregarded the directive. During the presidential inauguration festivities, in an "act of defiance," Weinberger invited Plimsoll to the concert at the John F. Kennedy Centre. He was the only ambassador to be seated in the same row as the Cabinet. Beforehand, the Weinbergers also had him to a small dinner of conservative Republicans; guests included Governor Ronald Reagan. It seemed like a sign to Nixon: "Don't boycott Australia, or you won't have even your conservatives supporting you."[80]

Plimsoll seemed despondent and unhappy at the direction of the Whitlam Government, and at constantly having to defend its new policies to the Administration.[81] He, nevertheless, continued to provide forthright advice to Canberra, warning about possible effects on relations with the US of the new government's moves.

Whitlam was "attached to the principle of universality in our diplomatic relations", especially with communist countries, to assist in achieving the more "independent" foreign policy to which he aspired.[82] Following an approach from Cuba about establishing consular relations, Plimsoll noted that many Latin American countries still did not support Cuban membership of the UN. Nor was there any US movement, either from the president or Congress, towards rapprochement with Cuba. For Nixon, Cuba was still "a very personal issue"; the 1962 missile crisis remained much on his mind, while Bebe Rebozo, a Cuban émigré, was one of his closest friends. The US would regard any Australian move towards Cuba as "a deliberately anti-American act since there would be little or no resulting benefit to Australia". Plimsoll "urged caution" and patience. To hold off was not a matter of "following" the US. Rather, looking at it from an Organisation of American States regional perspective, "there should be no conflict with the idea of the independent foreign policy in waiting on the countries of Cuba's own region to develop a position". Canberra accepted Plimsoll's comments as "generally valid" and was persuaded not to respond to the Cuban approach.[83]

Whitlam wanted to move quickly towards recognising North Korea. Plimsoll had had years of involvement in policy towards Korea. The Foreign Minister of South Korea, who frequently consulted him when visiting Washington, was "very hurt" that Australia, as an old friend and ally, "had canvassed its new moves with a number of other countries before talking them out with Seoul".[84] Green told Plimsoll that the US disagreed with Australia "making any decision at this stage in favour of recognition or diplomatic relations with North Korea or even saying that it was an objective".[85] Plimsoll advised Canberra to proceed cautiously: "Let the contacts with the Democratic People's Republic of Korea grow rather than be created overnight,"[86] he wrote before Whitlam received the visiting South Korean Foreign Minister in Canberra. Plimsoll recalled how earlier Australian policy on Korea had been bipartisan, noting Dr Evatt's support in 1950 of the Menzies Government's decision to commit Australian forces in the defence of the South. Australia was well respected in Seoul; that was "not something that should be lightly cast aside".[87]

Getting Whitlam to the White House

During the first six months of 1973 Plimsoll assisted no fewer than six Whitlam ministers visiting Washington: Frank Crean (Treasurer), Lionel Murphy (Attorney-General), Ken Wriedt (Primary Industry), Fred Daly (Services and Property), Al Grassby (Immigration) and C.K. Jones (Transport). But Nixon had let it be known at the end of March that he was "so displeased" that he would not receive Whitlam himself. Whitlam professed surprise. He had thought that for him to visit the president should be "as natural and relatively informal as his visit to a British Prime Minister".[88] Getting Nixon to reverse his decision presented a major challenge.

Whitlam's first idea was that, on his way to the Commonwealth Prime Ministers' meeting in Ottawa, he could pass through the United States. Chances of seeing the president would be improved if an ANZUS Council meeting could be held in Washington. "He considers it would not be well understood if," in this itinerary, "he did not receive such an invitation to Washington".[89] When Plimsoll raised with Rogers the possibility of Whitlam coming to Washington for an ANZUS meeting, the latter instantly reacted that this would include Whitlam meeting the president. "Now was not the time to raise that" with Nixon, not until

Green arrived in Canberra as the new US Ambassador early in May. Nixon was "still smarting". Plimsoll reported that he "spoke frankly to Rogers about forces at work inside the political parties in Australia and the resulting pressures and also limitations on freedom of action". He pressed the desirability of the two leaders having "a frank personal talk" soon.[90]

Whitlam did not appear overly concerned, yet he did not want to be thought an unreliable ally or not a friend of the US.[91] The prospect of being unwelcome at the White House in his first year in office would not have appealed either. He was sensitive to questions in the House of Representatives about whether he would be invited.[92]

Whitlam next tried sending Peter Wilenski, his principal private secretary, to Washington to talk to Dr Kissinger. This cut across the normal role of the ambassador. Whitlam, although he respected Plimsoll, felt that it would be more appropriate to get a message of reassurance through to Nixon about the nature of the new Australian government through Wilenski, who would be more familiar with the new ministers, not least the three "mavericks". Whitlam noted also, with his fascination with European history, that Kissinger and Wilenski each had been born only a few hundred kilometres apart.[93]

Wilenski's mission was most secret. Not even Plimsoll was informed. Whitlam had been afraid that a request to see Kissinger through the normal diplomatic channels, if refused, would leak to the press and make his government seem "isolated from America" or even "anti-American". Whitlam personally telephoned Professor Ross Terrill at Harvard to ask him to arrange a meeting. Terrill, who knew Kissinger, was an Australian Sinologist among those who accompanied Whitlam on his visit to China in 1971. It was only an hour before the meeting with Kissinger on 2 May, that Plimsoll, who happened to be in the embassy, was informed of Wilenski's arrival, and that Wilenski had asked to see him.[94]

Wilenski had been among those present at Plimsoll's earlier meeting with Whitlam in Sydney. Aged 33, he had worked in Foreign Affairs and then the Treasury briefly, and had degrees from the universities of Sydney, Oxford, Carleton (Canada) and Harvard – "more degrees than an obtuse angle". He was the foremost example of the new kind of personal staffer that "assumed an importance unmatched by the personal staffs of previous prime ministers".[95] Whitlam had been impressed by him. Plimsoll's first impression of the people around Whitlam, including Wilenski, however, had not been favourable.[96]

In Washington it was not an easy meeting. Wilenski sought Plimsoll's help in preparing to talk to Kissinger. Plimsoll was unhappy at being kept out of the picture, at Whitlam not asking him to talk to Kissinger, at the short notice of Wilenski's arrival, and at this last minute request for advice before such an important meeting. He hardly knew Wilenski, and would have wondered what Wilenski could hope to achieve with Kissinger, 20 years his senior, and one of the most powerful people in Washington. Not surprisingly Plimsoll, according to Wilenski, was "not at all helpful".[97] Searching quickly for something to say, he annoyed Wilenski, of Polish background, with a suggestion that he refer to the common English-speaking background of both countries. Later in the evening Wilenski called on Plimsoll at the Residence to give him some account of his meeting,[98] but Wilenski's subsequent written report to Whitlam was not copied to Plimsoll.[99]

Wilenski later told Terrill that with Kissinger there had been a "reasonably conciliatory tone" and "talk of wiping the slate if not clean, partly clean, reopening direct line of communication between the prime minister and the president". On matters that they disagreed on, Kissinger "adopted a lecturing tone," and kept reminding him "of the responsibilities of a great power". There were, nevertheless, hopeful signs that a Whitlam visit would take place.[100]

At least one embassy officer considered Whitlam's initiative was "an appalling, insensitive, stupid thing to do to Plimsoll", risking undercutting his standing with the Americans.[101] Plimsoll kept his counsel. It was the new way.[102]

Next month, June, Andrew Peacock MP, a minister in the previous government, visited Washington on a US Leadership Grant. Plimsoll talked to him about the problems confronting a prime ministerial visit. He had a dinner for Peacock at which Republican Senator Charles Percy was a guest. Percy later helped Peacock to meet other prominent Republicans, among them George H.W. Bush, then National Chair of the Republican Party.[103] Bush took Peacock to meet the Vice-President, Spiro Agnew.

Agnew had his feet up on the desk, eating a sandwich. A bit of beetroot had fallen on the floor. In an "ugly fifteen minutes", Agnew said the US was sick of being criticised by banana republics, and then having people (like Peacock) creep in to back down. Peacock replied that this was not the point. A refusal to receive Whitlam would boost his standing in Australia and, in the longer term, would have a bad impact bilaterally. Agnew would not budge, but Bush was impressed, and arranged for Peacock to see Nixon, who listened and said he would think about it. Next day, Bush, after accompanying Nixon on a plane flight, phoned Peacock to say that Nixon had taken the point: he did not want Whitlam to get a boost in the Australian electorate as a result of no invitation. Peacock told Plimsoll this before leaving the US on 15 June.[104]

The next morning Plimsoll was telephoned by Lieutenant General Brent Scowcroft, Kissinger's deputy, and "one of the Nixon administration's most powerful men".[105] He extended "an invitation on behalf of the president for Mr Whitlam to see him on 30 July". Plimsoll immediately informed Canberra.[106] Scowcroft recalled that Nixon had been persuaded that refusing to receive Whitlam "would be an affront", and regardless of what he and his ministers had said, "would not be the right thing".[107] Although the invitation came soon after the Peacock visit, Nixon's reversal was probably the cumulative effect of a number of such demarches and conversations, in Canberra as well as in Washington.[108] Plimsoll certainly pushed hard on this. Scowcroft recalled Plimsoll as a "very skilful advocate at a very difficult time, trying to explain very different attitudes and policies".[109]

When Whitlam came to Washington, he had some 40 minutes with Nixon during which he tried to establish "some rapport and mutual confidence". He felt this "crucial test" came off very well. He was accompanied only by Plimsoll, whom he told not to give an account of the talk to anyone, "and that includes Wilenski".[110] Along with others, Plimsoll also accompanied Whitlam on calls on the Vice-President, Spiro Agnew, the Secretary of State, William Rogers, Dr Kissinger, and congressional leaders.[111]

The programme for the visit was a shadow of the normal one for an Australian prime minister. There was no invitation to stay at Blair House, by no means always extended to previous prime ministers, but which had been to McMahon in 1971. There was no joint press conference and no lunch or dinner at the White House. The sole hospitality on the US side was tendered by Rogers and his wife, who had the Whitlams and Plimsoll to a late afternoon drink at their home on a Sunday afternoon. By contrast, some weeks later, Nixon hosted a dinner in honour of the Prime Minister of New Zealand, Norman Kirk.[112]

Plimsoll filled the gap in local hospitality by hosting three dinners and a working lunch at the Residence. His personal standing was such that, despite the coolness from the White House, he was able to attract many significant Americans to meet and talk with over meals, opportunities which Whitlam "fully used".[113] These included five Cabinet members: Rogers, Elliot Richardson, Caspar Weinberger, Earl Butz (Agriculture), and Claude Breniger (Transportation). Others had been prominent in previous Democratic administrations: Robert S. McNamara, President of the World Bank and former Secretary of Defense, and Arthur Goldberg, former Labor Secretary, Justice of the Supreme Court and US Permanent Representative at the United Nations. Other guests included Senate Democratic Leader Mike Mansfield, and leading congressional figures, the Administrator of NASA, and Leonard Woodcock, President of the United Automobile Workers.[114] Graham Freudenberg, a Special Adviser to Whitlam, recalled that as the most "junior" Australian at the dinner which he had attended, he had sat between George Meany, President of the AFL-CIO, and Katharine Graham, publisher of the *Washington Post*.[115]

At the Residence Freudenberg had a sometimes spirited discussion with Plimsoll about the speech which Plimsoll had drafted for the prime minister's address to the National Press Club in Washington. One issue was the US F-111 aircraft for the RAAF, costs of which had escalated in the ten years since the original agreement. Freudenberg wanted Whitlam to attack the F-111 project. Plimsoll disagreed: regardless of the rights or wrongs of the original decision, Australia had the aircraft and "ought to make the most of it. It's an asset, don't throw it away". Freudenberg was "angry and rude", with comments like: "It's a Labor Government, and you're putting forward Liberal Party views." Whitlam said nothing, but later privately told Plimsoll that he would not mention the F-111 in the speech. "In fact I'm glad we have got it, because I think it is a good thing for the populous countries to the north of us to know that we've got a weapon like that. And I'm not going to do anything to disparage it."[116]

The important thing about the visit was that it took place at all. Whitlam, moreover, felt that it had "gone very well", and "had more than achieved the purposes we had in mind".[117]

Few knew that Plimsoll's presence during the visit had been by no means assured. His health was "beginning to play up a bit".[118] At 5am on 19 July, nine days before Whitlam and his party arrived, Plimsoll had "fainted in his bathroom and fallen unconscious to the floor". On coming to, he had gone back to bed, slept until morning, and then carried on as if nothing had happened. During the next few days he had visited two specialists, including a neurologist, and had undergone various tests: encephalogram, an ECG, blood test and x-ray. On 21 July, during a weekend, he was confined to bed with a cold and a temperature of 101F. He had accompanied Whitlam on his subsequent visit to New York and, on return to Washington, he had a proctoseginoiscopic examination. Ultimately he was assured that he was in good health but should reduce his weight.[119]

Eviction from Washington

Plimsoll had come to relish his role as ambassador, including "the intellectual challenge presenting Australia's case at the highest level". The richness of US political life "was a source of endless fascination for him".[120] He was well settled in Australia's most important post, from where he could exercise some moderating influence on the emerging foreign policy of the new government, given his attachment to providing frank and fearless advice, and his relationship with Whitlam. But others had other ideas. During Whitlam's visit, Plimsoll received a personal letter from Whitlam notifying him of the end of his posting in Washington and of his transfer to Moscow.

The news would not have been a complete surprise. Some weeks earlier Whitlam had told him that he was thinking of replacing him: where would he want to go? Plimsoll had asked for Moscow, Port Moresby, or OECD in Paris. Whitlam had ruled out OECD as "not big enough". He said it would probably be Moscow, and then afterwards another big post such as London. Plimsoll said he would fit in wherever he was wanted. Whitlam later told Woolcott that he had been enormously impressed with Plimsoll's "dedication and decency," in that few of Plimsoll's stature would be prepared to go from Washington to Port Moresby.[121]

At the same time Plimsoll, for all he had said about being willing to fit in with changes, would have preferred to stay longer in Washington. And he found the rationale for his move unconvincing and upsetting. Unknown to him, a manoeuvre, involving movement of others as well, had been under way for some time. Whitlam had wanted to find a post for Bruce Grant, a leading journalist, one who had given him public support before the election.[122] Whitlam suggested Washington; Grant was hesitant. Then it was suggested that Grant become permanent representative at the UN in New York: Waller argued successfully that McIntyre should be allowed to remain because Australia had been elected to the UN Security Council. Wilenski suggested either Tokyo or Delhi. Grant was interested in Delhi, which he had discussed in the past with Plimsoll.[123] Sir Patrick

Shaw, who had been in Delhi for more than three years, and wanted to end his career there, was informed that Grant would take his place. He was then offered either Tokyo or Washington. He preferred Tokyo, his wife preferred Washington; they chose Washington.[124]

The Shaws were good friends of Plimsoll, although he was surprised to be replaced, not by a political appointment, but another career officer, one whom he thought was "less in sympathy with the Whitlam Government than I was".[125] Plimsoll was upset that the first he heard of his move was as a *fait accompli*, and that no one in the department, especially not Waller, had seen fit to tell him what was afoot.

Waller had wanted to be helpful to Shaw. Although not close personally, they were of similar age and background: the same school and then Arts at the University of Melbourne. Yet Waller had been sensitive that he had become secretary and Shaw had not.[126] They had both been much longer in the department than Plimsoll: Waller started in 1936, Shaw in 1939. In the 1950s they had seen Plimsoll shoot ahead of them and many others. Waller understandably harboured some annoyance for the administrative problems in the department which Plimsoll had bequeathed to him.[127]

Plimsoll found an opportunity to discuss the matter privately with Whitlam while he was in Washington. Recapitulating their talk in a later letter, Plimsoll said he knew some "might consider that I was unduly pro-American" but Whitlam had reassured him that he was "not dissatisfied" with his performance. Nor was Whitlam "doubtful of my loyalty as Ambassador to your Government". Plimsoll undertook to go to Moscow if things had gone too far for the decision to be reversed. Whitlam told him he had been advised that Plimsoll's term had expired. Plimsoll contested this: since 1946 all his predecessors had served six years or more. Whitlam had said he would look into that.

Some weeks later, in the absence of anything further from Whitlam, Plimsoll wrote to him, more in sorrow than anger. He had already been instructed to seek agrément for Shaw, while agrément had been sought for him in Moscow. Having rehearsed the points they had already discussed, he took issue again with the department's assertion that his term had expired. He felt "particularly strongly that neither Waller nor any other officer should have been in touch with me at any time for the advice that my term here had expired". He repeated his view about the need for a five-year posting, given the time it took to get to know the US. He noted that nearly 40 foreign ambassadors currently in Washington had been there longer than he had.[128]

Whitlam replied three weeks later. The department had told him that "a move now for you would not be seen as premature in terms of the normal length of postings for ambassadors". (That is, at the general run of posts, whereas Plimsoll's point was specifically about Washington.) Whitlam "did not take issue" with what Plimsoll had told him about the Washington posting, but this was now "water under the bridge". As to why neither Waller nor others had been in touch with Plimsoll about the expiry of his time in Washington, Whitlam expressed "regret that events took this course".[129]

Waller had not been in good health after his time in Washington: this had been widely known. Plimsoll had later learned that Waller felt strongly that three years as ambassador in Washington was "as long as flesh and blood could stand".[130] This was perhaps a view that few knew, and which he evidently had not shared with Plimsoll: not in three separate private talks which Plimsoll had had with Waller during his Consultations in August 1972, nor during the four talks during Plimsoll's short visit at the end of that year.[131] Plimsoll considered that capacity to stand the strain of Washington depended on the individual. For his part, he "certainly wasn't worn out",[132] an assertion that is at least open to question in view of his collapse before the prime minister's visit.

Whitlam expressed understanding that "your letter to me can have been no easier to write than has been this reply". He assured Plimsoll of his confidence in him, and of his interest in Plimsoll's forthcoming posting to Moscow.[133]

On 26 September Whitlam announced Grant's appointment to New Delhi, Plimsoll's to Moscow, Shaw's to Washington, and Shann's to Tokyo.[134]

Final weeks

In December 1973, during a BBC-TV interview, Whitlam was asked whether there were any circumstances in which "the taking of life in an organised way is justified". He replied that in southern Africa such action by the liberation movements "would be justified".[135] This created a stir at home and abroad.

Plimsoll, with his knowledge and interest in southern Africa and in human rights, contacted the State Department on his own initiative, in support of the prime minister. He explained that Whitlam's position accorded with the third paragraph of the preamble of the 1948 Universal Declaration of Human Rights. Whitlam had not been "urging Africans to take up arms or kill people". It was a matter of "last resort", of "how long people could be urged to remain passive" in a situation where human rights were non-existent and there was "almost no possibility of bringing about change by peaceful or constitutional means". Such prospects in South Africa were "not good" and, in Rhodesia, "worse than they were ten years ago". David H. Popper, Assistant Secretary of State for International Organizations, warned about the danger of "appearing to endorse terrorism by liberation movements" but conceded that "any early peaceful movement forward in southern Africa was difficult to foresee".[136] A day later, Whitlam's letter of explanation that went to two major newspapers seemed to draw on Plimsoll's point about the difference between incitement to violence and recognition that "oppressed people may be driven to rebellion to secure their natural rights" in accordance with the Human Rights Declaration.[137]

The year 1973 drew to a close. In January 1974, in his final weeks in Washington, the question of relations with North Korea rose again. It had been understood that Canberra would not move on this until March, which would have been after Plimsoll left. But it was decided that the issue should be "out of the way" before the ANZUS Council meeting in February, but more especially by the beginning of February, before the resumption of Parliament. Whitlam and Willesee (now Foreign Minister) feared that otherwise the Labor Caucus might "seize the initiative" and press for relations quickly, which would suggest that "Caucus is running foreign policy rather than the Government itself". Willesee also directed that relations should be established "even if the price for this would be to open an office with a Chargé in Pyongyang", although Alan Renouf, the new secretary, had pointed out that the department thought this would be undesirable.[138]

Plimsoll, disappointed, said he had hoped that Australia would have delayed establishing relations in order to try further to get Pyongyang's agreement to the admission to the UN of both Koreas "in accordance with the principle of universality", and because this would give an additional degree of recognition to the international status and *de facto* boundaries of the two governments "and would make it clear that an attack of one on the other would be an act of aggression".[139] He gave up on getting approval to visit Seoul on his way to Moscow to discuss the development of relations between Seoul and Moscow. This had been at the invitation of Kim Dong-Jo, his former ROK colleague in Washington, now Foreign Minister of Korea.[140]

In a farewell call, Kissinger told him that basically bilateral relations were good. "We had so many interests in common that it took a great deal of ingenuity on both sides to create trouble between us." Although the US was "unhappy" about the Australian approach to North Korea, it was not something that would affect the relationship.[141] Looking back later, Plimsoll recalled Kissinger as "an able man with a nimble mind, a profound thinker. But quite ruthless and completely cynical".[142]

The United States was becoming increasingly divided over Watergate. Plimsoll was guest of honour at a dinner in Spokane, Washington.

Following the usual toast to the Queen, he responded with a toast to the President of the United States. More than half those present refused to drink to the second toast, even though it was to the Office, not the incumbent.[143]

Upon reflection, Plimsoll considered that, as prime minister, Whitlam did not pay enough attention to fostering public opinion. Whitlam "liked dramatic things and so he would do things in a dramatic way which often made it impossible to get them accepted". Altogether "he was visionary in many respects, but if he'd had a better personal staff it would have helped. But they also liked to make things appear revolutionary in a way. And that's not what the public wanted".[144] However, his cordial personal relationship with Whitlam remained unaffected.

It was ironic for Plimsoll to be moved not only when he was at his peak in Washington, but after the considerable help he had rendered the prime minister by his role over the meeting with Nixon. Not long before Plimsoll's departure he accompanied the visiting Lance Barnard, Deputy Prime Minister and Minister of Defence, when the latter called on Kissinger. Kissinger told Barnard: "You're mad to move Plimsoll. He's got contacts here and great influence, and you're mad to move him."[145]

Yet he was moved, as part of "musical chairs" to facilitate a political appointment elsewhere. Since Plimsoll's time in Washington, most incumbents have served for around three years.

At the core of the relationship was the ANZUS Treaty, by then more than 20 years old. There were times when Plimsoll felt that through ill-considered actions, its future was uncertain. On return home, in a speech early in 1974 in Melbourne, he said that Australia must "hang on" to the ANZUS Treaty.

> Under it the President is able to act to help us without first consulting Congress. That was achieved in a climate that might be impossible to rediscover. ANZUS is like a precious vase, it could be broken into pieces, it is irreplaceable.[146]

Endnotes

1 Owen Harries, letter, 12/11/04.

2 President Nixon's speech in reply when Plimsoll presented his credentials as Ambassador. I.3417 of 11.6.70. JP papers, DFAT.

3 WRC Jnl, 22/4/70, xx, 4583.

4 Waller found that out of 116 foreign ambassadors in Washington in President Johnson's time, he had become "one of a small bunch whom he recognizes". Waller to Lord Casey, 7/10/66, Waller papers, DFAT.

5 "His extraordinary intelligence and profound understanding of issues made an indelible impression". *RN – The Memoirs of Richard Nixon*, London, 1979, 120-1.

6 Lt-Gen Brent Scowcroft, conversation, 4/4/08.

7 JP, unnumbered Washington memo of 30/11/72. A1838/385 683(72)57 NAA.

8 Waller to Plimsoll, 10/4/1972; *Australia and Recognition of the People's Republic of China 1949-72, Documents on Australian Foreign Policy*. S Doran and D Lee (eds), DFAT, Canberra, 2002, 730-1.

9 "Both were intensely political but in ways that inevitably brought them into conflict. Neither man had a strong commitment to the party ..." Otherwise they "had very little in common apart from ambition and mutual dislike." Graeme Starr, *Carrick. Principles, Politics and Policy*. Connor Court Publishing, Ballan, Vic 2012, 190.

10 JP to Waller, 25/6/70. JP papers, DFAT.

11 Tange, conversation, 6/1/98. He heard this from Plimsoll; and Sadleir, letter of 29/1/00, who heard this from Woolcott, who was also present.

12 Sadleir, letter, 29/01/00.

13 *Reminiscential Conversations between Hon Clyde Cameron and Sir James Plimsoll 1984.* TRC 1967, ii,177; JP diary, 9 and 10/3/71.

14 J.E. Ryan, unpublished diary, 16/3/71. Held privately. Ryan was No.2 in the embassy.

15 Kissinger told him things – on condition he not tell "those S.O.B's in State". R.R. Fernandez, conversation, 19/3/97. Fernandez succeeded Ryan as deputy at the embassy.

16 JP diary, 7/8/70.

17 Peter Costigan reported in the Melbourne *Herald* from Washington that

"although they rarely made the social columns of the *Washington Post*, the dinners and lunches hosted by Sir James became a legend among the top officials in State, the Pentagon, the White House and the Congress". Quoted by Cameron in Cam/Plim, ii, 337.

18 *Reminiscential Conversations between Hon Clyde Cameron and Sir James Plimsoll 1984*. TRC 1967, ii, 337. NLA. Hereafter cited as Cam/Plim.

19 He worked the Residence staff very hard. He had to be reminded about the need for some days off for them. Marjorie Knight, Ambassador's Social Secretary, conversation, 30/5/97.

20 P.G. Timmins, letter, 21/12/99.

21 This illustrated Green's high regard for Plimsoll's knowledge and judgment, not to mention his memory for detail. This often later led to phone calls from the State Department to Counsellors at the Embassy. "What's this about the Soviet position in the UN First Committee in 1952 ?" Mack Williams, conversation, 2/7/98.

22 Sadleir, conversation, 11/4/97.

23 M.J. Hughes, conversation, July 2000.

24 Sisco, for his part, recalled that he had had no hesitation in doing this for "one of the best diplomats I dealt with during my entire career". Sisco, letter, 20/8/96.

25 US officials were "conscious we were hanging on their every word". Williams, conversation, 2/7/98.

26 Cable I.116091 of 15/11/71. A11536/1 NAA.

27 Sam Lipski, Washington correspondent for *The Australian*, conversation, 28/8/97.

28 In the event the main demonstrations were held elsewhere in the city. JP diary, 2/5/71.

29 One who penned some thoughts on China policy doubted that "in the prevailing political climate here" his ideas would "get far in the immediate future". H.D. Anderson, handwritten note, 2/10/1970. A1838/2 3107/38/20 Pt 1 NAA.

30 Sir Keith Waller, *A Diplomatic Life*, 44.

31 During discussions with a counsellor at the embassy Plimsoll referred to China as "the enemy". Lavett, letter, 29/8/2002.

32 Sadleir, letter, 15/1/2002. JP diary, 15/7/71.

33 Although a Foreign Affairs policy planning paper had warned that, as a great power, the US would act in its own interests and could change policies quickly. See *Facing North: A Century of Australian Engagement with Asia*, David Goldsworthy (ed), MUP, 2001, vol. 1, 1901 to the 1970s, 332ff.

34 Australia needed to consider the "implications for trust in US good intentions". Shann continued: "Our foreign policy must be conducted in the total dark for many months – and has been for the past three." He observed that "Nixon is not only tricky but a bastard." Shann to Roger Holdich, head of the department's Policy Planning Group, 19/7/71. A1838/361 625/10/1/1 Pt 1 NAA.

35 Lavett letter, 25/3/2002.

36 Plimsoll, Washington memo 1976 of 17/8/1971, A1838 625/14/23, NAA.

37 Kissinger, quoted in Nixon, *Memoirs*, 527.

38 *Soviet-American Relations, the Detente Years 1969-1972*, Department of State publications 11438, Washington DC, 2007. Chapter 5, "A watershed in our relationship", 15/11/71-31/12/71.

39 *Soviet-American Relations*, 537-8.

40 Plimsoll "even had meetings in his office with emerging Bangladeshis – at that time no doubt regarded as dissident Pakistanis – to give them advice and encouragement". Lavett, letter, 25/3/2002.

41 Waller, *Diplomatic Life*, 45.

42 The message to Plimsoll came in such a way that the Indian Ambassador was unaware of it. Williams, conversation, 2/7/1998.

43 Cam/Plim, ii, 313-315, and Washington cable I.127272 of 15/12/1971, A1838/272 169/11/148, Pt. 51, NAA.

44 Post Annual review 1971-72. A1838/346 TS 693/3 part 14 NAA.

45 "Mr Ambassador – flags, pomp and a changing role". *Christian Science Monitor*, 26/5/72. JP papers, 8048/16/3, NLA.

46 J.P. McCarthy, conversation, 28/6/02.

47 Marjorie Knight, conversation, 30/5/1997.

48 Cam/Plim, ii, 166-168; JP diary, 14/6/1973, 25/6/1973, 22/8/1973 and 23/10/1973.

49 Washington cables 3834 and 5805 of 19/7/73 and 21/10/73. JP papers, DFAT.

50 Cam/Plim, ii, 166.
51 P.G. Timmins, letter, 21/12/1999.
52 Sir Patrick Shaw Post Annual Review, March 1973-February 1975, of 28/5/1975. A1838/357 250/9/29 Part 1 NAA.
53 JP diary.
54 JP diary, 4/12/1972.
55 JP diary, 15-19/7/1970, 26-29/1/1972.
56 Whitlam had been impressed that in 1972 Plimsoll had had James Mollison, Director of the National Gallery of Australia, to dinner in Washington, along with directors of the major galleries in Washington. Whitlam believed that Australia had never had a gallery director who knew anything about US art. Plimsoll was introducing Mollison to a new world. One outcome was the purchase for the NGA in 1973 of Jackson Pollock's *Blue Poles* painting. Whitlam, conversation, August 1996, and JP diary, 16/5/72. Plimsoll held a similar lunch for Mollison again on 25/10/73. JP diary.
57 Whitlam had mentioned that Kim Beazley (Senior) would like Foreign Affairs, but Whitlam ruled this out on account of his Moral Rearmament background. "He would never lie – a Minister for Foreign Affairs has to be prepared to lie sometimes." Cam/Plim, ii, 308.
58 Waller, *Diplomatic Life*, 48.
59 Marshall Green, *Pacific Encounters, Recollections and Humour*, DACOR Press, Bethesda MD, 135.
60 Plimsoll, Washington-Post annual report, March 1972-February 1973, para 15. JP papers, DFAT.
61 E.G. Whitlam, *The Whitlam Government*, Penguin, Melbourne, 1985, 43.
62 Waller, *Diplomatic Life*, 47-8.
63 Fernandez, conversation, 19/3/97.
64 Peter Edwards, *A Nation at War: Australian Politics, Society and Diplomacy During the Vietnam War*. Allen and Unwin and AWM, Sydney, 1997, 324.
65 JP diary, 12/72.
66 Cam/Plim, i, 436.
67 Woolcott, *The Hot Seat*, 112. Text of Whitlam statement is in *Australian Foreign Affairs Record*, vol. 43, December 1972, 619.

68 Plimsoll, Washington memo 1976 of 17/8/71. JP papers, DFAT.
69 Cam/Plim, ii, 301-2.
70 Fernandez, conversation, 19/3/1997.
71 Roy Macartney, Washington correspondent, *The Age*, 5/2/1974.
72 Cam/Plim, i, 454.
73 Washington cable I.2602 of 8/1/1973, A7976/1, NAA.
74 Cam/Plim, ii, 176.
75 Washington cables I. 13166 of 2/2/1973, I. 13039 of 2/2/1973, I.12399 of 6/2/1973, A1838/2 3020/10/3, Part 1, NAA.
76 Edwards, *Nation at War*, 326. Cable I.11925 of 31/1/1973, A7976/1, NAA.
77 Fernandez, conversation, 19/3/1997.
78 Cam/Plim, i , 455-6.
79 Marshall Green, letter, 13/4/1997.
80 Cam/Plim, i , 455-456; JP diary, 19/1/1973.
81 Fernandez, conversation, 19-20/2/2001.
82 Statement by the Prime Minister. *Australian Foreign Affairs Record*, December 1972, 59.
83 Washington cable 2124 of 20/4/1973; and Canberra cable 1933 of 27/4/1973. JP papers, DFAT.
84 Washington O.1775 of 24/2/1973, JP papers, DFAT.
85 Washington O.2045 of 3/3/1973, JP papers, DFAT.
86 Washington O.0883 of 29/1/1973, JP papers, DFAT.
87 Washington O.4147 of 9/5/1973. JP papers, DFAT.
88 Whitlam, *Whitlam Government*, 46. Whitlam wrote that this message came via a "planted story" in the *Washington Post*.
89 G.N. Bilney, who was in Whitlam's office, seconded from Foreign Affairs. Note to Secretary of Department, 28/2/73, A1838/369 686/2/15, Part 1, NAA.
90 Washington cable I.30601 of 16/3/1973, A1838/369 686/2/15, Part 1, NAA.
91 Bilney, conversation, 3/3/2008.
92 *Whitlam Government*, 46.
93 Whitlam, conversation, 27/3/2008. See also Gough Whitlam *Abiding Interests*. University of Queensland Press, Brisbane, 1997, 286.

94 Ross Terrill, *The Australians – In Search of an Identity*. Simon and Schuster, London, 1987, 89. Terrill, letter, 16/07/2008.
95 Alan Reid, *The Whitlam Venture*, Hill of Content, Melbourne, 1976, 59.
96 Fernandez, conversation, 19/3/1997.
97 Terrill, letter, 10/7/2008.
98 JP diary, 2/5/1973; Terrill, letter, 10/7/2008.
99 Fernandez, conversation,19/1/1997.
100 Terrill, letter, 10/07/2008.
101 M.J. Hughes, conversation, 2000.
102 Later that year in China Waller found it "a bit gratuitous" that, given the limit on numbers present, Whitlam preferred to take Wilenski in to see Chairman Mao in preference to the Secretary of his Department. Waller, *A Diplomatic Life*, 50.
103 Later President of the United States, 1989-93.
104 Peacock, conversation, November 1996. Plimsoll saw Peacock several times at dinners between 1 and 15 June 1973. JP diary.
105 Bob Woodward and Carl Bernstein, *The Final Days*, Simon and Schuster, New York, 1976, 196. Scowcroft was later National Security Adviser to President Ford (1974-76) and to President G.H.W. Bush (1989-93).
106 JP diary, 16/6/1973.
107 Scowcroft, conversation, 4/4/2008.
108 Fernandez, conversation, 20/2/2001.
109 Scowcroft, conversation, 4/4/2008. Also Roy Macartney, *The Age*, reported from Washington that "the Australian Ambassador's enhanced standing at the White House had helped prepare the way". Quoted by Cameron in Cam/Plim, ii, 333.
110 Cam/Plim, ii, 332; Washington cable 0.7136 of 1/8/73. JP papers, DFAT.
111 JP diary, 30-31/7/1973.
112 A dinner which Plimsoll attended. JP diary, 27/9/1973.
113 Washington cable 0.7136 of 1/8/73. JP papers, DFAT.
114 JP diary, 28, 29, 30 and 31/7/1973.
115 Freudenberg, conversation, 2003.
116 Cam/Plim, i, 392
117 Washington cable I.7136 of 1/8/73. JP papers, DFAT.

118 Fernandez thought Plimsoll had collapsed on two occasions in the Residence. Plimsoll had reminded Fernandez of standing instructions for the No. 2 to inform Canberra when the HOM was ill – at the same time he did not want Fernandez acting "precipitately" on this. Fernandez, conversation, 19/3/1997.
119 JP diary, 19, 21, 22, 23/7, and 2/8/1973.
120 Sam Lipski, conversation, 28/8/1997.
121 Cam/Plim, ii, 324; Woolcott, conversation, 12/12/97.
122 In late 1972 Grant, along with others including Kenneth Bailleau Myer and Walter Crocker, had written a letter to the editors of leading Australian newspapers advocating a change of government.
123 Bruce Grant, conversation, 1997. Waller emphasised to Whitlam the "highly professional position" of the PR at the UN. Waller, *A Diplomatic Life*, 48-9.
124 Karina Campbell, conversation, 19/2/2004. See also "Musical Chairs in an Embassy" by Roy Macartney, *The Age*, 5/2/1974.
125 Cam/Plim, ii, 324.
126 Henderson, conversation, 25/9/08. He had been told this by Shann.
127 Waller, *A Diplomatic Life*, 42.
128 JP to Whitlam, 3/9/1973, 8048/16/3. JP papers, NLA.
129 Whitlam to JP, 9/1973, 8048/16/3. JP papers, NLA.
130 Cam/Plim, ii, 324.
131 JP diary references to talks with Waller: 15/8/1972, 18/8/1972, 25/8/1972; and 22/12/1972, 28/12/1972, 29/12/1972, and 4/1/1973.
132 Cam/Plim, ii, 324.
133 Whitlam to Plimsoll, 9/73 8048/16/3. JP papers, NLA.
134 *Australian Foreign Affairs Record*, vol 44, No 9, 1973, 622.
135 Canberra O.131759 of 13/12/1973, A1838/372 916/1, Pt 38, NAA.
136 Washington I.145457 of 13/12/1973, 1838/372 916/1, Pt 38, NAA.
137 Canberra O.132616 of 15/12/73, 1838/372 916/1. Pt 38. NAA.
138 Renouf, note of conversation with Senator Willessee, 12/1/1974, A1838/2 3125/10/1/3, Part 2, NAA.
139 Washington I. 8128 of 17/1/1974, 1828/2 3125/10/1/3, Pt 2, NAA. In fact things moved slowly. The Australian Chargé did not arrive in Pyongyang until 30/4/1975, more than a year later.

140 Washington I. 144009 of 11/12/1973, I. 149483 of 21/12/1973, A1838/2 3127/10/1, Pt 13, NAA.
141 Wash I.14594 A1838/2 3125/10/1/3/ Pt 2 NAA.
142 Cam/Plim, ii, 170.
143 Cam/Plim, ii, 168.
144 Cam/Plim, ii, 301-2.
145 Cam/Plim, ii, 325.
146 Plimsoll speech to AIIA, Melbourne, 25/2/1974. As recorded in diary of Alfred Stirling for that date.

9

Moscow, 1974-77

Jim clearly understood the great impending changes in world affairs, as Soviet power crumbled and the Cold War was soon to end.[1]

Early in 1974 Plimsoll returned on home leave and consultations. Alan Renouf had succeeded Waller as Secretary of the Department. The major new appointment was that of Plimsoll's old friend, Sir John Kerr, as Governor-General. A day or two after Kerr's appointment, Plimsoll saw Menzies, who told Plimsoll that he thought Whitlam had "made a mistake" in recommending Kerr for the job. Menzies declined to elaborate, but went on to say that if he had been still in office, he would have recommended Plimsoll. "You've got a feel for politics, and you're accepted by all parties".[2]

Plimsoll's move from Washington to Moscow was from the capital of one super power to the other, with all the differences involved. Americans were obsessed with the Soviet Union; Moscow was among their most important diplomatic posts. For Australia, the attitude was different. The Soviet Union was regarded suspiciously but not obsessively; as a diplomatic post, Moscow was of less importance, although for long the sole Australian embassy in a communist country.[3] The relationship had little substance apart from trade. Earlier attempts to develop the relationship had failed, not helped by Soviet espionage in Australia.[4]

Plimsoll remains the most senior Australian appointed to Moscow. Some saw it as a demotion although, after being secretary and then ambassador in Washington, any other posting would have looked like a step down. Although Whitlam primarily needed Plimsoll out of

Washington, his letter offered Plimsoll a challenge. The time "has come for Australia to put its relations with the Soviet Union on a new basis"; Australia, with its "more independent foreign policy", should not leave it to others to end "Russian isolation". Although "a mature relationship with Moscow will not be easy," he did not believe that the Soviet Union "represents a threat to Australia". It was "time Australia broke out of the straitjacket of cold war attitudes". A small start had been made with some exchange of visits. Whitlam planned to visit in 1974. But all that was "no substitute for the work of an experienced Ambassador".[5]

During the course of 1974, leaving Washington and the manner of his going still caused Plimsoll "considerable personal distress".[6] Whitlam later recalled that he sensed that Plimsoll "was not particularly pleased about going to Moscow, though not resentful". Australia should be taking the Soviet Union more seriously in case detente led to opportunities in the bilateral relationship: "We had never sent our best to the Soviet Union." He wanted Plimsoll there.[7] The prime minister was interested and had personally asked him to go: for Plimsoll that made acceptance a matter of duty, whatever his personal feelings. It was an unusual opportunity to attempt a new start with the USSR. Plimsoll's positive, open instructions from Whitlam, combined with his own curiosity, interest and talent, led to his becoming absorbed in the country and, in the end, unhappy to leave it.

Roving Ambassador

He arrived in Moscow in mid-March, and for the first time in his career started lessons in the local language. But during the next nine months he was frequently away from the USSR. In May, federal elections at home prevented Australian ministers and senior officials in Canberra from attending conferences abroad. Plimsoll led Australia's delegation to the Commonwealth Senior Officials Meeting in London, and then to the Ministerial Council of the OECD in Paris. From August to the end of November he was almost continually absent.

In August he visited Scandinavian capitals as part of a campaign for the election of the foreign minister, Senator Willesee, as President of the UN General Assembly for 1975.[8] He saw much of the Soviet Union by returning to Moscow from the east: by plane to New York, then Tokyo, and then by sea, and train via Khabarovsk, Yakutsk, Irkutsk, Lake Baikal, and Omsk. He had "a childlike delight in gazing for ever at the boring, featureless landscape".[9]

Then he flew back to Tokyo for an East Asian heads of mission meeting. Two weeks later he spent three weeks at the General Assembly in New York, where he helped to draft major addresses by Senator Willesee and the Prime Minister respectively.[10] He also lent his expertise to negotiations on Korean representation at the UN, on which the Foreign Minister for South Korea, Kim Jong Do, also sought his counsel.[11]

In November he visited Canberra to attend two sets of bilateral talks with the Soviet Union in political and then trade matters. He discussed with Whitlam the Prime Minister's forthcoming visit to the Soviet Union, and spent time with the Governor-General, Sir John Kerr, whose wife had recently died.[12] On return to Moscow, Plimsoll had been authorised to stop in Delhi, so that the President of India, Fakhruddin Ali Ahmed, could present him with a major Indian scouting award, the Silver Elephant, in recognition of his support and encouragement while based in Delhi more than ten years earlier.[13]

In any spare moments during his travels he visited art galleries, museums and the theatre. In Iceland he visited every art and history museum in Reykjavik. He asked questions about "nineteenth century cod fishing, and about where the wood and pipes for all three of Iceland's church organs came from (there are no trees in Iceland)".[14]

Outwardly he was in good health, despite at least two recurrences of blackouts. In Khabarovsk he injured his hand in a fall "of which he has very little recollection". A doctor set it in plaster in Tokyo shortly afterwards. He had another blackout, in Tokyo, when he fell in the bathroom of his hotel. Medical examinations later pronounced him "completely healthy," but Shann, the ambassador, thought that "he is neither happy nor well".[15]

Baltic states

In July 1974, Plimsoll's visit to Tallinn, the capital of Estonia, led to criticism of the Australian Government. Estonia had been forcibly incorporated into the USSR in 1940, along with Latvia and Lithuania. Hitherto most Western countries had declined to accord *de jure* recognition; only junior Australian embassy officers had visited these states, without calling on local officials.

The question of Australian recognition of the incorporation arose after New Zealand indicated that it was considering recognition by sending a parliamentary delegation.[16] The Department of Foreign Affairs consulted especially the UK, US and Canada. While in London Plimsoll talked to Sir Thomas Brimelow, permanent under-secretary of the Foreign and Commonwealth Office. Plimsoll thought "it was dangerous and unsettling to try to perpetuate an artificial state of affairs which had no basis in current realities". He added, presciently, that "if in some remote contingency the three Baltic States again became independent, it would be possible to accord recognition to them again".[17]

The department accepted Plimsoll's view.[18] Recognition might help to improve bilateral relations, and enable better consular assistance for the Baltic community in Australia, some 25,000, mainly living in Sydney, Melbourne and Adelaide, who could not visit their families at home without a visa from the Soviet Union.

On balance recognition was recommended, discreetly and unobtrusively. The best option would be for Whitlam himself quietly to explain Australia's intentions when he visited Moscow. But, as the visit had been postponed until 1975, it was recommended that the ambassador signify the change in policy by visiting a Baltic state. Plimsoll had suggested that, given the likelihood of domestic criticism, the government should "state right away publicly, though undramatically, what we had done". Renouf personally signed the submission, addressed to Whitlam as acting minister, Willesee being abroad. Although the matter was not one Whitlam had pressed, it interested him; there were numerous people from Latvia and Lithuania in his electorate. He minuted his agreement, noting that the matter could await the return of Willesee. On return Willesee, who had earlier seemed cautious, although "not unduly concerned" about adverse domestic reaction, felt that Whitlam's agreement was decisive. Privately he would not have approved the proposal.[19]

Plimsoll was instructed to visit Estonia, where he called on senior local representatives of the Soviet regime thereby symbolising *de jure* recognition by Australia of Estonia's incorporation in the USSR. Plimsoll reported that the atmosphere of Tallinn was of "a Western European, relaxed town", very different from what he had hitherto seen of Moscow and other parts of the Soviet Union. The best that the West could do was help them maintain their contacts with the outside world, and thus "maintain their own culture and personality and liveliness of thought within the Soviet Union".[20]

News of the visit quickly became known, with uproar from the Baltic communities in Australia and elsewhere, notably the US. Those in Australia felt betrayed and concerned lest other, more important, countries might follow suit, but no other Western countries did. Plimsoll was instructed not to visit Latvia or Lithuania.[21]

Whitlam visit

Among Whitlam's many visits abroad during 1973 had been as the first Prime Minister of Australia to visit China. This, and postponement of his visit to the USSR, led to suspicion in Moscow. A visiting Soviet official told Whitlam that his government "appeared to be placing great emphasis on the advantages of relations with China". Whitlam denied

With Prime Minister Gough Whitlam at Moscow airport (Russian Foreign Ministry, Moscow)

this: "Australia had no wish to take sides between Moscow and Peking. Australia wanted good relations with China but not at the expense of its relations with the Soviet Union."[22]

Whitlam's Moscow visit, also the first by a Prime Minister of Australia, took place 12-15 January 1975.[23] Doug McKay, Secretary of Overseas Trade, one of Whitlam's accompanying party, recalled it as the "blandest, flattest, most uneventful, least exciting" prime ministerial visit he had been on. This was perhaps partly due to Plimsoll ensuring it all went smoothly in this, "the grimmest of countries".[24] It was not entirely smooth, however. The Russians handed Plimsoll the programme for the visit only 30 minutes before Whitlam's arrival. At the airport it was discovered that the hosts had the New Zealand flag flying in his honour.[25]

Some weeks before, Barry Hain, the commercial counsellor at the embassy, had felt obliged to inform Plimsoll (although he had been instructed not to) that he had heard by telephone that Dr Cairns, Deputy

Prime Minister and Treasurer, would visit Moscow a week before Whitlam, and that there was to be no reference to this in cables. Plimsoll was horrified, both at the possible effects on Whitlam's visit, and that the Russians undoubtedly would have heard the telephone call, including that the ambassador was not to be told. Plimsoll wrote to Renouf in Canberra, who told Whitlam. He, in turn, promptly forbade Cairns making the visit.[26]

Whitlam arrived on his own plane with a retinue of 60-80, "a flying circus",[27] including another minister, Lionel Bowen, and three departmental heads: Bunting, McKay, and Hewitt, other officials, and media.

Plimsoll thought all that "outrageous". He recalled Menzies once arriving in Washington as prime minister, walking along the tarmac, and collecting his own bag.[28] The visit started in Leningrad, as requested by Whitlam; and he enjoyed visiting palaces there. Whitlam queried a visit to the Antarctic Institute, which Plimsoll had added to the programme. Plimsoll explained that Soviet-Australian cooperation in the Antarctic suggested such a visit would provide appropriate balance to the programme, given media criticism at home of his extensive "tourist activity" during a long odyssey involving visits to a succession of countries.[29]

Whitlam handled himself with aplomb and style. Two agreements were signed: on scientific cooperation and on culture. Culture was a personal interest of Whitlam's, and a field with potential for progress. Whitlam noted: "Plimsoll was already thoroughly steeped in Russian culture and history. Russians knew it and appreciated it. He got on with the locals so well. Not sycophantic, but genuinely interested as a cultured, educated person."[30]

Whitlam had meetings with President Podgorny and Prime Minister Kosygin, who interrupted a holiday to meet him.[31] (Plimsoll had tried in vain to secure a meeting with Brezhnev.) Whitlam spoke on Soviet TV – with an estimated audience of 100 million.[32] Plimsoll felt the Prime

Minister had handled himself well. He approved of how Whitlam had started his talks with Kosygin on a "realistic basis" by making clear that Australia was an ally of the US; otherwise "the Soviets might have been misled by his geniality". But, with the long itinerary, Whitlam was too tired to prepare himself to get the most out of his talks with Soviet leaders. He did not respond to an invitation to discuss trade, the most substantive part of the relationship.[33]

As the Prime Minister's plane departed Plimsoll stood outside at the airport without hat and coat in a temperature of minus 17 which gave him momentary fame on TV throughout the USSR.[34]

Decline and fall of the Whitlam Government

Follow-up visits to Moscow of Whitlam Government ministers were not what they might have been, largely due to political developments at home, culminating in the dismissal of the Government.

The impending visit in June of the science minister, W.L. Morrison, in the wake of the signature of the Science Agreement, was awaited by the embassy with more than usual interest. A former Australian diplomat – Plimsoll knew Morrison well – and a Russian language speaker, he had served in Moscow twice.[35] But on 6 June, on the eve of his visit, a reshuffle of the ministry in Canberra led to Morrison's promotion to Defence. Clyde Cameron, formerly Minister of Labor and Immigration, took his place. Cameron had hardly been sworn in to the new portfolio, but followed through on the programme prepared for Morrison. The visit was "a total embarrassment, a nightmare". Cameron showed no interest in his portfolio or in science. He was "full of invective" about Whitlam. Plimsoll was "partly annoyed and embarrassed, while enjoying it when talking about it afterwards".[36]

In July Senator Ken Wriedt,[37] Minister for Agriculture, visited with officials for discussions about a long-term grain agreement. At the joint meeting with 15 Soviet officials of the trade and agriculture ministries,

Wriedt unexpectedly gave the Russians his personal and confidential brief for the meeting. Plimsoll was angry: slapping his thigh, he muttered: "like Paddy's Market". Wriedt had seemed upset on hearing that Cairns had been dismissed from the ministry in Canberra.[38] He left several days ahead of schedule, "because of the political troubles in Australia".[39]

Frank Crean, Minister for Overseas Trade, and the new Deputy Prime Minister, came in August.[40] His interest seemed to have waned: in an official meeting with Archipov, deputy to Kosygin, after pleasantries, there was a deafening silence. Plimsoll jumped in and asked a question, and muttered to Hain: "get one ready, Barry".[41]

The deadlock over the budget in Canberra and the dwindling of supply reduced international travel by ministers and offiicals. A round of bilateral officials talks in Moscow and an Eastern Europe heads of mission meeting, planned for October, were cancelled. The department warned that "because the Senate has not approved Supply, all expenditure that is not absolutely essential and unavoidable will have to be cut".[42] In Moscow and other overseas posts economies were put in place; staff felt remote from the situation and anxious.

Plimsoll would have felt briefly involved when on 28 October he received a surprise phone call over the open line from Malcolm Fraser, Leader of the Opposition, about a parliamentary question which had alleged that Fraser had complained about his treatment by the High Commission in Singapore during the period that Plimsoll had been department head.[43]

On 11 November 1975 Plimsoll heard on BBC shortwave radio that Kerr had dismissed Whitlam and commissioned Fraser to form a ministry and that the budget had passed, with an election to follow.[44] Plimsoll kept his own counsel, and gave no outward expression of view about these developments.[45] Privately, however, during the crisis he had recalled "several times" the earlier compliment of Menzies about the post of governor-general. He had wondered: "What would I have done in that position?" He concluded that he would not have "done the same as Kerr". He would have been "on a more intimate basis with the Prime Minister than Kerr was". He was surprised "that the Prime Minister and the Governor-General so rarely seemed to talk to one another, man to man,"[46] and thought that the Constitution should be amended so that the Senate could no longer block the budget.[47]

On 13 December 1975, election day, Plimsoll was visiting Ulan Bator. In that remote place he heard through BBC radio of Fraser's victory.[48] With a new government in power it was timely for home leave and consultations: Plimsoll secured agreement for this.

Advent of Fraser

In Canberra Plimsoll saw Kerr several times. He called formally and attended the Governor-General's lunch for the Vice-President of the United States, Nelson Rockefeller, whom Plimsoll knew. Kerr also included him in a lunch for the Prime Minister of Mauritius. Next morning Plimsoll had over an hour with Kerr and then walked in the garden with his new wife, Anne, a contemporary of Plimsoll's at university.[49]

He saw Whitlam, now Leader of the Opposition. As for the new Government, he had known many of them before. He saw Peacock, now Foreign Minister; and Anthony, Deputy Prime Minister and Nixon, Minister for Transport, both of whom would shortly visit Moscow. During Plimsoll's leave and consultations in 1974 Senator John Carrick had had Plimsoll to dinner along with a much younger man, the Liberal "candidate-designate" for the seat of Bennelong, in Sydney.[50] By 1976, John Howard was already a minister (business and consumer affairs), but neither Plimsoll nor those arranging his programme had seen any need for him to call on Howard. No one could have foreseen Plimsoll's dealings with Howard 18 months later.

While he took the measure of the new government, he did not address AIIA meetings or other public or semi-public gatherings, as he usually did. But given his standing he addressed no fewer than four different meetings of officers in the department. At the senior officers meeting, a participant could not recall any other head of mission drawing such a huge group for a policy discussion – "most Heads of Mission didn't have the intellectual depth and sweep".[51] Another present recalled "the air of authority – professional and intellectual – and high seriousness that his dark-suited figure conveyed".[52] He spoke at meetings of the branch heads, the Foreign Affairs Association and the 1976 graduate entry to the department.[53] He also addressed the Senate Foreign Affairs and Defence Committee.[54]

Over a year earlier Whitlam had claimed that, in Australia, "Old Cold War emotions and fears had subsided greatly".[55] Fraser's views made them rise up again. Before Christmas Peacock had told the Soviet ambassador that "he wished to work for the development of closer relations with the USSR not only in a business-like but in a cordial manner", and expressed support for détente.[56] It became evident that Fraser's foreign policy would be different from that of Whitlam, and that the tone at least would differ from that of Peacock.

Not long before the 1975 election was called, Renouf had predicted that it would be a domestic political imperative for Fraser, if elected, to revert to the old line on the Baltic states: "The cost to our relations with the Soviet Union of any change in policy on [the Baltic states question] would not worry the Liberals or the electorate at large."[57]

Plimsoll was among others who realised this, and Fraser's scepticism about advice from foreign affairs, "which remained in his view, encumbered by the personnel appointments and the policy legacies of the Whitlam era," particularly in relation to détente and Soviet aspirations in the South Pacific and Indian Oceans.[58]

Yet Plimsoll called on Fraser, believing it was his duty to flag with him possible consequences for Australia of withdrawing recognition of Soviet incorporation of the Baltic states.[59] According to Fraser, their conversation went on for 90 minutes. Plimsoll's argument was that "the USSR would neither forgive nor forget if we changed". Fraser told

Plimsoll he was representing the USSR to him, accusing him implicitly of "localitis", that he, Fraser, was certain the USSR would not refer to it or mention it, but would let it go.[60] Fraser could not have been certain of this; what was certain was the domestic political necessity for him to reverse the policy, regardless of how the Soviets might react. In the event the Soviet Union did not respond adversely.

Plimsoll returned to Moscow. On 1 June Fraser made a statement on international affairs in the House of Representatives. The Department of Foreign Affairs, consistent with Fraser's distrust, had little role in preparing the speech which was mainly drafted by Fraser's own department and Sir Arthur Tange, Secretary of Defence.[61] There was a cold, analytical tone: a return to emphasising the importance to Australia of the USA and ANZUS. Fraser was critical and suspicious of the USSR, while forthcoming about China, which he would shortly visit. He spoke of the importance of the Indian Ocean to Australia, and noted that the USSR had significantly increased its "permanent presence in the vital north-west sector of the Ocean". He spoke of the importance of China. Australia could expect "Chinese support for our own views on the need for an effective American presence in the Pacific and Indian Oceans. Such support has been given".[62]

No one told Plimsoll to stop trying to develop the USSR relationship; but Fraser's speech showed that the difficulties in that task had increased. Suslov of the Ministry of Foreign Affairs told Plimsoll of Soviet "unhappiness" about parts of the speech, but "reiterated a desire to have a good working relationship". He hoped that the Deputy Prime Minister, Doug Anthony, would be in Moscow in July as scheduled.[63] In other words, given Moscow's superpower preoccupations, the comments of the leader of a minor Western country were not of great concern.

Earlier Renouf, the head of the department, had planned a meeting in Brussels of a select group of senior ambassadors based in Europe. As one participant, John Ryan (ambassador in Rome), put it, the aim of the meeting was to "try and obtain unanimous opinion of a bunch of old hands (some of them respected) that there would be little profit in the Australian Government embarking on a public-hate-Russia-campaign".[64] But the meeting was on 6 June. As Fraser had already declared his policy, he was unlikely to take much account of the meeting's conclusions.

Renouf, whom Ryan observed was "an extremely indiscreet man", outside the meeting described Fraser's statements about the USSR's malevolent influence in the world as being based on not much more than his "gut-feeling". Plimsoll attended, armed with a personal briefing from General Haig, supreme commander of US and Allied Forces in Europe, whom he had known in Washington. On his arrival at Brussels airport Haig had arranged for a car to take Plimsoll straight to a meeting with him at NATO military headquarters at Mons.[65] Ryan noted a consensus in the meeting to the effect that NATO was not unhappy with its balance of strength *vis–à-vis* the Warsaw pact.[66]

Ryan also noted that "Plimsoll's view of the Russians is that growing material wealth and availability of consumer goods, plus a growing importance of public opinion, make Russia less of a threat than it was" in earlier years.[67]

Trade and ministerial visits

The Fraser Government was still interested in any new trade opportunities with the USSR. Bilateral trade had burgeoned, following signature of the 1973 trade agreement. Doug McKay recalled that Plimsoll was a very positive help: knowledgeable and interested, he contributed to discussion at meetings and generally went out of his way to assist.[68]

Late in June 1976, Fraser asked Peter Nixon, Minister for Transport, who was travelling in Europe, to visit Moscow at short notice. Plimsoll had been worried that Australia was being ignored.[69] Plimsoll advised Nixon and his wife to wait in Leningrad, make some calls there, until a response came from Moscow. After three days and no word about a programme, they caught the overnight train to Moscow, dressing informally as Plimsoll advised no one would meet them.

But on arrival they were greeted by three members of the Presidium – the ministers for navy and shipping, for army, and for transport (air force and civil) respectively, and a brass band. Speeches and toasts followed, also details of a programme of meetings with ministers. A low key visit to repair relations had become high profile. Plimsoll took it in his stride, organised briefing notes, and hosted a lunch which four members of the Presidium attended. A waiter tipped an ice dessert into the waist of the Soviet Minister of Trade. Plimsoll, mortified, cleaned him up. Undaunted, the same minister hosted a return dinner by the Presidium.

By the end of what had turned into a very successful visit, Nixon felt he was on a "very cordial basis" with the transport and trade ministers. There were some possible commercial opportunities arising from Russian plans to build a new Trans-Siberian Railway. Although he had visited Moscow before, Nixon felt there was nothing of his making that would have caused the three members of the Presidium to turn up like that. It had been a high regard for Plimsoll personally that had triggered the Soviet response to his visit:

> Plimsoll was master of his responsibilities – advice always impeccable – great knowledge and intellect. The way he handled difficult issues was superb. He was extraordinarily calm. Very aware of people, he had a great capacity to make people feel comfortable, at ease and relaxed.[70]

Two weeks later came the scheduled visit of Doug Anthony, Deputy Prime Minister, Minister for Overseas Trade and Minister for National Resources. Anthony recalled that he found some ambassadors tended to "heavy" him, thinking he did not understand. Plimsoll never did that. Anthony felt more comfortable with someone like Plimsoll beside him, and had respect for his judgment. Plimsoll allowed his staff, especially trade people, to advise a visiting minister. If something was sensitive politically, then he was to the forefront.[71]

Early in 1977 Plimsoll noted continued increase in Australian exports to USSR, Australia's fifth biggest customer.[72] He fretted, however, about Fraser's repeated remarks about the "unwelcome Soviet naval presence in the Indian Ocean". Plimsoll once complained in the embassy, as the prime minister answered another parliamentary question in a manner not to his liking: "We have important interests in this country. The Prime Minister should realise this." Plimsoll worried that the Soviets might retaliate by reducing trade with Australia.[73] But they chose not to.

Soviet Foreign Ministry

The pace in Moscow was slow, after being head of the department and then ambassador in Washington. The high level of access to which he had been accustomed elsewhere was not possible in a communist regime.

Plimsoll's official access was largely restricted to senior Foreign Ministry officials with whom he established excellent relations. They admired his professionalism, sensed his enthusiasm, and responded positively: "The USSR under Brezhnev was not promising territory for an Australian diplomat, but Plimsoll was able to work his magic." The remarkable response which he drew from people was the product of "a highly distinctive and likeable personality . . . an almost unworldly selfless quality, an earnestness and warmth towards others and an ability to convey his genuine interest in them. There was something about him that inspired an instinctive liking and trust".[74]

Plimsoll formed a close friendship with V.P. Suslov, then Head of the Second European Department, which was responsible for Australia. Suslov was very senior, immediately below the level of vice-minister. He was a member of the Collegium of the Foreign Ministry, which gave him "an access and influence beyond his direct functional responsibility".[75] Plimsoll and Suslov had "a genuinely warm relationship, going well beyond the usual professional cordiality and convenience, and it gave Plimsoll exceptional access in the Ministry of Foreign Affairs when he needed it. Suslov was formidably intelligent, widely read, and given the right interlocutor and circumstances, willing to chance his arm in reflecting on international developments in terms which left aside the ideologies which placed him and Plimsoll on opposite sides".[76]

Plimsoll's usual diary entries for 25 April did not refer to his birthday. 25 April 1977, his sixtieth birthday, was different. Led by Suslov, his MFA interlocutors of the Second European Department presented him with a gift on behalf of the ministry and the Soviet Government. This was an oil painting by L. Mazanov, entitled "Spring". His birthday present was "a most unusual gesture for a senior Soviet official in those days".[77]

A month earlier there had been "the most extraordinary demonstration" of Plimsoll's standing in the Soviet Foreign Ministry. It followed Indira Gandhi's unexpected loss of the Indian elections of March 1977. "This was a painful reverse for the Russians who had invested a great deal in their relationship with Gandhi and now worried

Being introduced to Soviet leader Leonid Brezhnev (Russian Foreign Ministry, Moscow)

that the influence they had enjoyed in India through her would be lost." The Russians, aware of Plimsoll's interest in India, had sought his advice on what they should do now. Plimsoll was invited to the Foreign Ministry for a discussion with a group of senior officials, almost certainly at Suslov's instigation.[78] Plimsoll had advised the Russians "to stay calm and in effect to sit tight and wait (sage advice in the light of Gandhi's return to power two years later)". John Burgess, the deputy in the embassy, to whom Plimsoll confided this, remembers being "astonished to learn that Plimsoll had taken it on himself to advise the Russians in a purely personal capacity. I am pretty sure he told no one in Canberra what he had done".[79]

The Russians would have known that it was then 12 years since Plimsoll's posting in Delhi. Nevertheless they thought it worthwhile to seek the view of someone whom they respected, and who seemed to have a special feel for India, to compare with the advice they were receiving from their own sources. Advice and exchanges of views are part of the daily diplomatic round. Plimsoll would not have been fazed by such a request: other governments had sought him out about their own matters of concern. His advice in this instance was cautious but sound. He advanced his own standing and that of Australia for his willingness to be helpful.

Plimsoll believed that it was not necessary to report everything. Such a conversation should have been reported. It would have been of interest to Canberra to know that the USSR, then one of two super powers, had sought the Australian ambassador's advice about an important matter to the USSR, and which related to a major Asian country. Further, it was a standing instruction to report conversations with officials of communist countries. Perhaps Plimsoll was worried about a leak. With Fraser's own approach to the USSR, what he had done might have been misinterpreted. Perhaps he did Canberra a favour by not reporting it.

Cultural relations and Moscow State University

Senator John Carrick, Minister for Education in the Fraser Government, recalled prophesying at the time of Plimsoll's appointment to Moscow that "he would make a go of it," that he would understand the history and the culture, whereas others "disliked the surface vulgarity of the place, and had not gone much further into it", that he would look wider than the cold war aspects.[80]

Plimsoll's strong belief in the importance of the US alliance did not change with a posting to Moscow. Freeth's 1969 speech had shown Plimsoll's interest in trying a different approach to the USSR. Whitlam had encouraged such flexibility.

Plimsoll believed his approach was based on realism – treating the USSR as it was, not how one would like it to be. He viewed the USSR as a positive force for stability with important interests, which should be acknowledged. He had no illusions about, for example, Soviet meddling in Angola, but saw the USSR as a significant building block in international security, which would be enhanced by cooperation with the West.[81] Plimsoll "was no great fan of their system", but we could not change it. "We had to get as close as possible to them in order to get information and to make things happen."[82]

Winning their confidence was part of his approach towards achieving Australia's ends. He tended not to be abrasive, censorious or critical. Generally Plimsoll had an unusually positive outlook towards the USSR. The burgeoning of bilateral agreements he exploited to open up new, less political, areas of the relationship, building on development in bilateral trade, but also in science and culture.[83]

Doug Anthony thought Plimsoll excelled in "sophisticated" postings, and in the way he could demonstrate a warm interest in concerts, ballet and literature. Locals responded positively. "They saw him as much more than a bureaucrat".[84] Plimsoll had been deeply interested in cultural aspects of every country to which he had been posted, but in Moscow this interest became of greater professional significance.

Plimsoll sought to make clear his desire to understand Russian culture. He persisted with Russian language studies despite distractions of a full-time job. His spoken Russian sounded like "morse code",[85] but he could read a Russian newspaper.[86] He enjoyed frequent evenings at the theatre, opera and ballet, other musical events, and the circus. He arranged to read translations of theatre performances beforehand. Plimsoll felt that getting involved in these fields "helps understand the USSR better". In particular "some of the contemporary plays really illuminate society in a way that I do not think anything else does".[87]

The cultural agreement, signed during Whitlam's visit, bore little fruit during Plimsoll's time. In 1977, however, Andrew Peacock, the Foreign Minister, noted that it was being "actively implemented".[88] What Peacock and the department were unaware of was a remarkable personal role that Plimsoll played in this field.

In 1977 Plimsoll took to lecturing in English literature at Moscow State University, the premier institution of its kind in the USSR, attended by the best students. He lectured at the Faculty of Philology and Linguistics (English), usually weekly for an hour on "whatever they asked me to do".[89] He provided a comprehensive literary survey, mainly of English poets. He lectured twice to teaching staff on "Fluctuations in the reputation of writers, with special reference to John Donne". Lectures followed on John Donne again, Gerard Manley Hopkins, and on "Why Saul Bellow?"[90] He spoke to first and second Year students on "Gray's Elegy," William Blake, with detailed analysis of "Tiger, Tiger, burning bright," and William Wordsworth.[91] Then he lectured first year students on Shelley's "Ode to the West Wind" and "Ode to a Skylark"; Keats's "Ode on a Grecian Urn" and "La Belle Dame sans merci"; then on Lord Byron's "So we'll go no more a-roving" and "Fare thee well, and if for ever"; and on Tennyson, especially on "Break, break, break" and "The splendour falls".[92]

He then spoke on wider subject matter, lecturing faculty staff on "Varieties of English—British, US, Canadian, Indian, West Indian and other," and then on "Australian literature".⁹³ He attended the final lecture of the academic year, and participated in discussions with the faculty on "Style in English," and "Descriptions of English voices".⁹⁴ Two weeks later he had a discussion with faculty staff about "Punctuation in English." In turn this led to a tutorial on the same subject, and then a seminar to post-graduate students.⁹⁵ There followed six more seminars on punctuation, also seminars for the faculty on "Some problems with English words," "Australian Poetry" and, finally, "The English Language in Australia" – at which he also offered "some final reflections."⁹⁶

Irina Gubbenet, an academic in the English Department at the University, recalled that Plimsoll's lectures were "very informative and lively, full of most interesting facts and sparkling wit and he enjoyed great popularity with students and teachers alike".⁹⁷ He "never used notes, spoke in a pleasantly animated manner". Plimsoll spoke for an hour "and was always willing to answer questions afterwards. Students and teachers never missed this opportunity. Very often their queries had to do with their own research upon which they wanted Sir James's advice and he was invariably generous with it".⁹⁸ He also examined a doctoral candidate.⁹⁹

Another who heard the lectures similarly recalled that "the quality of his lectures was superb both in form and content. We were not an easy audience. Indeed, we were all experts in philology, English language and literature being our special interest. We appreciated his lectures very highly. Each time it was a special occasion. We even dressed up for his lectures as if we were going to a theatre or to a party". It was remarkable that, during the Cold War, a Western diplomat should have been permitted to lecture to faculty and students of the elite Soviet university.

> Even now that Russia is open to all the winds, with all curtains raised: and colours flying, a course of regular lectures given by a [foreign] ambassador would be sensational. At the time of the Soviet Union such a thing was unimaginable, unheard of and next to impossible.¹⁰⁰

Plimsoll derived some wider benefits. Given foreign diplomats' restricted access to all sections of Soviet society, this access at the University "provided some contact with ordinary Russians and a small insight into their lives".[101] It also led to access to all sorts of Russian theatre, including fringe-plays that were hypercritical of the status quo. Members of the Politburo often were present, and spoke to him. He was the only ambassador accorded that privilege.[102]

Only just before leaving Moscow did he tell the department about this lecturing.[103] But it was an activity consistent with the objectives of the Cultural Agreement.

It was Professor Olga Sergeevna Akhmanova, head of the Faculty of Philology and Linguistics (English), who arranged for Plimsoll to lecture. Over the years she had known many foreign diplomats.[104] Wives of British diplomats had also provided some assistance to the teaching staff. There was no formal sanction by the authorities of this free "Commonwealth" assistance. Professor Olga was "a fairly senior member" of the Communist Party, which "helped a great deal. She once said that she never asked permission from anyone". The authorities were "somehow persuaded to accept the situation or turned a blind eye. There were anomalies such as this even during the Cold War".[105]

Plimsoll's involvement was valued, at a time when there were so few native language teachers and when opportunities for Russians to travel to English-speaking countries were "few and far between". In the selection of those few who went abroad, many factors apart from academic need or merit were involved. Party membership was a prerequisite for a successful career and most members of the English Department joined the party.[106] "In those days, when our contacts with foreigners in general and diplomats in particular were rather limited, Sir James, together with the British Ambassador, Sir Terence Garvey and his wife, were among the trail-blazers in establishing friendly ties between the two worlds that seemed at the time to be poles apart."[107]

Plimsoll enjoyed a warm friendship with Professor Olga, a widow, nine years older. One Sunday he went to her dacha for lunch and afternoon tea,[108] he had her to lunch at the Residence,[109] and she had him to lunch at her apartment.[110] At all of these functions there is no mention in his diary of others being present. Irina Gubbenet thought it was a relationship of *"'amitie amoureuse'* or loving friendship, based entirely on the inimitable kinship of spirit".[111]

But this friendship seemed doomed not to progress during the Cold War. Both were committed to their respective careers, the one an eminent Western diplomat, the other an academic of some international standing, and a senior member of the Communist Party. It was doubtful "if she would have done anything to prejudice her official position in spite of her strong character".[112]

Assessment of the USSR

Peacock, as Minster for Foreign Affairs, thought some of Plimsoll's reporting on the USSR, "by despatch especially, was outstanding".[113]

Owen Harries recalled hearing Plimsoll talk in the department while on leave and consultations in 1976, and "his firm conviction that profound changes were underway, that the regime's control of things was slipping (I remember being sceptical, but he was right, of course)".[114] Marshall Green recalled that Plimsoll was, according to US diplomats in Moscow:

> one of the best informed diplomats about basic attitudinal changes taking place throughout the Soviet Union. Jim pointed out to me how deeply American culture was penetrating almost everywhere, including rock music, grade B westerns, hair and clothing style – all bespeaking a kind of youth revolution in Soviet attitudes which must have been deeply worrisome to the old guard in Moscow. Jim clearly foresaw how the penetration of American "culture" was perhaps even more threatening to the regime than American economic and military power.[115]

There was also criticism of his approach. John Rowland, as deputy secretary of the department, visited Moscow early in 1977 on a post-liaison visit. A Russian speaker and former ambassador in Moscow, he thought Plimsoll was generally "inclined to take on local colouration too much at posts". He considered that earlier ambassadors like Waller had "grasped the sinister aspects of USSR, whereas Plimsoll was inclined to trust people".[116] Another contemporary, John Ryan, ambassador in Rome, while attending Renouf's heads of mission meeting in Brussels in 1976, similarly noted that "Plimsoll has a tendency to fall in love with the less comfortable posts in which he has served." Ryan thought that at the meeting Plimsoll's "anecdotes relate a certain tenderness towards the Russian system as it operates today".[117]

Peacock recalled that Fraser, too, was critical. In particular, Plimsoll had assessed that however much one might disagree with communist philosophy and think it repugnant, Russian officials truly believed in it. "Malcolm couldn't accept that they believed it. He thought Plimsoll had gone nuts".[118] On the other hand, Sir Arthur Tange thought that, generally, "while never losing sight of Australian interests, wherever he was posted Plimsoll had enormous capacity to discover what was good and admirable".[119] Similarly, Richard Woolcott, who had served in Moscow twice, the second time under Waller, was doubtful that Plimsoll was any more guilty of "localitis" or being "pro-Soviet" than was Waller.[120]

Much as they liked and admired him, Plimsoll's embassy staff were often critical of his inclination to gloss over the bad and to overlook the defects and failings of the system. His positive outlook on life and enthusiasm for the work was such that he never saw the need to take leave trips to Finland or the UK, to which they and their families were all entitled, and valued highly, to offset the difficulties of life and work in Moscow. Some thought that, as ambassador, life was much easier for him than for them. But he was conscious of their difficulties, and tried to do what he could. For example, soon after arrival he noticed the cramped working conditions of junior diplomatic staff, all in one room, and gave them more space by letting them have his bigger room. It was easier for him than for them to get tickets to the theatre and ballet, and he obtained tickets for staff as well.

He took an interest in the avenues available for schooling of embassy and other Australian community children. He acted decisively when the illness of the wife of a commercial counsellor had remained undiagnosed after the normal avenues of enquiry, including a visit to doctors in nearby Helsinki, had been exhausted. On his own authority he had her medically evacuated to London, leading to successful diagnosis and treatment.[121]

Fire broke out in the embassy in June 1976. The building, which housed the office on the first floor and the ambassador's residence on the ground floor, dated back to 1902. Built by the architect Schaktel for a sugar baron, who had housed his mistress, Drynshaya, a singer, there, it was a spectacular structure. Plimsoll loved the building and liked to show visitors over the residence. The fire, probably started by fused wires, had burned for some time in the cork which was between ceiling and floor for insulation, before being detected. Much of the damage was caused by the fire brigade rather than the fire itself. It damaged Plimsoll's bedroom. Afterwards he took his pillows and blankets and slept in his bath.[122]

Plimsoll was distressed both by the fire in the building and by the loss of books and papers. He was not precise about the extent of his loss.[123] Some staff were under the impression that he had lost the manuscript of memoirs which he had been writing. Two, on the other hand, were convinced that this was not the case. He told one that "he would never contemplate writing anything which would reveal any of the matters of state in which he had been involved. I gained the distinct impression that he considered such revelations improper". Another was similarly convinced: "Trust was important to Plimsoll. Unless he was going to write something very bland, it would be a betrayal of trust to write memoirs."[124]

Departure

His posting ended early in September 1977. He had become well settled and, despite the difficulties of a Moscow posting, he wanted to stay longer. He was fascinated by the work:

> I shall be very sorry to leave here and would have preferred to complete five years. It is an interesting and inexhaustible country and I am sad to think that I am leaving it while there is still so much to do.[125]

The night before he left, he held his last dinner at the residence, a small gathering with Suslov and Bukin of the Ministry of Foreign Affairs, and three of his senior embassy staff, all with their wives. Plimsoll noted that "we drank some Armenian wine (madeira type) presented to me by the Mayor of Yerevan and bottled in 1917".[126] The dinner was "an emotional occasion and Suslov's affection for Plimsoll was very apparent". Suslov was in tears as he spoke of Plimsoll.[127] Next morning at 7:30 Plimsoll left the residence "after going round the building, including the burnt area, a last time", farewelled the domestic servants,[128] and boarded the plane to his next posting, Brussels.

He had told an official of the Soviet Ministry of Foreign Affairs that Brussels was not a more important post for Australia than Moscow, but "it was going to be more difficult".[129] It would prove to be more difficult than he could have anticipated.

* * *

While in Washington Plimsoll had had reason for concern about Whitlam's approach to the relationship with the US. In Moscow, however, he felt in greater harmony with Whitlam's approach, using the opportunity of détente to try to make something of the relationship with the Soviet Union, including in cultural matters. Whitlam visited, but increasingly with the distractions of domestic developments in 1975, there was less support from home. This continued with the advent of the Fraser Government: for different reasons, improving bilateral relations was the last thing on his mind. No one told Plimsoll to stop trying to build up the relationship, but, in the new climate, anything achieved was despite the attitude of Canberra rather than with its active encouragement.

Plimsoll understood Fraser's approach: after all, he was only reasserting, if in rather strident terms, the conventional Cold War approach to the Soviet Union with which Plimsoll had long been familiar. He would have doubted whether what Fraser said in public would have achieved anything substantial. It was the first sign of difficulties that Plimsoll had in serving Fraser as prime minister, which continued in the years ahead.

Two years later the Soviet invasion of Afghanistan in 1979 might seem to justify Fraser's attitude towards the USSR. On the other hand, ten years later, with the end of the Cold War and of communist rule in Moscow, it might be said that Plimsoll had been more farsighted.

Plimsoll's work in Moscow was an attempt to try a new approach towards the USSR. He would look back on his experience in Moscow as one he would not regret, unlike what was to come in the next few years.

Endnotes

1 Marshall Green, letter, 13/4/97.

2 *Reminiscential Conversations between Hon Clyde Cameron and Sir James Plimsoll 1984*. TRC 1967, ii, 377.

3 Until the opening in Belgrade in 1967. Later the Whitlam Government opened Peking, Warsaw, Berlin, Hanoi and Pyongyang.

4 The cases of Petrov(1954) and Skripov (1963).

5 Whitlam to Plimsoll, c 9/7/1973. JP papers, DFAT.

6 Shann to J.R. Burgess, 17/3/1975, courtesy Burgess. Shann saw Plimsoll several times in 1974 both in Tokyo (where Shann was ambassador) and in New York.

7 Whitlam conversation, 1996. The era of détente followed signature of the first Strategic Arms Limitation Treaty (SALT 1) and Nixon's visit to Moscow in 1974 – the first by a president of the United States.

8 Cisca Spencer, letter, 31/3/2006. As third secretary in Copenhagen, she accompanied Plimsoll on the visit.
9 R.G. Crick, who accompanied him. Conversation, 23/11/1999.
10 JP diary, September-October 1974.
11 JP diary, 8/10/1974. Bilney, conversation, 4/2/1998.
12 JP diary, 16, 22, 23/11/1974.
13 JP diary, 9-11/11/1974.
14 Cisca Spencer, letter, 31/3/2006.
15 Shann to Burgess, 17/3/1975; and JP diary.
16 Renouf conversation with F. Corner, Secretary Ministry of External Affairs, Wellington, 6/5/1974. A9828, 61/1/3/8, NAA.
17 Moscow Memo 551 of 27/5/1974, A9828 69/1/3/8, NAA.
18 Canberra Memo 202 of 11/6/1974, A9828 69/1/3/8, NAA.
19 Note of 21/5/1974 by F.B. Cooper; Moscow Memo 551 of 27/5/1974; submission of 2/7/1974; note by L.H. Border 15/7/1974. A9828 69/1/3/8, NAA. Bilney, conversation, 4/2/1998.
20 Plimsoll, Despatch on Estonia, No. 3/74 of 8/8/1974, A9828 69/1/3/8, NAA.
21 Cam/Plim,ii,64.
22 Whitlam conversation with V.P. Suslov, Canberra 3/4/1974. A18838/272 69/1/3, Pt 35, NAA.
23 Since that time Prime Minister Bob Hawke visited late in 1987.
24 Doug McKay, conversation, 29/6/2000.
25 Barry Hain, conversation, 5/3/1998. Rod Tier, letter, 4/8/2007.
26 Cam/Plim, ii, 335.
27 Hain, conversation, 5/3/1998.
28 Hain, conversation, 5/3/1998; Crick, conversation, 23/11/1999.
29 Cam/Plim, ii, 62.
30 Whitlam, conversation, 1996.
31 Crick, conversation, 23/11/1999.
32 Whitlam, *The Whitlam Government*, 145.
33 Cam/Plim, ii, 59, 63-4.

34 Hain, conversation, 5/3/1998.

35 Each time his posting had ended in unusual circumstances: in 1954 when the embassy had been closed following the break in relations, and in 1963 he had been declared *persona non grata*. 1954 was precipitated by the Petrov affair; 1963 was in the wake of Australia declaring the Soviet diplomat Skripov *persona non grata*.

36 Crick, conversation, 23/11/1999. JP diary, 18-20/6/1975.

37 Also Government Leader in the Senate since the elevation of Senator Murphy to the High Court.

38 Hain, conversation, 5/3/1998.

39 JP diary, 4/7/1975.

40 L.H. Barnard was the first. Dr Cairns had been Deputy Prime Minister since 10/6/1974.

41 Hain, conversation, 5/3/1998.

42 JP diary, 18/10/1975.

43 JP diary, 28/10/1975.

44 JP diary, 11/11/1975.

45 Crick, conversation, 25/11/1999.

46 Cam/Plim, ii, 377-8.

47 He told Whitlam this later. See 12.

48 JP diary, 13, 14 and 16/12/1975.

49 JP diary, 29/3/1976, 22/4/1976 and 23/4/1976.

50 JP diary, 2/1974.

51 Dalrymple, conversation, 4/4/1998.

52 Owen Harries, letter, 12/11/2004.

53 JP diary, 23, 30/3 and 7, 9/4/1976.

54 JP diary, 1/4/1976.

55 Whitlam conversation with V.P. Suslov, 14/11/1974, A1838 694/7, Pt 9, NAA.

56 Peacock conversation with M.A. Basov, Soviet Ambassador, 23/12/1975, A1838/347, Pt 2, 69/1/3/3, NAA.

57 Renouf conversation with Sir Michael Palliser, Permanent Under-Secretary, FCO, 15-16/10/1975, 1838/2 67/1/3, Pt 13, 2, NAA.

58 Prof John Fitzgerald, *Australia-China relations 1976 looking forward*. RG Neale Memorial Lecture 2007, 8; Margaret Simons and Malcolm Fraser, *Malcolm Fraser. The Political Memoirs*, Miegunyah Press, Melbourne, 2010, 456-7.

59 Fraser claimed Plimsoll was making this call at the behest of the Department. It is much more likely that he did it at his own initiative, because he, as Ambassador, thought it appropriate. Malcolm Fraser and Margaret Simons, *Malcolm Fraser, the Political Memoirs*, Miegunyah Press, Melbourne 2010, 456.

60 Fraser, conversation, 28/8/1997.

61 Fitzgerald *Australia-China Relations*. Fraser and Tange had long been close personally; see Edwards, *Tange*, 184-90.

62 Fraser speech to House of Representatives, 1/7/1976, quoted in *Australian Foreign Affairs Review*, vol. 47, 303-9.

63 O.MS3590 of 2/6/1976, A1838/345 919/8/9, Pt 18, NAA.

64 J.E. Ryan, diary, 7/6/1976.

65 JP diary, 5/6/1976.

66 J.E. Ryan, diary, 7/6/1976.

67 Ibid.

68 McKay, conversation, 29/6/2000.

69 Peter Nixon, conversation, 25/8/1997.

70 Nixon, conversation, 25/8/1997.

71 J.D. Anthony, conversation, 19/2/1998.

72 JP to R.J. Fisher, 12/1/1977, courtesy Fisher.

73 Dr John Gee, letter, 5/5/1999.

74 J.R. Burgess, letter, 25/8/1997.

75 Plimsoll, cable I.43815 of 27/3/1974; and Whitlam, record of conversation with Suslov, 3/4/1974. A1838/272 69/1/, Pt 35, NAA.

76 Burgess, letter, 25/8/1997.

77 JP diary, 25/4/1977; Burgess, letter, 25/8/1997.

78 The Indian election result became known on 20 March. Plimsoll's diary records a meeting with Suslov on 23 March.

79 Burgess, letter, 25/8/1997.

80 Carrick, conversation, 3/3/1999.

81 P.M. Knight, conversation, 11/8/1998.
82 Hain, conversation, 5/3/1998.
83 P.G. Bassett, conversation, 26/9/1996.
84 J.D. Anthony, conversation, 19/2/1998.
85 Hain, conversation, 5/3/1998.
86 Cam/Plim, i, 58.
87 Cam/Plim, i, 29.
88 Peacock speech to House of Representatives, 15/3/1977. Quoted in *Australian Foreign Affairs Review*, vol 48, 21-36.
89 Cam/Plim, i, 60,
90 JP diary, 4, 11. 28/1 and 4/2/1977.
91 JP diary, 14, 21 and 28/2/1977.
92 JP diary, 14, 21/2 and 4/4/77, 11/4 and 25/4/77.
93 JP diary, 4 and 11/5/1977.
94 JP diary, 16/5/1977.
95 JP diary, 1/6, 13/6 and 20/6/1977.
96 JP diary, 5/7, 13/7, 27/7, 1/8, 8/8, 15/8, 22/8, 29/8, 5/9, 19/9/1977.
97 Irina Gubbenet, letter, 21/9/2007.
98 Gubbbenet, letter, 29/10/2007.
99 Cam/Plim, i, 60.
100 Professor Svetlana Ter-Minasova, letter, 12/2/2008.
101 Lady Sutherland (see below), letter, 6/11/2007.
102 Don Dobinson, conversation, 8/2/1999.
103 Burgess, letter, 25/8/2007.
104 Richard Woolcott and the ambassador, Keith Waller, had known Professor Olga when posted in Moscow in the early 1960s. Woolcott, conversation, 10/3/2008.
105 Sutherland, letter, 26/10/2007, and 1/11/2007. Wife of the UK Ambassador in Moscow, she was one who assisted at the English department.
106 Gubbenet, letter, 22/10/2007.
107 Gubbenet, letter, 21/9/2007.

108 JP diary, 10/7/1977.
109 JP diary, 30/8/1977.
110 JP diary, 8/9/1977.
111 Gubbenet, letter, 14/10/2007.
112 Sutherland, letter, 2/11/2007.
113 Peacock, conversation, 11/1996.
114 Harries, letter, 12/11/2004.
115 Marshall Green, letter, 13/4/1997.
116 J.R. Rowland, conversation, 12/8/1996.
117 J.E. Ryan, diary, 7/6/1976.
118 Peacock, conversation, 11/1996.
119 Tange, conversation, 1996.
120 Woolcott, conversations, 10/3/2008 and 2/4/2008.
121 R.J. Fisher, letter.
122 Bassett, conversation, 26/9/1996; Crick, conversation, 23/11/1999.
123 Plimsoll's diary for June onwards in 1976 was destroyed, while diaries for 1965 and 1966 were totally destroyed. Superb conservation work undertaken years later by NAA and NLA respectively has preserved other papers that were badly damaged.
124 Rod Tier, letter, 4/8/2007; Fisher, letter.
125 JP to Fisher, 30/8/1977. Courtesy Fisher.
126 JP diary, 23/9/1977.
127 Burgess, letter, 25/8/1997; Hain, conversation, 5/3/1998.
128 JP diary, 24/9/1977.
129 Bassett, conversation, 26/9/1996.

10

Brussels, London, Tokyo, 1977-82

After Moscow, frustration and disappointment marked Plimsoll's remaining years as a diplomat.

Now that he had passed 60, less than five years remained before the then normal age of retirement, a prospect he dreaded. Retirement at 60 had no appeal. With his standing he could have taken his pension, and pursued options as a consultant, company director or academic. Plimsoll was not interested. He was devoted to continuing work as an Australian diplomat for as long as possible.[1] But now he wanted to have a say in where he went.

The ideal would have been one suitable posting up to retirement at 65: instead he had three postings in the course of five years. It was a case of talent badly used. He became increasingly alienated from Canberra, especially from the Prime Minister, Malcolm Fraser.

Plimsoll's fascination with Papua New Guinea had continued ever since his work during the War. He wanted to be high commissioner in Port Moresby, dealing with the questions of development in Australia's newly independent northern neighbour. He was "very aware" of the need for sensitive building of new links based on PNG's interests in the relationship, and "work out gradually the way in which Australia's own role and influence are to be shaped".[2] He wanted Moresby so much that "he would have swapped the experiences of being Ambassador in either Washington or Moscow to get it". National development especially would be a testing assignment, "for which Australia bore a primary responsibility".³ Early in 1974 Michael Somare, who became PNG's first prime minister, had told Plimsoll that he would like him to succeed the current high commissioner, who was about to leave. Plimsoll said he would be glad to, and Somare took the matter up in Canberra.⁴ But the Prime Minister, Gough Whitlam, had rejected a recommendation from Renouf to appoint Plimsoll, on the ground that he would be too tall;⁵ and Plimsoll was earmarked for Moscow. A similar proposal was also rejected in 1976, when the Foreign Minister, Andrew Peacock, judged that he would be too senior and old for a very young country going through a special stage.⁶

Plimsoll's next preference was to be high commissioner in London. The appointment had been the preserve of former ministers. London remained important, although less so than before. Like many of his colleagues, Plimsoll had long felt that a career diplomat should be appointed. In 1974 Whitlam had appointed Sir John Bunting, previously Secretary of the Department of Prime Minister and Cabinet, to the post. Home on leave and consultations early in 1976, Peacock told him that Bunting would have to quit on account of ill-health, and that he wanted Plimsoll to replace Bunting. Peacock had not yet talked to Fraser, but did not foresee any problems. Later Renouf told Plimsoll he was going there, and the British high commissioner intimated that they would be seeing him in London, leading Plimsoll to assume that the British already had been told informally.

A day or two later Plimsoll lunched alone with the Governor-General and Lady Kerr. The decision to dismiss Whitlam two months earlier had led to continuing controversy and criticism of Kerr. Plimsoll told his old friend that his post was a focus of national unity, accepted by everybody. But as Kerr was no longer accepted, "I think you ought to resign." Kerr took this well. He replied that if he resigned he would want another job: perhaps a diplomatic post. He would like London. Plimsoll explained that Peacock wanted Plimsoll in that post, and that he thought the Prime Minister would agree. Plimsoll said he would not stand in Kerr's way "if the Government wants to appoint you". A week later Kerr told him he had seen Fraser who had said that he did not want Kerr to resign, and that there was no question of replacing Bunting, who could stay as long as he wanted, "whether he can do the work or not".[7]

A year later, in February 1977, Bunting had left London. Peter Henderson, acting head of the department in Canberra, wrote to Plimsoll in Moscow. Noting that Peacock's "first reaction" on hearing of the vacancy in London was that Plimsoll "would be the obvious choice", Henderson and Nick Parkinson, Secretary of the department, had "tried our hardest to get you to London". For Fraser, however, London was part of another strategy. John Menadue had been Whitlam's appointment as secretary of the Department of Prime Minister and Cabinet. Peacock successfully resisted Fraser's proposal to appoint Menadue as Secretary of Foreign Affairs. Menadue instead became ambassador in Tokyo. But, in June 1976, Fraser had promised Keith (Mick) Shann, who had been ambassador in Tokyo since 1974, that he could stay there until he retired. Fraser now appointed Shann to London.[8]

Shann was not enthusiastic; eventually he returned to Canberra as chairman of the Public Service Board. Fraser then reverted to the conventional view that London "was best occupied by a former Minister".[9] He did not appoint one of his serving colleagues, but reached back into the past, appointing Gordon Freeth, former Minister for External Affairs, who had been ambassador to Japan from 1970 to 1974. Having resumed his legal career in Perth during the next two years, Freeth was surprised to be approached.[10]

Plimsoll was offered Brussels. Henderson told him that Peacock, Parkinson and he "could think of no other appropriate policy post for you". Given the Government's increasing interest in the European Community, someone of Plimsoll's stature was needed there. Further, although Plimsoll did not speak French, he could get by in English in Brussels.[11] Plimsoll was unhappy[12] but eventually resigned himself to going. In his own words, it proved to be not his "most agreeable post".[13]

At about the same time Fraser had agreed that Plimsoll be sounded out about becoming the first head of the newly-formed Office of National Assessments (ONA) in Canberra. This was ironic given that Fraser, according to Peacock, thought Plimsoll was "too soft on Russians".[14] Plimsoll turned it down. He later explained: "Intelligence is not my métier – it wouldn't have interested me." Further, he thought it would look bad for him to go "to head intelligence". He had never been in intelligence, and the Russians would think he had been.[15] Probably there were other reasons as well. Although eminently qualified in some respects, he would have had to oversee establishment of this new organisation – management not being his strength. He would also have been disinclined to return to a job in Canberra, and to work closely with Fraser.

Of all the prime ministers after Menzies that Plimsoll served during his career, Fraser was in a different category. Plimsoll had come to know each of Fraser's predecessors through work dealings or social functions either in Canberra or when they were visiting posts where he was based, in most cases before they became prime minister. And, despite some disagreements and critical feelings about their performances, he had maintained good, or at least reasonable, personal relations with each of them, lasting into their respective retirements.[16]

That could not be said with respect to Fraser. Compared to the interest shown by his recent predecessors in office, Fraser took minimal interest in where Plimsoll was to be deployed. Despite his interest in international affairs Fraser had travelled little as a backbencher or as a minister. Fraser knew few people in the department, of which he was suspicious. Previous prime ministers either had been older than Plimsoll or were his contemporary; Fraser was 13 years younger, the youngest prime minister at 45 since Menzies at 44 in 1939. Fraser was "shy and awkward",[17] not easy to get to know; he was complex and unpredictable.[18] Apart from Menzies, Fraser lasted longest in office, nearly eight years, but was the one with whom Plimsoll had had the least direct dealings.

Plimsoll would have applauded Fraser's contribution on Zimbabwe. Was Fraser aware of Plimsoll's role on Rhodesia and other African issues when he was at the UN?

But from Fraser's viewpoint their differing views about the Soviet Union were a problem that could not be underestimated. There had been the question of the three Baltic States a year earlier, and in 1969 the passage in Freeth's speech about the Indian Ocean, of which Fraser probably disapproved. According to one close observer: "Fraser was obsessed and alarmist about the Russian threat. Although you could argue with him, to disagree with him on the Soviets gave you a serious black mark in his mind."[19]

One encounter Plimsoll recalled occurred late in 1969. Fraser, then defence minister, asked Plimsoll as secretary of external affairs for some information and then said that Plimsoll was not to tell McMahon, Plimsoll's minister. Plimsoll refused: Fraser was "silly" because there was "no reason" why McMahon should not get the information. "But once he told me not to tell my own Minister, I just could not live with that."[20] Plimsoll held to standards of correct dealings with his minister, despite his attitude to McMahon. Plimsoll increasingly was to form a negative impression of Fraser.[21]

Brussels

Fraser's short visit to Brussels in June 1977 had a profound effect on his approach to the European Community (EC), and so on Plimsoll's time in Brussels.[22] By 1977 there was resentment and dissatisfaction in Canberra about a continuing lack of provision for regular consultations with the EC for countries like Australia which were adversely affected by the UK's membership of the EC (since 1973) and a sense that Australia's interests had been betrayed under the Whitlam Government.[23] Fraser wanted quick progress for Australia in respect of the EC, with agreement to regular consultations. He was dealing with not one government but (at that time) nine, which were accustomed to moving with deliberation. Perhaps he had not been well informed about this. As part of a wider visit to Europe he came to Brussels for less than 48 hours, much of which was taken up with calls on key figures in NATO and on leading Belgians.

Fraser first had a *tête-à-tête* with the President of the EC, Roy Jenkins. It was not a happy day for either. As a former senior member of the Wilson Labour Government in Britain, Jenkins had bad memories of dealings with Australia.[24] Fraser told Jenkins that he wanted to be able to leave Brussels, the next day, with a written agreement from the EC to annual negotiations with Australia about trade difficulties. Jenkins said he could not guarantee this outcome.[25] The working lunch that followed with Jenkins and other European commissioners was an acrimonious affair. The antipathy and hostility between Jenkins and Fraser was palpable. Jenkins was rude, Fraser arrogant.[26] Fraser, "who had no time for European courtesies, got stuck straight into the EC"[27] and its protectionism.[28]

After lunch Jenkins suggested they leave it to the "chaps"; he would guarantee Fraser's desired result. Fraser instructed his officials to reach an acceptable written agreement with the EC by next morning.[29] The negotiations went on through the afternoon and evening. Crispin Tickell, Jenkins's *Chef de Cabinet*, had some "pretty acerbic exchanges" with Fraser over the phone. Peacock, accompanying Fraser, told Tickell not to be put out by Fraser's manners. "He is much worse with us."[30] Fraser obtained his written agreement but at the cost of putting the EC's most powerful officials offside.[31] What he sought involved the Common Agricultural Policy (CAP), a sacred cow of the EC; to say that "some adjustments can and should be made"[32] was anathema.[33]

Fraser decided that the EC was "so uncooperative, so unhelpful, unwilling to treat Australia in a realistic, decent way, that if Australia was going to get anywhere, it would need a sharper focus".[34] Dissatisfied with the performances of the departments of Foreign Affairs and

Overseas Trade respectively, Fraser decided that what he wanted to achieve from the EC – better access for agricultural exports – called for special measures.

Fraser persuaded Cabinet to adopt a "head-on tack" towards the EC,[35] the instrument for which was creation of a new department, Special Trade Representations (STR), staffed by a small group of senior officials, seconded mainly from trade, but also from Foreign Affairs and Prime Minister and Cabinet. STR's charter was an intensive attempt to improve Australia's EC trade access, especially in agricultural produce.[36] Trade matters normally were the province of the Country Party in the Coalition. Fraser appointed a minister in charge of STR, who would work under Anthony's direction. The minister chosen was John Howard, a Liberal, who had previously been Minister for Business and Consumer Affairs. The minister and STR team would conduct an intensive series of visits to Brussels and to other EC member capitals. Fraser was "convinced that the only way we would make real progress would be, effectively, to have a resident minister in Europe banging on doors the entire time".[37]

Plimsoll had no inkling of what was in store. He was well-versed in the evolution of the EC and of the development of Australian policy. But he lacked briefing in Fraser's thinking because, in this case, Plimsoll had decided to proceed straight to the new post, settle in for a few months, and only then take home leave and consultations. Plimsoll flew from Moscow to Brussels on Saturday 16 September. I met him at the airport and introduced him to John Howard who, accompanied by officials, had arrived only a few minutes earlier, on his first official visit to Europe.[38]

Next day, Sunday, Plimsoll attended a special briefing laid on for Howard and his team in the mission office. The main speaker was Dr Jim Cumes, Plimsoll's predecessor as ambassador in Brussels, who had come from his new post in Vienna for this purpose. This Sunday briefing was an early indication of the extent to which the team was coming to its task "cold" and under pressure for early results. Of the Canberra officials accompanying Howard, only Colin Teese had had extensive experience of international trade negotiations. The most senior official, Philip Flood, had been withdrawn at short notice from his post as deputy ambassador in Washington to join STR. Twenty years before Plimsoll had interviewed him for recruitment to the department.

On the Monday there occurred what Plimsoll later described as a defining moment in his relationship with Howard and his team. This was at a meeting with them at the embassy. Plimsoll had not been specifically invited, but "naturally turned up", taking it for granted that, as ambassador, he would participate. He found, by contrast, that "it was clear that I was not expected and that my presence was not wanted".[39]

The meeting had considered how Australia might be able to apply leverage on the EC: nuclear safeguards and the supply of Australian uranium was seen as one possible avenue for dividing the Europeans against each other. Plimsoll spoke out against this proposition. Firstly, it was not in Australia's political and security interest to break Western European unity. Secondly, Australia wanted the EC as a whole to agree with our nuclear safeguards policy (not least so that they could qualify as approved customers to purchase Australian uranium). Plimsoll felt that the objections he had expressed to the STR team "irritated them", and may have been why he was neither informed nor invited to any subsequent STR delegation meeting held in Brussels. Further meetings were held away from the embassy.[40]

It was all "rather humiliating for me".[41] Many times in his career his advice had not been accepted. Now he was to find that his advice was not even sought. It was a new and unpleasant experience to find himself uninvolved in a major negotiation going on around him, virtually a spectator, despite his considerable experience, not least in multilateral diplomacy.

STR's game plan had been hatched in Canberra at high level. It allowed little room for manoeuvre, and was one which they did not share with Plimsoll or any other Australian representatives stationed in

Europe. Plimsoll assessed that there was nothing personal in this. Rather it had been decided that Australian posts in Europe generally would be "difficult" and the team had arrived "with its mind virtually made up to by-pass them".[42] Plimsoll and his staff, including those working on trade policy, took no part in the drafting or discussion of the "Howard memorandum," which was to be the basic statement to the EC of Australian intent. One day before the memorandum was submitted to the EC Plimsoll was asked for comments but he declined:

> I did not feel myself able to comment at short notice on a long paper in whose preparation I had played no part and where I had no first hand knowledge of the team's discussions with other parties.[43]

Plimsoll accepted the desirability of better agricultural access. But he was "very put off by the style of the STR exercise – a bit gung ho, very confrontational, megaphone diplomacy". Nor did he like other retaliatory options, such as proposals to involve Australian defence procurement and export of European cars to Australia. "He was visibly turned off by the whole thing",[44] he was "exercised, anguished" and he disliked the "abrasions" of the STR exercise.[45] It went against the grain of normal diplomatic negotiation. It would affect normal working relations with the EC, in particular with the UK, whom Plimsoll believed could contribute to reform of the EC to ways more compatible with trade interests of the wider Western world. Teese told Plimsoll that Fraser did not accept this, that the STR approach would be "difficult and abrasive", but there was no alternative.[46]

Plimsoll felt that the STR took "a most narrow view of their task. They were a 'task force', and everything was to be subordinated to it". He "tried to keep the widest conception of our interests before Canberra, and to argue against our relations with Europe revolving around a few tons of beef". Plimsoll noted that the Department of Foreign Affairs "has a greater tradition of speaking frankly than some other departments".[47]

That tradition must have surprised Howard. In his late thirties, he had been a member of the House of Representatives for three years, and a minister for less than two. He had been given a task in which the Prime Minister would take a particular interest in his performance. Trying to carry out what Howard thought was an agreed government policy, it must have been surprising to be confronted by an ambassador with 30 years of high level experience who, having been newly exposed to the STR strategy, instantly expressed profound disagreement.

In accordance with his usual practice Plimsoll had Howard and his accompanying officials to meals at the Residence. Although included in STR meetings with officials of the Belgian Government, Plimsoll was excluded from the key ones, those with European commissioners. The EC had offered two lunches for Howard and asked who he would like invited in addition to the ambassador. Plimsoll learned that Howard said "he did not want me invited".[48]

Howard later recalled having spent "seven weeks tramping round Europe, not making a great deal of progress".[49] He left Brussels on 28 October. He never returned: he was very shortly appointed Treasurer, and was confirmed in this post following the federal elections on 10 December 1977. Plimsoll's disenchantment with Fraser was not lessened by the holding of these elections, "after only two years in office when the Government had a more than comfortable majority". In a letter written before the elections he said:

> Whatever the outcome, I think it was wrong to have an election. People expect governments, in normal circumstances, to serve the major part of the period for which they have been elected.[50]

It was not like him to express such a view of the government of the day on paper.

At the end of 1977, Plimsoll returned to Australia for leave and consultations. Ironically, given what he had just been through in Brussels, in the Australia Day Honours list for 26 January 1978, Plimsoll was appointed a Companion of the Order of Australia, a very high Australian award, which is "for eminent services to Australia or to humanity". Of the messages he received, one was from Gough Whitlam, under whose government the Order of Australia had been instituted. "Am delighted with your award. You are eminently the sort of person whom our national system was designed to honour." The other was from Sir Walter Crocker, who noted that Plimsoll was the first serving Australian diplomat to receive the AC: "It is right that you are the first, for no member of the service has approached your contribution."[51] Plimsoll was only the second serving public servant to receive the award, Tange having been the first six months earlier. Of the two other ACs awarded that day, one was to his old friend Emeritus Professor Sir John Crawford.

Howard's place as Minister for Special Trade Representations was taken by Victor Garland. Plimsoll, who already knew Garland, had him to a meal in Canberra, and visited him and his wife at their home in Perth, en route back to Brussels.[52] But dealings with the STR team did not improve. The Australian mission in Brussels was still "in the dark as to the STR thinking or what they were doing". There was in fact "resentment if we tried to get into the act". STR often dealt directly with the EC by telephone without informing the mission. Talks were held in Geneva with EC commissioners and their officials, but neither Plimsoll nor any of his staff were invited. Contrary to normal practice, STR were reluctant to leave a copy of their brief with the mission when they visited Brussels.[53]

As Plimsoll saw it:

> Howard, and to a lesser degree Garland, acted as though he were the head of mission, with Flood as the Deputy. The Mission's function was in effect reduced to providing transport, arranging accommodation, secretarial assistance, and obtaining information for them.[54]

In mid-1978 the agriculture commissioner, Finn Gundelach, was to convey the EC reply to the Howard memorandum at talks with Garland. The talks were preceded by a meeting at officials level, in which the Australian delegation was led by Flood. The latter informed Plimsoll that Garland would expect him to attend "in order to give weight by your presence to what I have to say". Plimsoll declined. He felt he could not attend because he had not seen the brief. "I would have had to let Flood play things as he chose and appear to be concurring, whether I thought the tactics right or not." Further, he did not see how he could have preserved his standing locally given the "important role" he understood he would play, when asked by the government to come to Brussels in the first place.[55]

One STR official told Plimsoll that in first announcing Howard's appointment as Minister for Special Trade Representations, Fraser had said it was to allow contact at commissioner level. The implication which Plimsoll drew was that he should leave it to Garland to talk to commissioners, but he declined. Plimsoll felt he had good personal relations with Gundelach, but left any dealings of substance to Garland. He felt he developed good personal relations with Jenkins, commission president, and with commissioners Haferkamp, Davignon and Tugendhat and with their staffs, and felt he was able to do something, in the way of "explaining things" and "picking up pieces and smoothing ruffled feathers or worse in the wake of STR visitations" or "shenanigans". Further he continued to give his usual frank advice to Canberra and to the visitors, although often this was not appreciated "and indeed resented by STR".[56]

Early in 1979 Plimsoll heard a report that he was "regarded as uncooperative and was about to be replaced by a Trade man" as ambassador.[57] In fact there was a proposal that Max Moore-Wilton, then a senior officer in trade, would become the top trade representative on Plimsoll's staff in Brussels but with a mandate to operate personally throughout Europe, and "fix the problem" of agricultural access. That did not happen.[58]

Plimsoll praised trade department officials based in Australian posts in Europe for the way they worked closely with their foreign affairs counterparts during this difficult period. Though his views, and those of other posts in Europe, may not have been palatable to STR and others, he felt "they helped to save the Government from itself".[59]

Early in 1979 Plimsoll felt he "could see our ship headed for the rocks". He cabled Canberra that he had called on Jenkins, "explained the situation very frankly to him, and urged the need to treat the situation on a broad political basis". He reported that Jenkins was impressed, and gave some instructions. On 7 June Plimsoll took a visiting Australian parliamentary delegation to call on Jenkins.[60] Jenkins said he was glad that an EC/Australia agreement under the framework of the Multilateral Trade Negotiations (MTN) had been reached. He continued: "The MTN is a personal triumph for your Ambassador. Without Sir James Plimsoll, there would have been no MTN agreement with Australia." At the time Plimsoll had told Alexander Downer, the third secretary who was present as note-taker, to omit that part from the record of the meeting, "first out of a sense of modesty" and partly because "it seemed desirable not to diminish any role of a Minister".[61]

The STR exercise did not achieve what Fraser wanted, apart from minor improvements. The outcome achieved in the Multilateral Trade Negotiations with the EC as part of the Tokyo Round of the GATT (started 1973, ended 1979) included slightly better access for beef and cheese. Whether the result was commensurate with the effort and the effect on Australia's general standing in Europe was another question. "In the long run it did little good. The Europeans, then as now, remained impervious to any but their own interests."[62]

In hindsight it is not easy to understand how the STR exercise could have had much effect. The fundamental difficulty was the Common Agricultural Policy (CAP). The confrontational style of STR reflected an impatience on the part of Fraser and his close advisers when a more

Call by Australian Parliamentary Delegation in Brussels, 1979, on Roy Jenkins, President of the European Commission. Left to right: Jenkins, Gordon Scholes, Stephen Lusher, Alexander Downer (Third Secretary, Brussels), Jim Short, Sir Billy Snedden, Senator Reg Withers, Ken Fry, Senator Don Grimes, and Plimsoll (European Union)

subtle, nuanced approach might better have achieved the desired goals. "It was just not the way the world works". There was "need for more respect and understanding of the Europeans".[63]

It was the STR exercise that made Brussels "professionally the least satisfying" of all Plimsoll's postings, because the Australian Government had "mishandled its negotiations with the EC and it was very difficult". Australia "gave undue prominence to beef. We have a lot more at stake in Europe than that".[64] Plimsoll was not alone in voicing misgivings. Apart from other Australian posts in Europe, there were reservations at senior levels in departments in Canberra. Peacock was advised to resist pressure from other ministers to make nuclear safeguards a leverage point with the EC. Australia could not afford to weaken nuclear safeguards policy in the unlikely hope that this would lead to greater access for Australian beef exports. Peacock succeeded but "at considerable personal cost".[65]

Outwardly Plimsoll carried on with his usual calm, grace, good humour and professionalism. One of his diplomatic colleagues recalled in discussions Plimsoll's "acumen, his sensitivity to the undercurrents in world affairs and the clarity of his expression".[66] Plimsoll took a considerable interest in the European Parliament, meeting in Strasbourg or Luxembourg. He spent hours listening to the debates, and talking to the members. It was part of a Plimsoll strategy to try to broaden the EC relationship with Australia, and develop more personal contact. In his successor's time in Brussels a European parliamentary delegation visited Australia for the first time.[67] He travelled extensively in Belgium and Luxembourg. Aside from official travel, whenever he could he would go alone at weekends for one or two nights to various cities in Belgium, visit local galleries, museums and bookshops and attend performances of ballet or opera, go for walks, and often, on a Sunday morning, he would sit on a park bench and read. Most people he knew well in Brussels were English-speaking, but he read much in French.[68] During 1979-80 he gained some solace from commuting to Geneva to represent Australia at meetings of the Committee for Disarmament, which Australia had joined at the beginning of 1979. At that time the department foreshadowed proposing that Plimsoll lead the Australian delegation to the Second Nuclear Non-proliferation Treaty (NPT) Review conference in 1980.[69]

London

In November 1979 Peacock had told Plimsoll that although he was still hopeful, he feared that Fraser would make another "outside appointment" to succeed Freeth in London.[70] Then the situation changed. On 10 January 1980, Plimsoll was in Luxembourg with Sir Billy Snedden, the Speaker of the House of Representatives, and was accompanied by the third secretary, Alexander Downer. After breakfast he received a "phone call from Australia – it was Peacock conveying an offer of appointment as high commissioner in London". Plimsoll was delighted to accept.[71]

Plimsoll's appointment, however, did not mean Fraser now favoured career officers for the post. This was far from the case, just as Fraser's intended appointment of Shann to London a few years before had been mainly to prise him out of Tokyo. Fraser did not want to appoint one of his current ministers and precipitate a by-election shortly before general elections, due by year's end. It would also have been too long to leave the post unfilled. He had told Peacock that the selection was his call, but that whoever was chosen should know that tenure might be short: after the elections Fraser might want to make a political appointment. He was trying to "warn off" whoever took the job.[72]

In agreeing to Peacock's nomination of Plimsoll, Fraser was agreeing to appointment for the first time of a career diplomat, one of some standing, and already well known in high places in London. Lord Carrington, the foreign secretary in Mrs Thatcher's Government, had a high opinion of Plimsoll formed over 20 years, going back to his time as high commissioner in Canberra.[73] With Plimsoll as the nominee, the

British naturally assumed that his tenure would be of normal length. How it might have looked to the British if Plimsoll was there such a short time did not seem to concern Fraser. Despite his period as a student at Oxford, Fraser seems to have formed no particular affection for the British and he had more personal liking for her Labour Party predecessor, James Callaghan, than for the current prime minister, Margaret Thatcher.[74]

Freeth had been in London for less than three years. He might have been persuaded to stay until at least the middle of 1980, thus avoiding the need for a new appointment until after the election. However, there was no inclination to extend Freeth's time.[75] The alternative would have been to send someone as acting high commissioner until after the election.

There is some question as to whether Plimsoll was told of the condition stipulated by Fraser before he accepted the appointment. Plimsoll later recalled that Peacock, when he made the offer, had said it would be for three years, and that he had no doubt it would be extended beyond.[76]

In August 1980 Plimsoll told a visiting colleague that Peacock had offered him the post unconditionally, that subsequently Henderson had informed him of Fraser's observation that he might want to put in a politician before or after the elections. Further, that when he, Plimsoll, later rechecked with Peacock, the latter had been "rocked" and had said such an appointment would be a breach of faith. Plimsoll had commented that Peacock might be "moved to other pastures, which would change all bets".[77] That is, if Peacock moved to another portfolio, he would no longer be in a position to protect Plimsoll's appointment. (In the event, after the election, Peacock became Minister for Industrial Relations.)

Whether or not he was "warned" in advance, Plimsoll was well aware in accepting the appointment, until then usually held by a politician, especially some eight or nine months before elections at home, that the length of his tenure could be uncertain. But he wanted the job and he wanted to leave Brussels.[78]

A "warning" of sorts appeared in a report that has the ring of authenticity in the Melbourne *Herald* on 4 February 1980.[79] Peter Costigan, one of the media accompanying Fraser on a European visit, noted that the prime minister had informed the Queen of Plimsoll's appointment at lunch at Sandringham. The appointment would mean that "Fraser will be free to appoint any of his senior Cabinet Ministers in the plum diplomatic post soon after the next election," because "Sir James will be 63 this coming Anzac Day. With holiday and long service leave entitlements he would be able to retire about a year after that, in other words about five months or so after the expected date of the next election in December". There was inherent in this an assumption that Plimsoll would accept an early departure from London, and would retire.

Plimsoll would have liked the appointment personally, both as a descendant of Sir Samuel Plimsoll, of the Plimsoll line, and as the first career high commissioner. He would have regarded it as a final posting that offered professional opportunities, and where he had a head start, given the vast range of political figures, diplomats, and others in London whom he already knew.[80]

Over the years he had developed views about the job. In 1972, after lamenting inadequate reporting from London, he wrote of "one asset which we have in Britain, which we do not take sufficient advantage of, is the number of important Englishmen with interests in Australia". Then there was the "close personal relations" between senior officials of the two countries, which needed to be continued and strengthened. "Britain is looking more and more to Europe, but we must not take it as inevitable that it will lose interest in Australia. Now, more than ever, it is necessary for Australia to keep hammering away in Britain at all levels and in many circles".[81] He would have seen the high commissioner being closely involved in this work.

Plimsoll chose to go directly to London from Brussels, arriving on 17 March 1980. He hit the ground running, both by inclination and on account of a helpful lack of formality.[82] He made an early call on Lord Carrington, who later recalled that Plimsoll "appeared to be totally at ease in London and greatly respected not just as Australia's representative but as a considerable person in his own right. He had so many friends in this country that he was regarded in a rather special way".[83] Plimsoll entertained extensively. His guest lists included old friends, but also others selected by thumbing through *Who's Who*, regardless of whether or not he had met them before.[84]

He set out to get to know every nook and cranny of the country.[85] He took a close interest in cultural activities of the high commission, appointing a Foreign Affairs officer as part-time cultural attaché. Events were organised in Australia House, frequently as often as two a week.[86]

In the period up to the Australian elections in October only two Australian ministers passed through London, Peacock and Senator Durack, Attorney-General. In 1980 there was no Commonwealth Heads of Government Meeting. With a wider canvass of activity than in Brussels, Plimsoll was somewhat more insulated from the STR people, though they frequently passed through London. The STR exercise continued to cause some angst for Plimsoll and others in posts in the EC countries. He composed a "masterly" reply to a cable from Canberra implying criticism of him, although Brian Hill, the senior trade officer in London, could see he was upset.[87] He was by no means the only head of mission in European posts to be criticised. The STR exercise was a major issue for discussion at a European heads of mission meeting held in London.

In the elections on 18 October, Fraser's Government survived with a reduced majority. Plimsoll took some leave. On 24 October he left for Ireland, where Ruth Dobson, a friend from the department, was ambassador. A week later the holiday was spoilt for him by a telephone call from Canberra:

> Peter Henderson phoned to say that Garland was being appointed High Commissioner in London; that Mr Fraser was telephoning

Mrs Thatcher to get concurrence; and that this would be announced publicly within the next 24 hours as part of the [post-election] Cabinet reshuffle.[88]

Henderson, on being informed by Sir Geoffrey Yeend, had said he assumed that the prime minister would personally contact Plimsoll. Yeend replied: "No. You are to do that".[89]

There was nothing Plimsoll could do. But he felt angry and let down. Usually an announcement about a new head of mission at least foreshadows an announcement about the next appointment of the incumbent. Garland's appointment, as indicated by Henderson's call, was geared solely to timing of the announcement of the ministerial reshuffle in Canberra, and disregarded Plimsoll's reasonable concerns about his future, not to mention how he would answer questions from all quarters. There would have been little he could have said, little he could have offered in the way of a credible explanation of the government's decision: certainly no one in Canberra offered him one. Many assumed that he was a victim of the vagaries of domestic politics.

The decision was no reflection on Plimsoll's performance: Fraser understood that Plimsoll had been doing well in the post.[90] The rationale for the decision to appoint Garland is not a part of Plimsoll's story.[91] The decision was probably taken without consultation with colleagues. Senior ministers like Killen and Carrick from the Liberals and Anthony, Nixon, and Sinclair from the Country Party all knew Plimsoll well and respected him. They may have regretted his summary eviction, but would have accepted that such appointments are ultimately for the prime minister.

Peacock, who was moving from foreign affairs, was not consulted. A letter which Hasluck, when minister, sent to Sir Keith Waller, ambassador in Washington, sheds light on approaches to matters of this sort. When Gorton became prime minister, Waller had sought Hasluck's advice about whether he should offer to stand down from his post. Hasluck strongly advised against this in the case of a career officer. No matter how important the post, a career officer's first responsibility was to the minister, not the prime minister. In other words to Hasluck, not to Gorton. Hasluck expressed the hope that "no matter how impetuous any Prime Minister might be, he would not assume that it was his prerogative to change diplomatic postings without seeking the views of his Minister, and paying considerable attention" to such views.[92]

Peacock had been unaware of any consideration being given to such an appointment for Garland. But, late in 1980, Peacock had intimated to Fraser that after five years in the portfolio, he would prefer to be moved to a domestic one.[93] If Peacock had remained as foreign minister, then Fraser might have felt obliged at least to consult him about moving Plimsoll. As Fraser moved Peacock to another portfolio at his own request, Fraser perhaps did not feel under any obligation to consult him.[94] Plimsoll had foreseen this possibility.[95] Peacock later told Plimsoll that he had immediately contacted Fraser to complain that the move was contrary to assurances given Plimsoll when appointed. Fraser had told Peacock: "We have got to do these things."[96]

Plimsoll completed his holiday in Ireland, and returned to London on 3 November. Outwardly with feelings well under control, he carried on as if nothing untoward had happened. A few days later Plimsoll was "invested with the livery of the Tallow Chandlers Company at a Special Court", having a few weeks earlier been made a Freeman of the City of London in that Company. He continued to travel extensively. Privately Plimsoll was hurt and distressed. He had been in London for only seven months. "Still only on my calls," he muttered to the deputy, Frank Murray.[97] High commission staff were "shocked and disgusted" when they heard of his removal. It was the way it was done as much as anything else. "He was very dignified about it, but you could see he was hurt, and seemed more tense than depressed."[98]

The British were not happy about the decision. They would have seen that this was treating the post in London as a "convenience", one that could be fiddled with at short notice like a game of musical chairs, in order to suit purposes unconnected with Australian representation in Britain. Carrington told Plimsoll at a social function in December: "I don't care who knows it, James, I think you have been treated very shabbily." Plimsoll conveyed this remark in confidence to a senior colleague in the high commission. Later it was leaked by an official in Canberra, and became front page news back home.[99] There was no retraction of the remark. Carrington, when it was suggested he should deny it, said: "Why should I deny it? How can I deny it? I did say it and I meant it."[100] Three years later Carrington, by then Secretary-General of NATO in Brussels, and talking to Australian ambassador, David Anderson, was still moved to express indignation about Plimsoll's removal from London.[101]

Carrington later recalled:

> ... it was, I know, a great blow to him that he was removed from the position when he was doing so well, and it caused an enormous amount of irritation in this country against those who had done it. It was not a very sensible move.[102]

A senior FCO official similarly recalled that "all of us in the FCO who had dealings with [Plimsoll] were extremely glad to have a career diplomat in that post, and one of such exceptional talent. It was a real disappointment when he was moved away after only a year".[103]

Having been evicted from London, and approaching 64, with much accumulated leave, he could have gone "on leave pending retirement" until he reached 65. But Plimsoll wanted another post;[104] also he dreaded the prospect of retirement.[105] If offered a post under Executive Council conditions, then age would not be a barrier.

Media reports in Australia about Lord Carrington's unusually blunt comment were followed by a statement by the major public service union, the ACOA, criticising the Fraser Government for "cronyism" and "shoddy disregard for the career public service". The ACOA commented that it was puzzling that someone of Mr Garland's low level of political importance "should be sent to London" – he had been ranked 23 out of 27 in the ministry. Senator Peter Walsh, an Opposition frontbencher, in a gesture of protest sent a message to the Queen.[106] Denis Warner, a well-known Australian foreign correspondent, described Plimsoll as "a man who has truly earned his country's thanks and gratitude". Praising Plimsoll's long devotion to the national interest, he questioned whether it was in the national interest "that a man of such distinction and so eminently qualified for the job, should be removed simply because of political expedience". If a post had to be found for Garland, why not Tokyo, which was vacant?[107]

The position of ambassador in Tokyo, one of the most important postings in the Australian service, in fact had been vacant since September 1980.[108] Plimsoll decided that he wanted Tokyo.[109] His scheduled visit to Canberra on leave and consultations enabled him personally to advance his cause. There he saw the newly-appointed foreign minister, Tony Street, and Bill Hayden, Leader of the Opposition, as well as numerous officials within the department and in other parts of the public service. He did not see the prime minister. On 17 December 1980 he accepted an offer of Tokyo. Plimsoll arranged with the department and with Garland that he would stay in London until March, when he would have completed a year there.

In Sydney for Christmas with the family, a particular concern was his brother John, in hospital for a major operation. Plimsoll visited him immediately on arrival, and several times thereafter. He saw Murray Bourchier, his successor in Moscow, whom he had visited in hospital in London where he had been medically evacuated, and who was now in hospital in Sydney. He had meals with Sir Garfield Barwick, Chief Justice of the High Court, and Sir Roden Cutler, Governor of NSW. He had a meal also with Sir William and Lady McMahon: there was "no personal bitterness", and he accepted the invitation. In Melbourne he called on Dame Pattie Menzies and on Lady Casey; and on Peacock, now minster for industrial relations.[110] In Perth, on the way back to London, he addressed a group of political science honours students at the University of Western Australia. Asked if he was annoyed about being recalled from London, he replied, "Yes."[111]

On return to London on 11 January, he continued with a busy programme of travel in the UK, and looked after visitors. Bill Hayden, Leader of the Opposition stayed with him at the Residence; Sir Phillip Lynch, Minister for Industry and Commerce also visited. Plimsoll "outwardly accepted the decision to move him with good grace".[112] Privately, he still felt deeply about what had happened. He liked the job in London, felt he was well suited and that he fitted in well.[113] His return had brought home to him again what he would have liked to achieve there. On 17 January Plimsoll talked with a senior official from Canberra whom he knew well, saying that it was clear that the relationship with the UK needed working on. He had been able to start getting through to areas in the UK of importance to Australia: "I am afraid that with my departure this will all go. I am not happy and I don't care who knows it." It was difficult to accept just being "shoved aside" for a politician.[114]

He paid a farewell call on the Queen and "kissed hands" on appointment to Japan. The Queen Mother hosted a farewell lunch, as did Lord Carrington. Carrington recalled that Plimsoll "at that time did stand out as an exceptional person . . . not just because of his personality but because intellectually he was a man of very considerable attainment. Gentle, kind, but at the same time tough and resolute".[115]

At the end of March Plimsoll left the office, in the centre of London, only 90 minutes before the departure of his plane from Heathrow. This reflected his usual problems of leaving, with a particular reluctance in this case, crowding in too many functions in the last few weeks, and leaving little time to pack and clean up both in the office and the residence. He gave Frank Murray a bag of coins found in his desk to bank for him. The suit he was wearing was the only one he had: he had given his second suit away.[116]

Although brief, Plimsoll's time in London set the precedent for career diplomats to be considered for the post. Of ten appointments made since 1983, four have been career diplomats. In retrospect he might have wryly noted that, of the two postings where he had to make way on account of a political appointment, on the first occasion (Washington) the move came from a Labor prime minister, on the second from a Liberal one.

Tokyo

For some years Japan had been Australia's biggest trading partner, exerting a major influence in the Asian region, economically and increasingly politically. Its "self-defence" forces, although constrained constitutionally, were now a major factor in combination with US forces stationed there and in Korea in the maintenance of regional stability. There was a certain symmetry about becoming ambassador in Tokyo at the end of Plimsoll's career which had begun about Japan in the Far Eastern Commission in Washington in 1945.

When he arrived in Tokyo, it was just before his 64th birthday. Henderson had informed him that Fraser had "guaranteed" that his posting would be extended beyond this birthday, so that he would serve there a normal three years.[117]

Tokyo was a large mission. As in Washington and London, sections of the embassy were headed by senior representatives of Commonwealth departments: Foreign Affairs, Defence, Trade, Treasury, Customs, and CSIRO. Following the 1982 Federal budget CSIRO's representation was to be withdrawn. Despite the difficulties Plimsoll managed to persuade Canberra about the importance of retaining CSIRO, and the adverse effects if withdrawn.[118] There was also the Consulate General in Osaka, while a number of Australian states, and major Australian companies like BHP, maintained resident representatives in Tokyo, as did the ABC and other Australian media outlets.

Unlike the EC and the US, Australia maintained a favourable balance of trade with Japan, given Japan's significant purchases of minerals and agriculture. Relations between Australia and Japan were well developed, with annual joint meetings of six senior ministers, and of officials.

For presentation of credentials to the Emperor of Japan, ambassadors had the choice of a car or a horse drawn carriage to take them to the palace. Plimsoll chose a car, being concerned about causing extra traffic disruption. For normal travel he was disinclined to fly the Australian flag on the ambassadorial car, but was persuaded that the flag would be helpful to the police.[119]

Plimsoll spent much time travelling in Japan, especially taking a close interest in cultural relations between the two countries. He had a "burning desire" to find out what was interesting, perhaps to gain better insight into Japan. He took no lessons in the Japanese language, but interested himself in it. Plimsoll went to Japanese operas and ballets, often accompanied by a Japanese-speaking officer and his spouse. He strongly supported the first comprehensive Japanese art exhibition in Australia, and hosted meals for officials of the Japanese museums which lent pieces. The exhibition came to Sydney after he left.[120]

Plimsoll was away from Japan a number of times, including three official visits home in the first 15 months, attending the extensive round of high level bilateral meetings. He travelled back to Australia for three weeks of consultations in June and July, with no more than a few days "holiday". Besides Canberra he visited Brisbane, Sydney, Melbourne, Adelaide and Perth. Despite the short time he had been in Japan, he spoke about it to AIIA branches in Canberra and Melbourne.[121] In November he returned for a fortnight's consultation in Canberra, Melbourne, Sydney and Hobart for the Committee for Consultation with Japan. In July 1982 he returned briefly once more, this time for the Japan/Australia Ministerial Committee meeting held in Canberra, and for consultations beforehand.

Plimsoll turned 65 in April 1982. The previous November in Canberra he had passed the periodic medical check required of all officers serving abroad. With the strenuous pace at which he continued to work, however, with little or no holiday – although he usually spent Sunday quietly – it was not surprising that he might have become more prone to ill-health.

During the night of 8 April a pain developed first on his back, and then the front. He had Sir Frederick and Lady Deer staying with him. Next day he travelled by train with them to Osaka, accompanied by Mr Dobinson, first secretary of the embassy. During the journey the pain grew worse and continued all day. In the evening he accompanied them to a music festival. At a buffet function afterwards, the local representative of the British Council came up to Dobinson: "Excuse me, but your Ambassador has just fallen over." Plimsoll had fainted. There was some general embarrassment. Plimsoll came to, and kept saying that he was all right, that this had happened to him before in Washington.[122] An ambulance took him to hospital where he was examined, and allowed to return to his hotel.[123] On 10 April, after a further examination, he was allowed to continue the journey. At the inaugural meeting of the Japan/Australia Society at Gifu, Plimsoll was one of the speakers, and had a radio telephone conversation with the Ambassador for Japan in Canberra. He left early and went to bed. Pain kept him awake most of the night.[124]

On return to Tokyo he was diagnosed with shingles. His butler changed his dressings for him three times in the morning, before a lunch he was determined to attend for members of the important Marubeni Corporation.[125] He took things quietly for a few days. On 16 April he actually cancelled his appointments but still worked in the office for part of the morning and afternoon.

In May 1982 he made a week's visit to South Korea. He received an emotional welcome from people who remembered him from the Korean War. He insisted on going through with this, with a shortened program and early bed some nights.[126] On return to Japan he generally maintained his schedule, including visitors amongst whom was the Prime Minister, Fraser, and party. Next time, in Canberra, he visited Dr Marcus Faunce, his physician, and noted, no doubt with relief, that he "passed me as fit".[127]

All in all, Plimsoll was assiduous in performance of his duties. There were no major policy issues that confronted him.[128] Though not his specialty he handled competently the important trade aspect of the relationship. Although he travelled extensively and took a deep interest in many aspects of Japanese life and culture, for someone who was not a Japanese linguist, it took longer to settle in. He came to Tokyo with no particular objectives, nor did the government set him any. If he had been there longer, undoubtedly he would have made a greater impact and drawn more from the staff of whom many were fluent Japanese language speakers, often on their second postings. However, within months of his arrival he knew that he would leave after only 18 months.

That said, his performance was not his best. One of his staff, John Graham, who had also worked for him in Washington a decade earlier, noticed the difference. He was not only older, but seemed less confident and happy, which Graham ascribed to the manner of his exit from London, although Plimsoll did his best not to show his disappointment. While he travelled extensively, he did it without the same keenness as in the US. Health problems also affected his performance.[129] Most of the Japanese diplomats he had known before had retired. Despite his dealings over many years with Japanese, and his intellectual curiosity about Asia, he seemed never entirely comfortable. Compared with Japanese specialists on his staff, he was not at one with the Japanese, with less understanding of their culture and the way they thought.[130]

Endnotes

1 Plimsoll had a lifelong "unswerving sense of idealism, commitment and dedication to the diplomatic career and beyond it, to the concept of committed Public Service". Bob Cotton, letter, 4/11/2004.

2 M.J. Hughes, letter, 10/11/1999; Plimsoll to Lavett, 15/9/1975, then deputy in Port Moresby. It would be "a most stimulating post to be in at this time". Letter courtesy Lavett.

3 Marshall Green, letter, 13/4/1997.
4 J.R. Burgess, conversation, 29/12/2007; Cam/Plim, ii, 250-1.
5 Lavett, letter, 25/3/2002.
6 Plimsoll wrote two "agonised" letters to Peacock about his wish for Port Moresby. Peacock, conversation, November 1996.
7 Plimsoll later observed that he was sure Kerr should have resigned after the 1975 elections. When Fraser said he did not want Kerr to resign, Kerr came under great strain. Cam/Plim, ii, 342-5.
8 Henderson to JP, 21/2/1977. Courtesy Henderson.
9 Henderson to JP, 21/2/1977.
10 Freeth letter.
11 Henderson to JP, 21/2/1977.
12 Pacing up and down his office in Moscow, in some agitation, he told a visiting colleague, Garry Woodard, ambassador in Beijing, that those in charge of postings in Canberra seemed now to "just think about moving people around every three years", unrelated to any policy considerations. C.G. Woodard, conversation, 16/7/1996. JP diary, 19-21/9/1977.
13 Henderson to JP, 21/2/1977; Cam/Plim, ii, 339. Plimsoll told Peacock he thought Brussels a "demotion". Peacock, conversation, November 1996.
14 *Reminiscential Conversations between Hon Clyde Cameron and Sir James Plimsoll 1984*. TRC 1967, ii, 344.
15 Cam/Plim, i, 307-8.
16 Although contemptuous of McMahon in many respects, he later once dined with the McMahons in Sydney and McMahon attended his State Funeral in Hobart.
17 Tange, conversation, 9/10/2000. A "lonely person who had great difficulty mixing freely and easily with people". Killen, *Inside Australian Politics*, 256.
18 Fraser "belonged to no known mould": the only member of cabinet sympathetic to blacks in southern Africa, but "just as troglodyte on other issues as his colleagues were on Southern Africa". One "could never predict how he felt". Parkinson, conversation, 29/11/2000.
19 Source anonymous.
20 Cam/Plim, i, 19-20.
21 Cam/Plim, i, 66.
22 I was Counsellor at the Australian Mission in Brussels, 1975-78, which

included Plimsoll's first year there. The following account of Plimsoll's time in Brussels contains some personal recollections.

23 D. Kenyon, conversation, 18/2/1999.

24 Jenkins told a meeting of the UK Parliamentary Labour Party on 19/7/71: "I am not a great believer in kith and kin politics." The Australians were "without exception the toughest, roughest and most self-interested government with which I ever had to deal". Cable, Downer to McMahon, 20/7/1971, M1003 NAA.

25 Fraser, conversation, 28/8/1997.

26 McKay, 29/6/2000.

27 Tange, conversation, 9/10/2000. Tange noted that he often was involved in matters for which he had no responsibility when accompanying Fraser overseas.

28 Jenkins thought Fraser was "a rather surly fellow who looks a mixture of the self-confident and the suspicious". He reminded him of a fast bowler on an "off day" in cricket, toiling away, but not getting any wickets. It was "a fairly rough discussion round the table". Fraser was "an awkward, aggressive man, who does not put his best face forward". Roy Jenkins, *European Diary 1977-81*, London, 1989, 118-9.

29 Fraser, conversation, 28/8/1997.

30 Sir Crispin Tickell, letter, 3/9/2001.

31 "He left with an array of enemies and tensions greater than ever before". J.W.C. Cumes, *A Bunch of Amateurs. The Tragedy of Government and Administration in Australia.* Macmillan, Melbourne, 1988, 100. Dr Cumes was the Australian ambassador in Brussels at the time. "Fraser's brusque diplomatic methods in a formal European environment might have been more likely to shock than to persuade." Tange, quoted in Fraser, *Political Memoirs,* 467.

32 Fraser statement on return home, June 1977. M1356, Item 10, NAA.

33 A year earlier Sir Christopher Soames, then EC Commissioner (External), told Renouf that the EC was a *"political* organization" and would increasingly become so. "Of course the CAP was protectionist but Australian Ministers should understand the political problems which agriculture everywhere presented. The worst thing Australia could do was to protest publicly about the CAP. This merely lowered Australia's already low reputation [in Brussels] and made alleviation of the CAP more difficult". O.BS3987 of 10/06/1976. A1838/332 3107/38/12/10, Pt.1, NAA.

34 Fraser, conversation, 6/6/2001.

35 Peter Nixon, conversation, 25/8/1997.
36 Fraser, conversation, 6/6/2001.
37 John Howard, *Lazarus Rising: a Personal and Political Autobiography*, Harper Collins, Sydney, 2010, 96.
38 In fact Plimsoll and Howard had met earlier in Canberra in February 1974, through Senator John Carrick. See chapter 9.
39 JP to Henderson, 10/5/1980. Courtesy Henderson. The letter was written after Plimsoll had left Brussels, and he judged its sensitivity to be such that he typed it himself.
40 JP to Henderson, 10/5/1980.
41 Ibid.
42 Ibid.
43 Ibid.
44 Kenyon, conversation, 18/2/1999.
45 Peacock, conversation, 29/11/2000.
46 Teese, conversation, 8/6/2001.
47 JP to Henderson, 10/5/1980.
48 Ibid.
49 Howard, *Lazarus Rising*, 96.
50 JP to RJ Fisher, 8/12/1977. Courtesy R.J. Fisher.
51 JP papers, NLA.
52 JP diary, 7/1/1978.
53 JP to Henderson, 10/5/1980. "After the Howard visits, I never again saw a brief".
54 JP to Henderson, 10/5/1980.
55 Ibid.
56 Ibid. Jenkins "became a close personal friend" of Plimsoll. "They'd have supper together on Sunday nights and discuss literature. And then Jim would throw in a request about sheep-meat quotas for Australian farmers." Alexander Downer, "A tough job with style," *Adelaide Advertiser*, 20/9/2009. Among senior officials of the European Commission, Sir Roy Denman recalled Plimsoll as "one of my abiding memories of Brussels ... one of the considerable international figures of his age". Despite trade problems with Australia, "Jim

impressed me at the outset with a massive authority, integrity and calm". Sir Roy Denman, letter, 29/3/2000.

57 JP to Henderson, 10/5/1980.

58 Instead, early in 1980 Alex McGoldrick, a senior Trade Department officer, became the new Minister (Trade) in Brussels with responsibility for the EC as a whole but working in close cooperation with Australian ambassadors in EC posts. He thought the establishment of STR was "the stupidest decision of any government in 40 years". McGoldrick, conversation, 16/3/2001. Also JP to Henderson, 10/5/1980.

59 JP to Henderson, 10/5/1980.

60 Delegation members were Sir Billy Snedden, Senators Withers and Grimes, and Messrs Fry, Lusher, Scholes and Short.

61 Plimsoll to Henderson, 10/5/1980. (That Plimsoll had asked Downer to omit that passage from the record was confirmed by Downer, conversation, 23/2/2001). Plimsoll added: "I do not exaggerate what may have been achieved (and STR were not happy that I had taken any initiative). But Loveday in Bonn, and Rowland in Paris [and HOMs in other EC capitals] were also directly and indirectly trying to keep before those to whom they were accredited the wider considerations and trying to keep lines open."

62 Fraser, *Memoirs*, 469. "33 years on the essential elements of the CAP remain in place". Howard *Lazarus Rising*, 96. See also Philip Flood, *Dancing with Warriors. A Diplomatic Memoir*. Australian Scholarly Publishing, Melbourne, 2011, 118.

63 McKay, conversation, 29/6/2000.

64 Cam/Plim, i, 66.

65 Fernandez, conversation, 19/3/1997.

66 Sir Donald Maitland, UK Ambassador to the EC, letter, 9/5/1998.

67 Fernandez, conversation, 19/3/1997.

68 During 1978 Plimsoll's reading included 120 of Georges Simenon's *Maigret* detective novels. JP diary, 1978.

69 J.R. Kelso to Peacock, 27/02/1979, A1838 919/10/5/2, Pt 8, NAA.

70 JP to Henderson, 29/11/79. Courtesy Henderson.

71 JP diary, 10/1/1980.

72 Fraser, conversation, 28/8/1997.

73 See chapter 4, footnote 27.

74 Parkinson, conversation, 29/11/2000.

75 Peacock, conversation, 29/11/2000.

76 Cam/Plim, ii, 340-1.

77 R.H. Robertson, Ambassador in Rome, letter to Henderson, 26/8/1980. Courtesy Henderson. Robertson was in line to be the next deputy in London in the event of another political appointment.

78 Fernandez, Acting High Commissioner in London until Plimsoll's arrival, had no doubt that Plimsoll was aware of this. Fernandez, conversation, 19/3/1997. Also John Sankey, letter of 17/6/2004. Although the Executive Council appointment of a Head of Mission normally lasts at least three years, it can be terminated at any time.

79 Melbourne *Herald*, 4/2/1980.

80 A.F. Dingle, letter, 4/8/1998.

81 Washington memo 52 of 7/1/1972, JP papers, DFAT.

82 The arrangement among Commonwealth countries which acknowledge the Queen as head of state is that their high commissioners can start making calls and doing business on arrival, and do not have to wait to present credentials first. Calls are made on the Queen and the Prime Minister later, as convenient.

83 Carrington, letter, 26/6/1996.

84 F.C. Murray, Deputy High Commissioner. Conversation, 30/12/1997.

85 Alexander Downer, on holiday from Brussels, attended an opera in Derbyshire and encountered Plimsoll there. Downer conversation, 30/3/1998.

86 D. de Stoop, conversation, 12/9/2000. He was the appointee.

87 B.J. Hill, conversation, 13/9/2000.

88 JP diary, 1/11/1980.

89 Henderson, conversation, 1997.

90 Fraser, conversation, 28/8/1997. Parkinson could not recall Fraser making any derogatory remarks about Plimsoll, although he often did about other senior members of the department. Nor could he recall him heaping praise on Plimsoll either as, for example, Menzies had. Parkinson conversation, 29/11/2000.

91 Plimsoll later recalled that he believed that Fraser, who never discussed the matter with him, wanted Garland out of the ministry, and that Garland had said he wanted the post in London. Plimsoll had heard that Garland "worked quite hard at his job and did quite well". Cam/Plim, ii, 224, 350. See also Anne

Summers, *Gamble for Power: How Bob Hawke beat Malcolm Fraser: the 1983 Federal Election*, Nelson, Australia, 1983, 51.

92 Hasluck to Waller, 27/2/1968. Waller papers, DFAT.

93 Peacock, conversation, 29/11/2000.

94 According to Fraser, relations between them were difficult at the time. Fraser, *Memoirs*, 479-81.

95 See Plimsoll's conversation with Robertson, 77 above.

96 Cam/Plim, ii, 225.

97 Murray, conversation, 30/12/1997.

98 De Stoop, conversation, 12/9/2000.

99 E.g., *The Age*, 12/12/1980.

100 Cam/Plim, ii, 224.

101 Anderson, conversation, 7/2/1997.

102 Carrington, letter, 26/6/1996.

103 R. Barltrop, FCO, letter, 22/9/2000.

104 Two months earlier he had told Robertson that "if he were displaced there'd be a special problem for all concerned", as he had another couple of years to go before retirement. R.H. Robertson to Henderson, 26/8/1980. Courtesy Henderson.

105 Ingram, conversation, 6/5/1997. Isla Stuart, who had known Plimsoll since his time in the Bank of NSW, told Rowen Osborn that even in his 40s she recalled Plimsoll worrying about retirement, that he could not drive a car, run a house, or generally look after himself. Osborn, conversation, 4/11/1997.

106 *The Australian*, 17/12/1980.

107 Melbourne *Herald*, 20/11/80.

108 On 5/8/1980 Henderson told Osborn, then Minister and Deputy Head of Mission in the Tokyo Embassy, of Ambassador John Menadue's impending departure. Osborn could expect to be Chargé d'Affaires probably at least until after the elections. Osborn, conversation, 4/11/1997.

109 He confided this to a visiting senior colleague, Jim Ingram. Conversation, 6/5/1997.

110 JP diary, December 1980, January 1981.

111 P.J. Boyce, conversation, 12/5/2007.

112 John Stone, conversation, 25/2/2001.
113 Cam/Plim, ii, 349.
114 Source anonymous.
115 Carrington, letters of 26/6/1996 and 1/7/1996.
116 Murray, conversation, 30/12/1997.
117 JP diary, 6/3/1981.
118 Osborn, conversation, 4/11/1997.
119 Ibid.
120 Dobinson, conversation, 8/2/1999.
121 JP diary, June-July 1981.
122 Dobinson, conversation, 8/2/1999. Osborn, conversation, 4/11/1997.
123 JP diary, 9/4/1982.
124 JP diary, 10/4/1982.
125 JP diary, 15/4/1982.
126 L. McLean, conversation, 27/2/1997.
127 JP diary, 30/7/1982.
128 Osborn, conversation, 4/11/1997.
129 J. Graham, Information Attache, conversation, 13/7/2001.
130 T. Wilson, conversation, 28/4/2000.

11

"A Great Tasmanian", 1982-87

He had no family in Tasmania when he came here, but in less than five years he made the whole state his family.[1]

Early in 1981, when Plimsoll moved from London to Tokyo, in Tasmania a discreet search was under way for a new Governor of the State. Sir Stanley Burbury, the first Australian-born incumbent, had been Governor since 1973. He made it known that he wanted to step down. The State Premier, Doug Lowe, asked Nick Evers, Secretary of the Premier's Department, and Edward O'Farrell, Official Secretary to the Governor, to assist him in finding a suitable successor. The first preference was a suitable Tasmanian but none was available. Two diplomat contemporaries of Plimsoll, both from Tasmania, Sir Laurence McIntyre and Ralph Harry, were among those approached.[2] The search was widened to seek someone from the mainland. Lowe later recalled that during 1980, when Evers had accompanied Lowe on visits to China and Japan, he had frequently mentioned Plimsoll in glowing terms. Evers had known of Plimsoll since his own time as a young Australian diplomat in the 1960s.[3]

Lowe had not met Plimsoll, but recalled hearing him mentioned favourably years before, when Plimsoll was secretary of the department in Canberra, and Lowe was Tasmanian State Secretary of the ALP. He recalled a discussion between Tasmanian senators Nick McKenna and Justin O'Byrne about SEATO. McKenna had said that he would check with Plimsoll to ensure that he understood the details. When Lowe asked McKenna about Plimsoll, McKenna gave him a "rapturous assessment".

He had "enormous faith" in Plimsoll.[4] Sir Roden Cutler, Governor of NSW, when visiting Tasmania, was informally consulted. He agreed with the view that being single had not been an obstacle in Plimsoll' s career as a diplomat.[5] Lowe decided on Plimsoll, sight unseen.

Plimsoll knew that Tokyo would be his last assignment. He was uncertain about the duration of his tenure. Despite assurances, Plimsoll knew there could be no guarantees. Executive Council appointments could end at any time. Given his experience in London, Plimsoll felt less certain about his tenure in Tokyo, where there was well-established precedent for non-career ambassadorial appointments.[6]

He had not made any definite plans about what to do after Tokyo. Becoming a company director did not interest him: he had been "thinking more in terms of becoming associated with an art gallery or educational institution".[7] He had had an invitation to join the Board of the Public Library in Sydney. He had thought of buying an apartment within walking distance of the Library and the Opera House, but had done nothing about it.[8]

Offer of appointment

One afternoon late in August 1981, Plimsoll returned to the embassy after an appointment. He found a message for him to call Nick Evers in Hobart. Evers said that he was calling on behalf of the Premier: would Plimsoll agree to his name being put forward to the Queen as the next Governor of Tasmania? Plimsoll was surprised and delighted, but asked if he could think it over.[9]

The offer of the appointment came as a complete surprise. He had had no inkling of it; he had had no connection with Tasmania. It was a signal honour, a fitting way to move on from being a diplomat. But his first instinct was to decline. Street, the Foreign Minister, had authorised him to tell the Japanese that he would be there for a normal three years. He had told a few Japanese that.

Plimsoll immediately wrote personally to Henderson in Canberra, asking him to talk to Street. Henderson later phoned him, on behalf of Street, that given Plimsoll's London experience, he should "keep in mind" that Fraser "might suddenly decide" he wanted to send a politician or someone else there. "He's done it to you once, he's capable of doing it again."[10] Plimsoll told Henderson that although he had been in Japan for a comparatively short period his treatment over his removal from London was a major reason in his decision to let his name be put forward for Tasmania. He could never trust a government again not to remove him at short notice, whereas in Tasmania he could look forward to some security of tenure.[11] But if Canberra had asked him to stay in Tokyo three years, he would have. Street asked that if he accepted the governorship, he should say to the Tasmanians that he should first complete 18 months in Tokyo.[12] He cleared with the Tasmanians that his arrival in Hobart would be delayed until October 1982.[13]

Lowe phoned Plimsoll and recalled that he showed "considerable excitement" at the prospect of taking up the post. He was looking forward to visiting Tasmania at the earliest moment in order to consult and make preparations.[14]

As Plimsoll's appointment would not take effect for more than a year, it would be premature for Buckingham Palace to be approached, or for the authorities in Tokyo and Canberra to be informed. Secrecy was more than usually important. In Tokyo, Plimsoll only told Rowen Osborn, the deputy in the embassy, whom he had known for nearly 30 years.[15] Keeping the decision under wraps for so long at home proved, in the event, too difficult. The appointment became widely known in Hobart. The Premier met local media chiefs, who agreed to respect an embargo. An announcement of the appointment was readied for release in six months.[16]

Premature announcement

In November 1981 Plimsoll visited Hobart during his normal leave and consultations. Discreet discussions about his future appointment were planned. But a Tasmanian journalist, travelling on an interstate flight, fell into conversation with another journalist and let drop Plimsoll's appointment, believing that his colleague, Richard Carleton, would respect the embargo. The latter did not feel under any such obligation, as he was not a Tasmanian. On 11 November, Lowe was deposed as premier in a party *putsch*. Carleton, in reporting this development on television, concluded with an afterthought: "funny the things you hear on an aeroplane. The next Governor of Tasmania will be Sir James Plimsoll". Plimsoll saw this on TV in his brother's home in Bondi. Scheduled to visit Tasmania the next day, he was acutely embarrassed. [17]

Meanwhile, Government House in Hobart immediately informed Sir William Heseltine, an Australian who was Principal Private Secretary to the Queen. The Palace was very accommodating, perhaps as the Queen, who already knew Plimsoll, was happy to approve the appointment.[18]

In Hobart Plimsoll was also worried whether he would be acceptable to the new Premier, Harry Holgate, with whom he had a talk and lunch. Other lunch guests included the Chief Justice, Sir Guy Green, who was also Lieutenant-Governor, and the State Attorney-General, Mr B.K. Miller. Miller had been a political ally of the deposed premier. What had been intended as a quiet, relaxed lunch, was a tense affair for the new premier as well as for Plimsoll.[19]

The appointment was formally announced. On 13 November Plimsoll gave a press conference, the first in Tasmania by a Governor-designate. With practised ease he made a favourable impression and avoided anything controversial. Next morning Plimsoll was back in Bondi, clipping the front hedge of his brother's house.[20] The Japanese accepted his appointment well.

A few months later, following State elections, Robin Gray became the Premier in a Liberal Government. A sufficient lack of partisan commitment to be able to take such changes in his stride, a must for a Governor, was something to which Plimsoll had long been accustomed as a public servant. "Working with Ministers, you tend to see the arguments of both Parties," so that generally he had "never been violently partisan".[21]

In June 1982 Plimsoll visited London for an audience with the Queen. Afterwards he lunched with Sir William Heseltine. Sir John Kerr arranged for him to talk with Eugene Forsey, a Canadian authority on the royal prerogative.[22] He stopped in New Delhi for a few days whilst returning to Tokyo.

Taking up appointment

After leaving Japan Plimsoll returned to Bondi for a few days, then went to stay with Sir Ninian and Lady Stephen at Government House in Canberra. He had first met the Stephens by chance in Ottawa a few months earlier, when he was en route to his audience with the Queen.[23] Later Plimsoll happened to be in Canberra in July when Sir Ninian was sworn in as Governor-General, and attended the ceremony. It was the beginning of a firm friendship.

On 1 October Plimsoll flew by RAAF VIP flight from Canberra to Hobart, where Gray Government ministers lined up to greet him on arrival. Only one, Geoff Pearsall, had met him before, while visiting Tokyo.[24] It was a day of pomp and ceremony, with guards of honour, the swearing in, a speech in reply to a welcome at the Town Hall, and many handshakes.

In Australia vice-regal appointees at that time had been drawn largely from the military, the law or politics. Plimsoll was the second former diplomat to assume the role after Sir Roden Cutler, who had been Governor of NSW from 1965 to 1981.[25] Plimsoll was more familiar with the role of the Governor-General, having long observed the incumbent in Canberra, and at close quarters in the case of Casey, Hasluck and

The Governor with Premier Robin Gray and Tasmanian Government Ministers, March 1986. Back row left to right: Peter Hodgman, Julian Green (Secretary, Premier's Department), John Bennett, John Beswick, Roger Groom, Nick Evers, Ray Groom. Front row left to right: Ian Braid, Gray, Plimsoll, Geoff Pearsall, Peter Rae (Newspix)

Kerr. The Queen seemed to have had his genuine support; he spoke of his meetings with her in "very favourable terms".[26] He liked the stability provided by the monarchy.[27] One leading Tasmanian Labor figure felt that Plimsoll's tolerant and balanced outlook reduced the level of anti-royalist feeling prevalent in ALP circles in Tasmania.[28]

Tasmania, the smallest Australian state both in area and population, is the most rurally-based, with scattered small communities. Its climate and scenery prompted the visiting Anthony Trollope, one of Plimsoll's favourite authors, to write: "'Were it my lot to take up my residence in Australia . . . I would pitch my tent in Tasmania.'"[29]

To be a governor from outside Tasmania can in some ways be an advantage, not seeming to be aligned to any particular part of the state, or group within it. Plimsoll knew he must not neglect any area. Incumbents each put their own particular stamp on the vice-regal role. As an ambassador Plimsoll had been used to travelling extensively and meeting the widest cross-section of people. Similarly, as governor, he wanted to see, to listen and to understand. He acquired a profound understanding of Tasmania's potential as well as its challenges.[30] He quickly identified himself with Tasmania. He saw it as part of his role to "represent" the state as he had represented Australia: his approach was one of instant total commitment and absorption.

Busy and informal

Plimsoll set a "breakneck" pace.[31] He was happy to attend functions throughout the state, with little concern for notice received, or for the number of people likely to be attending. If there was a function on in Hobart and one elsewhere, he would tend to choose the latter.[32] He travelled extensively, 40,000 kilometres in his first nine months. His official car was often filthy, after long stretches on side roads.[33] Premier Robin Gray found that "one could hardly go anywhere in the State without finding that Sir James had been there last week or would be coming next".[34] The Official Secretary once went through the governor's programme with Plimsoll for the next six months. Plimsoll, on finding he had a spare weekend, said: "Find me a show to open or something."[35] The one part of Tasmania that Plimsoll did not visit was Macquarie Island, situated well to the south, which necessitated a lengthy voyage by ship.[36] His informal style "endeared him to the community". Usually at functions, "the person least concerned with formality and protocol is Sir James Plimsoll".[37] He was "most brilliant at really 'connecting' with people," regardless of background.[38]

He delivered speeches at between a third and half of the functions. These were often reported in the Tasmanian media. He sought to interest the audience in front of him, and Tasmania. He resisted any temptation to attract wider attention: such an approach would have gone against instincts developed during 35 years as a public servant.

Accustomed to preparing his own speeches, he saw no need for a speechwriter. He delved into the detail and complexity of the varied subjects, speaking without notes, and with "a flow of speech and a capacity to find just the right word".[39] In his keynote address at the Australian Road Safety Conference, he spoke for 40 minutes, and at the National Potato Conference for 30 minutes.[40] He spoke for an hour "On collectors and on museums" to the Friends of the Tasmanian Museum and Art Gallery.[41] He delivered an address in St David's Cathedral in Hobart on the history of religious art. John Bennett, Tasmania's Attorney-General, was sitting next to the leader of the Russian delegation when, late in 1986, Plimsoll opened an international conference on the Antarctic, speaking for more than 30 minutes: "Where did you find HIM?" asked the Russian in awe.[42]

He was assiduous in going to women's functions. He became President of the Girl Guides as well as Chief Scout in the State, and agreed to be patron of many women's organisations. To some women he came across as shy, almost dismissive, but he enjoyed the company of women. Many women friends were among guests who stayed at Government House.[43]

As patron of many community and welfare organisations Plimsoll was kindly rather than compassionate. He did not lack compassion, but it was balanced by awareness of dignity of the office. He did not actively promote causes, nor wear his heart on his sleeve. His was a realistic concern for people. He wanted to know about people's miseries and difficulties, but did not seem absorbed by them, or take them on as a personal duty; it was part of a lifelong instinct to be more aware of what was going on.[44]

Plimsoll filled in travelling time by his usual reading diet of novels, including some in French and Russian, and the *Economist*.[45] He liked to stay overnight where he was visiting, just as he had as a diplomat, content to stay in hotels or motels, no matter how basic, whereas predecessors had stayed privately.[46] He stayed in the one pub on Flinders Island and King Island respectively.[47] At the latter, one of his staff noticed the poor bedside light that Plimsoll was reading from in his room, and removed the lampshade to improve things. Plimsoll would not have countenanced making a complaint.[48]

Despite his reticent, understated style, there developed a genuine affection for him throughout Tasmania. His attitude, body language, and voice, relaxed people.[49] He related to where people had come from in Tasmania. Often he had already been there and could remember. At agricultural shows Plimsoll used his remarkable memory to recall the names of farm people, even of their animals.[50] Plimsoll liked impromptu opportunities to talk to people, for example, visiting farmers in their homes in the same district of an agricultural show he was attending.[51]

He was the first governor to conduct an investiture for the Girls Brigade,[52] and the first to attend the trotting, which delighted the trotting people.[53] The Sir James Plimsoll Plate became an annual event on the trotting calendar.[54] On the way to his first trotting meeting, the official car broke down. Checking with Government House, it was found that no backup car was readily available. Then a passing police car stopped: "You want a lift Your Excellency?" Plimsoll consulted his ADC: "What do you think? I have never been in a Police car before." It was a case of accept or be late arriving. They got into the back seat, pushing aside sneakers, old clothes, and the remains of lunch. The receiving line at the trotting was surprised at the Governor's mode of transport. Plimsoll enjoyed it all.[55]

He was able to combine dignity appropriate to the office with a kindly, benign personal manner and ability to be himself. "He took pomposity away, yet never lowered the dignity of office. In fact he gave it added quality, a new dimension."[56] He did not like outward trappings of office, he shied away from using the large formal car (a Daimler Princess) except for occasions like the opening of Parliament.[57] He would personally meet at the airport guests coming to stay at Government House, standing informally among others in the terminal building. He liked to slip off alone, and did not like being cooped up. He would stroll to the centre of town, a distance of three kilometres, and browse in bookshops or music stores, or arrive unannounced at the university bookshop.[58]

Becoming governor caused little if any change in his frugal living habits, and his lack of interest in his outward appearance. He used the same limited range of clothing, and ill-fitting suits. Once, given the frayed condition of his shirts, the butler, without approval, went and bought him some new ones. Plimsoll threw them in a corner, and never wore them.[59]

He was surprised when people noticed him.[60] One afternoon Plimsoll took some personal friends to Port Arthur. The young woman at the entry refused to accept payment. "Oh, you recognised me did you?" he asked. "No, but I recognised the car," she replied.[61]

Helping Tasmania

He entertained at Government House more often than his predecessors and with as wide a selection of Tasmanians as possible: the public sector, business, university, music, art, sport and other walks of life.[62] Donavan, President of the Hobart Waterside Workers Union, an older man, used to come to lunches. He and Plimsoll were by no means similar characters, but there was "definitely a bond".[63] Dress for dinner became lounge suit for men, instead of black tie as before.[64] "He was exceptionally good both at mixing together all manner of folk and at putting them, individually and collectively, at their ease".[65] At the same time functions normally served a broader community purpose. During one dinner in the winter of 1986, it snowed heavily. With a "minimum of fuss but a maximum of care", Plimsoll arranged accommodation at Government House for those unable to drive home due to road closures on higher ground.[66]

Sometimes functions tended to go on a long time. Previous governors would rise, signaling it was time for guests to leave. Plimsoll, however, was enjoying the company, and reluctant to see them go. Sometimes guests found it necessary to excuse themselves after lunch, as they had to return to work.[67] A degree of personal indulgence, perhaps, but often it was Plimsoll's own money that contributed to the costs, such was the importance which Plimsoll attached to this aspect of his role. Plimsoll would use up his annual entertainment allowance of about $20,000 within six months. Instead of asking for more money, he preferred to pay the extra expenditure himself. He arranged for his salary as Governor, some $60,000 p.a, to be paid into a trust account, to be drawn on for official entertainment, of which the overall annual expenditure in his time was between $70,000 to $90,000. The trust account was regularly audited.[68]

Plimsoll used his position to promote Tasmania. Economic problems had caused the population to decline; good people left. Tasmanians at the time were tending to fight over a diminishing pie instead of trying to increase it. Plimsoll tried to get away from "this snake swallowing its tail approach".[69] Tasmania needed all the help it could get. There was an opportunity discreetly to do what he could to promote the state's development. Plimsoll accepted this challenge. He was a master in "doing good by stealth. One often only became aware in considerable retrospect of what he had done".[70]

He kept abreast of current developments and considered how these could be applied to Tasmania's advantage. As "ambassador for business," he went to great lengths with offering meals for visiting groups to ensure that the right Tasmanians were there, both from government and business. He was very strongly directed in this way, not just reacting to advice.[71]

Functions were planned carefully. He preferred small groups and guest lists which included enough people of sufficient substance to ensure value as well as enjoyment for principal guests. He scrutinised seating plans, always searching for relevance and connections. Sometimes he would display art pieces, especially paintings, in the hall of Government House as a potential icebreaker for a particular guest. He would want to ensure that a visiting guest of honour got the most out of talking to other guests, especially the Premier, if they otherwise would not meet. The menu was always distinctively Tasmanian, trout, quail – of which he was particularly fond – apple pie, King Island brie, and he would point it out. The menu did not vary much from this fare, as frequent guests discovered.[72]

Plimsoll brought together over lunch Sir Harold Cuthbertson, head of the Tasmanian Savings Bank and a leading figure in the leather industry, and the visiting Major-General R.L. Hughes, the head of Army Logistics Command, Melbourne. Earlier Tasmania, which used to make army footwear, had lost the contract. The two talked at lunch, leading to further discussions in Melbourne which resulted in an army order for footwear for three years.[73]

Ambassadors and high commissioners of the diplomatic corps in Canberra and their spouses had a standing invitation to stay at Government House. This way he encouraged some to visit Tasmania more often than they might otherwise have done. Further, when he judged it appropriate, he would personally "take over" the planning of their visits to mutual benefit, including hosting functions for them.[74]

Saudi Arabia had placed an embargo on the import from Tasmania of lamb carcasses, which had been a valuable trade. Plimsoll invited the Saudi Ambassador in Canberra to stay at Government House. He arranged a lunch, including industry representatives, followed by discussion through the afternoon. The outcome was that a local Muslim Imam went and blessed the Tasmanian abattoir in question, enabling the trade to resume. His initiative led to the resolution in a day of what had been a problem for some time.[75]

He was helpful to visiting Japanese delegations. He interested the Fuji clan in Tasmania and, years later, Fuji made a major economic investment. Somewhat unusually, Plimsoll allowed a Japanese film star and his bride to be photographed at Government House. He had wanted to let them be married and have their reception there, but was advised not to go so far. With Plimsoll's help "the event generated millions of dollars worth of invaluable coverage for Tasmania in Japan".[76]

Many significant visitors came to Tasmania just to see Plimsoll and renew acquaintances. General Vernon Walters visited Canberra, as an emissary of President Reagan, to brief the Australian Government about the US bombing of Libya in 1986. Afterwards he flew to Hobart to "have a chat" with Plimsoll.[77] Plimsoll badgered the Department of Foreign Affairs in Canberra to send more international visitors to Tasmania, and more of Australia's own heads of mission to Tasmania as part of their briefings and mid-term consultations.

University Visitor

At the University of Tasmania Plimsoll was active as *ex officio* Visitor.[78] Out of 35 graduation ceremonies he came to 34, including the relatively small ceremonies, seven a year.[79] He thought nothing of attending one graduation ceremony after another, usually four in a row over three days. Sometimes he would deliver the address. He would hold a Government House function to introduce new professors to the wider community. He took a particular interest in students of international affairs, and sometimes delivered lectures. As Patron of the Tasmanian Branch of the AIIA, he initiated an annual Patron's dinner, which proved a useful focus for the Branch's public outreach, and which would bring in new members. About once a month he would ask the Branch to take a visitor staying at Government House out for a meal. The Branch responded enthusiastically, members paying for themselves.[80]

Involvement in the University arose from his lifelong interest in such institutions and his belief in the importance of education generally. He liked to encourage and help young people. One of his ADCs mentioned to the Governor at dinner that as part of a junior naval staff course by correspondence, he was writing an essay about Dutch New Guinea. The next morning a stack of 12 books on the subject from Plimsoll's library was on the ADC's desk, with slips of paper in each, highlighting important passages.[81]

In September 1983 Plimsoll delivered two Arthur Yencken lectures at the ANU in Canberra on "The third world and Australia; an historical survey." [82] In October 1985 he declined an invitation from Don Ranard, Director of the Centre for International Policy in the US, to chair a conference on South-East Asia and the problem of Cambodia at the Rockefeller Foundation Centre in Bellagio, Italy, in December.

The arts

He considered encouraging local arts as part of promoting the state. He opened exhibitions, attended performances, and made visits. He became a frequent visitor to the Tasmanian Museum and Art Gallery in Hobart, sometimes privately if he had a free Saturday morning, entering by a side door. He came to know the paintings well enough to notice when they had been moved, sometimes asking the reason. Once he gave an address to the Friends of the Museum in which he spoke of his impressions of art galleries and museums which he had visited over 40 years in many parts of the world, as well as on his time as member of the interim Council of the Australian National Gallery. He displayed Tasmanian contemporary art at Government House.[83] He became interested in the work of Stephen Walker, a local artist. It was traditional for governors to leave a personal gift to the garden at Government House. In 1986 Plimsoll commissioned Walker to make some brolga statues to put in a garden bed just outside the front door.[84]

The constitutional role of the Governor

The governor acts on the advice of ministers, has the right "to be consulted, to encourage and to warn", and needs to monitor the legality and procedural regularity of action he is being advised to take.[85] Plimsoll was conscientious, if perhaps not so interested in the constitutional side of his role.[86] This included presiding at regular meetings of the Executive Council, and sessions for giving assent to Acts of Parliament.

Before Executive Council meetings, he was "fastidious" about satisfying himself that something he would have to sign, such as the appointment of a judge or head of a department, had been to cabinet, or such other prescribed process. If he saw a problem with a minute, he would ask if the minister concerned could withdraw it, so as to avoid embarrassing him at Executive Council, and to resubmit it later after the problem had been addressed. Unlike some other governors, he did not want to rewrite minutes.[87] He was always interested to know the premier's views in advance of Council meetings. Cautious, courteous and tactful, he understood the limitations of the governor's role, and was conscious of the proprieties as between governor and premier, and of the role of parliament and its privileges. "Unambiguously proper" about the conventions relating to the separation of powers between the different arms of government, he was uninterested in "clever deals or quick fixes". He looked for a solution, but always worked from the basis of principle, or adherence to statutory requirements.[88]

At Executive Council meetings Plimsoll was courteous and amiable. But around the table there was a "consciousness that Plimsoll was not someone you could baffle with bull. He was treated with respect". He was prepared to exercise his limited prerogatives if necessary. He was his own man. On one of the parole cases that came before cabinet, John Bennett as Attorney-General decided he would not recommend release. His colleagues agreed. Plimsoll later told Bennett that he would have overridden any recommendation for parole.[89]

Plimsoll enjoyed getting to know the ministers personally. After Executive Council meetings, he would stay for coffee with the premier and ministers, and chat for up to half an hour, during which a friendly and intelligent exchange took place, which all enjoyed. His intellect was pervasive but not flaunted.[90] He ensured that ministers all came to meals at Government House.

Ministers were full of praise for Plimsoll: "Courteous, considerate, humane, dutiful, conscientious, yes, but a humanity, interest in human beings. He cared about people."[91] "Took his role very seriously but didn't stand on dignity: humble, not aloof, compassionate."[92] When Bennett contracted glandular fever, Plimsoll visited him at his home. They were sitting having tea, when a large blowfly started buzzing everywhere. Bennett was wondering what to do about it, when the governor remarked on the similarity between blowflies and politicians: "Here today, gone tomorrow – don't worry about it".[93]

Keeping in touch with the Labor Opposition was made easier as he already knew Ken Wriedt, the Leader, from Wriedt's time as a minister in the Whitlam Government.

Plimsoll, who felt comfortable about his relationship with Premier Gray, did not insist on having regular meetings with him. Although Gray did not go and see the governor often, they developed a good relationship. Gray admired Plimsoll and enjoyed his company. He thought Plimsoll was the "sort of bloke one would like to have as a father to talk to". Plimsoll got to know Gray's family. Sometimes he had them to Sunday lunch; sometimes he would visit their home in Launceston for afternoon tea. Plimsoll "went to a great deal of trouble on our behalf, especially at difficult times, to show that he cared".[94]

Plimsoll "had long developed a superb gift of distilling views and imparting calm, wise advice, which was rarely if ever resented, and usually prized".[95] Gray found that if the governor wanted to give advice, "he did it in such a way you didn't know you were getting it".[96] He described Plimsoll as "a tremendous source of advice and counsel. His wisdom and experience often enabled him to assist our consideration of important issues, without in any way trying to impose upon Cabinet a particular point of view".[97] Bennett described Plimsoll as the "world's best poker player". He had no idea what his politics were. "He was so consummate a professional, he never said anything that would lead one to attribute a personal view to him about any issue of the day."[98] But he was intensely interested in the ins and outs of local politics. Once, at a Government House dinner, he was chatting with a well-known local public affairs commentator who, after touching on some current allegations of political misconduct in the local scene, told Plimsoll that he was not sure he should be relaying such rumours to him. The governor called the butler and told him to give his guest another brandy.[99]

The Franklin River Dam was a major issue that confronted the Tasmanian Government early in Plimsoll's tenure. Should Tasmania negotiate with the Commonwealth or take the matter to the High Court? Plimsoll privately saw risks in giving up on the negotiating process and losing flexibility. He felt it was important to avoid handing the matter over to lawyers, and was concerned that Tasmania seemed to be making a policy choice without an exit plan. Where would that leave Tasmania in future? The Commonwealth position centred on the external affairs provision in the Constitution. A judgment in favour of Canberra would have wide ramifications. It could close things off for the Australian states, diminish their position in cases where treaties applied domestically.[100] The Commonwealth, however, was leaning hard, and the Tasmanian Government, which was not prepared to negotiate, decided to go to the 'High Court.

Plimsoll's feeling for Tasmania became personal. Once asked where he regarded home, he replied that "this" was the first home he had had. It was heartfelt.[101] He became attached to living in Government House, perhaps the most beautiful of vice-regal residences in Australia.[102] He was to live there longer than anywhere else since he first left home, apart from his time in the Hotel Canberra. Plimsoll liked taking guests on a tour of the building with its superb position and commanding view, surrounded by beautiful grounds and adjoining the attractive Botanical Gardens, out of a desire to share Government House, a generosity of spirit.[103] It was also because a visitor might feel more at ease and open in conversation. Walking was Plimsoll's only exercise. A walk could take anything from 30 to 45 minutes, while to look at the view from the tower in Government House meant a climb of some 180 steps up and down again.

Through people he knew in Tokyo, he initiated establishment of a Japanese garden in the adjoining Botanical Gardens. He would walk in the Gardens, sometimes alone, sometimes accompanied by guests; one recalled that "people knew, respected and liked him. They were constantly greeting him, or coming up to talk and he was constantly attentive".[104]

He took little time off, such was his absorption in the job. He did not make any visits abroad, although he enjoyed visits by friends from overseas. He made brief trips to the mainland, mainly to Canberra, Melbourne or Sydney, often in the nature of "busman's holidays", staying at Government House in each, except in Sydney where he would stay with his brother's family, especially for a few days at Christmas. But that break was always cut short by the Sydney-Hobart yacht race, a major event in the Tasmanian calendar which starts on Boxing Day. The Melbourne to Devonport and Melbourne to Hobart races took place at about the same time. He presented prizes at the end of these each year.

Cricket

Attendance at sporting fixtures was a duty, except for cricket. It was a lifelong interest.[105] He attended at least one day of each Sheffield Shield match in Tasmania. He watched in Launceston and Devonport as well:

"It is remarkable how often – by pure coincidence of course – Sir James finds it necessary to conduct some Vice-Regal business" in those cities, when the cricket was on.[106] David Boon, former Test cricketer from Tasmania, recalled: "Sir James always had a presence that endeared him to you, and as a young man he made you comfortable in that presence and never had a negative comment or thought." It was "always nice to know that the Governor was on your side and irrespective of the result he was always there watching and supporting". Plimsoll knew everyone's name in the Tasmanian team and their role and performance.[107] During Shield matches he frequently held receptions for both teams. For touring Test teams he sometimes had some 200 guests to dinner in the ballroom.

Plimsoll seemed totally relaxed at the cricket. He liked to talk about it, and his knowledge of the game was considerable. He had met a number of prominent cricket people from his postings in New Delhi and London. He was stronger on the personalities of the game than statistics.[108] He put on a dinner once for visiting Australian Cricket Board members, and on another occasion a small dinner at which Colin Cowdrey, former England captain, Kim Hughes, then the Australian Test captain and Lazenby were the only guests. At the same time he always had an agenda, for example, putting in a word here or there in the right places in order to encourage the Australian cricket authorities to play a Test match in Tasmania.[109] The first such match was played in Hobart in 1989.

Aside from where to hang his art works, he took no interest in the furnishing of his surroundings. Nor had his predecessors: items like curtains, bedclothes and table cloths had not changed since the first post-war governors. His extensive personal library in his own rooms at Government House was messy, with unpacked cardboard boxes everywhere.[110] He was "paranoid" about fire precautions[111] but generally did not involve himself in day-to-day administration of Government House and its staff, to whom he was kindly but detached. When one long-serving member's father died, Plimsoll comforted her with a hug.

Heart attack, May 1985

Plimsoll normally breakfasted alone in his room at about 7am, retired by 11pm, and was not asleep until at least midnight. He enjoyed walking but not as part of any regimen. He was "pretty unfit", though never puffing. Episodes before coming to Tasmania in which he suffered fainting fits and loss of consciousness have already been described. The shingles contracted in Japan continued in Tasmania. Although often in discomfort, even excruciating pain, he never complained.[112] Plimsoll had always had a good appetite. At Government House he used to have tripe and offal at least weekly.[113] These factors, as well as his self-imposed work pattern, probably contributed to a heart attack in May 1985.

This may have been precipitated following a minor controversy, the application of the Council Amalgamation Act to two councils in Launceston: St Leonards councillors wanted to see the governor to persuade him not to give assent. He was advised not to see them, which led to the council at its final meeting criticising the governor, then cabling Buckingham Palace, asking the Queen to revoke Plimsoll's commission as governor. The Hobart *Mercury* editorial labelled this "ill-conceived, ill-advised and shabby". It said Plimsoll had "brought to the vice-regal office in this State the same qualities that distinguished his diplomatic career".[114] In a letter to the *Mercury* next day Brian Miller, a member of parliament, described Plimsoll as "an ornament to the office" of governor. Plimsoll did not want the premier to defend the position of the governor publicly, but Gray decided to do so and, on 16 May, publicly criticised the St Leonards Council.[115]

It was a storm in a tea-cup, but Plimsoll may have been upset. On Sunday 26 May in Hobart he had back pain, seemed ill, and may have had a minor heart attack, but would not listen to suggestions that he cancel a visit to the Eisteddfod at Burnie the next night. At the Eisteddfod he came up on stage, and remained standing there, so as to avoid going up and back. When Plimsoll sat down he was in severe pain, but would not leave. As was common, the show ran two hours over time. Back at the motel he said he was all right. The next morning he looked unwell. He agreed to see a doctor, then collapsed in his room, but came round easily enough. His brother John flew in from Sydney.[116] One immediate problem was that the Letters Patent for his appointment as governor did not provide for an automatic successor in the event of incapacity. With difficulty he had to sign the papers to enable Sir Guy Green, as Lieutenant-Governor, temporarily to take over the reins.

After a few days in intensive care at Burnie Hospital he flew by air ambulance to the cardiac care unit in the Royal Hobart Hospital for a week, where he was under Dr Michael Loughead, head of the unit. Plimsoll wanted to convalesce at Government House, despite the difficulties of being alone. One of the personal staff was on hand round the clock. Early in July he returned to the Royal Hobart for 24 hours for an operation in which electrical impulses were administered to correct an irregular heart beat.[117] He was provided with an emergency button for summoning an ambulance. Sometimes he absent-mindedly pressed it; at other times with good reason.[118]

After a few weeks he gradually resumed duties. At first he stayed put in Government House, only receiving callers, and presiding over Executive Council meetings there, then resuming having guests to meals, and then undertaking functions outside, judging "in the light of experience how far and how fast I can go". It was not easy to help him see the need to go carefully. Plimsoll wrote to a friend that he expected to be "fully active again" by the end of the month. Forceful directives from Dr Loughead helped to slow him down.[119] He also convalesced for a few days early in August at Government House, Canberra, with Sir Ninian and Lady Stephen. "Convalescence" included calls on the Foreign Minister, Bill Hayden, and on old colleagues from Foreign Affairs. He radically changed his diet and may have tried harder to take regular walks, mainly around the gardens. He stopped walking to the city and back. His face took on a more emaciated look.[120] By late September he was undeterred about doing his own tax return, as was his custom.[121] In late November he said that his health was standing up to the job.[122]

In November 1986 it was announced that Plimsoll's term of office, which was due to end in October 1987, had been extended three years to October 1990. This was the normal length of extension, although there are some indications that Plimsoll, having sought longer, was disappointed.

Apart from prescribed medical checks he was not inclined to bother doctors. One day Dr David Crean (later Treasurer of Tasmania) was at Government House with his parents, his father being the former Deputy Prime Minister, Frank Crean. He felt sufficiently concerned to get his medical kit out of his car, examine Plimsoll and prescribe some medicine for "a mild case of influenza", when he declined to see his own doctor.[123]

Except for diet Plimsoll made little change to his approach to his duties. He was soon back on his usual demanding schedule. One weekend, early in 1987, he went to Launceston on the Friday, next day to the races in Hobart for the Governor's Cup, to a function in Devonport in the late afternoon, then attended a function outside Launceston, followed by another in Hobart.[124] Gray thought Plimsoll at this time looked tense, and suggested that he should take things more quietly. "I'm all right" was the reply.[125] Sir Guy Green similarly asked Plimsoll about his renewed level of high activity, while not trying to persuade him to change. Plimsoll replied that he was not being stupid, but he felt that to change his normal ways would restrict life too much, would make the job not worth doing, and life would not be worth living.[126]

Last days

On 5 May Plimsoll visited Stephen Walker's studio at Campania. Three weeks before, on a visit to look at Walker's drawings of the Antarctic, Walker had broached doing a bust. Somewhat enigmatically Plimsoll had replied, "you'd better do it soon". He had started the next week, and now this was the fifth sitting, each of two hours. Plimsoll was tense, and sat vigorously drumming his fingers on his satchel, placed across his knees, partly perhaps having just heard that morning of the death of Judy McIntyre.[127]

At dinner at Government House on 7 May, Dorothy Beswick, wife of the Minister of Education, thought Plimsoll seemed fine. He was looking forward to visiting Ringarooma, in the Beswick's home area next year, for the local show that would celebrate Ringarooma's centenary in the same year as the national Bicentenary.[128] Sir Donald and Lady Tebbit, who were staying at Government House, were also at the dinner. "He was as minutely and helpfully interested as ever in everything and everybody." After dinner Plimsoll, as usual, insisted on accompanying the Tebbits up the 90 steps to the top of the tower of Government House to see the view. The next morning, 8 May, after breakfast, Plimsoll farewelled them, "apparently in the best of health and spirits".[129]

The day was the anniversary of the Battle of the Coral Sea. There were five functions to attend, including a ball in the evening. At the memorial service at the Cenotaph Plimsoll read the lesson and laid a wreath. At lunch at Government House, the 12 guests included Sir Guy Green, and Rear Admiral Horton RAN. Plimsoll seemed quiet and preoccupied. The guests left at 2:15.[130] Plimsoll returned to his office, where, at about 3pm, Peter Manton, Deputy Official Secretary, brought him some briefing papers, and talked to Plimsoll, seated at his desk. He seemed fine. Fifteen minutes later, Lieutenant Simon Schiwy RAN, the ADC, told Manton that he had just been in the Governor's office. Was it normal for him to be asleep at this hour? Manton went in again with Schiwy. He noticed Plimsoll had moved from his desk to an armchair. A briefing paper was on his lap. A doctor was summoned, and arrived instantly, but Plimsoll had already died of a heart attack.[131]

Death and Funeral

The Premier was at an agricultural festival between Carrick and Longfield, south of Launceston. Immediately informed, he was deeply shocked. Alexander Downer wept when he heard the news on his car radio in Adelaide.[132] Plimsoll's passing was reported nationally, and in London in *The Times*. In Montevideo an international Antarctic committee was meeting. Plimsoll had delivered the opening address to the previous meeting of the committee in Hobart and had held a reception for the delegates. The Chairman, Chris Beeby of New Zealand, paid tribute to Plimsoll and called for a minute's silence. The Department of Foreign Affairs described him as "one of Australia's most distinguished and respected professional diplomats" whose "long and brilliant career of public service" was "unlikely to be surpassed". The former US diplomat, Marshall Green, described Plimsoll as "one of the great diplomats of our times".[133] Downer wrote that Plimsoll "was one of the greatest men Australia has produced . . . We should be proud that as a nation we produced such a man".[134]

For someone who had always been so totally absorbed in his work, who had such dread of retirement, perhaps it was fitting that he should depart in the course of busy activity: "Up to and including his very last day on earth, Jim Plimsoll was maintaining and exercising to the full the wonderful qualities that made him such a great public servant and such an admirable human being."[135]

In Tasmania some had not found him easy, had indeed found him daunting, disinclined to converse if not in "professional mode". Despite that quietness and reserve, Sir Guy Green felt he had never seen anything like the way that Plimsoll had gained the affection of the state. He was "a great Tasmanian". On his death, a deep sense of personal loss was widely evident. Every Tasmanian that Green talked to seemed to regard Plimsoll as someone with whom they had a personal relationship.[136]

A State Funeral was held at the Anglican Cathedral of St David. The Governor-General and four state governors, (NSW, Victoria, South

Australia and Western Australia), all attended. Former holders of viceregal office, Sir Paul Hasluck and Sir Roden and Lady Cutler, were there. Hasluck, in the cathedral congregation, thought of the Plimsoll he had known and worked with, and of the work over the greater part of his life that had "established his place in Australian history".[137]

Senator Michael Tate of Tasmania represented the Prime Minister, Bob Hawke. Sir William McMahon came. There were heads of mission from the diplomatic corps in Canberra, including those of the UK, Japan, Korea and New Zealand. The packed cathedral and street outside included many who came from all over the state. The service in the cathedral was broadcast into the street, and throughout Tasmania.

Robin Gray delivered the eulogy. He and four former premiers of Tasmania carried the bier out of the church. A tri-service guard of honour and the police pipe band were drawn up. There was a stillness in the streets, lined with people who were concerned rather than curious, having lost someone known to them. Huge numbers followed the hearse on its journey to the airport. The Government House staff were all there. As the hearse was driven up the ramp onto the waiting RAAF Hercules, it was sunset, and there had been a thunderstorm. A number of "tough characters" among prominent locals were openly weeping.

Proceedings at the airport before the plane departed took longer than expected. The lone police piper had to go on playing for an hour. He later complained of sore fingers to the Police Commissioner: "Boss, don't drop one like that on me again."[138]

The body was flown to Sydney where, after a funeral service at St Matthew's, Bondi, burial took place in the Northern Suburbs general cemetery, North Ryde. There was a memorial service some days later at St John's in Canberra. In delivering the eulogy, Sir Arthur Tange said that "the Plimsoll story is a story for Australians to treasure. He achieved so much for his country in high places while exhibiting so many of the qualities which we Australians value".[139]

At the next meeting of the Tasmanian State Parliament in July, a number of members spoke about Plimsoll's contribution as governor. One, Dr Bob Brown (Denison), later Federal Senator and Leader of the Australian Greens, said:

> He was a generous man and that generosity flows on now, after he is dead, because everybody here really feels good – all Tasmanians feel good – for his having been with us for five years and for his having given us so much.[140]

In Australia, vice-regal appointments partly recognise distinction already achieved. Not all are especially remembered as having been memorable in the office, because of the nature of the role, discreet and non-controversial. In Tasmania, however, years afterwards, Plimsoll was still regarded as having been among the best governors. "In the most benign and gentle way, he had acquired the aura, status and influence of a longstanding constitutional monarch. He had no airs whatsoever but displayed a constant, quiet, imperturbable and unself-seeking dedication to every good, or even reasonably good cause."[141] As an outsider, his instant identification with Tasmania, and constant striving to do what he could to help, were warmly remembered.

His name is commemorated by Lake Plimsoll in western Tasmania. In 1984 Plimsoll's *alma mater*, the University of Sydney, had conferred an honorary doctorate. On 3 April 1987 the University of Tasmania had conferred an honorary doctorate "for the enormous contribution he has made to the life of Tasmania".[142] In May 2007, at the University, Alexander Downer, as Foreign Minister, delivered the inaugural Sir James Plimsoll Memorial Lecture. In the Department of Foreign Affairs and Trade in Canberra, there is the Plimsoll Room.

Plimsoll's contribution in the cultural field is particularly remembered – the Plimsoll Gallery at the Tasmania University Fine Arts Department was a joint decision of the government and the university. The bust by Stephen Walker is in the foyer. There were generous provisions in his

Will. After the National Gallery of Victoria and the Art Gallery of NSW had received, between them, his Asian art, the Tasmanian Museum and Art Gallery received the remainder of his collection, mainly Australian pieces, plus a bequest of more than $550,000. This money contributed to the purchase at auction of two paintings of historical importance, John Glover's *River Derwent and Hobart Town*, and Francis Low's *Old Government House*.[143]

Plimsoll's greatest legacy to Tasmania was the way he carried out the role of governor, making it more relevant to the times, and transforming expectations for his successors. He upheld the office with dignity, but used it to promote possibilities that the state had to offer, rather than simply to preserve the status quo. He did this because he thought that was what he should do.[144] His contribution affected perceptions of the importance of the role of governor – people had been coming to expect less. Partly this was the impact of Plimsoll himself, an unusual and unforgettable human being. Somewhat unworldly but highly intelligent and knowledgeable, with wide interests, and energetic, he stimulated and brought out the best in people. He bore himself with natural dignity and aura, so that many may not have noticed or, if they did, forgave how uninterested he was in his clothing and appearance. Stephen Walker recalled that while intensely private – he could "retreat behind his eyelids, and lower his shades" – on the other hand, "he never shut you off".[145]

Endnotes

1 R. Gray, Eulogy, 13/5/1987.

2 Evers, conversation, 5/12/1996; R.L. Harry, conversation, 1998; D.J. Pitchford, conversation, 8/1996.

3 D. Lowe, letter, 13/10/1998.

4 Lowe, letter, 13/10/1998.

5 Cutler, conversation, 7/1996; Evers, conversation, 5/12/1996.

6 Among his predecessors three, Sir Allen Brown, Sir Gordon Freeth, and John Menadue had been non-career appointments.

7 JP to Tange, 18/6/1982.

8 Dobinson, conversation, 8/2/1999.

9 JP diary, 27/8/1981; Evers, conversation, 5/12/1996. In 1986 Evers joined the Gray Government on being elected to the House of Assembly in Tasmania.

10 Cam/Plim, ii, 227 and 342.

11 Henderson, conversation, 27/2/2003.

12 Cam/Plim, ii, 227.

13 JP diary, 1 and 2/9/1981; Evers, conversation, 5/12/1996.

14 Lowe, letter, 4/11/1997.

15 Osborn, conversation, 4/11/1997.

16 Evers, conversation, 5/12/1996; Pitchford, conversation, 8/1996.

17 JP diary; E. O'Farrell, conversation, 5/12/1996.

18 O'Farrell, conversation, 5/12/1996.

19 Sir Guy Green, conversation, 5/12/1996.

20 JP diary, 12-14/11/1981.

21 Cam/Plim, i, 93.

22 JP diary, 22 & 26/6/1982.

23 JP diary, 19 and 20/6/1982.

24 Pearsall, letter, 26/1/2002.

25 Another diplomatic colleague, Sir Walter Crocker, was Lt-Governor of South Australia, 1973-82.

26 Sir Ninian Stephen, conversation, 23/7/2000.

27 Lt R.J. Griggs ADC RAN, later Vice-Admiral Griggs, Chief of Navy, conversation, 2/3/1998.

28 K. Wriedt, conversation, 1/4/2001.

29 Trollope, *Australia and New Zealand*, 1873, quoted in, Victoria Glendinning, *Trollope*, London, 2002, 414. Trollope was thinking particularly of climate and scenery.

30 Evers, conversation, 5/12/1996.

31 O'Farrell, conversation, 1996.

32 K. Von Bibra, conversation, 22/9/2001.

33 D.J. Pitchford, who succeeded O'Farrell as Official Secretary, conversation, 8/1996; and Lt R. Menhinnick, ADC, RAN, conversation, 20/8/2000.

34 Gray, Eulogy, 13/5/1987.

35 Parsons, 6/5/1997.

36 Griggs, conversation, 2/3/1998.

37 Citation for Honorary Degree at the University of Tasmania, 3/4/1987.

38 R.J. Groom, letter, 22/5/2000.

39 Bishop P.K. Newell, letter, 22/9/2000.

40 Griggs, conversation, 2/3/1998.

41 JP diary, 28/6/1983.

42 J.M. Bennett, conversation, 19/9/2001.

43 Evers, conversation, 5/12/1996; Griggs, conversation, 2/3/1998.

44 Dr R. Herr, conversation, 20/9/2001.

45 Menhininck, conversation, 20/8/2000.

46 M. Robinson, Police Commissioner of Tasmania, conversation, 29/9/2000.

47 Menhinick, conversation, 20/8/2000.

48 P. Manton, Deputy Official Secretary, conversation, 19/9/2001.

49 Evers, 5/12/1996.

50 Once, however, in a story which Plimsoll told against himself, his memory was not quite accurate. A show exhibitor received Plimsoll's kindly greeting by reminding him that they had met before at Dairyville. "And Your Excellency will remember Matilda too." "Yes indeed," replied the Governor, "and how is your wife?" "No! No!", replied the exhibitor. "You gave Matilda the blue ribbon for being best cow." Tange Eulogy.

51 Menhinick, conversation, 20/8/2000.

52 Robinson, conversation, 29/2/2000.

53 Griggs, conversation, 2/3/1998.

54 Lowe, conversation, 4/6/1998.

55 Griggs, conversation, 2/3/1998.

56 S. Walker, conversation, 23/9/2001.

57 Menhinick, conversation, 20/8/2000.
58 Pitchford, conversation, 8/1996; Professor A Lazenby, conversation, 10/2/1998; Griggs, conversation, 2/3/1998.
59 Manton, conversation, 19/9/2001.
60 Griggs, conversation, 2/3/1998.
61 Sir David Hay, conversation, 10/10/1996.
62 Dr M. Vertigan, conversation, 28/8/1997; Lt S. Schiwy ADC, conversation, 18/2/2000: Sir Max Bingham, conversation, 20/9/2001.
63 Evers, conversation, 5/12/1996; G. Green, conversation, 5/12/1996.
64 J. Beswick, conversation, 21/9/2001.
65 H. Gelber, letter, 4/2/2002. A local resident once remarked that he now always read the vice-regal court circular in the *Mercury* newspaper: "It has become such good reading to see who has been at Government House and where the guests have come from." Henderson, conversation, 27/2/2003.
66 Newell, conversation, 22/9/2000; Robinson, conversation, 29/9/2000; JP diary, 24/7/1986.
67 D. Gregg, conversation, 19/9/2001; G. Green, conversation, 19/9/2001; K. Von Bibra, conversation, 22/9/2001.
68 Pitchford, conversation, 8/1996; Manton, conversation, 19/9/2001.
69 J. Green, conversation, 20/9/2001.
70 "He was nothing short of brilliant at smoothing the path with people for things that needed to be done, or that would be useful. And always without in any way going, or being seen to go, beyond the proper gubernatorial impartiality, let alone intervening in political affairs. It was quite admirable." Gelber, letter, 4/2/2002.
71 Gray, conversation, 21/9/2001; Vertigan, conversation, 28/8/1997.
72 Pitchford, conversation, 8/1996; Griggs, conversation, 2/3/1998; Lazenby, conversation, 10/2/1998.
73 Cam/Plim, ii, 106.
74 Pitchford, conversation, 8/1996.
75 Pitchford, conversation, 8/1996.
76 Manton, conversation, 19/9/2001; G Pearsall, letter, 26/1/2002.
77 G. Green, conversation, 5/12/1996.

78 Ibid.

79 Chagrined that he was unable to come to the one that he missed, he asked for more notice. Lazenby, conversation, 10/2/1998.

80 Pitchford. conversation, 8/1996; Herr, conversation, 20/9/2001.

81 Griggs, conversation, 2/3/1998.

82 JP diary, 13-14/9/1983, and 10/85.

83 Gregg, conversation, 19/9/2001; S. Walker; conversation, 23/9/2001; JP diary, 28/6/1983.

84 Walker, who had been going through difficult times financially, was grateful for the commission. Plimsoll paid in advance, while the publicity Walker derived from this work served as a "stamp of good housekeeping". Walker, conversation, 23/9/2001; JP diary, 27/8/1986.

85 Sir Guy Green "Governors, democracy and the rule of law," *Constitutional Law and Policy Review*, vol. 9, no. 1, June 2006, 11-16.

86 G. Green, conversation, 5/12/1996.

87 Julian Green, conversation, 20/9/2001.

88 Ibid.

89 Sir Max Bingham, conversation, 20/9/2001; Gray, conversation, 21/9/2001; Bennett, conversation, 19/09/2001.

90 Evers, conversation, 5/12/96.

91 Bingham, conversation, 20/9/2001.

92 Beswick, conversation, 21/9/2001.

93 Bennett, conversation, 19/09/2001.

94 Gray, Eulogy and conversation, 21/9/2001; Evers, conversation, 5/12/1996; Manton, conversation, 19/9/2001.

95 Sir Donald Tebbit, letter, 7/1/1998; Tebbit was UK High Commissioner, Canberra, 1977-80. On later visits to Tasmania, he stayed twice with Plimsoll at Government House.

96 Gray, conversation, 21/9/2001.

97 Gray, Eulogy and conversation, 21/9/2001.

98 Bennett, conversation, 19/9/2001.

99 J. Green, conversation, 20/9/2001; Herr, conversation, 20/9/2001.

100 J. Green, conversation, 20/9/2001.

101 G. Green, conversation, 5/12/1996.

102 In 1875 Anthony Trollope had observed that in Hobart "the Government House is, I believe, acknowledged to be the best belonging to any British colony". Anthony Trollope *Victoria and Tasmania*, London 1875, 161.

103 Robinson, conversation, 19/1/2002; Von Bibra, conversation, 22/9/2001.

104 Keith Douglas Scott, letter, 6/11/2004.

105 His attendance at one day matches, "pyjama cricket," was more out of a sense of duty. He was unhappy with this innovation, though he kept that to himself. Griggs, conversation, 2/3/1998.

106 A tongue in cheek observation in the Citation that was read out when Plimsoll received his honorary degree from the University of Tasmania.

107 David Boon, letters 22 and 26/9/2000.

108 Lazenby, conversation, 10/2/1998.

109 Griggs, conversation, 2/3/1998.

110 Sir Ninian Stephen, conversation, 10/8/1998; O'Farrell, conversation, 5/12/1996; General Sir Phillip and Lady Bennett, conversation, 10/7/1996.

111 Probably in the wake of his experience of the fire in the Embassy in Moscow. Pitchford, conversation, 8/1996; Manton, conversation, 19/9/2001.

112 Griggs, conversation, 2/3/1998.

113 Ibid.

114 Hobart *Mercury*, 7 and 8/5/1985.

115 Griggs, conversation, 2/3/1998; Gray press release, 16/5/1985.

116 Griggs, conversation, 2/3/1998.

117 Pitchford conversation, 8/1996; JP to BJ Hill, 12/7/1985, JP papers 8048/21/91, NLA.

118 Griggs, conversation, 2/3/1998.

119 Pitchford, 8/1996; JP to B.J. Hill, 12/7/1985; JP papers, 8048/21/91, NLA.

120 Pitchford, conversation, 8/1996; Lazenby, conversation, 10/2/1998; JP diary, 5-9/8/1985.

121 JP diary, 29/9/1985.

122 JP to Griggs, 27/11/85, JP papers, 8048/21/92, NLA.

123 JP diary 30/9/1986; F. Crean, conversation, 8/6/2001; Dr David Crean, letter, 17/8/2001.

124 Lt S. Schiwy, ADC, RAN, conversation, 18/2/2000.
125 Gray, conversation, 21/9/2001.
126 G. Green, 5/12/1996.
127 Walker, conversation, 23/9/2001; JP diary, 5/5/1987. Lady McIntyre was the widow of Sir Laurence.
128 D. Beswick, 21/9/2001.
129 Sir Donald Tebbit, letter, 7/1/1998.
130 Schiwy; Rear Admiral Horton, conversation, 3/7/1998.
131 Manton, conversation, 19/9/2001; Schiwy, conversation, 18/2/2000.
132 A. Downer, conversation, 30/3/1998.
133 DFAT News Release 9/5/1987; Marshall Green letter to Sir Arthur Tange, 6/3/1988, Tange papers.
134 Downer, letter to *Canberra Times*, 20/5/1987.
135 Tebbit, letter, 7/1/1998.
136 G. Green, conversation, 5/12/1996.
137 Hasluck to Crocker, 2/6/1987, Hasluck private papers, courtesy Nicholas and Sally Hasluck.
138 Robinson, conversation, 29/9/2000.
139 Tange, Eulogy, Anglican Church of St John the Baptist, Canberra, 21/5/1987.
140 Dr Bob Brown, *Tasmanian House of Assembly Proceedings*, 7/7/1987, 1954.
141 Tebbit, letter, 7/1/1998.
142 Citation read out at the ceremony by the Vice-Chancellor.
143 Gregg, conversation, 19/9/2001.
144 Manton, conversation, 19/9/2001.
145 Walker, conversation, 23/9/2001.

Epilogue: Ambassador Extraordinary[1]

Plimsoll's time was one in which a fledgling diplomatic service struggled to become a recognised arm of government and to organise itself. People were frequently posted abroad at short notice. Language training for non-English speaking posts was recognised as being desirable but was spasmodic. By today's standards, communications were primitive. Thereced limited policy guidance from Canberra. Many, if not all, posts were short-staffed. Plimsoll, however, seemed to revel in adapting to all this, although foreign languages was not a strength; and later to the role of Governor of Tasmania. Plimsoll's service as an ambassador no fewer than eight times (a normal number would be about three), and all in major centres, is a record unlikely to be matched. In a small, developing diplomatic service it was not uncommon for relatively young officers to be thrust into important positions abroad. That Plimsoll preferred the work abroad, and that he did not have the family responsibilities which prompted others to seek more time at home, were other factors. But his appointments also reflected his talent and the high regard in which he was held at home and abroad.

Diplomacy was a little known profession in Australia when Plimsoll started. He participated in establishing standards and style. He was among those who helped Australia's political leaders to recognise the need for, and to accept the value of, a professional diplomatic service. In the intervening sixty years much has changed but not the need for a foreign service of the highest quality: its officers need to be individuals who can make a difference. Plimsoll's career is evidence of this.

---

1 In the text of the Credentials which a new ambassador presents, the ambassador is formally described as "Ambassador Extraordinary and Minister Plenipotentiary".

Acknowledgements

Sir James Plimsoll clearly intended to write his memoirs; unfortunately this did not happen. The idea of a biography was well received, but it has taken 17 years, part-time. Many people have given all kinds of help, for which I am very grateful.

At an early stage I contacted both John Poynter and Geoffrey Serle, two of my lecturers many years ago at the Melbourne University History School. Each provided excellent starting advice.

Many helped with access to the considerable documentary material relating to Plimsoll, to which in some instances Special Access was granted. In Canberra I am grateful to Bill Hudson, Liz Nathan and Moyra Smythe in DFAT, while in the Library there many thanks to Kathy Stapleton, Marissa Vearing, Jenny Ensbey and Michaela Laus; in the National Library of Australia, Graeme Powell and staff in the Manuscripts Room, and Shelley Grant and her colleagues in the Oral History Collection; in the National Archives of Australia, Elyse Boutcher and Kylie Scroope, also to my nephew David Hearder. I would like to commend the National Library and the Archives for their conservation skills in preserving a much as possible of Plimsoll's papers that were affected by the fire in the embassy in Moscow. Elsewhere I am grateful to Susan Woodburn, the Special Collections Librarian in the Barr Smith Library at Adelaide University; Tony Miller at ANZ Group Records Management and Archives, Melbourne; and Lucy Rantzen and Julie Gleaves at Westpac Historical Services, Sydney. I was also much helped by libraries of the ANU and Flinders University, and Archives of Melbourne and Sydney universities respectively.

I have benefited from the recollections and comments of many people who knew Plimsoll. I am particularly grateful to the following for their help: at the Federal level former governors-general Sir Zelman

Cowen and Sir Ninian Stephen; former prime ministers Sir John Gorton, Gough Whitlam and Malcolm Fraser; former foreign ministers Sir Garfield Barwick, Sir Gordon Freeth, Andrew Peacock, Bill Hayden and Alexander Downer, to whom I am also indebted for his gracious foreword.

At the state level former NSW governors Sir Roden Cutler and Air Marshall Sir James Rowland; former Tasmanian governors General Sir Phillip Bennett and Sir Guy Green; and former Victorian governor Dr Davis McCaughey; former Tasmanian premiers Doug Lowe, Robin Gray, and Ray Groom. Further afield I am most thankful to Lord Carrington, Field Marshall Lord Carver, Sir John Cornforth and Philip Ziegler in Britain; Brent Scowcroft in the US; C.V. Narasimhan and Sir Brian Urquhart at the United Nations in New York, and Pote Sarasin in Thailand.

Sir Arthur Tange, who had known Plimsoll for most of his life, was generous with his time on several occasions. I benefited from talking to other former heads of the department who knew Plimsoll well: Dr J.W. Burton, Alan Renouf, Sir Nicholas Parkinson, Peter Henderson, Professor Stuart Harris, Richard Woolcott, and Philip Flood. Although this book has been a private venture, I am also grateful to subsequent Secretaries, Dr Ashton Calvert, Michael L'Estrange, Dennis Richardson and Peter Varghese for their encouragement. Sir Walter Crocker allowed me special access to his personal papers. Vice-Admiral Ray Griggs, Vice Chief of the Defence Force, talked to me about his time as ADC to Plimsoll as Governor of Tasmania.

Many of Plimsoll's former colleagues and friends shared their memories and impressions of him, providing valuable information as well as improved understanding of the background in which he worked in Sydney, Melbourne, Canberra and Hobart, as well as in all his postings abroad. The bibliography lists 140 people with whom I was in contact. I am also grateful to the following: Professor Don Aitkin, Lesley Alcorso, Peter Bailey, Jean Battersby, Joan Beaumont, Alan Behm, Hazell Bell, Dr

Harold Bell, M.R. Booker, Denis Brophy, Syliva Brown, Meredith Buring, Peter Costigan, Frank Crean, John Dauth, Barry Dexter, Tony Eggleton, F.S. Fry, Narelle Gibson, Ainsley Gotto, Bob and Patsy Hamilton, Ralph Hillman, Joan Hird, Kathy Howes, S.H.R. Hume, Garth Hunt, Hershel Hurst, Kim Jones, Lesley and Keith Jones, Lance Joseph, Noel Kelly, J.R. Kelso, Sir Richard Kingsland, Justice Michael Kirby, Joyce Koch, Dame Leonie Kramer, Sir Peter Lawler, Charles Lloyd Jones, Mary McPherson, Elaine Miller, Ian Nicholson, D.G. Nutter, Rae Oldfield, Sir John Overall, Roger Pescott, P.F. Peters, John Piper, George Pooley, Paul Potter, Cassandra Pybus, Peter Rae, Rear Admiral Ian Richards, Richard Rowe, Ian Sinclair, J.T. Smith, Pat Stanner, F.H. Stuart, J.W. Sullivan, John Thorpe, Michael Thwaites, R.J. Tyson, Nancy-Bird Walton, Sir Eric Willis, and Reg Withers. If there are others whom I should have mentioned, my humblest apologies.

I am indebted to people who kindly read drafts of chapters as they emerged, offering suggestions and criticism: Peter and Heather Henderson, Ian Hancock and Bill Pritchett. Dr David Lee, Professor Peter Boyce, Ric Smith, Jim Ingram, and Professor Geoffrey Bolton have all read the completed text. Others who provided valuable comment on particular chapters were: Colonel Graeme Sligo, Peter Ryan, Michael Cook, Peter Curtis, Bob Robertson, Dr Ric Shand, Dick Smith, Geoff Miller, David Sadleir, John Burgess, David Pitchford, and Nick Evers.

I am grateful to the following for various assistance or advice: Rob Laurie, Robert Dessaix, Dr Cassie Ryan, Jim Merralls, Garry Woodard, Michael Wilson, Dr A.W. Martin, Nicholas and Sally Hasluck, Peter Edwards, Andrew Hay, Associate Professor John Lack, Davey Ryan, Bob White, and Galina Lazareva.

I value the help and friendship over the years from a group of special colleagues: Ian Brown, John Moore, Michelle Marginson, Ian Wille, Bill Nelson, Bruce Hunt, Lee Kerr, Barbara Cooper, Matt Jordan, Moreen Dee, Wendy Way, Stuart Doran, Leith Douglas, Gordon Murphy, Steve Robinson, Paul Lawson-Brown, Geoff Stroud, Don Haig, Roger

Holdich, Jeanette Ryan, Janet Tomi, Dara Williams, Robyn Mudie, Ruth Pearce, Chris Taylor, Liz Frazier, Maxine Hewitt, and more recent colleagues, Wanda Oram-Miles, Brooke Rogers, and Peter Lockey.

Plimsoll's brother John's family has been encouraging and helpful throughout. I am especially grateful to Patricia and to Kathleen.

I am most grateful to Dr Anthony Cappello, of Connor Court Publishing, for his support. I will always remember my first visit to Ballarat, when, at very short notice, he had invited me to coffee at the Golden Nugget Bakery. Warmest thanks also to Michael Gilchrist.

I have special gratitude for John Nethercote, Adjunct Professor, Canberra Campus, Australian Catholic University, who has acted as guide, philosopher and friend, with his editorial skills, his understanding of publishing, and his extensive knowledge of governance in Australia and elsewhere.

Over the many years my family has been very supportive and helpful in all kinds of ways; not least in solving IT challenges, in which our young grandchildren have especially contributed. Our historian daughter, Dr Rosalind Hearder, kindly read through the draft chapters and made many valuable suggestions: and while visiting London, interviewed Alec Adams, Plimsoll's British colleague in Korea. The usual disclaimer applies: responsibility for the final text is shouldered by me alone.

This book is dedicated to the memory of my father and mother.

Select Bibliography

The following lists those sources that I found most useful:

Archival sources

The main source was Plimsoll's personal papers, which initially had been divided between the National Library of Australia [NLA], the National Archives of Australia [NAA] and the Department of Foreign Affairs and Trade [DFAT].

Australian and New Zealand Bank Archives

Letter of 23/2/98 from Tony Miller, ANZ Group Records Management and Archives.

Australian War Memorial

Australian Military Mission, Washington messages.

Land Headquarters, Melbourne messages.

Barr-Smith Library, University of Adelaide

Papers of Sir Walter Crocker.

Department of Foreign Affairs and Trade [DFAT]

Plimsoll personnel file

Personal papers of Sir Arthur Tange, Sir Keith Waller and Sir Alan Watt.

W.D. Forsyth, Recollections, (unpublished manuscript).

Alfred Stirling, Diary, (unpublished).

DFAT *Documents on Australian Foreign Policy* series.

Doran, SR (ed), *Australia and Papua New Guinea 1966-69: Documents on Australian Foreign Policy*, DFAT, Canberra, 2006.

Doran, SR and D Lee (eds), *Australia and Recognition of the People's Republic of China 1949-72. Documents on Australian Foreign Policy*, DFAT, Canberra, 2002.

National Archives of Australia [NAA]

Plimsoll papers CRS M2203/5 Canberra.

Hasluck papers MS 5274 Foreign Affairs, vol. II, 1964-66, Box 37, Canberra.

National Library of Australia [NLA]

Manuscripts.

Plimsoll Papers MS 8048.

Casey Papers MS6150.

Oral histories.

Reminiscential Conversations between Hon. Clyde Cameron and Sir James Plimsoll 1984 TRC 1967; Tange Oral History TRC 1023 1981; TRC 2482 1989 and 1992.

Sir David Hay Oral History TRC 121/65-1.

AP Renouf Oral History TRC 2981/6.

Sir Laurence McIntyre Oral history TRC 121/67.

Westpac Archives

Correspondence of Sir Alfred Davidson, General Manager.

Correspondence of Professor Torleiv Hytten.

Manuscript of *Bureaucracy and Democracy* by J Plimsoll.

Public Record Office, London

B Cockram, Deputy UK High Commissioner, Canberra, conversation with Plimsoll 8/1/53, DO35/5821 PRO London. Courtesy Dr Rosalind Hearder.

Fisher Library, Sydney University

Union Recorder.

Soldier Career Management Agency, Melbourne

Details of Major J. Plimsoll.

Privately held records

Alec Adams, interviewed by Dr Rosalind Hearder, August 1998.

HW Bullock, *My Time in Korea 1950-52: a Personal Memoir*, unpublished, 2000.

Sir Owen Dixon papers – courtesy J.D. Merralls.
Ruth Dobson to John Plimsoll, 27 May 1987.
Robin Gray, *Eulogy at State Funeral for Sir James Plimsoll*, Hobart, 13 May 1987.
Sir Paul Hasluck to Sir Walter Crocker, 2 June 1987. Hasluck Private Papers, courtesy of Nicholas and Sally Hasluck.
Sir Paul Hasluck to AW Martin, 13 January 1988, courtesy AW Martin.
C.T. Moodie, unpublished memoirs, 1992.
Plimsoll's letters home, 1945-46.
John E. Ryan, unpublished diary.
Sir Arthur Tange, interviewed by AW Martin, 7 August 1987.
Sir Arthur Tange, *Eulogy, Memorial Service for Sir James Plimsoll*, St John the Baptist, Canberra, 21 May 1987.

Interviews, conversations and written communications

Bruce Allen; HD Anderson; JD Anthony; Keith Baker; Laurie Baragwanath; Roger Barltrop; Patricia G. Barnett-Brubaker; Dr Tom Bartlett; PG Bassett; John Bennett; Gordon Bilney; Barrie Blackburn; LH Border; HW Bullock; JR. Burgess; Betty Burke; C.L. Burns; I. Butchart; A.D. Campbell; Karina Campbell; Sir John Carrick; RLC Cotton; Hazel Craig; Bob Crick; TK Critchley; Sir Roden Cutler; FR Dalrymple; Vesta Davies; Owen Davis; John Deeble; Sir Roy Denman; D de Stoop; Basil Dickinson; AF Dingle; Don Dobinson; HA Dunn; DW Evans; Nick Evers; K Farnham; AC Farran; RR Fernandez; R.J. Fisher; Brian Fleming; Graham Freudenberg; RW Furlonger; Pat Galvin; Dr John Gee; H Gilchrist; John Graham; Bruce Grant; Marshall Green; RJ Greet; Harold Groves; Irina Gubbenet; Barry Hain; Owen Harries; RL Harry; Sir David Hay; Gerald Hensley; Prof Richard Herr; Sir Lenox Hewitt; Dorothy Higgins; BC Hill; Brian J Hill; RF Holder; Peter Howson; MJ Hughes; PNB Hutton; Walter Ives; Professor Marjorie Jacobs; GA Jockel; RE Johns; ML Johnston; TN Kaul; Lionel Kentwell; Don Kenyon; Sir Richard Kingsland; DJ Kingsmill; Marjorie Knight; PM Knight; JA Lavett; Em Prof John Legge; Sam Lipski; Max Loveday; Sir Donald Maitland; John Malone; P Manton; JP McCarthy; Michael McGeorge; Alex McGoldrick; Doug McKay; Lyndal McLean; Sir Leslie Melville; Ronald Mendelsohn; Commodore Richard Menhinick; Em Prof JDB Miller; James Mollison; Malcolm Morris; FC Murray; Bishop Philip Newell; Peter Nixon;

Mervyn Norrish; Edward O'Farrell; RF Osborn; AR Parsons; Geoff Pearsall; DJ Pitchford; GJ Price; Judge Ray Reynolds; RH Robertson; Max Robinson; Judge Hugh Robson; JR Rowland; John Sankey; Lt Simon Schiwy; James Scott; Joseph Sisco; RJ Smith; Cisca Spencer; John Starey; John Stone; Lady (Jean) Sutherland; Colin Teese; Professor Svetlana Ter-Minasova; Professor Ross Terrill; Sir Crispin Tickell; Rod Tier; Peter Timmins; Rosemary Viret; Kenneth Von Bibra; Stephen Walker; Jack Walshe; Geoffrey White; Margaret Whitlam; Mack Williams; Trevor Wilson; Warwick Mayne Wilson; Mervyn Wood; Ken Wriedt; Throsby Zouch.

Memoirs and secondary sources

Beaumont, Joan, Waters Christopher, Lowe David, with Woodard Garry, *Ministers, Mandarins and Diplomats: Australian Foreign Policy Making 1941-1969*, Melbourne University Press, Melbourne, 2003.

Casey, RG, *Friends and Neighbours: Australia and the World*, FW Cheshire, Melbourne, 1954.

Edwards, Peter, *Arthur Tange: Last of the Mandarins*, Allen and Unwin, Sydney, 2006.

Evatt, HV, *The Task of Nations*, Duell, Sloan and Pearce, New York, 1949.

Flood, Philip, *Dancing with Warriors: A Diplomatic Memoir*. Australian Scholarly Publishing, Melbourne 2011.

Goldsworthy, David (ed), *Facing North: A Century of Australian Engagement with Asia*. Vol. 1, 1901 to the 1970s, MUP, 2001.

Green, Marshall, *Pacific Encounters, Recollections and Humour*, DACOR Press, Bethesda, Maryland, 1997.

Harry, Ralph, *No Man is a Hero: Pioneers of Australian Diplomacy*, Arts Management, Sydney, 1997.

Hasluck, Sir Paul, *The Chance of Politics*, edited by Nicholas Hasluck, Text Publishing, Melbourne, 1997.

Hasluck, Sir Paul, *Diplomatic Witness: Australian Foreign Affairs, 1941-1947*, MUP, 1980.

Henderson, Heather (ed), *Letters to My Daughter: Robert Menzies, Letters 1955-75*, Pier 9, Sydney, 2011.

Henderson, Peter, *Privilege and Pleasure*, Methuen Haynes, North Ryde, NSW, 1986.

Hudson, WJ, *Casey*, Oxford University Press, Melbourne, 1986.

Martin, AW, *Robert Menzies: A Life* .Vol. II, 1944-1978, MUP, Melbourne, 1999.

O'Neill, Robert, *Australia in the Korean War 1950-53*. Vol. 1, Strategy and Diplomacy, Australian War Memorial and Australian Government Publishing Service, Canberra, 1981.

Parsons, Alf, *South East Asian Days*, Australians in Asia Paper No 22, Griffith University, Brisbane, April 1998.

Simons, Margaret, and Fraser, Malcolm, *Malcolm Fraser: the Political Memoirs*, Miegunyah Press, Melbourne, 2010.

Sligo, Graeme, *The Backroom Boys: Conlon and Army's Directorate of Research and Civil Affairs, 1942-46*, Big Sky Publishing. Sydney, 2013

Sugarman, B, Stone, Julius and McIntyre Neil (Eds), *Alfred Conlon: A Memorial by Some of His Friends*, Benevolent Society of NSW, Sydney, 1963.

Urquhart, Sir Brian, *A Life in Peace and War*. Norton, New York, 1991.

Waller, Sir Keith, *A Diplomatic Life: Some Memories*, Australians in Asia, Griffith University, Brisbane, 1990.

Watt, AS, *Memoirs of Sir Alan Watt*, Angus and Robertson, Sydney, in association with the AIIA, 1972.

Watt, AS, *Evolution of Australian Foreign Policy 1938-1965*, London, Cambridge University Press, 1967.

Woolcott, Richard, *The Hot Seat: Reflections on Diplomacy from Stalin's Death to the Bali Bombings*, Harper Collins, Sydney, 2003.

Articles, periodicals, chapters and entries in biographical dictionaries

Crawford, Sir John, "The role of the Permanent Head," *Public Administration*, Sydney, Vol 13, No. 3, September 1954, 153-65.

Downer, Alexander, "A tough job with style," *Advertiser* [Adelaide], 20 September 2009.

Edwards, PG, "The origins and growth of professional diplomacy in Australia," *Australian Foreign Affairs Review*, Vol. 56, 1985, 1069-1076.

Farran, Andrew, "The Freeth Experiment," *Australian Outlook*, Vol. XXVI, No. 1, April 1972, 46-58.

Greenwood, Gordon, "Australian foreign policy in action," in *Australia in World Affairs 1961-65*, Gordon Greenwood and Norman Harper (eds), FW Cheshire, Melbourne, 1968.

Hancock, Ian, "The VIP Affair, 1966-67," *Australasian Parliamentary Review*, Vol 18(2), Spring 2003.

Hearder, Jeremy, "Plimsoll, Sir James (1917-1987), public servant, diplomat and governor," *Australian Dictionary of Biography*, Vol 18, MUP, 2012.

Hearder, Jeremy, "Casey and Plimsoll: a close working relationship" in Melissa Conley Tyler, John Robbins, and Adrian March (eds), *R.G.Casey: Minister for External Affairs 1951-60*. AIIA Canberra, 2012, 61-80.

Plimsoll, James, "Towards a wider conception of our common humanity," in *The Emerging World. Jawaharlal Nehru Memorial Volume*. Asia Publishing House, Bombay, 1964.

Plimsoll, James, *Asian issues in the Australian Press*, 28th A.N. Smith Memorial Lecture in Journalism, Melbourne University, 23 November 1965.

Plimsoll James, "In Canberra as new policies emerged 1954-60," in *John Paul Quinn –Recalled by Some of His Friends for His Children*, privately printed, 1968.

Ryan, Peter, "Conlon, Alfred Austin Joseph (Alf) (1908-1961) army officer, medical practitioner," *Australian Dictionary of Biography*, Vol. 13, MUP, 1993.

Sawer, Geoffrey, and Hudson, W.J., "The United Nations," in Gordon Greenwood and Norman Harper (eds), *Australia in World Affairs 1956-60*, FW Cheshire, Melbourne, 1963.

Sawer, Geoffrey, and Hudson, W.J., "The United Nations," in Gordon Greenwood and Norman Harper (eds), *Australia in World Affairs 1961-65*, FW Cheshire, Melbourne, 1968.

The Record: The Magazine of the Sydney Boys High School.

"A watershed in our relationship," *Soviet-American Relations, the Detente Years 1969-1972*, Chapter 5, 15/11/71-31/12/1971. Edward C Keefer (ed), Department of State publications 11438, Washington DC, 2007.

"Unique era in Australian Banking," *Australian Financial Review*, 5 February 1965, 2-3.

Woodard, Garry, "The politics of intervention: James Plimsoll in the South Korean constitutional crisis of 1952," *Australian Journal of International Affairs*, vol. 56, no. 3, 2002, 473-86.

Newspapers

Australian Financial Review
Canberra Times
Christian Science Monitor
Current Notes on International Affairs (later Australian Foreign Affairs Review)
Daily Mirror
Sydney Morning Herald
The Age
The Herald (Melbourne)
The Times (London)
The Advertiser (Adelaide)

INDEX

Acheson, Dean 78
Agnew, Spiro 236, 246-7
AN Smith, Memorial Lecture in journalism 197
Anderson, David 200, 315
Andrews, Prof John 26, 28, 39
Anthony, Doug 106, 274, 276, 280, 309, 313
ANZAM 93
ANZUS 93, 192, 207, 229, 254, 274
ANZUS Council 243, 253
Apartheid in South Africa, 131-2
Army 25ff, 33, 36, 39-40, 42, 46-7, 166, 172
Asia 68, 79, 111, 132, 169, 206, 279, 318, 321, 342, 355

Baillieu, Clive, Lord 137
Baltic states, recognition of incorporation in USSR 266-7
  policy following return of Fraser Government 273
Bangladesh 234-5
Bank of Australasia 10, 12
Bank of NSW 45, 61
Barnard, Lance 254
Barwick, Sir Garfield 111, 127-8, 135, 138-9, 148-9, 156ff, 185, 213, 316
Beale, Sir Howard 110-11, 125, 128, 164
Bilney, Gordon 80, 200

Blamey, General Sir Thomas 27-9, 35
Bland, Sir Henry 190-1, 197, 211, 268, 286
Border, L.H. 187
Breniger, Claude 247
Brennan, K.G. 203
Brezhnev, Leonid 205, 269, 277
Brown, Dr Bob 354
Bullock, Harry 43, 67-8, 70
Bunting, Sir John 148, 165-6, 182, 197, 209, 269, 295-6
Burke, Betty 14
Burns, Creighton 101
Burton, Dr J.W. 46, 54-6, 59, 94, 364
Bush, George H.W. 246
Butlin, S.J. 14
Butz, Earl 247

Cairns, Jim
  visit to Moscow cancelled, 269
Calwell, Arthur 94, 111
Canada 130, 138, 159, 241, 245, 266
Carrington, Lord 90, 111, 147, 309, 312, 315, 317
Carver, General Sir Michael (later Field Marshall Lord) 191, 354
Casey, R.G., (later Lord)
  views on Australian accommodation in Korea 69
  visit to Korea 68-70

first impressions of Plimsoll 73
considers talks in China with Chou En-Lai 98
performance in Cabinet 98
Casey, Maie 98
Castro, Fidel 127, 146
Central African Federation 136, 139
Chifley, J.B. 42, 55-6
Chilton, Sir Frederick 87
China, People's Republic of 29, 64-5, 74, 156-8, 172, 189-93, 206, 231-4, 236, 240, 244, 267-8, 274, 329
Chivers, Joyce (later Lady Wilson) 58-9
Clark, General Mark 77, 79
Christmas Island
  transfer to Australia 105
Cohen, Sam (later Senator) 30, 32
Cold War 61, 92, 111, 263-4, 273, 280, 282, 284, 288
Confrontation of Malaysia 212
Congo 134, 194
Conlon, Alf 23, 26-31, 33, 38-9, 41, 45
Cook, M.J. 365
Coombs, H.C. 13, 42
Cornforth, Sir John 6-8, 364
Crawford, Sir John 196, 212, 237, 304
Crean, Frank 243, 271
Critchley, T.K. 14, 79
Crocker, W.R. (later Sir Walter) 87, 95, 101, 111-12, 132, 161-3, 182, 190, 197, 200, 203, 205, 211, 304, 364
Cuba
  Cuban missile crisis 140, 145, 157, 242

Davidson, Sir Alfred 12-14, 18, 31
Davies, Vesta 13-14
Davis, Owen 16, 106-7
De Gaulle, General Charles 133
Dean, Sir Patrick 140, 148
Defence, Department of 68, 102, 106
Democratic Labor Party 206
Deschamps, N. 187
Directorate of Research and Civil Affairs (Army) 25ff, 39
Dixon, Sir Owen 61, 111, 160
Dulles, John Foster 57, 62, 91

Eastman, A.J. 147
Economics Society of Australia and New Zealand 12, 14, 93, 100
Economic Record 14
Eban, Abba 183
Eggleston, Sir Frederic 43, 198
Egypt
  Australia's relations with after Suez crisis, 105-7, 132-3
Eisenhower, President Dwight 37, 57, 79, 110, 127-8
European Community
  Australia's relations with, after UK entry 298-9

INDEX

Evans, G.C. 202
Evatt, Dr H.V. xii, 39-42, 45-7, 54ff, 77, 94, 100, 111, 181, 186, 209, 243
Evers, Nick 327, 330, 334, 365
External (later Foreign) Affairs, Department of
  communication with overseas posts 95
  overseas representation 199
  growth 200-01
  new posts abroad 201

Far Eastern Commission
  frustrations with USA and with General MacArthur 43
Farmer, W.J. 201
Fernandez, Roy 238-40
Flood, Philip 301, 305
Ford, President Gerald 231
Forsyth, W.D. 39-41
France, nuclear tests in South Pacific, Australian reaction, 239
Fraser, Malcolm 271-3, 275, 279, 285, 287-8, 306, 309-11, 313-4, 320. 331
  statement on foreign policy (1976) 274
  Plimsoll's anxieties about effect of views on Australia-Soviet trade 277
  attitude to Soviet Union 298
  Plimsoll's attitude towards 298
  seeks regular consultations with European Community 299
Freeth, Gordon (later Sir Gordon)
  Indian Ocean and Soviet presence 205-08
Freudenberg, Graham 247-8

Gandhi, Indira 167, 234, 278-9
Ghana 104, 132, 136, 194
Gilchrist, Hugh 89
Goa 172-3
Gorton, J.G. (later Sir John) 152, 184-5, 204, 206-8, 210, 229-30
  and Soviet shipping in Australian waters 185
Gotto, Ainsley 230
Graham, Katharine 248
Grant, Bruce 249
Gray, Robin 332, 334-5, 353, 364
Green, Marshall 231, 241, 284, 352
Griggs, Vice-Admiral Ray 364

Haig, Alexander 232, 274
Hammarskjold, Dag 95, 122, 127
Harper, Norman 101
Harriman, Averell 158, 172
Harry, Ralph 39, 329
Hartnett, L.J. (later Sir Laurence) 63
Hasluck, Paul (later Sir Paul) xiii, 55, 149, 163, 166, 174, 182-4, 185-9, 192-7, 199, 204, 208-9, 212-3, 333, 353

as minister, 185-9

relations with media and consequences, 196

views on responsibilities of career heads of mission, 313-4

Hastings, Peter 147

Hawke, Bob 353

Hay, Sir David 124

Hayden, Bill 316-7, 349, 364

Helms, Richard 329

Henderson, Peter 296, 310, 312-3, 318, 331, 364

Hensley, Gerald 143

Herring, Sir Edmund 111

Herter, Christian 128, 130

Hewitt, Len (later Sir Lenox) 109, 198, 209, 212, 269

Heydon, P.R. (later Sir Peter) 161

Hicks, Sir Edwin 132, 190

Hodgson, Colonel W.R. 63

Holgate, Harry 332

Hollway, D.A. 202

Holt, Harold

foreign relations generally 183

VIP planes affair 184

Hood, John 124

Horne, Donald 17, 32, 147

Howard, John 300, 303

Hytten, Professor Torleiv 13, 31, 45, 61

India 29, 43, 127, 156-60, 162, 164ff, 180, 189, 191-2, 122-2

Indian literature 168

attitude to Australian immigration policy 169

India-Pakistan relations 234-5

Indian Ocean 205-6, 273-4, 277, 298

Indonesia xi, 57, 94, 109, 135-6, 166, 192-3, 212

Australia's concerns re Dutch New Guinea 136

Israel 183

Japan 29, 34, 40-2, 46, 70, 75, 103, 107-8, 172, 233, 296, 318-20, 331, 333, 348

Australian attitudes towards, 104

Jenkins, Roy viii, 299, 305-7

Jockel, Gordon 17

Johnston, M.L. 167

Kashmir dispute 60, 157-8, 160, 192

Kaul, T.N. 170

Kennedy, President John F. 140, 145, 171, 190, 241

Kerr, J.R. (later Sir John) 28-9, 35, 88, 198, 263, 271, 295-6, 333

Plimsoll visits in Canberra (1976), 272

Keynesian economics 14

Khrushchev, Nikita 130

Killen, D.J. (later Sir James) 206, 313

INDEX 379

Kissinger, Dr Henry 233-4, 239, 241, 244-7, 253-4
Korea 54ff, 189, 191, 227, 318, 353, 366
  Unification, proposal for UN mediator, 71
Korea, North (Democratic People's Republic) 242-3, 252-3
Korea South (Republic of Korea) 242-3, 253, 265, 320
Korean War 61, 92, 320
Krishnamachari, T.T. 159-60, 162-3

Legge, Professor John 29, 32
Liberia 130-1
Lie, Trygve 74
Lodge, Henry Cabot 140
Loomes, A.H. 7
Louw, Eric 130
Loveday, Max 69, 187
Lowe, Doug 329-30, 332
Lowndes, Arthur 95
Lyon, M.E. 178

MacArthur, General Douglas 35, 40, 43, 46, 64-5, 70-1
Makin, Norman 46
Marcos, Ferdinand (later President) 142
Macmillan, Harold 128
McAuley, James 26, 29
McEwen, John (later Sir John) 98, 210

McGeorge, Michael 101
McIntyre, L.J. (Jim), (later Sir Laurence) 137, 164, 181, 185, 209, 230, 249
  as Deputy Secretary 199-200
McMahon, W. (later Sir William) 182, 185, 208-11, 228ff, 247
McMahon Ball, Professor W. 55, 101
McNamara, Robert S. 247
McNicol, D.W. 60
Meany, George 248
Menzies, R.G. (later Sir Robert) 59, 63, 103-8, 129, 144-6, 149, 161, 163, 165, 192, 228, 263, 297
  capacity to think ahead 104
  limited reporting of discussions with heads of government 104
  preference for oral briefing 105
  visits Asian countries, 1957 107
  relations with senior officials 108
  Minister for External Affairs 126-7
  intervention in UN General Assembly (1960) 128-30
  praises Plimsoll's intervention in UN debate on apartheid (1961) 132
  possible visit to India 166
  retirement (1966) 182
  comments re Sir John Kerr's appointment as Governor-General 263

Military Mission, Washington DC 35, 37ff
Miller, Professor Bruce 197
Minho, Suh 78
Mollison, James 198
Moodie, C.T. 209
Moore-Wilton, Max
  Proposed trade role in Europe (based in Brussels), 305
Muccio, John (See United States, representation in South Korea) 66, 71-2

Nasser, President Gamal Abdul 105, 127
Nehru, Jawaharlal 128, 130, 157, 159, 166, 169, 170, 191
New Delhi 189, 202, 213, 234, 252
Nigeria 132-3
Nixon, President Richard 207, 227-31, 233-8, 242-4, 246-7, 254
Nkrumah, President Kwame 104, 127
Non-Proliferation Treaty 191

O'Brien, Archbishop Eris 88-9, 147
Organisation of American States 242
Osborn, Rowen 331

Pakistan 60, 65, 77, 100, 157-8, 160, 167, 192, 234-5
Palestine 57-9
Papua New Guinea 107, 135, 188, 191, 294
  major Australian interest at UN 135-37, 138, 193ff, 195
  question of independence 195
Parkinson, N.F. (later Sir Nicholas) 128, 296, 364
Parsons, A.R. 209
Peacock, Andrew 246, 272-3, 281, 284-5, 295ff, 306ff, 316, 364
Percy, Senator Charles 246
Petrov affair 92, 142
Plimsoll, James, (later Sir James)
  family background 1-4
  school 4-8
  Bank of Australasia 8-12
  Economics Department, Bank of New South Wales 12-15
    contribution to Department 15
  University of Sydney
    Economics degree 15
    Arts degree 15
    extra-curricular activities and social life 15
    develops skill at public speaking and debating 15-16
    student societies 16-17
    President of Sydney University Union 17-18
    article re Keynesian theory for *Economic Record* 14
    criticises University Senate re proposed cancelling of professorial appointments 18
  joins militia (1939) 18-19

INDEX

exempted from call up 19

enlists on Army (1942) 19

joins Army Directorate of Research 25

Papua New Guinea, major part of work 28

also covers USA 29

reports on war-time Chinese economy 29

personal reading (1942-44) 30

writings 31

writes manuscript, *Bureaucracy and Democracy* 31

joins group interested in China 32

Canberra, early views of 32-33

selected to attend School of Military Government, Charlottesville, Virginia 33

decides to keep diary 34

course in military government 34

learns to salute 35

promoted major 35

joins Australian Military Mission, Washington DC 35

travels USA 35-37

assumes diplomatic role re Japan (1945) 39

staff work for Far Eastern Commission conference 39-40

elected chair of FEC subcommittee re Japanese economy 40

Sent to Japan (1946) 40

de facto Australian representative at FEC 40

Dr H.V. Evatt, criticisms of as Minister for External Affairs 41

travels to Japan with FEC member delegations 41

with FEC in Japan 41-42

reports to Australian Government on Japan 42

establishes Australian delegation office to FEC 42f

accustomed to working on own; 43

life in Washington DC (1945-47) 43-45

invests in BHP shares 45

looks for post-war employment 45

personal crisis re instructions from Canberra about reparations 45-6

visits Japan with Evatt 46

talks with Evatt re joining External Affairs 46

joins External Affairs,47

Secretary-General Commonwealth conference on Japan 47

accompanies H.V. Evatt to UNGA 1947 47

starts work in DEA (1948) 54

works closely with HV Evatt 55

demobilisation 56

resigns from Bank of New South Wales 56

drafts and arranges publication of book for H.V. Evatt 57-8

offered UN Secretariat posts 59, 74

liaison officer to Sir Owen Dixon 60

works closely with John Foster Dulles 62

holds out for UNCURK staying put in Korea as Communist forces advance 66

leaves Seoul as Communist forces near Seoul 67

accommodation in Pusan (1951) 67-8

Casey visit to Korea 68-70

relations with Syngman Rhee (President, South Korea) 72

Casey's first impressions of Plimsoll 73

declines offer of UN Secretariat post of Director of Social Affairs 74

returns to Canberra from Korea 74

returns to Korea 74-5

proposed appointment as Head of Mission, Jakarta 78

posting in Korea, retrospect 79-80

settles into Canberra in unusual way (1953-59) 86-87

personal reading in 1955-58 88

recognition of China 92

Defence expenditure (1954) 94

Watt criticises reports of conversation in Asia(1956) 96

assists Casey with *Friends and Neighbours* 99-100

proposed closure of School of Oriental Studies at University of Sydney 100

Casey's retirement and peerage (1960) 102

valedictory report to Casey 102-3

relations with Tange 108-09

appointment as permanent representative at United Nations, New York 110-111

influence on US at UN (1960) 130

visits to Africa 132-36

attends independence celebrations of Cameroon 134

activities re Southern Rhodesia (later Zimbabwe) 137-40

possibility of UN assignment (High Commissioner for Refugees) 141

possible mediation on Cuba 141

displeases Joshua Nkomo 143-4

speaking method 144

life in New York 144-6

knighthood 146-7

posting to India as High Commissioner 148-9

seeks to strengthen relations with India 167-73

INDEX 383

visit of Krishnamachari, Minister for Defence production) 159
term in India 163-4
appointment as Secretary, Department of External Affairs 160-165
hopes for Washington posting 164
interests in Indian art, culture, literature 168
visit to Goa (1964), protests by Portugal 172-3
visits Korea December 1963 173
visits Japan (1963) 173
departure from India.(1965) 174
routines as Secretary 181-2
relations with Gorton 184
Gorton and visits abroad 184
Ministers for External Affairs 185ff
Hasluck 185
visits abroad as secretary (1965-68) 189
policy matters as secretary 189-93
leads delegations to UNGA (1965 and 1966) 193
approach to African issues 194
votes at UNGA(given discretion) 195
active in public relations 196-8
establishes historical documents program 196
lecture on "Asian issues in the Australian press" 197

Walter Crocker's *Australian Ambassador* 197
personal reading as Secretary 198
and National Gallery of Australia 198
and Boy Scouts 198
Hasluck sends paper on overseas representation to 199
administration of department as Secretary 199
making decisions 200
overseas conditions of service 200
interest in staff 201
staff postings abroad 202-03
Freeth speech re Soviets in Indian Ocean 205-08
attitude to McMahon 208-09
relations with McMahon as Minister 209-10
appointment as Ambassador to the USA 210
reputation in Washington on arrival as ambassador 227
handling relations in Washington 228-229
activities in USA 230-1
Nixon gratitude towards Plimsoll 235
observes Watergate affair develop 236
offered appointment as Master University House ANU 237.

Nixon Administration contacts continue despite White House bans 241

argument with Graham Freudenberg about the F111 248

end of Washington posting, and transfer to Moscow 249ff

departure from Washington 253-4

arrival in Moscow 264

special assignments (1974) 264-5

Whitlam's view of acceptance in USSR 269

reaction to dismissal of Whitlam Government 271-2

presentation to by Soviet Foreign Ministry on 60th birthday 278

Soviet officials seek views re electoral defeat of Indira Gandhi 279

seeks to develop Australia-Soviet relationship 280

cultural interests in USSR 281

lectures in English literature at Moscow State University 281-4

friendship with Professor Olga Akhmanova, Moscow State University 283-4

professional opinions of (1976-7) 284-5

staff relations 285-6

fire in Moscow embassy 286

attitude to memoirs of officials 286

departure from USSR 287-8

discontent with Canberra, especially prime minister 294

desire for Port Moresby posting 294-5

possible appointments after Moscow 295-6

lunches with Kerr early in 1976 295-6

appointment to Brussels 296-7

declines offer of director-general of Office of National Assessments(ONA) 297

relations with prime ministers 297

lack of briefing on Coalition Government's policies re EC 300 and STR delegation 301

not invited to STR delegation meetings in Brussels 301

put off by style of STR 302

thinks holding of Federal elections in 1977 wrong 303

appointed a Companion of the Order of Australia 303-4

meetings with Victor Garland (later Sir Victor), new Minister for STR 304-5, 312-6

declines to participate in STR meeting with EC 304-5

praised by Roy Jenkins, President of European Commission 306

Brussels "least satisfying" posting 308

INDEX

interest in proceedings of European Parliament 308
represents Australia at meetings of Committee for Disarmament in Geneva 308
appointed High Commissioner in London 309-10
possibility appointment might only be brief 309-11
entertains extensively in London 312
holidays in Ireland 312
learns Victor Garland is to be appointed to London 312-3
reactions to removal from London 314-6
appointed Ambassador to Japan 316-7
presents credentials in Tokyo 319
performance in Japan 321
appointment as Governor of Tasmania 329-33
Sen. Nick McKenna gives "rapturous assessment" 329
settles in in Hobart 333-4
activities in Tasmania 335-8
entertaining at Government House, Hobart 338
Visitor, University of Tasmania 341
Patron, Australian Institute of International Affairs (Tasmania Branch) 341-2

constitutional role of the governor 343-6
relations as governor with the Opposition 344
the Botanical Gardens, Hobart 346
cricket 346-7
controversy surrounding legislation for a local government amalgamation 348
funeral and burial 352-4
honours 354
legacies as Governor 354-
health 112, 211, 248, 265-66, 319-20, 348-51
attitude to media 100-01,196

Plimsoll, James Ernest 1-2, 4
Plimsoll John 3-6
Plimsoll, Kathleen 366
Plimsoll, Patricia 20, 366
Plimsoll, Sir Samuel 1, 311
Portuguese Timor 136
Powles, Sir Guy 46
Pritchett, W.B. 167, 365
Pyun, Y.T. 74
Quaison-Sackey, Alex 136, 194
Quinn, John 7, 90

Radio Australia 101, 165
    Hasluck's frustrations 189
Reagan, Governor Ronald (later President) 242, 341

Rebozo, Bebe 242
Renouf, Alan 6-7, 253, 263, 267, 269, 273-5, 285, 295, 364
Restricted immigration policy 169
Reynolds, Ray 35
Rhee, President Syngman xii, 66-7, 69, 71-3, 77-9
   reelection as President of South Korea 75-6
Rhodesia (Southern Rhodesia, Zimbabwe) 194
   Holt, handling of 183
Richardson, D.J. 202, 364
Richardson, Elliot 236-7, 241, 247
Robertson, R.H. (Bob) 365
Rogers, William 207, 229, 233, 235, 240-1, 244, 247
Ryan, J.E. 274-5, 285
Ryan, Peter 26, 28-9
Rusk, Dean 61, 166, 169, 194

Sandys, Duncan 137-9, 147, 158, 160
Sanson, Sir George 46
Sarasin, Pote 65, 69-70
Scherger, Air Marshall Sir Frederick 198
Scowcroft, Brent 246
SEATO 91, 93, 100, 107, 166, 329
Shann, KCO (Mick) (later Sir Keith) 96, 211, 233, 252, 266, 296, 309
Shaw, P. (later Sir Patrick) 194, 237, 250, 252

Shedden, Sir Frederick 147
Sisco, Joseph 232
Smith, R.C. 202
Smith, R.J. 169
Smith, Vice Admiral Sir Victor 185
Smyth, O.W. 67-8
Soviet Union (see USSR)
Special Trade Representations (STR), Department of 305-8, 312
   creation 300
   most of team lack experience in international trade negotiations 301
   Plimsoll in Brussels 301
   by-passes Australian posts in Europe 302
   deals directly with EC, excludes Mission in Brussels 304
Spender, P.C. (later Sir Percy) 59, 61-4, 67-8, 73, 75, 110
Spry, Sir Charles 87
Squire, Betty 44
Stephen, Sir Ninian 333, 349, 364
Stevens, Sir Bertram 62
Stevenson, Adlai 147-8
Stewart, Michael 194
Stirling, Alfred 112
Stone, Professor Julius 18, 26
Stuart, F.H. 187, 364
Suez Canal
   nationalisation of, Australian policy 105-06

INDEX 387

Sukarno, President 127, 135
Sutherland, Dame Joan 148
Sydney Boys High School 1, 5
Sydney University 13, 18, 25-6, 29-30, 89, 100, 197
Syme, Sir Colin 111

Tange, Arthur (later Sir Arthur) 13-15, 61, 69, 86, 108-10, 125, 127-8, 135, 145, 160-6, 171, 174, 185-8, 192, 200, 203-4, 211-3
  Relations with Plimsoll 108-09
  Opinion of Plimsoll's role under Hasluck 188
  Delivers eulogy at Canberra memorial service for Plimsoll 353
Terrill, Professor Ross 244-5
Tito, President Joseph 127-8
Toure, President Sekou 127
Truman, President Harry 239

U Thant 134, 138, 144, 211
UK x, xii, 40, 90, 96, 101, 106, 109, 111, 128, 137-8, 140, 143, 158, 164, 194, 317
  Withdrawal from Far East 191
United Nations
  decolonisation 95
  General Assembly (UNGA) xi, 47, 110, 124-5, 127-8, 130, 133-6, 138, 142-3, 147, 191, 193-5, 198, 208, 265
  ECOSOC 55-7, 59

UN Commission for Korea (UNCOK) 62
UN Commission for Unification and rehabilitation of Korea (UNCURK) xii, 62-7, 70-3, 75, 77-8
  Australia's permanent representative at ii, 123-6, 140
  increasing anti-colonialism 135
  issues in late 1960s, 193ff
Urquhart, Sir Brian 134, 364
United States of America 33-8, 58, 60, 140, 166, 227ff
  visit by President-elect Dwight Eisenhower to Korea 79
  Kissinger visit to China 233
  relations with China 233
  relations with Australia-trade union boycott (1972) 240
  concern re relations with Australia (1973) 240
USSR 192, 205-8, 231, 234-6, 264, 266-7, 273ff, 279ff, 284-6
  invasion of Czechoslavakia 205
  Australian interests 263
  Whitlam Government's objectives in 1974 264
  visit by Clyde Cameron, Minister for Science 270
  visits by other Whitlam ministers 270-271
  Australian Embassy in, effect of Supply crisis (1975) 271

visit by Peter Nixon, Minister for Transport 275-6

Vietnam war
  Australian involvement 190ff, 192, 212, 232-3
Vietnam North
  Whitlam Government initiatives, US disquiet 240
Viret, Rosemary 370

Walker, Dr E.R. (later Sir Ronald) 31, 56, 74, 95
Waller, J.K. (later Sir Keith) 184-5, 204, 210-11, 228-9, 233-4, 249-51, 263, 284, 312
Watergate xiii, 228, 236-7, 253
Watt, A.S. (later Sir Alan) 6, 39, 59, 61-3, 67. 69, 74, 87, 95-6, 105, 197
Weinberger, Caspar 241, 247
Wensley, Penny 202
Wentworth, W.C. 125-6
West New Guinea 94
Wheeler, Sir Frederick 45, 197, 200

Whitlam, Gough 30, 142, 182, 229, 237-44, 247ff, 254, 262, 264-70, 280-1, 287, 295-6, 304, 344, 364
  desire to visit Nixon at White House 243-248
  visits USSR (1975) 268
  size of travelling party 269
  itinerary 269
  tired by long itinerary 270
  Plimsoll calls on (1976) 272
Whitlam government and relations with the USA 237ff
  reaction to renewed US bombing of North Vietnam (1972) 238-9
Whitlam, Fred 114
Wilenski, Peter 6, 244-5, 247, 249
Willesee, Senator Don 253, 265, 267
Willis, Eric (later Sir Eric) 26, 365
Wilson, Sir Roland 44, 58, 109, 111
Woolcott, Richard 249, 285, 364

Yom Kippur War 232

Zimbabwe 138, 143, 298

www.ingramcontent.com/pod-product-compliance
Lightning Source LLC
Chambersburg PA
CBHW072118290426
44111CB00012B/1698